Understanding Third World Politics

Understanding Third World Politics

Theories of Political Change and Development

Third Edition

B. C. Smith

INDIANA
University Press
Bloomington & Indianapolis

This book is a publication of

Indiana University Press
601 North Morton Street
Bloomington, Indiana 47404-3797 USA

http://iupress.indiana.edu

Telephone orders   800-842-6796
Fax orders   812-855-7931
Orders by e-mail   iuporder@indiana.edu

© 1996, 2003, 2009 by B.C. Smith

Printed and bound in Great Britain by CPI Antony Rowe, Chippenham, Wiltshire

Cataloging information is available from the Library of Congress.

ISBN 978-0-253-35346-7 hardback
ISBN 978-0-253-22104-9 paperback

1 2 3 4 5 14 13 12 11 10 09

For Liam and Laura

Contents

Tables and Figures

Tables

Figure

Preface

The main aim of this third edition is to update data, case material and conceptual discussion, while keeping to the original aims and objectives of earlier editions, namely to provide an introduction to the attempts of political science to understand politics in less developed countries. Revisions also focus the discussion more closely on *political* theories, taking as given the sociological basis of functionalist political theory and the economic foundation of dependency theory. The second aim has been to focus more closely on *contemporary* politics in developing countries, making reference as far as possible to current political developments.

This has entailed deleting the chapter on theories of imperialism and colonialism, which analysed explanations of relationships between rich and poor countries which are now of largely historical interest, having been replaced by forms of neo-colonialism, the subject of the new Chapter 3. However, material on the varied political and economic experience of colonialism from the old Chapter 2 has been incorporated into the opening chapter in order to identify key historical legacies which help shape contemporary politics in post-colonial states.

In order to identify the types of society with which the book is concerned Chapter 1 deals with the concept of a 'third' world, distinguishing between the different meanings that have been attached to the term 'Third World', and explaining why doubts have been expressed about the legitimacy of such a label. The main socio-economic problems facing Third World countries and the major changes that have taken place since the end of the Second World War are described. The chapter has been updated with economic, social and political data from the World Bank's *World Development Indicators*, and UNDP's annual *Human Development Reports*, under the headings 'Political independence', 'National incomes', Industrialization', 'Integration into the world economy', and 'Human development'. The discussion of the concept 'Third World' has been revised to reflect the implications of developments both among poor countries, and between them and other regions of the world which no longer fit easily into the categories of 'first' and 'second' worlds. Two alternative categorisations for understanding divisions within the world – the 'end of history' and 'clash of civilisations' – are critically examined in the light of continuing conflicts and tensions within the Third World and between it and developed countries, and of new relationships between regions of the Third World, especially Africa and Asia, and especially China.

The next two chapters deal with the main theoretical perspectives on the overall quality of political change in the Third World which explain the situation in which societies find themselves in terms of 'modernization', 'development', 'neo-colonialism' and 'dependency'. Chapter 2 locates the origins of modernization theory in evolutionary social theory and its key concepts of continuity, progress, increased complexity and specialization. The material on sociological foundations of functionalist politics has been condensed to make space for more contemporary illustrations and tests of utility. The material on 'differentiation', 'secularization' and cultural modernity is used to enrich the discussion of 'political culture' in functionalist political science. The chapter focuses more closely on the political aspects of modernization theory. More illustrations of how political functions are performed in contemporary Third World countries are given to show how far contemporary Third World politics deviate from the model of a modern political system formulated by the functionalists. The problematic aspects of functionalism – its concept of tradition, secularization, change, ethnocentricity and integration – are placed in the context of current developments in different regions of the 'third world'.

Chapter 3 examines the concept of neo-colonialism and the significance of formal independence for post-colonial societies. The governments of newly independent states soon found that constitutional independence did not mean that they had sovereign state power at their disposal. This was the result of economic resources remaining under the control of foreign interests located in metropolitan centres that before independence had ruled directly. The difficulty of describing the *political* manifestations of this domination is explained, with reference to the political influence of external economic interests, comprador elites and aid dependency. A contrasting perspective arguing that formal independence fundamentally changed political life in new states is examined.

Dependency theory takes the neo-colonial interpretation further with its conceptualization of hierarchy, underdevelopment and disarticulation. The key aspects of a debate about the nature of capitalism in post-colonial society are presented. The relationships between dependency and economic performance, social class and democratisation are explained.

The next four chapters turn to specific institutional arrangements and the attempts by political scientists to produce valid theoretical statements about the most significant political institutions in Third World societies: the state, political parties, the bureaucracy and the military. Interest in the post-colonial state has in part been a reaction against the economic reductionism found in dependency theory and in part an extension of a resurgence of interest in the nature of the capitalist state within mainstream Marxist thought. In Chapter 4 a pluralist view of the political system is contrasted with Marxist theorizing about the state in Third World societies. Contemporary Third

World politics is shown to be far removed from the pluralist model. Different Marxist conceptions of the state are illustrated by reference to Pakistan, Zimbabwe and Thailand, before the Bonapartist model is applied to Pakistan and Tanzania. Two models emphasizing the role of the bureaucracy in the post-colonial state are examined. A comparative framework of state–society dialectics is an alternative view of the state which shows how state action and structure is not only influenced by the political environment, but actually influences political culture and collective action. A controversy about the implications of globalization for the state is also examined.

Chapter 5 deals with theories explaining the role of political parties in Third World politics. Ideological foundations in class, European political ideas, religion, ethnicity and populism, with its attendant factionalism and patronage politics, are explained. Explanations of the single-party system are illustrated by the cases of Uganda and Zimbabwe. The relationship between party systems and democratization in the Third World is examined utilizing the concepts of institutionalization, partisan dealignment, and the multi-party system. The survival of parties as institutions is also of concern as the movement for democracy gathers momentum in the Third World. The conditions required for organizational survival are illustrated by experience from Latin America, Zambia, Taiwan and Uganda.

Bureaucracies are important political organizations in all political systems. Chapter 6 distinguishes between different concepts of bureaucracy and shows that all are contained in the analyses that have been carried out of the role of the bureaucracy in Third World societies and states. Sources of bureaucratic power are categorized, as well as bureaucratic features which have been taken to be signs of the emergence of a new kind of ruling class. Bureaucracy also implies a certain kind of rationality in the context of the official allocation of scarce resources. Thus Chapter 6 considers the theory of 'access'. Attempts to reduce the political significance of bureaucracy, such as economic liberalization, and new principles of public management are explained. These entail contracting public services out not only to the private sector but also to the 'third sector' of non-governmental organizations, creating problems of accountability.

Chapter 7 is concerned with military intervention and the *coup d'état*. Methodological problems encountered when explaining military intervention are set out. Different types of military intervention in politics are distinguished and illustrated by the cases of Burma, Iran and Thailand. Explanatory factors identified as accounting for the *coup* as the most extreme form of intervention are considered: social mobility, the demands of the middle class, level of economic development, the political culture, the military's organizational strength and culture, and foreign influences. Finally, hypotheses about the conditions necessary for ensuring that the military 'remain in barracks' after democratization are considered.

The final chapters deal with challenges to the status quo and therefore the political instability which is so frequently found in Third World societies. First, Chapter 8 examines the demand for independence on the part of ethnic or national minorities: the phenomenon of *secession*. This is a widespread feature of Third World politics and the response to it is usually severe, as shown by recent events in Tibet and Sudan. The nature of nationalism is illustrated by Tibet and elsewhere. The primordialist, situationist and constructivist theories of nationalism are compared. Four theories of separatism are examined: political integration, internal colonialism, 'balance of advantage' and class structure, with illustrations from Bangladesh, South East Asia, Palestine, the short-lived Biafra, Kurdistan and Sri Lanka. It is argued that explanations of nationalism and secession need a class dimension because of the social stratification found within cultural minorities, the petty-bourgeois leadership of ethnic secessionist movements, and the significance for the outcome of nationalism of the reaction of the dominant class in the 'core' community to nationalist political mobilization.

After identifying some conceptual problems associated with the analysis of political instability – its normative content, the type of regime involved, and the lack of a satisfactory operational definition of 'instability' – Chapter 9 examines the theoretical preconditions for stability that have been formulated in terms of levels of poverty, rates of economic growth, the revolution of rising expectations, foreign influences, ethnicity, the political culture, inequality, crises of authority and political institutionalization. The discussion of state crisis takes in the question of 'failed' states such as Somalia. The theoretical or empirical weaknesses of some of these conclusions are identified, namely that correlation does not necessarily prove causality, that poor and underdeveloped countries can be stable especially if authoritarian, that political stability might *cause* affluence and economic growth, and that high rates of growth and stability have gone together in some countries.

Chapter 10 first discusses the contested concept of democracy, before moving on to theories of democratic transition which identify the main causes of authoritarian breakdown as elite conflict, domestic crisis and international pressure. The variability of democratic transitions has generated controversies about the relative significance of elite and popular pressure for change, the frequency of democratic regression and the neglect of persistent authoritarianism. The prerequisites of democratic consolidation are identified as national affluence, with its implications for equality and class development; the 'autonomy of political factors'; the political culture and the problem of the direction of causality; civil society as a counterbalance to the power of the state; the balance of power within democracies; the importance of institutional development to democratic consolidation;

and pressure from foreign sources seeking to promote democracy and good governance. Political institutionalization is one aspect of the 'new institutionalism' that has provided another framework for comparative political analysis.

The concluding chapter considers the prospects for Third World democracy in the light of the theories of political change discussed in the previous chapters, and examines the argument that development and democracy might not be compatible, especially in view of the success which some authoritarian states have had in developing their societies economically and socially. However, the weight of evidence suggests that a democratic developmental state should be able to secure economic progress, as well as providing political benefits in terms of political rights, freedoms and participation, while authoritarianism has often failed to provide economic and social progress, Zimbabwe and North Korea being leading instances. The study of developmental states, whether authoritarian or democratic, reveal that a particular type of state intervention is required, together with a unified and competent bureaucracy, nationalistic political and bureaucratic elites, and 'embedded autonomy' in relationships between state and society. Regrettably, the requirements of democratic developmentalism are all too rare in the Third World.

A debt of gratitude is owed to Steven Kennedy and Stephen Wenham at Palgrave Macmillan, and three anonymous reviewers, for support, encouragement and constructive criticism. Jenny Brooks, librarian at the University of Exeter, also provided invaluable assistance, as did David Smith's computing skills. Keith Povey once again performed editorial tasks meticulously. My wife Jean extended a long tradition of patient comfort and reassurance. I hope they feel the result is worth their efforts.

B. C. SMITH

1

The Idea of a 'Third World'

A definition

Since this chapter examines a controversy over the label 'Third World' it is appropriate to begin with a definition. In order to identify the subject-matter of this book, to convey the diversity of the social and economic conditions within the Third World, and to provide an outline of the major changes taking place in Third World countries, an indication of the key characteristics of Third World status must be given. For the purpose of this survey the Third World will be defined as a group of countries which have colonial histories and which are in the process of developing economically and socially from a status characterized by low incomes, dependence on agriculture, weakness in trading relations, social deprivation for large segments of society, and restricted political and civil liberties. This definition acknowledges the process of change and therefore the likely diversity of countries within the group.

The following sketch of Third World status and trends will follow the components of the definition: the achievement of political independence; average income levels; industrialization; integration into the world economy; and human development. By this definition the Third World comprises approximately 100 states in Africa, Asia, the Middle East, Latin America and the Caribbean. Their combined population of over 4.8 billion accounts for 75 per cent of the world's total and their territories cover nearly 58 per cent of the world's land area (World Bank, 2001b).

Political independence

Only a tiny minority of countries that would be regarded as part of the Third World by other criteria have not experienced colonialism at some stage in their recent histories. The picture of the Third World in this respect is becoming more complex with the dissolution of the Soviet Union and the emergence of a number of independent states that were formerly part of it (Berger, 1994). Most of these, such as Tajikistan and Uzbekistan, rank as lower-middle-income countries along with, for example, Senegal, Thailand and Peru.

A significant variation in Third World status is the length of time that countries have been independent from their colonizers, with most Latin American countries gaining political independence in the early nineteenth century and most African countries only after the Second World War. Experience of imperial political control and economic penetration varied considerably, as did the routes to independence that were taken (roughly divided between constitutional negotiations and armed struggle). However, the legacy of imperialism and colonialism was everywhere profound, transforming political institutions and processes. New geo-political boundaries were drawn. Reactions against alien rule mobilized new political forces and alliances. Indigenous social structures and political systems were altered by European economic interventions and settlement.

In fact, the imperialist impulse produced a complex pattern of colonial intervention in the world's pre-industrial societies. In addition to the varying balance of economic, strategic and diplomatic interests, and cultural expansionism prompted by a confidence in the superiority of Western civilization, there were highly variable local factors that conditioned the impact of European intervention. These included material conditions and the different political organizations encountered when the decision was taken to move from a purely commercial relationship with pre-industrial societies to their political incorporation into an imperial structure.

Nor did the European powers promote their cultures in the same way and to the same degree. It is possible to contrast the approaches of the British and French or Portuguese to their imperial possessions. Britain's approach to the dissemination of its culture was far more pragmatic than some of its continental neighbours, in that it sought to preserve indigenous cultures, values and social structures where it suited the colonial power politically to do so. It was possible for British imperialists to talk at one and the same time about the great benefits to their colonial dependencies of the liberties that followed the flag, while at the same time respecting and reinforcing caste and feudalism. Britain's need for political control and the maintenance of stability was consistent with the preservation of indigenous practices. In many parts of West Africa, for example, with the exception of inhuman punishments for criminal offences defined according to local customary law, existing customs and laws were left intact. It was far easier to keep a population quiescent when it was partly governed by its own institutions, laws and customs, although ultimately subject to the local representatives of the British Crown. A hierarchy of colonial officials extended from the Secretary of State for the Colonies at the apex down to district commissioners in charge of large populations and supervising the exercise of customary law by indigenous judges and lawmakers regarded as legitimate by the local population.

The French and Portuguese, by contrast, attempted assimilation. This meant that native peoples were to be turned into Europeans, particularly through Western education. This had significant implications for the devel opment of areas in which local political élites identified closely with Europe and European culture. There was a much more vigorous policy, albeit in reality aimed at a select minority and with limited effect (Berman, 1984), in French than in British territories of turning local people into local versions of the populations of the imperial power. The assumption was that local culture was an obstacle to the spread of European civilization.

The availability of fertile land and the possibility of utilizing it for peasant cash cropping or plantations for tea, coffee, sugar and cotton also varied. Sometimes the land could only be exploited for produce that was already indigenous to the area. The introduction of cash crops from abroad (such as rubber into Malaya from Brazil) was not always feasible. The availability of deep-water harbours which could be linked to the interior by railways and roads also affected the pattern of colonial intervention. The whole structure of communications and transportation was a highly variable factor. Initially rivers were the key to expansion, allowing penetration into the interior without any significant capital outlay. Traditional communication routes tended to determine the spatial pattern of colonial investment. The presence of minerals was another factor – copper in East Africa, gold and diamonds in Southern Africa, and tin in Bolivia, for example. Climatic conditions also differed, making East Africa far more conducive to European settlement than West Africa.

A further variable was the indigenous social structures of the colonized territories. Some local communities were extremely simple in their economic activities, being based on hunting and gathering. Some were nomadic pastoral communities, surviving on the basis of livestock which was grazed over regular transhumance routes. Other societies had complex agrarian systems with highly elaborate organizations for production, distribution and exchange. Levels of urbanization varied considerably, too, with some societies based on towns that performed the roles of administrative and commercial centres. Some societies were highly feudalistic in terms of relations between landowners and their tenant cultivators, whereas elsewhere more egalitarian systems were found, with land held in common and individual plots cultivated by families without rights to alienate or accumulate. Concepts of rent and tenancy were absent from such cultures, as were the political relationships that accompany them.

Different forms of political organization were encountered. There were centralized state structures immediately recognizable as such by Europeans: ancient kingdoms had clearly articulated forms of political authority and leadership, with state functionaries recruited according to explicit rules; traditional leaders were surrounded by civil and military officialdom; territorial divisions were created for purposes of administration, taxation and the enforcement of laws. Such structures of government were highly suitable for the purposes of colonial administration, especially in the context of the pragmatic approach to managing dependent territories mentioned earlier. Indirect rule meant using the indigenous political structures for imperial objectives. There were obvious political advantages in using the legitimacy conferred upon traditional leaders who were at the same time loyal to, and dependent on, the colonial administration. Exploiting military and commercial superiority was thus made easier.

The colonial powers found it relatively easy to persuade indigenous rulers to accept this integration of their own traditional systems of decision-making and adjudication into the colonial state hierarchy. Claimants to the throne received the support of the colonial authorities in return for their loyalty and co-operation. Corrupt, incompetent or insubordinate rulers were easily deposed and there were always more co-operative princes, chiefs and emirs to replace them (Berman, 1984). British officials became the real power behind the thrones of indigenous rulers, intervening according to the precise needs of the European presence. Such interventions had to be greater if there was a need to remove local people from their land through legislation and other instruments of colonial policy. Elsewhere there was simply a need to preserve conditions under which cash crops could be produced by peasant cultivators according to traditional methods of cultivation. Here indirect rule was a most appropriate form of colonial administration.

Indigenous political structures were not always so familiar and useful to colonial government. In the acephalous societies, without formal positions of permanent leadership, government was organized without separate institutions for making laws, adjudicating in disputes and performing other civil and military functions on behalf of the community. Far less familiar forms of authority were used to manage society's communal affairs, such as age groups, lineages, clans or elders. An interpretation of the wisdom of ancestors might be needed to solve disputes over land, family affairs or economic activities, make decisions concerning the welfare of the community, or deal with conflicts with neighbouring communities. In societies without obvious structures of chieftaincy or other political offices it was much more difficult to integrate indigenous political authority into an imperial system. Offices had to be artificially created for the purposes of colonial government, a source of great discontent and alienation in the communities affected, sometimes leading to political instability and problems of social order.

A consequence of such local economic, social and political variety, combined with the varying motivations of the imperialists, was that different forms of colonial intervention developed. In some areas plantations were set up in which industrialized forms of agricultural production were created, requiring large numbers of wage labourers and European managers. Elsewhere mining activities required the encouragement of the local population into the formation of an industrial labour force. In other areas imperialism required the encouragement of peasant cash cropping without changing the relations of production by the introduction of wage labour or new technology. Another variation on the colonial theme was European settlement on the best land available, leading to permanent commitments on the part of white minorities. It was common to find more than one form of colonial intervention in a single colony – as in Kenya and Tanganyika, where peasant production was combined with plantation and settler agriculture. Economically one form was usually dominant, as in the Gold Coast, where peasant commodity production dominated a colonial economy that included European-owned mining operations (Berman, 1984).

National incomes

The majority of countries in the Third World are found in the low-income or lower-middle-income categories used by the World Bank and defined in terms of gross national income per capita. Differences in per capita incomes vary greatly between regions of the world and, as Table 1.1 shows, the Third World continues to lag behind the developed economies.

The gap in real incomes between some Third World countries, such as those in East Asia, and the industrialized countries has narrowed considerably since 1945. East Asia's share of developing countries real income

Table 1.1 *Per capita national incomes 1966–2007*

Economy	2005 GNI per capita (US$)	Annual average % growth in GDP			
		1966–73	*1974–90*	*1991–97*	*1998–2007*[1]
High income	35,131	3.8	2.0	1.4	2.0
Low and middle income	1,610	3.9	1.2	1.6	3.0
Asia	1,155	2.9	4.3	6.9	4.3
Latin America and Caribbean	4,008	3.9	0.3	1.5	2.2
Middle East and North Africa	2,241	5.8	–2.0	0.6	0.9
Sub-Saharan Africa	745	2.0	–0.9	–0.2	1.0

NOTE: [1]Estimate.
SOURCES: World Bank (1999), Table A2–4, p.197; World Bank (2007c), Table 1, p. 289.

increased from 22 per cent in 1965 to 50.2 per cent in 2005. Per capita incomes throughout the Third World rose relatively quickly in the 1960s and 1970s. Despite a levelling out in the 1980s, the average level of per capita income in developing countries rose by 2.1 per cent per year from 1960 to 1997. Their rate of economic growth accelerated between 1995 and 2005. Poverty, as measured by the number of people living on less than $1 a day declined by over 260 million between 1990 and 2004. This is mainly due to achievements in East Asia, especially China. Positive economic growth during the first 5 years of the twenty-first century meant that growth in incomes in low-and middle-income countries accelerated. For the first time in post-colonial history incomes grew faster than in rich countries (UNDP 2001; World Bank 2007b).

However, in some regions of the Third World incomes have stagnated or fallen. The divergence between regions mainly occurred in the 1970s so that whereas by 1980 per capita GDP was growing at 6.7 per cent in East Asia and 3.2 per cent in South Asia it was falling in Latin America and Sub-Saharan Africa. Per capita incomes in Sub-Saharan Africa fell in real terms between 1975 and 1999, the number of those living in poverty increased by almost 60 million. Currently the Sub-Saharan region accounts for 30 per cent of the world's poorest people, up from 11 per cent in 1981. Many Third World countries, especially in Africa, will not achieve the UN's Millennium Development Goal of halving the proportion of poor people by 2015. Even under the most optimistic assumptions about economic growth between 1998 and 2015 – an average annual growth in GDP per capita of 3.7 per cent – it is likely that there will still be 2.3 billion people attempting to survive on less than $2 a day (UNDP, 2001; World Bank, 2001c).

The situation will be made worse by the steep rise in food prices between 2005 and 2008, estimated to have already increased poverty by 3 percentage points. For many countries and regions where progress in reducing poverty has been slow, the impact of rising food prices risks undermining the poverty gains of the last 5 to 10 years (World Bank 2008a).

The gap between developed countries and those of the Third World widened until the end of the twentieth century. The income difference between the fifth of the world's people living in the richest countries and the fifth in the poorest was 74 to 1 in 1997, up from 60 to 1 in 1990 and 30 to 1 in 1960. By the end of the 1990s the fifth in the highest-income countries owned 86 per cent of the world's GDP compared to the bottom fifth's 1 per cent (UNDP, 2001). However, the World Bank predicts that the income gap will close over the next 25 years, though it will remain substantial for the foreseeable future. There is also no sign of convergence between low- and middle-income economies.

Industrialization

Low per capita incomes have been related historically to the Third World's economic dependence on agriculture. Incomes tend to rise as countries industrialize and the size of the manufacturing sector increases. These are important goals for developing countries.

All regions of the Third World have shown a decline in the contribution of agriculture to GDP since 1990 (see Table 1.2), though where there is subsistence farming much agricultural produce is not exchanged, making it difficult to assess changes in production accurately. Employment in agriculture has also declined, though the sector still employs 40 per cent of developing countries' workers. In 2005 the International Labour Organization found that the agriculture sector is still the main employer in 65 of the 162 developing economies for which employment data are available by sector. The agricultural share of employment is higher in Sub-Saharan Africa and Asia than in the Middle East, North Africa, and Latin America.

The general trend in the structure of Third World output has been from agriculture to manufacturing and services. The annual average growth in agricultural output was 2.4 per cent from 1990 to 2000, and 3.4 per cent between 2000 and 2005. But, over the same periods, industrial output grew by 4.6 per cent and 6.2 per cent, manufacturing by 6.8 and 7.2 per cent and services by 4.1 and 5.2 per cent. Expansion of the service sector has been particularly pronounced, both in terms of growth in output and value added as a proportion of GDP.

Table 1.2   *Value added as a percentage of GDP 1990–2006*

Economy	Agriculture		Industry		Services	
	1990	*2006*	*1990*	*2006*	*1990*	*2006*
Low income	29	20	31	28	41	51
Middle income	13	9	39	36	47	55
Lower-middle	21	12	39	43	40	45
Upper-middle	8	6	39	31	53	63
Low and middle income	16	10	38	35	46	55
East Asia	20	12	40	46	40	42
Europe and Central Asia	17	9	43	30	40	61
Latin America	9	6	36	30	56	63
Mid. East and N. Africa	15	11	38	41	47	48
South Asia	30	18	26	28	44	54
Sub-Saharan Africa	18	15	34	32	48	52
High income	3	2	33	26	64	72

SOURCES: World Bank, (2001c) Table 12, p. 297; World Bank (2008b) Table 4, p. 341.

Table 1.3   *Regional employment by sector, 1996–2006*

Region	Agriculture (%)		Industry (%)		Services (%)	
	1996	2006	1996	2006	1996	2006
East Asia	48.5	40.9	24.3	25.6	27.2	33.5
S-E Asia and Pacific	51.0	45.4	16.5	18.6	32.5	36.0
South Asia	59.7	49.4	15.2	21.0	25.1	29.6
Latin America and Caribbean	23.1	19.6	20.7	20.8	56.1	59.6
North Africa	36.5	34.4	19.8	20.0	43.7	45.6
Sub-Saharan Africa	74.4	65.9	7.5	10.0	18.1	24.1
Middle East	21.2	18.1	25.2	25.6	53.7	56.3

SOURCE: ILO (2007), Box 4b.

Average annual growth in the service sector remained constant from 1980 to 1998. The contribution of the service sector to GDP rose from 46 to 55 per cent between 1990 and 2006. Third World manufacturing, generally the most dynamic part of the industrial sector, has actually declined since 1990.

In the last decade agriculture has provided a declining share of employment in all regions of the Third World, though it is still the main source of employment in the poorest regions, notably Sub-Saharan Africa and South Asia (see Table 1.3). In most regions employment in services has grown faster than employment in industry, throwing doubt on the theory that economic development produces a shift from agriculture to industry.

Integration into the world economy

The growing involvement of Third World economies in trade is bringing about closer integration into the global economy. In all regions of the Third World except the Middle East and North Africa foreign trade has increased as a percentage of GDP. Growth in merchandise trade by low- and middle-income countries increased from 32.5 per cent of GDP in 1990 to 59.2 per cent in 2005 (see Table 1.4). Over the same period trade in services increased from 7 per cent to 10.8 per cent . Average rates of annual growth in the export of goods and services from low- and middle-income economies have almost equalled those by high income economies since the mid-1960s. Exports increased from 19.8 per cent of GDP in 1984 to 35.1 per cent in 2004. However, though the Third World's share of global trade has increased, it still only accounts for less than a third.

Table 1.4 *Integration into the world economy, 1990–2005*

Economy	Merchandise trade (% of GDP)		Trade in services (% of GDP)		Total trade (% of GDP)	Foreign direct investment (% of GDP)	
	1990	2005	1990	2005	2005	1990	2005
High income	32.3	43.9	7.9	11.1	50	1.0	2.1
Low income	23.6	41.1	6.2	9.8	53	0.4	1.5
Middle income	34.5	62.1	7.1	10.5	67	0.9	3.1
Lower middle	31.6	58.9	6.4	10.0	75	0.8	3.1
Upper middle	38.3	66.4	8.0	11.1	61	1.2	3.1
Low and middle income	32.5	59.2	7.0	10.8	65	0.8	2.9
East Asia and Pacific	47.1	74.6	7.3	10.3	86	1.6	3.2
Europe and Central Asia	49.7	68.6	7.1	12.6	77	1.0	3.5
Latin America and Caribbean	23.2	44.2	5.7	6.8	48	0.8	2.9
Middle East and N. Africa	43.5	57.6	9.2	..	73	0.3	2.4
South Asia	16.5	31.2	4.2	8.2	44	0.1	1.0
Sub-Saharan Africa	41.9	57.8	10.8	13.1	68	0.4	2.7

SOURCES: World Bank (2007b), Table 6.1; World Bank (2008b), Table 5.

A major economic problem of the early post-colonial years was the Third World's dependence on the export of small numbers of primary commodities whose prices were subject to severe fluctuations. Even as late as 1990 only in South and East Asia did the value of manufactured exports exceed that of primary commodities. Manufactured exports from Third World countries have grown and the export of primary commodities has declined as a percentage of merchandise exports. Low- and middle-income economies accounted for 16 per cent of world merchandise exports in 1990. By 2005 this had risen to almost 30 per cent. But the value of manufactured goods in total exports varies considerably from one Third World region to another.

The growth in Third World exports has been achieved despite the protectionism practised by the Western industrial countries which are the markets for the bulk of Third World exports. In the 1980s quotas and other measures are estimated to have cost developing countries a loss of export earnings nearly equivalent to the value of official aid.

The growing globalization of international economic relations has certainly not shifted economic power towards poor countries. Most international trade is still between a small number of rich, developed countries. Trade liberalization benefits these rather than poor countries. Foreign direct investment increased by nearly six times between 1985 and 1995, and tenfold over the following 10 years. Two-thirds of total FDI went to just 10 countries in 2005, mainly located in the wealthier regions of Latin America, and East and Central Asia. In 2005 South Asia received net inflows amounting to only 1 per cent of GDP (World Bank, 1991, 2007a, 2007b).

Human development

Despite progress in human development over the past 30 years, measured by life expectancy, educational attainment and the purchasing power of incomes, there are still substantial contrasts between the developed and developing worlds, as well as between groups of poorer countries (see Table 1.5).

Human development has thus been uneven across the Third World. Trends have reflected overall economic performance. Progress was made between 1965 and 1985, with per capita consumption increasing by nearly 70 per cent in real terms, average life expectancy rising from 51 to 62 years, and primary school enrolment rates reaching 84 per cent. Progress in child mortality rates and primary school enrolments continued in the 1980s in most developing countries. In 1950, 28 children in 100 died before their fifth birthday; this number had fallen to 10 by 1990. Smallpox has been eradicated, whereas it claimed more than 5 million lives annually in the Third World in the early 1950s (World Bank, 1993).

Such averages conceal variations between countries, regions and, of course, social groups within countries. Sub-Saharan Africa, for example, with the highest infant mortality and lowest primary education enrolment, saw only a small improvement in infant mortality in the 1980s and a decline in the enrolment rate. Several Latin American countries, by contrast, saw infant mortality declining at a rate faster than that achieved in the 1960s and 1970s. The economic recession of the early 1980s resulted in substantial declines in real per capita spending on education and health in Sub-Saharan Africa and Latin America. In East Asia the poor have had more access to primary education than in Sub-Saharan Africa. Progress in extending health care to the poor has been slow in all regions of the Third World. East Asia has made most progress in expanding education and improving survival rates, while South Asia and Sub-Saharan Africa still lag behind, with adult literacy rates well below the average for developing countries. Life expectancy, infant mortality and adult literacy have all improved in the Arab states.

Table 1.5 *Human development 2005*

	Life expectancy at birth (years)	Infant mortality (per thousand live births)	Maternal mortality per 100,000 live births	Educational enrolment (%)[1]	Adult literacy (% aged 15+ 1995–2005)	HDI[2]
Low income	60.0	115	684	56.3	60.2	0.570
Middle income	70.9	37	150	73.3	89.9	0.776
Arab states	67.5	52	183	65.5	70.3	0.699
East Asia	71.7	33	117	69.4	90.7	0.771
Latin America	72.8	54	194	81.2	90.3	0.803
South Asia	63.8	83	564	60.3	59.5	0.611
Sub-Saharan Africa	49.6	163	919	50.6	60.3	0.493
High income	79.2	7	14	92.3	..	0.936

NOTES: [1] Combined primary, secondary and tertiary average for each age group.
[2] The United Nations Development Programme's Human Development Index (HDI) is derived from scores given for life expectancy at birth, adult literacy levels, average years of schooling and real GDP per capita (to indicate purchasing power). The two educational variables are combined but with different weightings and growth in the human development value of increases in income is assumed to fall after a certain level is reached. The three indicators are averaged to provide each country with a score from 0 to 1.

SOURCES: UNDP (2007), Table 1, p. 232; World Bank (2008b), Table 3, p.339.

Absolute mortality levels in developing countries are high. It is estimated that decades of improvement in mortality rates will be wiped out by the AIDS epidemic, causing 1.8 million deaths annually. Malaria is proving resistant to treatment, and tobacco-related deaths are likely to increase to more than 12 million a year by 2025 (World Bank, 1993). To achieve significant improvements in health and education in the Third World requires higher levels of expenditure on the social sectors. It is difficult to see how these can be provided by governments that are under pressure to reduce public expenditure as part of economic restructuring.

Child mortality has improved in all regions of the Third World, yet each year over 10 million children die before the age of five. While infant mortality fell in developed countries by over 36 per cent between 1990 and 2005, it did so in developing countries by only 20 per cent. Under-five mortality is 15 times higher in low-income countries than in high-income countries. The main causes are AIDS, measles, respiratory infections and malnutrition – all of which are linked to poverty. Maternal mortality remains high, mainly as a result of malnutrition, inadequate health care and frequent pregnancies. Millions of people still lack access to modern health services and medicines, leading to premature deaths from preventable and curable diseases. In Sub-Saharan Africa almost half the population cannot obtain essential drugs. Immunization coverage remains inadequate. Over a billion people in the Third World have no safe drinking water, although the proportion of people with access to an improved water supply increased from 73 per cent in 1990 to 80 per cent in 2004.

Progress in education includes an increase in the average primary school completion rate from 62 per cent in 1994 to 72 per cent in 2004, and a reduction in gender disparities. However, some 100 million primary school-aged children were not attending school in 2002, three quarters of them in Sub-Saharan Africa and South Asia.

Inequalities in social well-being, as indicated by health and education, are found between urban and rural areas, between men and women, and between income groups. There is generally greater poverty in rural areas and more severe problems of malnutrition, lack of education, life expectancy and substandard housing. Infant mortality rates are above average for rural populations and among the poor, since access to health care is dependent upon income. The disabled are found disproportionately among the poor. Levels of inequality vary among regions of the Third World, with Africa and Latin America having the world's highest levels of inequality (World Bank, 2006).

In all regions of the Third World women do worse than men in terms of health, nutrition and education. Women can also be expected to work longer hours for lower wages than men. They face more cultural, legal, economic and social discrimination than men – even poor men (World

Bank, 1990). When a country's Human Development Index is adjusted for gender disparity, every country's value declines. Rankings change too, showing that some countries do better than others. The most significant disparities for women lie in employment opportunities, earnings (also the main factors in industrialized countries), health care, nutrition and education. It has been estimated that in South and East Asia there are some 100 million women fewer than there would be were it not for maternal mortality rates, infanticide and the nutritional neglect of young girls (UNDP, 1993).

Although human development remains a severe challenge for poor countries, variations in levels occur between developing countries regardless of wealth. For example, Vietnam has achieved more in human development than Pakistan, despite similar levels of per capita GDP.

One of the factors holding back human development in the fourth quarter of the twentieth century has been mounting debt. During the 1970s the volume of international bank lending increased by nearly 800 per cent to reach $800 billion. The scale of indebtedness reached crisis proportions in the early 1980s when a combination of high interest rates, adverse trade balances and a world recession caused severe debt servicing problems for many Third World countries. With a total external debt of US$2.74 trillion in 2005, the cost to developing countries of debt servicing is the equivalent of 6 per cent of GDP. This limits the resources available for human development (as well as discouraging economic growth), so that most poor countries spend more on debt servicing than on basic social services, including education and health care, safe water, sanitation, family planning and nutrition.

Human development is increasingly being thought of as encompassing political factors, such as the level of democratization and the protection afforded to human rights. In 1987 roughly three-fifths of the developing world's governments were not democratic. However, in the late 1980s pressures towards democratization and the rule of law built up from a number of factors acting in unison. One was the economic failure of authoritarianism. Another was the highly political consequence of the structural adjustment programmes demanded by multilateral and unilateral aid donors.

The structural adjustment programmes required of many developing countries as a condition for receiving assistance from international development agencies such as the World Bank and IMF have had far-reaching political consequences for the governments concerned. Public enterprise reforms and privatization have usually meant substantial job losses. Devaluation and increases in agricultural prices can increase food prices and malnutrition. Public expenditure cuts usually mean a decline in social spending – particularly health and education – per capita. These consequences and their distributional effects can cause social unrest, and have done so in a number of Third World countries. Structural adjustment also limits the scope for political patronage (Herbst, 1990). When it became clear to aid donors and international agencies that successful adjustment required political commitment as well as competent and accountable public services, this was interpreted as a need for democratization (Hawthorne, 1992; Leftwich, 1993). However, despite their 'good governance' rhetoric, Western aid donors have been remarkably reluctant to take positive action in support of Third World democracy, especially when their own foreign interests have been at stake.

Other factors contributed to the 'good governance' orthodoxy: the rise of Western neo-liberalism in the late 1970s; the spread of pro-democracy movements in all regions of the Third World as well as Eastern Europe; and the collapse of communism. This last and most momentous development strengthened confidence in the presumed link between political pluralism and economic success and left space for an extension of influence by the capitalist West within a 'New World Order' (Riley, 1992; Webber, 1993).

Despite some advances towards less authoritarian forms of government – in Zambia, South Korea and Taiwan, for example – the prospects for democratic development and survival do not appear to be too bright. The experience of the Third World with democratization has been mixed. By the end of the century democracy and freedom were the dominant trends in Latin America and the Asia Pacific region. In Africa by contrast, a minority of countries had free societies and electoral democracy. No countries in the Arab world were rated 'free'. Furthermore, all the downward trends are found in developing countries. Between 1998 and 2006 democratic gains in countries such as Mexico, India, Nepal and Indonesia were offset by regressive developments in Pakistan, Fiji, Sri Lanka, Malaysia and the Philippines. The Arab Middle East still has a huge 'democratic deficit', with no states rated 'free' in 2006 (respecting a broad array of basic human rights and political freedoms). All but 4 of the 45 countries rated 'not free' by Freedom House in 2006 were in the Third World. Most Third World states fall into the 'Partly Free' and 'Not Free' categories. Democratization has stagnated in recent years, with governments in all regions guilty of suppressing political opposition, civil society, and freedom of assemble. There has been something of a backlash against democracy (Freedom House, 2007).

Non-democratic regimes are by no means all associated with low incomes, spanning as they do a diversity of levels of economic development (for example, Saudi Arabia and Sudan) as well as cultures (for example Cuba and North Korea) and regions (Burma and Syria). However, the economic conditions associated with Third World status clearly remain significant. While it is possible for relatively rich countries to do badly in terms of political and civil rights violations and repression (e.g. Brunei), and for a poor country such as Benin to be rated among the countries with the highest level of political freedom, generally there is a correlation between levels of political freedom and economic prosperity (Freedom House, 2001).

One of the greatest threats to democracy in developing countries is militarization. This may take the form of overt military rule or disproportionate expenditure on the military compared with social welfare. Over 30 developing countries have had more than 20 years of military rule since 1960. Developing countries spend on average 15 per cent of central government budgets on the military. In several countries military spending amounts to over 10 per cent of GDP. Economic growth, especially in China and India, has fuelled increases in military expenditure. Many countries spend considerably more on the military than on social sectors, despite the desperate need for health care, education and the relief of poverty. The lower the per capita income group, the higher the priority given to military spending compared with social spending (SIPRI, 2005).

A further threat to democracy in the Third World is posed by forms of religious fundamentalism which violate principles of toleration and equal rights. In India, for example, Hindu nationalism is believed by some experts to threaten the very survival of the political system as a pluralist democracy (Chiriyankandath, 1994). To a considerable extent such movements reflect disillusionment with political and economic developments which leave large sections of the population marginalized both materially and politically as power is accumulated in the hands of new ruling classes. Religious fundamentalism provides an ideological focus which asserts the relevance of forms of traditionalism to the modern world.

The concept of a 'third' world

Gunnar Myrdal, winner of the Nobel Prize for economics in 1974, once said that in the relationship between rich and poor countries there has been diplomacy by language, meaning that in the developed, and to a lesser extent the underdeveloped, countries there has been a constant search for an acceptable label for this latter group. We sometimes refer to 'the South' rather than use 'developing countries' or 'Third World'. Others prefer 'less developed countries', while still others prefer 'underdeveloped', a concept that has taken on a very specific meaning and which, as we shall see in Chapter 3, denotes a particular kind of interrelationship between countries and a particular process of change.

No one has come up with a label that claims universal acceptance. The search is fraught with difficulties, not least ideological ones. As Goulbourne points out, the terminology of comparative politics, particularly as far as the

Third World is concerned, is largely expressive of attitudes rather than precise analytical concepts (Goulbourne, 1979). Cannot all countries be described as 'developing' in some direction or another? If we reserve 'development' for movement in a particular direction, then it has to be made explicit what path should be regarded as development and what should not. 'Modernization' similarly risks all the dangers of ethnocentric evolutionism, though as a conceptualization of social and political change it has had an enormous impact on development studies and comparative politics.

The concept of the 'South' reflects some of the frustrations felt when trying to differentiate between countries in terms of meaningful indicators that show why grouping countries is helpful to analysis. It is also possible to talk about rich and poor countries, but this draws a boundary between countries which many people interested in the Third World wish to treat as a single grouping. It is easy to understand the appeal of 'underdevelop' as a transitive verb in distinguishing those countries whose exploitation made possible the development of their exploiters. The idea that advanced societies secured their own advancement by underdeveloping poor countries is at the heart of dependency theory.

Such difficulties form the substance of the rest of this chapter. The purpose of examining the concept of the 'Third World' is that one can gain a preliminary insight into some of the problems experienced by such countries by examining the validity of using a single category for such an amorphous group.

Meanings and objectives

To be able to evaluate the different positions adopted by those who have entered into dispute about whether 'Third World' is a meaningful concept it is necessary to separate out the different perceptions that people have about the countries which they think deserving of the label.

The original meaning of the term 'Third World' referred to a group of *non-aligned* countries outside the great power blocs. There has been a lot of discussion as to who first used the term, but it is generally accepted that it was the French demographer and economic historian, Alfred Sauvy who coined the term in the early 1950s. However, there is also the view that it should have been translated as 'Third Force' because Sauvy seemed to have in mind the problem of power blocs during the Cold War, and of a Third Force distinct from the Western bloc and the Eastern bloc. Nevertheless, 'non-alignment' in the military and diplomatic spheres is one of the earliest qualities associated with Third World status (Wolf-Phillips, 1987; Love, 1980). This stance was most strikingly represented by the Bandung Conference attended by the representatives of 29 African and Asian countries in 1955 (Berger, 2004).

Another early idea associated with the Third World conveys *solidarity* among developing countries based on their primary producing economic status, their relative poverty, their dependence on agriculture, and their distinctive forms of economic regime neither modelled on the Eastern bloc of planned economies nor the Western, free market system. The Third World was seen to fall outside the first world of the advanced capitalist democracies and the second world of industrially advanced communist countries. The Third World was not just a residual category of states that were neither liberal-democratic nor communist-totalitarian. It was a significant grouping in that its members lay outside Europe, mainly south of the fortieth parallel, were mainly agrarian, were much poorer than northern states and had been subjected either to colonialism or 'deep diplomatic and economic penetration by the Western powers'(Finer, 1974, p. 98).

However, there was an important deviation from this perception of the world's economic divisions. China's Mao Tse-tung produced a very different categorization in which the USA and the USSR constituted the first world, Japan, the European countries and Canada constituted the second world, while Africa, Latin America and most of Asia formed the third world. The claim being made here was that *both* the USA and the USSR were imperialistic, with their developed satellites as the second world and the primary producing former colonial possessions of the first and second worlds forming the third world. So the OPEC countries would, despite their wealth, fall into this third group (Dirlik, 2004).

Mao was clearly influenced by current relationships between China and the USSR, worse at that time than between China and some capitalist states. From other socialist perspectives, developing countries have been seen as predominantly dependencies of the major capitalist powers. This led to the belief that one could only meaningfully talk about two worlds, not three, one capitalist, one socialist (Griffin and Gurley, 1985).

Thirdly there has been the idea of an *anti-imperialist* alliance against colonialism, neo-colonialism and racialism. So the Third World stood for solidarity against the continuing intervention and involvement of the powerful economies in the developing economies and polities of the world, in an attempt to strengthen economic sovereignty at a time when it was very obvious that political and economic autonomy did not necessarily go together, and that the achievement of constitutional independence did not guarantee freedom internally from external constraints. This idea will be taken up again when we come to look at the concept of 'neo-colonialism' and the way in which interpretations of political and economic development have been formulated in such terms. The idea of a Third World thus tries to capture a common experience of exploitation by richer and more powerful societies. All Third World countries have experienced such exploitation to some degree, and it was strongly felt by many Third World leaders that it was persisting even after independence.

Fourthly, Third Worldism has been associated with the idea of *regional coherence* through pan-nationalist movements. The Third World might not represent a grouping of countries all with identical interests, but within the Third World there could be groups of states that shared interests cutting across national boundaries – for example, the pan-Arab world or the pan-African world. Such concepts were important to political leaders in developing countries in the 1960s. Here was an attempt to prove that national boundaries were not going to be as important as they were in other parts of the world. National boundaries were seen as the creation of European colonialism, especially in Africa. Thus they were to some extent alien, reflecting a colonial past. Institutions were set up to reflect this internationalism and some still exist though without the significance that they were originally intended to have.

Fifthly, since the early 1970s Third Worldism has reflected a campaign for a *new international economic order* under which developing countries would secure greater national control of their natural resources, and try to protect their economies by collectively agreeing to the prices of raw materials upon which so many of their economies were dependent. Third Worldism has been to some extent driven by a sense of grievance against the developed countries which appear to have rigged the rules of the international economy against less developed countries (Rothstein, 1977). The objective has been to strengthen through collective action the position of individual Third World countries vis-à-vis their main trading partners and sources of foreign investment.

Third World countries also want to gain greater access to markets in industrialized countries for their own manufactured goods by persuading the governments in those countries to lower the trade barriers that protect domestic industries from competition from Third World products. This call has been taken up by the United Nations and the World Bank, both arguing for the liberalization of global markets and a reduction in the level of protectionism in the OECD countries. The costs of protectionism in the rich countries of the world extend beyond blocking imports from the Third World to include negative capital transfers, higher real interest rates, unequal competition in international services and closed markets for technology. A more rapid transfer of technologies to give Third World countries access to the advanced technologies required by the industrialization process, and which were proving so successful in some developing countries, also forms part of this aspect of Third Worldism.

Related proposals have included a World Development Fund to which all countries would contribute on a sliding scale related to their national income; the development of the sea bed to provide new sources of food; and the international development of alternative energy sources. Through UNESCO Third World countries try to act collectively to resist the pressures from the Westernized mass media, and the cultural, educational and scientific imperialism which introduces inappropriate technology and educational values into their societies. Solidarity was also shown at the World Trade Organization meeting in Doha in 2001 when developing countries formed effective alliances on intellectual property rights, drug patents, and the agenda of future negotiations, shifting the balance of power away from the rich industrialized nations.

Changing worlds

The Third World has changed much since the earliest visions of solidarity and continues to do so. Political culture may be the defining characteristic of the Third World, rather than level of economic affluence or diplomatic orientation. What distinguishes membership of the Third World is the lack of consensus over the rules of the 'game' of politics (Kamrava, 1995). Consequently, a label that conveys a message of homogeneity of socio-economic conditions and political purpose is increasingly unacceptable by commentators from both North and South (Leftwich, 1983; Hulme and Turner, 1990).

The first form of heterogeneity that needs to be recognized is cultural. The term 'Third World' has been considered by some as insulting to the diverse range of polities, cultures, histories and ideologies found within it (Rothstein, 1977). It may convey the idea that responsibility for Third World poverty lies wholly with the developed world, a view that might be regarded as patronizing and condescending. The Third World is not a 'uniform stagnant mass devoid of distinctive character'. The peoples of the Third World should not be denied identity, character, personality and responsibility (Bauer, 1981, pp. 83–4). However, rejecting the concept because it treats the Third World as an undifferentiated mass risks over-looking the psychological and political connotations of Third Worldism in favour of an interpretation that 'denotes an association of countries dedi-cated to the moral blackmail of a guilt-afflicted West' (Toye, 1987, p. 6).

A growing heterogeneity is in economic strength. As was shown earlier, there are great disparities of wealth within the Third World. Wide dispari-ties are developing in per capita GNP, levels of food production, annual growth rates and rates of industrialization. Expert observers and interna-tional organizations such as the World Bank now distinguish between the rich poor countries, the middle poor and the poorest countries, even to the extent of referring to the last group as the Fourth World – the poorest of the poor or the least developed of the developing countries (Rothstein, 1977). World Bank statistics are presented in such categories, and other organizations such as the UN also differentiate in their policy-making (Hoogvelt, 1982). Some of the cut-off points between these categories are pretty arbitrary (Worsley, 1984) but nevertheless there are real differences when one compares Bangladesh with, say, Malaysia. Some aid donors, such as the British Government, distinguish between the poor and the poorest with the aim of directing their development assistance at the poorest countries, many of which are among the countries of the British Commonwealth, which fits nicely with its policy of directing aid towards its ex-colonies.

Nor has the Third World's experience of globalization been uniform. It has been argued that the 'globalization' of market economics and pluralistic democracy, apparently heralded by the end of the Cold War, further challenges the validity of the concept of a Third World (Berger, 1994). The process of globalization integrates economies, cultures and technology. The end of the cold War and the demise of communist regimes in Russia and Europe, it has been argued, meant that all countries were converging politically on liberal democracy and economically on capitalism. Democratization seemed to be on the advance. The main sources of international conflict seemed to be irreversibly weakening. The world had reached, according to Francis Fukuyama (1992), the 'end of history' beyond which there could be no further evolution.

Whether such convergence ever occurs remains to be seen, but as Fukuyama himself recognized, it remains a distant prospect for most of the Third World. The 'end of history' concept is also of little help in understanding conflicts between Third World countries, such as Venezuela and Colombia, or the tensions between the so-called Democratic Republic of Congo and its neighbours in central Africa. Nor does it accommodate ethnic strife, as in Kenya, where the malfunctioning of electoral politics led to unanticipated violence in 2008 between the five tribes that make up the majority of the population of 43 tribes and 34 million people. Over a thousand people died and more than a quarter of a million were displaced to become internal refugees. It also seems unrealistically optimistic to expect a convergence on liberal democracy in Zimbabwe or Burma.

Part of the Third World diversity lies in conflicting ideologies, economic systems and forms of government. The consensus about liberal democracy, in so far as one is emerging, is certainly not shared by much of the Islamic world. In fact Islamic regimes are diametrically opposed to the basic tenets of democracy, especially freedom of speech, freedom of belief, political equality, the rule of law, and the separation of state and religion. Many Third World regimes that call themselves democratic find it difficult to operate democracy's formal procedures, such as free and fair elections, correctly, and virtually impossible to provide the material and social foundations for the enjoyment of full political rights and participation. Within the Third World there are also those who regard the claim that history is ending in liberal democracy and capitalism as yet another form of Western neo-colonialism.

An alternative view of the post-Cold War era is that, far from reaching a consensus on economic and political values, ideological conflict has been replaced by a clash of cultures and religions, or 'civilizations' as Samuel Huntington would have it (1996). The dominant post-Cold War conflict from this perspective is between Islam and the West.

Such categorization again offers an excessively uniform and inclusive image of the two contestants. It also falsely equates culture with religion. The Third World in the post-Cold War era consists of far more societies and cultures than allowed for by a duality of civilizations. Large regions of the Third World can be subsumed under neither category. Political and diplomatic relations between the West and other countries include tensions which are hard to fit within this view of the world order, such as the United States' relations with Venezuela, China and Cuba, or the UK's relations with Zimbabwe. America's relations with China and India are high on the State Department's list of priorities, and the UK's diplomacy is as much concerned with illegal immigration, drug trafficking, relations with Europe, and the country's economic interests, as with counter-terrorism. When the West is involved in societies that are predominantly Islamic, it is always in alliance with one or more Moslem-based factions or elites, rather than hostile to Islam as such. Iraq, Afghanistan, Saudi Arabia and Pakistan are the most obvious examples.

Significant changes within the international order are also taking place within the Third World, most notably between Asia and Sub-Saharan Africa. Africa's exports to Asia grew by 20 per cent between 2000 and 2005, making Asia the third most important destination for African exports after the EU and USA, and the region taking the fastest growing share. Both the EU and USA saw their shares of African exports fall between 1990 and 2005. Africa's imports from Asia have also grown faster than from other regions, with the EU and USA again accounting for declining shares of Africa's imports.

African development is becoming especially dependent on trade, investment and aid from China. African exports to China rose from negligible levels in 1990 to US$5 billion in 2000, accelerating to US$19 billion in 2005, or 15 per cent of the region's total exports. China is Africa's fastest growing destination for its exports. Imports from China have also increased in value, from US$3.5 billion in 2000 to over US$13 billion in 2005, or almost 15 per cent of Sub-Saharan Africa's total imports. Trade between China and Africa increased by 50 per cent in 2002 and by a further

60 per cent in 2003. Chinese investment in Africa includes offshore oilfields (Nigeria), petrochemicals (Sudan), mobile phones (Zimbabwe), roads (Rwanda and Kenya), railways (Angola) and forestry (Mozambique). China has also significantly increased aid to Africa, to US$19 billion in 2006, and intends to double this by 2009 (Jacoby, 2007), raising concerns that an absence of political conditionalities with Chinese aid could put human rights in Africa even further at risk.

The benefits of globalization – increased trade, foreign investment and the dissemination of technology – are by no means spread equally across the Third World. Some regions, such as East Asia, have taken advantage of globalization to generate growth in manufactured exports. Others remain marginalized because of their continuing dependence on primary commodities. Within East Asia, recovery from the financial crisis of 1997–99 has been uneven. The spread of information and communications technologies is very uneven. The poorest countries of the Third World have dangerously small shares of world trade and access to foreign investment.

Consequently, many developing countries are falling further and further behind developed countries economically, while a few have economies growing faster than those of developed countries. Notable here are India and China, the former doubling its growth rate between 1980 and 2000, the latter averaging almost 8 per cent per annum per capita since the late 1970s. Since these two countries account for over half the world's poor, their achievements have brought about a reduction in global poverty. However, the majority of poor countries have not only seen poverty increase. They also tend to lack the governmental capacity to cope with the threats of globalization, especially financial instability, bioinvasion, international crime and terrorism, the power of international institutions (such as the World Trade Organization and IMF, over 26,000 international NGOs, and transnational corporations), and the growing gap between rich and poor.

As some less developed countries have welcomed or at least accepted the inevitability of foreign investment and the dependency that it brings, including subordination in the international division of labour, non-alignment is undermined as a defining quality of Third World states. So even by the end of the 1960s Third World countries were by no means behaving in unity towards East–West relations. A stridently anti-communist group of Asian states emerged – Indonesia, Malaysia, Singapore, Thailand and the Philippines. This brought an end to the Third World as a coherent voting block in the United Nations, splitting it along ideological lines. Similarly, in 1979 at the United Nations Conference on Trade and Development (UNCTAD V) the more industrialized of the Third World countries vetoed a code of conduct for multinational corporations (MNCs) that the less industrialized Third World states wanted to bring in, demonstrating their need to avoid antagonizing MNCs on whose presence even the rich Third

World countries so heavily depend for their development. The material, economic basis of non-alignment had become very weak by 1980, making it difficult for dependent economies to form a solid bloc hostile to the major economic powers in the developed world upon which they depend for foreign investment, technology, aid and technical assistance. Politically, the majority of Third World countries have long been very 'aligned' (Worsley, 1984, p. 324).

Solidarity has been undermined by a number of other developments. First, many organizations expressing regional common interests have been weak or disappeared. Those organizations that have survived have been geared to the economic interests of particular regions, for example, the Central American Common Market, the Latin American Free Trade Association, and OPEC. The relationships have sometimes developed into international organizations with memberships cutting across the North–South divide, bringing together countries from the First and Third Worlds. An important recent example is APEC – Asia-Pacific Economic Co-operation – whose membership includes the USA, Japan, South Korea, Taiwan, Malaysia, Thailand, Singapore, China and Australia. The member-states of APEC account for more than half the world's economic output and two-fifths of its trade.

Secondly, domestic economic problems in Third World countries have undermined solidarity such as those reflected in demands for a new international economic order. Policy failures, mismanagement and debt have forced some Third World countries to become inward-looking, leading some to the conclusion that 'Third World solidarity has become a thing of the past' (Westlake, 1991, p. 16).

Thirdly, the demise of communist regimes in eastern and central Europe and the former USSR has produced a degree of homogeneity between the First and Second Worlds, at least in terms of economic systems, which makes references to developing countries as a 'Third' group or force less and less meaningful. It has been argued that the globalization of market economics and pluralistic democracy, apparently heralded by the end of the Cold War, further challenges the validity of the concept of a Third World (Berger, 1994), although this ignores the uncomfortable fact that markets may dominate economies in societies in which tyrants dominate government.

Finally, solidarity has been seriously undermined by warfare between Third World states, notably the Iran–Iraq conflict, the Gulf War, conflict between India and Pakistan, war in Southeast Asia in the late 1970s, and war in the centre and Horn of Africa. The consequent human suffering and economic loss cannot be underestimated when considering Third World 'solidarity'.

Another serious objection to the concept of a Third World has been raised by people who find difficulties with its association with poverty. The concern is that if a group of countries is defined as poor it might obscure the fact that there are in such countries classes that enjoy immense wealth. To talk about poverty-ridden peoples in less-developed countries (Meier, 1976) can act as a form of mystification deflecting attention away from internal stratification. Poor countries do not consist entirely of poor people. Great internal inequalities exist. The economic differentials between Third World countries have not eradicated poverty within the more successful ones. Inequalities persist and sometimes increase regardless of a country's overall economic performance (Toye, 1987). At the same time elites in Third World societies often appear to have more in common with Western elites than with their own dispossessed masses (Berger, 1994).

So, global stratification into rich, middle income and poor countries must not be allowed to conceal internal social stratification. This is not to say that the poverty that poor people in poor countries experience is solely to do with the domestic maldistribution of power. It is not to say that it has nothing to do with dependence on the more powerful economies in the world. But it does alert us to the possibility that those two things are related – that dependency within the world economic system actually benefits some classes in the Third World. The term 'comprador bourgeoisie' was coined to convey the idea of an alliance between an indigenous middle class and foreign investors, MNCs, bankers and military interests. There is thus a need to relate thinking about global stratification to how that division and the relationships between those global strata affect relations between internal social strata. To what extent would redistribution within a poor country be made easier if there was no dependence on more powerful trading partners and sources of foreign exchange?

There is thus a risk that the expression 'Third World' might obscure the heterogeneity of social classes, each with its own political objective. The concept of a Third World has consequently been denounced as mystification designed to conceal dependency and exploitation, as well as a device allowing rulers of Third World countries to present a common interest between themselves and the masses to disguise their own alliance with metropolitan interests (Debray, 1967).

Conclusion: Third World values

Though there are powerful arguments for concluding that 'the age of the Third World has passed irrevocably into history' (Berger, 2004, p. 30), some think it is still important to preserve the term in order to convey key values associated with it. It could be dangerous to stop talking about the Third World and so further fragment that group of countries. Their solidarity must be somehow preserved simply because as individual states they are bound to be weak in their relationships with the developed world. The 'Third World' is thus seen as 'a sound concept' and a 'flexible, resilient category'. Attempts to question its validity may be mischievous and misleading. It implies neither inferior values nor some lower numerical order, but rather a set of specific characteristics that are unique in more than one way to the countries of Asia, Africa and Latin America. It represents the broadly similar, though not exactly identical, nature of these countries' experiences in the processes of development, processes that were arrested in the past, are discouraging and uncertain at present, and are likely to be unprecedented in the future (Muni, 1979). Even if Third Worldism only means building regional alliances to present a united front economically, that in itself is important.

One such significant characteristic is global inequality, and the position of the Third World within this. The term serves the very important function of reinstating the significance of global economic relationships, and the disastrous social and political consequences for countries with such a small share of the world's income, notably civil war. It also provides a 'vital corrective' to the idea that international politics can only be seen in terms of a 'clash of civilizations' or religious traditions (Randall, 2004).

But most importantly, many of the problems which characterized the group of countries originally labelled the Third World by Western analysts, and which prompted solidaristic action by Third World leaders, persist. The countries conventionally categorized as part of the Third World do not all rank the same in terms of the indicators of Third World status used here. But all confront some of the problems associated with Third World status, and most of the 50 low-income countries experience them all. So while Brazil, an upper-middle income country, has a GNP per capita of $4,420, life expectancy is lower than Vietnam's with a GNP per capita of $370. Tanzania, a low-income economy, has a higher ratio of trade to GNP than upper middle-income Mexico. Manufactured goods account for only 10 per cent of middle-income Ecuador's exports of merchandise, compared with 84 per cent of low-income Pakistan. Diamonds may contribute 80 per cent of Botswana's foreign exchange earnings, 50 per cent of government income and 33 per cent of GDP. Yet dependence on this single commodity has transformed the country from one of the poorest in the world to one of the richest in Africa. However, life expectancy is 40 years, mainly due to a high incidence of HIV infection, and attempts to diversify industry have faltered. Infant mortality is high in most low-income countries, but so it is in upper middle-income Gabon. Almost as large a proportion of Bangladesh's population has access to safe water as Uruguay, though the latter has a per capita GNP 16 times greater.

Subsequent chapters will consider the political importance of such characteristics as poverty and inequality, dependence on foreign investment for economic development, industrialization and urbanization as aspects of modernization, and progress in the protection of human rights and freedoms. The dependency which has featured in much of the discussion about the nature of the Third World has also been central to interpretations of the changes which are taking place there. In one sense the expression 'Third World' represents a challenge to 'development' as autonomous growth and progress. The controversies within the social sciences about development, underdevelopment, and the consequences of contacts between rich and poor countries will form the substance of later chapters. The next chapter examines an approach to understanding political change in terms of the relationship between social and economic modernization and the emergence of western political institutions.

2

Modernization and Political Development

Social evolution

Modernization theory has its origins in classical evolutionary explanations of social change. Its intellectual roots are in the European evolutionists of the eighteenth and nineteenth centuries: the French philosophers and founders of modern sociology Auguste Compte and Emile Durkheim; the British philosopher Herbert Spencer; and of course Marx. All were in their different ways trying to explain the transformation from pre-industrial to industrial society. Two elements in particular from that early theorizing were carried over into debates about modernization in the Third World. One is the belief that social change involves continuity. The other is a belief in progress (Tipps, 1973; Varma, 1980; So, 1990).

Continuity is not seen as neutral but as progressive. The transition from pre-industrial to industrial society entails advancement and improvement, and progression from tradition to modernity (Hoogvelt, 1978). Progressive continuity involves two sets of transformations: increased complexity; and greater specialization, or 'differentiation', in human organization and activity in the social, economic and political spheres.

Modernization theory inspired an organic approach to comparative politics which was intended to integrate Third World political phenomena into a new theoretical framework. In this chapter the main arguments of the functionalist perspective on comparative politics are presented, especially the concepts of function and 'structural differentiation' when applied to political systems, the motivation behind this theoretical position, and the main criticisms that have been levelled against it.

Modernization theory, like other evolutionary explanations of society, had its own view of the end of the evolutionary process. Modernization meant advancement towards a condition corresponding to the industrial capitalist societies of the West. A society that is becoming modern is one that acquires characteristics common to more developed societies, achieving things that modern societies have in common (Eisenstadt, 1966.

27

Traditional societies will gradually eliminate their economic, political and particularly cultural institutions and values, replacing them with modern ones.

The attributes needed for modernization were seen as interrelated. Economic and social values were linked through such individual values as the work ethic, needed to support the kind of activities upon which modern industrial society depended but not found in traditional society. Modernization theory thus relied heavily on Max Weber's view of religious beliefs as sustaining certain kinds of economic relationships. Modernization theorists, while not necessarily wanting to disseminate Protestantism, nevertheless accepted that normative values were extremely significant as a foundation for launching new kinds of economic initiatives.

From tradition to modernity

Modernization theorists identified the features of the process by which it was thought the undeveloped societies of the world would become modern. First, they contrasted the characteristics of an ideal-type which was designated 'modern' with one that was designated 'traditional'. Development is then viewed as the evolution of the former into the latter as less developed countries evolve into developed societies (Nash, 1963; Blomstrom and Hettne, 1984).

Secondly, the importance of structural differentiation in the social changes accompanying economic development was emphasized. Differentiation occurs with the transition from domestic to factory production, the replacement of family and church by the school in the education function, and the substitution of the complex political party structure for tribal factions.

Thirdly, modernization theorists also asked what needs must be satisfied to maintain a social system in a healthy state. Following Parsons, they accepted there were general functional prerequisites in society: *adaptation*, so that a social system can survive in its environment; *goal attainment* – the need to be organized so as to achieve collective objectives such as waging war; *integration* or maintaining social support for the system; and *pattern maintenance*, or the need for stability and continuity. However different societies might be in other respects, they all have to develop ways of performing these essential functions if they are to survive.

Adaptation was thought to be particularly important. It meant that societies could change in response to changes in the environment. In the natural world biological organisms can adapt to a changing environment, albeit over very long periods of time. They can cope with change and survive. Societies and political systems, it was argued, have to do the same.

The application of modernization theory to politics was combined with a particular approach to social anthropology to produce a *functionalist* interpretation of political change. It had a major impact on the comparative study of politics when the existing tools of political analysis were deemed inappropriate for the task of including within a comparative analytical framework the new states appearing in the international political arena after the Second World War.

The organic metaphor

The concept of 'function' suggests among other things an analogy between a society and a biological organism. In biology 'function' refers to the contribution that different parts of an organism make to its maintenance. This biological analogy is useful to remember in order to get a grip on the presuppositions that were articulated about politics and government by this school of thought. Organizations such as political parties or administrative agencies could only be explained by reference to the purposes they serve for the functioning of the organism as a whole (Almond, 1965).

Political development theory borrowed two other key ideas from biology: *interdependence* and *equilibrium*. Interdependence means that when one component of an organism changes, the organism as a whole is affected. For example, the emergence of mass political parties or the mass media 'changes the performance of all the other structures of the political system, and affects the general capabilities of the system in its domestic and foreign environments'. If the change is dysfunctional to the system 'the dysfunctional component is disciplined by regulatory mechanisms, and the equilibrium of the system is re-established' (Almond, 1965, p. 185). Political systems tend towards equilibrium. Institutions preserve their character or at most change slowly.

Structure and function

Functions have to be performed by social structures, or sets of roles performed by individual members of the set. Roles are thus distinguished from persons. When roles are performed in a particular set they constitute a social structure. Individuals thus make up numerous different structures. A member of the role set of the family contributes to that structure as well as to the other structures to which they contribute roles – at work, in religious ceremonies, in the interpretation and enforcement of law and custom, in community associations, in political organizations, and so on. In premodern societies age may determine to which set an individual contributes.

Age-grades then become an important structure for the performance of political functions.

The relationship between structure and function gave rise to the label 'structural functionalism', an extremely influential theory for a while that, ironically, was all but abandoned by sociologists outside the USA when it was taken up by American political scientists in their efforts to devise a means of comparing all known political systems. They perceived a need for a theoretical framework that could cope with a bewildering variety of exotic political systems that could not be accommodated within existing modes of comparison (Holt and Turner, 1972; O'Brien, 1972; Varma, 1980).

Structural functionalism was intended to provide such a comparative framework of analysis. In non-Western societies unfamiliar structures were performing functions that seemed to be needed in all political systems. New concepts were needed to understand such phenomena. The concepts of contemporary political science were not, it was decided, equipped for the task. Western political science up to this point had been based on the comparison of institutions and, even more restrictedly, institutions found in Western industrialized societies and their processes of democratization.

Once again biology provided the required insight:

> The problem of developing categories to compare the conversion processes of different kinds of political systems is not unlike the problem of comparative anatomy and physiology. Surely the anatomical structure of a unicellular organism differs radically from that of a vertebrate, but something like the functions which in the vertebrate are performed by a specialised nervous system, a gastro-intestinal tract, are performed in the amoeba by intermittent adaptations of its single cell' (Almond, 1965, p. 195).

By analogy, complex political systems have specialized structures for performing distinctive tasks while simple ones do not.

Functionalism became the political interpretation of modernization theory in order to find a way of addressing societies that were rapidly achieving the status of nation states with apparently modern political institutions such as legislatures, parties, constitutions, and executives, but grafted on to structures that were totally unfamiliar to most Western observers other than anthropologists. The functionalists therefore abandoned comparative methods based on structures in favour of one based on functions. If structures were persisted with, the resultant analytical tools would be inappropriate. The search for constitutions, parties, pressure groups, legislatures and bureaucracies would be fruitless in societies whose government did not depend on such structures.

A set of functions has to be performed in all societies no matter how complex or simple, industrialized or agrarian. The task is to establish what these are and then seek out the structures that perform them in different societies. Comparative politics could no longer prejudge the question of structures. If communities are found to enforce their rules not by courts, police forces, prisons and the other institutions of the state but by contests between the injured parties, tempered by public opinion within lineages, as in the Nuer of the southern Sudan, it should not be assumed that such societies were disorganized, chaotic or without the means of governing themselves. They might be societies without Governments but they were not societies without government, or regular ways of performing necessary political functions. Structures existed to perform those functions. Familiar legislative structures might not exist to make legally binding rules but other social structures would exist to perform this function of articulating rules, perhaps by age-groups.

Another major contrast drawn by the functionalists between developed and developing societies was in the existence of boundaries between social, political and economic systems. In traditional societies these often appeared to be lacking, whereas in a modern society, according to the functionalists, it was possible to separate structures that were primarily economic from those that were primarily social or political.

The functionalists needed both a theory of the political system – a more appropriate label than 'state', given the existence of stateless societies – and a theory of change or development. Like all modernization theorists they wanted to incorporate into their thinking the idea of progressive change. Societies were seen as not merely moving from one condition to another but from being traditional to being developed, implying improvement and progress in the way that societies are governed.

The political system

The functionalist theory of the political system rests on five key concepts: politics; system; structure; culture; and function.

By *politics* the functionalists mean social relationships involving the legitimate monopoly of physical coercion, following the Weberian definition of the state (Almond, 1965). Political activities are directed at control of or influence over the use of coercive power. Whatever the values prompting demands for action by the authorities, and whatever the nature of the action called for, ultimately these relate to the coercive power of the political system.

The concept of *system* conveys the interrelationships between the parts of a polity so that when there is change in one part of the system other parts will be affected. A political system is made up of particular roles involving the monopoly of physical force and the establishment and maintenance of a process by which inputs are converted into outputs. The political process generates both demands for policies and a number of supports for governmental outputs. Those demands and supports on the input side are converted into outputs through political processes. All societies have ways of converting inputs into outputs. They constitute its political system. In all societies there are interactions which produce political outputs by means of the employment or threat of employment of legitimate physical compulsion.

The political system was thus perceived as a legitimate set of interrelated structures for maintaining order and responding to the changing pressures of the environment. Those structures would in part be regulative and coercive, concerned with the suppression of dissent. They would also be distributive, shifting resources between sectors of society. Extractive structures would draw resources from society through such means as taxation.

The idea of *structures* as sets of interrelated roles that make up the political process enables the functionalists to identify how functions could be performed without preconceived ideas associating particular functions with corresponding structures. So a legislature, for example, was a set of interrelated roles performing the function of making legally binding rules.

Functionalists developed the concept of *culture* to bring into the framework of political analysis the idea that all societies contain discernible attitudes and dispositions towards politics. Parsons's pattern variables are utilized in political development theory, sometimes to dichotomize traditional and modern systems of politics, as in Riggs' (1957) models of Agraria and Industria, and sometimes to demonstrate a 'dualism' of political structure found in all societies, as in Almond's distinction between primary and secondary structures in societies where primitive or premodern political structures persist in modern political systems (Almond, 1960).

A society in crisis is often a society in which the dominant political culture is being undermined by competing sets of beliefs. It can no longer sustain the level of support needed by the political system for it to survive. The political culture thus consists of values about how politics should actually be conducted, and how the processes of government should be carried on. The legitimacy adhering to the structures and processes of government is expressed through a society's political culture. The obligations that are the consequence of that legitimacy relate to the rules of the political system.

In any given society there may well be different political cultures that give rise to conflict. One of the problems of becoming modern was seen in cultural terms as a problem of persuading people in post-colonial societies to accept the boundaries of the nation-state as legitimate when those boundaries had their origins in alien rule. The processes of government might also lack legitimacy if they were based on unacceptable forms of authority again derived from an alien source. Thus adaptation to forms of democracy inherited from foreigners may also be difficult. This is frequently referred to as the problem of political integration, a major source of political instability in Third World societies. Political integration will be returned to in Chapter 8 when different explanations for nationalism and secession are considered.

Finally, there is the concept of *function*, central to the needs of the comparative analyst. The universal attributes of political systems can only be conceptualized in terms of functions. The functionalists claimed that every society, however organized politically, at whatever level of development, and whatever the political structures through which government is carried on, will perform eight political functions.

First there is *interest articulation*, or the ways in which demands are formulated and brought into the political arena so that the conversion process can transform demands into outputs. What for the West might be the most typical structure performing that function (pressure groups and similar forms of association) will not necessarily be found in pre-industrial or transitional societies. The development of civil society varies from one country to another, and the equality of treatment and freedoms, assumed by the functionalist model of a developed political system, is rarely found. For example, the Philippines has a strong civil society, with many organizations incorporated into decision-making. Such groups are capable of concerted action to remove corrupt and authoritarian leaders, as in the case of Ferdinand Marcos in 1986 and Joseph Estrada in 2001. However, left-wing pressure groups and church activists are vulnerable to military intimidation, undermining political dialogue and damaging democracy.

Bangladesh also has a wide range of active associations, think tanks, development NGOs, advocacy groups and voluntary bodies concerned with human rights and public policy, and representing the interests of vulnerable and marginalized sections of society, including women and the rural poor. But some NGOs are punished financially for being critical of government. The freedom of association which underpins interest articulation is not enjoyed equally, with discrimination against ethnic groups, such as the Chittagong Hill Tribes, religious minorities such as Hindus, and workers, notably women in the garments industry. Freedom to organize in trade unions is vulnerable to physical assaults by gangs hired by factory owners, and freedom of assembly is curtailed by violent police repression of opposition rallies and protests (Freedom House, 2007).

Secondly, demands and expressions of political interest have to be combined. This is the function of *interest aggregation*. Coalitions have to be formed that are powerful enough to overcome other combinations of interests. In an absolute monarchy or an African chiefdom interests of different sections of the community would be 'aggregated' by rulers enjoying the right to interpret the wishes of their people. In a modern society the classic structure for interest aggregation was, for the functionalists, the political party. Unfortunately for political legitimacy and stability, political parties have too often aggregated too few interests in an exclusive way, for example, by defining 'interests' in terms of ethnic identity. In Kenya, the reflection of ethnic divisions in party competition has been a major source of instability. Even parties that have attempted to appeal to interests that cut across tribe, such as the Forum for the Restoration of Democracy, have split into ethnically-based groups (Carey, 2002). In Ethiopia, it has been necessary to aggregate over 20 different political movements, all based on ethnicity, into blocs that could form governments capable of holding this multiethnic society together. Some political parties, for example in Thailand, resemble pressure groups representing the interests of powerful political bosses rather than organizations for aggregating interests behind ideologies or policy platforms.

Thirdly, the function of *rule making* has to be performed in all societies by some type of political structure. Political systems have to make authoritative and legitimate rules that can be supported by legitimate sanctions. Modern societies have developed specialized structures for this known as legislatures. In traditional societies such structures will be absent but the function will be performed somewhere in the political system. Most Third World countries have functioning legislatures, one exception being Saudi Arabia where rule-making is in the hands of an absolutist monarchy. But not all legislatures have sovereign law-making powers. In Iran, for example, a Council of Guardians consisting of Muslim scholars and lawyers can veto legislation passed by Parliament (Majlis) that does not conform to its interpretation of Islamic law. Rule-making powers may also be shared between legislatures and executives, especially in presidential systems, for example South Korea.

Fourthly, rules once made have to be enforced and applied. The modern structure for the function of *rule application* is bureaucracy. Countries vary in the extent to which their public bodies display the positive characteristics of bureaucracy. Too often bureaucrats are inefficient, recruited by patronage rather than on merit, and corrupt. The abuse of official powers for personal gain is a major problem of governance in developing countries. In Libya, for example, the tax system is especially vulnerable to corruption, with arbitrary decisions made about tax liabilities. In Laos, corruption is particularly evident in administrative agencies concerned with forestry, land ownership and environmental protection. In Bangladesh corruption is particularly intense in the police, customs and National Board of Revenue.

Conflicts arising from the application of rules to specific cases and circumstances require structures for adjudication. *Rule adjudication* was therefore identified as a universal political function. In modern societies the judiciary would be the specialized structure performing this function. However, most political systems draw the judiciary into rule-making as well as arbitration, especially when courts are empowered to rule on constitutional matters. For example, in 2006 the Colombian Constitutional Curt decreed that, under the Justice and Peace Law, illegally obtained assets should be used to compensate victims.

The importance for political development of specialized judicial structures lies in their separation from the other branches of government and thus their ability to adjudicate free from political interference. Unfortunately, this independence is too often compromised. In Tunisia, for example, the executive interferes in the judiciary through control of appointments, the Tunisian Association of Magistrates, and the legal profession generally.

Judicial impartiality may also be damaged by corruption. In 2006 surveys revealed that the majority of people in Bolivia, Cameroon, Gabon, India, Mexico, Morocco and Pakistan experienced extensive corruption in the judicial system. In Paraguay more than one in three court users admitted to paying a bribe. The majority of those polled in Africa regarded the judiciary as corrupt, with over 20 per cent of those having dealings with the courts having to pay bribes (Transparency International, 2007).

All political systems equally require means for the communication of demands and rules between the authorities and the people. In modern society the mass media constitute the social structures responsible for the function of *political communication*. In traditional society structures would reflect the technology available as well as the type of social organization that had developed.

For political modernization to occur, the social structure of the mass media should ideally be independent of the state. Private ownership and dependence on advertising revenue will introduce biases in the information provided, which only a diverse range of outlets in each type of media can guard against. But freedom from state control (if not ownership) should prevent governments from using the mass media to ensure only its interpretation of events reaches the public. In the Third World such independence is all too often lacking. In all regions the majority of countries have media which are restricted by the state in some way (see Table 2.1).

New incursions into the freedom of the press have been particularly noticeable in recent years in Venezuela, Thailand, the Philippines, Ethiopia, Eritrea, Uganda, Argentina, Peru and Bolivia. The main methods used by the state to suppress political opposition are the take-over of media outlets (Cote d'Ivoire), the withholding of licenses (Zimbabwe), libel

Table 2.1   *Freedom of the press, 1996–2008: percentage of countries rated unfree or partly free*

Region	1996	2006
The Americas	46	54
Asia-Pacific	65	60
Middle East/North Africa	95	95
Sub-Saharan Africa	89	85

SOURCE: Freedom House (2008b).

actions and violence against journalists (including state sponsored murder in the Philippines, Pakistan and Sri Lanka), control of the Internet (China and Iran) and restrictions on media coverage (Malaysia).

All societies have to transmit their dominant political values from generation to generation. All have ways of conveying to the younger generation what they ought to believe about political obligation, authority and the rightful exercise of power. How the function of *political socialization* is performed varies considerably from one society to another. The relative prevalence of the family, educational institutions or other associations will differ from society to society. The role of different social structures in processes of socialization will depend upon the development of the educational system and access to it, the opportunities offered by civil society for political experiences, and the status of the mass media. In the Third World, political socialization too often occurs in divisive contexts which emphasize exclusive identities such as ethnicity or religion. Parochial loyalties prevent the development of consensus about the basic principles of government. Such divisions may be further exacerbated by experiences of political instability or civil war which leave groups permanently hostile to fellow citizens, whether divided by class, ethnicity or religion. The danger then is that the current holders of state power will attempt to impose an ideological consensus by restrictions on freedom of association (as in the single party state), or through government agencies charged with indoctrination, such as Iran's Ministry of Islamic Guidance (Kamrava, 1995).

Finally, individuals have to be recruited into roles and offices. The function of *political recruitment* requires some kind of routinization in both traditional and modern societies. Processes of political succession have to be devised – election, inheritance, merit, physical might and other principles by which people are recruited into political roles and perhaps permanent offices. The roles that perform the universal political functions have to be filled by acceptable methods. These clearly change over time.

Many Third World states depart from modern principles of political recruitment into both political and administrative offices. Rather than filled on the basis of merit, recruitment into public offices is often based on nepotism or patrimonialism. Formally, and in constitutional documents, there may be a structure of rational-legal authority, but informally political and administrative authority operates according to different rules – those of patrimonialism (Brinkerhoff and Goldsmith, 2002). In Bangladesh, for example, this results in the occupation of public office for personal gain rather than public service, representation based on personalized favours and obligations rather than the interests of constituents, 'non-compliance with the formal rules of democratic politics' rather than political and administrative accountability, and distrust of politicians and bureaucrats rather than state legitimacy (Wood, 2000).

Political change

Functionalism tries to do more than just provide a new language for identifying the universal features of political systems. It seeks to provide a framework for understanding change. In practice the functionalists were more concerned with the characteristics of societies in some process of transition, rather than with the elaboration of models for 'simple' or 'primitive' societies. Their major areas of interest were the new nation states emerging on the international scene into which virtually all traditional societies had been more or less fully incorporated, usually through the operation of colonialism. Comparative politics was redesigned to explain the effects of the interactions between the traditional structures and cultures of communities incorporated into the new states that had been produced by colonialism and nationalistic reactions to it.

The most important change for the political functionalists was the association of increasingly specialized structures with single functions in modern societies. Political change is seen as the movement away from traditional politics towards the modern political system. Change takes place in both structure and culture. The examples given above of how political functions are performed in Third World countries indicate to functionalists that such systems are in the process of transition, and are yet to achieve modernity.

Structures, it was argued, become more specialized and differentiated as societies become more modern. This is an application of those parts of modernization theory that postulate the growing differentiation, specialization and complexity found within modernizing societies. Specialization of political roles was seen by the neo-evolutionists as part of becoming a modern polity. Whereas in a traditional absolute monarchical polity there would be found, bound up in a single structure, that of the royal court, a multiplicity of functions such as rule making and rule adjudication, in a

modern society with its pluralist democracy there would be found specialized structures performing single functions. Traditional social structures
were described as typically 'multifunctional'. As societies develop structures become less multifunctional.

When dealing with change in political cultures, the functionalists took
the concept of secularization from modernization theory. Secularization is
a process by which societies become more rationalized. It occurs when
people perceive that the circumstances around them are changeable by
human intervention. If religious belief, such as fatalism, prevents society
from seeing the environment in that way then religion may become an
obstacle to modernization. A rational or secular basis of social values does
not accept the facts of life as unalterable or sacred. Secularization means
enabling people to differentiate between the sacred and the profane, the
religious world and the world of material objects. It does not interpret
everything in terms of a set of beliefs about what is sacred and what is
handed down from time immemorial. Those beliefs may remain, but
people begin to separate them from secular concerns, the latter then being
exposed to rational scrutiny.

The precursor of this aspect of modernization theory was the German
sociologist Max Weber whose theory of social action distinguished
between actions determined by reason and actions determined by habit or
emotion. Bureaucracy was Weber's model of rational government. In the
domain of the state, bureaucracy epitomized the idea of linking means to
ends, and of defining an objective and calculating what needed to be done
to achieve it. Bureaucracy, based on rules, expertise, plans and calculations, was the ideal form of authority for the rationalization of politics.
Rational-legal authority combines the idea of means being related to ends
with the idea that rules, offices and public action would no longer reflect
heredity, tradition, custom or charisma. Rules reflect an understanding of
cause and effect in the political sphere. Rather than respect rules simply
because they are endorsed by custom, religion or traditional values, rules
are respected because they are instrumental.

Greater rationality is supported by the growth of scientific and technological knowledge in particular and socio-economic development in
general, as has been born out by cross-national surveys of social and political values comparing developed and developing societies. Development
shifts people's attitudes 'from an emphasis on traditional values to an
emphasis on secular-rational values' (Inglehart and Welzel, 2005, p. 6).

Modernization theory requires us to think about the way in which traditional social structures and values somehow hinder or present obstacles to
modernization (Higgott, 1978). The values and institutions of traditional
society are seen as causing underdevelopment and blocking modernization. For example, traditional societies are sometimes said to have failed to

understand the problem of over-population and therefore fail to adopt appropriate methods of birth control. Or they fail to see the dangers of over urbanization, leading to the appalling squalor of Third World slums and shanty towns. These failures of perception are associated with what is seen as a lack of rationality in the sense of being able to relate means to ends and so produce policies, strategies and interventions that will deal with problems. So part of the idea of a society becoming modern is a society which not only develops the administrative capability to embark upon policies but also develops the very way of thinking that permits phenomena to be confronted, a mode of thought which accepts that things can be changed by human agency, by setting goals and working out the means of achieving them. As societies develop they acquire systems of government that are problem-oriented and designed to perceive, analyse and meet the needs of society as articulated through political demands.

Survey evidence comparing attitudes and behaviour in developed and developing countries supports the theory that secularization increases with modernization. More prosperous societies have become more secular, while a particular feature of poor societies – insecurity – accounts for the persistence and growth of 'religiosity' in the Third World. As societies become more modern, the threat of poverty, disease, malnutrition and premature death recedes, and good governance, human rights, equality and political stability become more secure. Modernization means that 'the need for religious reassurance becomes less pressing under conditions of greater security' (Norris and Inglehart, 2004, p. 18).

In addition, members of a modernizing society experience cultural change. Secularization and rationalization require changes in cultural patterns. These changes were categorized by Parsons (1951, 1960, 1966) as 'pattern variables', variable patterns of related values with which people make judgements about other members of their society or the way people orient themselves within social relationships. He argued that social change was essentially a matter of how we perceive people with whom we come into contact, whether in the family, wider social organizations, territorial communities, or occupations.

Parsons saw traditional society as characterized by *particularism* whereas modern society is characterized by *universalism*. A particularistic judgement of, or response to, a fellow member of society applies special values because of a unique relationship between the people involved. Members of a kinship group or family will judge each other according to criteria applicable to that group relationship alone. When one only has values that can be utilized in the context of unique social relations a society is at the traditional end of the continuum. When judgements can be made on universal criteria, regardless of other dimensions of social relationships, society is at the modern end. When there are standards which can be applied to any individual, regardless of their position in society, universalism is said to exist. Criteria of performance that are defined independently of the status of those being evaluated constitute a pure form of universalism.

Parsons then contrasts *ascribed status* with *achieved status*. The former implies the existence of inherent qualities associated with the specific individuals concerned. For example, in a society which respects the wisdom of its older members that wisdom is assumed to exist by definition as soon as one becomes an elder. It is not appropriate to apply independent tests of competence. Achieved status depends upon a capacity to satisfy independent and abstract criteria that are defined independently of the other qualities of the individual concerned. When status is inherent in the person, society is traditional. Where status is acquired by the achievement of abstract qualities defined in terms of objective criteria, such as educational qualifications, society is modern. Ascriptive political office would be represented by an inherited position whereas achievement would be exemplified by a bureaucrat recruited on the basis of acquired characteristics defined as necessary for particular tasks to be performed.

A third pair of cultural patterns contrasts *affectivity* with *neutrality*. 'Affectivity' refers to emotional attachments between people. Neutral attachments are based on instrumentality and objectives external to personal relationships.

Finally *diffuseness* is contrasted with *specificity*. Diffuse relations refer to the complex web of interconnections that link people together involving many roles and aspects of their lives. Here judgements can only be made about a total person. Their different roles cannot be separated for purposes of evaluation and the definition of social relationships. When society is formed on the basis of specificity it is possible to distinguish the different roles performed by individuals and to be concerned with just one of them – as employer or employee, landlord or tenant, for example. Individuals in modern societies are seen as involved in a multiplicity of single-stranded relationships. Specificity signifies the separateness of social relations and their relative independence from each other. Diffuse relations combine all aspects of the individual's role in society and it is not possible to exclude consideration of some of these different aspects when individuals interrelate. Relationships are multistranded. No individual can abstract one of those relationships and give it an independent existence.

Such variables enable us to see how far a society has changed along different dimensions. The assertion of the individual's value in universalistic terms supports political equality and mass participation on an individual basis. Individuals would not see political roles as being ascribed by tradition and custom to predetermined groups. Political power could be enjoyed by all on an equal basis.

In functionalist development theory, political change affects both structure and culture. A combination of changes in these two spheres produces integration into the modern nation-state. The secularization of government is directed in part towards nation-building This process enables the political system to supersede sub-national loyalties such as tribe or religion, seen as parochial and pre-modern. It involves creating a consensus to support the new order by mobilizing the community to regard the nation-state, not some primordial grouping, as the legitimate political unit. Communities would be mobilized to articulate demands and supports; communications between leaders and led would be improved. This is all part of not just becoming modern but of producing an integrated society, a major achievement of a developed political system.

A further aspect of change in developing societies emphasized by functionalism are the 'capabilities' of political systems to formulate policies, enforce decisions throughout the territory, and develop a problem-solving capacity, especially through bureaucracy, so that public policies can be executed effectively and efficiently. Almond classified capabilities into five groups: extractive; regulative; distributive; symbolic; and responsive (Almond, 1965), having earlier defined political change in terms of the acquisition by a political system of some new capability and its associated changes in political culture and structure (Almond, 1963). A modern political system would, unlike traditional polities, be able to use such concepts as effectiveness and efficiency. Such a capability was seen as dependent on the system's resources in terms of powers to regulate, extract and distribute. The more modern the political system the more able it would be to build up its resources and in turn that would be dependent on the existence of differentiated and specialized political structures.

A central case in point is the bureaucracy. Only with a highly efficient bureaucracy, based on the principle of merit recruitment and organized rationally as a specialized institution, can a political system develop its full capabilities to provide itself with resources and powers.

The contribution of modernization theory

The conceptual apparatus of modernization theory had a profound influence on the analysis of political change. Secularization has important political consequences both for the role of the individual in the political system and for recruitment into political office. The emergence of rational-legal authority has profound implications for the nature of the state, not least in the opportunity which it opens up for bureaucratization. Clusters of pattern variables provide models of social organization in which the political significance of universalism, achieved status, neutrality and specificity is plain. Of particular importance to the study of political development is the effect of structural differentiation on the specialization of political roles in transitional societies.

Equally, much of what is expressed by functionalism has become almost commonplace and integrated into political analysis. Its enormous appeal is quite understandable. It attracted much criticism, particularly in its developmental aspects. But as a way of organizing information about political phenomena, it has become an integral part of political science. It is also questionable whether students of comparative politics have developed superior theories. It may be that structural functionalism was rejected because it failed an unfairly severe test, that of providing comparative politics with a scientific unity and an all-encompassing theory of politics (Lane, 1994).

Functionalism drew attention to the importance of seeing societies as consisting of interdependent parts so that one could adopt a dynamic rather than static approach to the analysis of systems of government. The study of politics had to a very large extent adopted a rather insular, normative and legalistic format which functionalism completely changed.

Political development theory inspired the production of a large number of monographs – over 200 by 1975 – yet many shared Eckstein's assessment that the result of all this effort was 'mostly muddle' (Eckstein, 1982, p. 451). However, the many criticisms to which functionalism has been subjected have themselves formed an important part of the process of acquiring a clearer understanding of political change in the Third World. A debt is owed to functionalists for stimulating so much debate about political change and for forcing critical assessment of their ideas. Nevertheless, the recent resurgence of interest in evolutionary theorising (Kerr, 2002) has yet to be applied to the politics of developing societies, where evolutionary explanations of change remain tainted by its association with functionalism. A number of theoretical and conceptual weaknesses leave functionalist approaches to politics critically flawed.

The problem of 'tradition'

The concept of 'tradition' as deployed by modernization theorists poses numerous problems. First, there is the tendency to see tradition as an obstacle to development. Resistance to change on the part of social groups is seen as the 'burden' of tradition and an inability to break with outmoded ways of perceiving the world, when in fact local people may be making very rational calculations about the economic and political risks that are inevitably associated with disturbances to the status quo. Resistance to change may reflect a different system of incentives operating under conditions that include poverty and dependency. Furthermore, the secular and the rational may benefit some groups in society much more than others. For example, a family planning programme may be readily taken up by wealthy families if they do not need children to assist in the cultivation of their land. It might not be accepted so readily by a poor family that cannot hire labour and whose existence as an economic unit depends upon their children; or by people who know that when they get old there will be no welfare state, or community care.

Secondly, ethnic conflict is similarly seen by modernization theory as a by-product of tradition. While it was recognized that the creation of colonies often meant grouping societies together in an arbitrary way, ethnic conflict after independence tended to be seen as a conflict between the primordial values of tribe and race and the modern values of nationalism, when people think of themselves as individual members of a nation state rather than as members of some sub-national collectivity such as a linguistic group. Again, there may be very 'modern' reasons, such as economic exploitation or political discrimination, for conflict between groups identified by reference to traditional attributes and perceptions.

Here modernization theory can be charged with ideological bias in the way it blames backwardness on the traditions of a people rather than on internal conflicts or external interventions, such as imperialism and war. Modernization theory is striking for what it leaves out in its attempt to produce an explanation of change, notably class conflict, colonialism and revolution (Rhodes, 1968).

The influence of external forces is the most noticeable omission from the modernization perspective. At the very most, external influences are perceived as limited to the diffusion of Western cultural attributes to non-Western societies. The colonial episode is notably problematic and can only be integrated into the 'traditional/modern' dichotomy with great difficulty, either as a hybrid or as a 'transitional' stage of evolution (Tipps, 1973, p. 212).

The static and uniform conception of tradition has also been criticized. Traditional cultures and social structures not only consist of diverse norms and values. Old traditions are not necessarily displaced by new norms and social structures. They can and do exist side by side. For example, in Asia political elites have drawn upon traditional values and perceptions, as well as modern cultural traits, in order to legitimize policies for economic development. In Thailand and Korea 'traditional and indigenous cultural symbols complemented modernity, which elites imported from abroad', with traditions present in varying degrees depending on whether 'traditional culture supplied appropriate tools for economic modernization', as Confucian respect for education and authority evidently did in South Korea (Compton, 2000, pp. 183–4).

In modernization theory 'tradition' is a residual concept, defined by reference to the logical opposites of modern. 'Tradition' is not defined by reference to observed facts and knowledge of societies prior to their contact with the West. If the dichotomy does not reflect reality, then all societies must be 'transitional', and modernization theory loses all value as an aid to understanding historical change. Modernization theory obscures the variability found both within and between traditional societies (Tipps, 1973).

Secularization and religion

The resurgence of religion in parts of the Third World, especially as a foundation for political mobilization, indicates that modernization does not necessarily bring about secularization. The growth of 'political religions' in the Middle East, Africa, the Caribbean, Asia and Latin America not only undermines the secularist assumptions of modernization theory. It raises the question of whether religious politics is a reversion to tradition. Whether Christian or Moslem, Hindu or Buddhist, progressive or conservative, religious politics has been in part a response to the failure of governments to secure economic prosperity and social well-being that is equitably distributed. It is also a reaction to the failure of secular ideologies to deliver socio-economic development, as well as a response to the undesirable consequences of modernity, including political repression, economic and political corruption, loss of cultural identity and community dislocation. While there may be continuity from pre-modern forms of politics in which religious and political authority and processes were undifferentiated, contemporary forms of political religion are formed by the impact of political and economic modernization (Haynes, 1993). Haynes claims that political religiosity 'is not a "return" to religion, but the latest example of a periodic utilisation – stimulated by perceived crisis – of religion to help pursue secular goals' (Haynes, 1999, p. 245). However, there seems sufficient evidence of political religion being a reversion to and revival of pre-modern traditions, values and practices, and a rejection of modernity, for the issue to at least remain unresolved.

In this context modernization theory can appear elitist and in contrast to the experience of the masses. Modernization theory depicts religion as a less real, evolved and rational alternative to politics, doomed to secularization, when in the otherwise contrasting cultures of Latin America, the Middle East, central and southern Africa, and South East Asia, religion remains a source of popular mobilization, alternative notions of legitimacy, resistance and even insurrection. It has come to fill an ideological vacuum. It can be revolutionary or reactionary (or evolve from one to the other). Where religion is identified with the state it tends to be a conservative force (as in Saudi Arabia) but where it is distanced from politics it tends to be anti-establishment, as in Central and South America (Kamrava, 1995, pp. 148–9).

In many parts of the Third World political choices and actions are increasingly the result of religious judgements. In India, for example, the last 25 years have seen 'a much more explicit expression of religion in public life', typified by Sikh extremism and Hindu nationalism. In Pakistan the influence of Islam now 'makes it very difficult for there to be open debate on such questions as women's rights, the position of minorities, and the rigid law on blasphemy' (Taylor, 2005, pp. 219, 225).

Liberation theology in Latin America has challenged the authority patterns of the Catholic Church as well as political regimes in its clerical populism, its ideology of democratization and equality, its stimulation of collective organization, and its recognition of the poor as a valid source of religious values and action. Its fusion of religion, social analysis (drawing inspiration from Marxism) and political activism has implications for the secular presuppositions of modernization theory in that religious values are not secondary to social and political reform. Religion is not merely being used as a convenient instrument of political mobilization and solidarity. It represents a new spirituality as well as a new awareness of class, conflict, exploitation – the spirituality of the exploited poor (Levine, 1986, 1988).

Liberation theology has also been a factor in South African politics, where it held some beliefs in common with Marxism, including challenging oppressive social structures, mobilizing the masses, and endorsing revolutionary action to overthrow the bourgeoisie. Libertarian theologians have had a considerable influence on constitutional developments in South Africa (Hilliard and Wissink, 1999). In Burma, the Buddhist monastic community plays a major role in mobilizing opposition to the military junta, secular pro-democracy groups having been virtually crushed.

Secularization of the state by technocratic elites in some Middle Eastern countries has magnified the ideological significance of Islam, especially for the poor and other excluded classes. As well as spiritual guidance it has provided a political framework and an alternative to the materialism and immorality associated with modernization and secularism (Kedourie, 1992; Omid, 1992). But in so doing it shows how politics based on religion combines traditional and modern elements. For example, millenarianism and commitment to an Islamic order (as in Iran) is accompanied by nationalism on the part of the clergy (Ram, 1997). Fundamentalist opposition in Saudi Arabia combines Islamic and modern Western concepts such as human rights and administrative probity (Kostiner, 1997). The appeal of religious movements such as the Iranian Shi'ites is related to secular concerns such as growing social inequality, political repression, corruption, foreign exploitation and cultural division (Banuazizi, 1987). Some interpretations of Islam find no difficulty in incorporating capitalism with the idea of the state as the realization of divine sovereignty and the source of law as transcendental (Judy, 1998). The notion that state and religion cannot be separated is a recent one in Islamic thought and, according to some Islamic scholars, not sanctioned by sacred prescriptions. Indeed, 'no Muslim society is governed solely with reference to religious law' (Filali-Ansary, 2003, p. 235).

While some interpretations of Islam accommodate political pluralism, and while some Islamic reformers are 'laying the foundations for an Islamic Reformation' (Wright, 1996: 66), the practical consequences of political Islam are rarely liberationist. With the partial exception of Turkey, Islamic societies are ruled by traditional or modernizing autocracies, or radical Islamic regimes, namely Iran and Sudan. Political Islam seeks to establish states governed by Islamic laws intolerant of alternative beliefs, and lacking the civil rights and political equality characteristic of liberal democracy. Political Islam may be motivated by a sense of injustice, social frustration, poverty and political exclusion, but it favours the Islamization of law and, ultimately, the rejection of democracy. The radicals want the Sharia to take precedence over laws promulgated by elected assemblies, and discrimination against minorities, women and other faiths to be legalized. Political Islam may not be a monolithic movement, and some moderates endorse consultation, consensus, majoritarianism, pluralism and respect for human rights. But both moderates and radicals seek to establish an Islamic state based on Sharia, in which there will be little room for tolerations of dissent, equality of civil liberties or political pluralism: 'when one focuses on their fundamental convictions, their most cherished values, and the kind of social and political order they aspire to create, moderates have far more in common with radicals than they do with Western-style democrats' (Denoeux, 2002: 73).

Dichotomous models

Modernization theory provided ideal types or models of traditional and modern society to show along which dimensions they could be said to differ. But these tell very little about the dynamics of transition from one cultural state to another (Kiely, 1995). For example, in terms of Parsons' pattern variables, developed countries can be shown to be particularistic in the behaviour of their social classes and private interests, as well as ascriptive, especially at the higher levels of business management and among the poor. Recruitment may be achievement based, but reward is often based on age and family obligations (e.g. in Japan). Roles are frequently 'diffuse' rather than functionally specific within such power structures as the military-industrial complex of the United States (Frank, 1972b).

Conversely, underdeveloped countries frequently demonstrate universalism in their educational systems and mass media, in labour unions and in liberation movements. The economic and political leadership thrown up by military coups and emerging bourgeoisies throughout the Third World cannot be described as normatively ascriptive (Frank, 1972b).

Role assignment by achievement is also widely found among the poorer classes of poor societies. In the distribution of rewards, achievement accounts for more than ascription in underdeveloped countries. Roles may be found to be functionally diffuse in underdeveloped countries, especially among the poorest and richest strata, though the middle-class military officers, police officers, bureaucrats, junior executives and administrators are functionally specific in their roles. Such people 'serve specific functions of making the whole exploitative system function in the diffuse but particular interests of those who have achieved control' (Frank, 1972b, p. 335).

Neither 'tradition' nor 'modernity' should be seen as packages of attributes. Modernization may be selective, with rapid social change in one area obstructing change in others, rather than tradition being the obstacle to development. Hence the eventual realization among political scientists of the modernization persuasion that modernization and political stability do not always go together: modernization in one sphere does not necessarily produce compatible ('eurhythmic') change in another. Once it is recognized that traditional values and practices may persist in otherwise modern societies, further doubt is thrown on the idea that tradition impedes change. Furthermore, if the destruction of tradition proves not to be necessary for 'modernisation', except in purely tautological terms, then traditional societies must be seen as being able to develop in directions other than towards 'modernity' (Tipps, 1973).

The important determinants of development *and* underdevelopment lie elsewhere than in ideal-typical models of tradition and modernity. In addition to questioning the empirical validity of the pattern variable approach, critics such as A. G. Frank have argued that it is theoretically inadequate not to differentiate between the importance of the roles to be affected by modernization, and not to recognize that the determinants of underdevelopment extend beyond the family, tribe, community or even a whole poor country taken in isolation.

The concept of 'integration'

Functionalism misjudges the level of harmony and integration in modern society. It tended not to accommodate the idea of conflicting interests and the differential power of groups in conflict with others. The idea that different parts of the political system are supportive of everything else, producing a functional unity, seems a distorted way of describing any society. The functionalists directed their attention mainly towards the factors in society which maintain consensus and stability. This is understandable, given the areas of natural science which they and their social anthropological precursors chose as analogous to social science.

Functionalism's systemic theorizing sees society in organic terms, with specialized and interdependent parts functioning to satisfy the requirements of the whole for survival. The structures of the political system are presented in a neutral light as a mere arena for the resolution of conflict that is impartial as regards the contestants. This conception of society as a functional unity is a mystification of social reality. However, we should remember that one of the sociological forefathers of functionalism, Robert Merton, explored the 'dysfunctions' that threaten social cohesion. This reminds us that what is functional for one group in society may be dysfunctional for another, perhaps to the extent of undermining the vitality of the whole.

Functionalism was more concerned with the integration of interests into a single normative pattern than with instability and conflict as sources of social change. Conflict over the allocation of scarce resources is seen as resolved within a framework of common values. Functionalism can be faulted for not being capable of explaining the very changes that were its *raison d'être* because it concentrates on the prerequisites of the maintenance of the *status quo*. The tendency to regard everything that exists, including the characteristics of the political system, as functional and therefore desirable becomes normatively supportive of existing social arrangements. Social inequality and stratification, for example, are functional because society has motivated people to seek higher rewards and induced people to perform the duties attached to their station in life. Functionalism begins to look like an arbitrary selection of values in so far as it fails to show how choices can be made between the values which, though functional to an existing system, would be dysfunctional to an alternative one. When utility is found in all patterns of behaviour conflict becomes regarded as pathological or abnormal. Such a view of society will be favoured by some 'parts' (or interests) but will work to the disadvantage of others. Thus political realities present a challenge to the functionalist paradigm.

This encourages a conservative bias in functionalism (Abrahamson, 1978). Some functionalists, such as Merton, argued that functionalism is radical. Institutions and practices are given no inherent value, only their consequences matter. They are only preserved until they cease to be of utility to society. That allows for as much change as a society feels it needs to achieve its goals. However, the main thrust of functionalism is towards a conservation of what already is in place. It encourages a search for the benefits of surviving institutions. New generations have to be socialized into the existing mores of society. Structures are expected to have positive, functional consequences, and so contribute to the persistence of a society. Functionalism guides enquiry towards explanations of how societies maintain themselves and survive under their present arrangements. Institutions are assumed to contribute to the health of the whole social and political fabric. Approaching institutions by seeing them as supportive of society implies some normative consensus which is then endorsed by the investigator who credits those institutions with positive values by deeming them to be functional.

The conservative bias of functionalism became increasingly visible as the focus of attention was forced to move towards explanations of crisis, instability and disorder. Crisis is seen to be a problem for elites. So a crisis is what the current élite deems to be so. Authoritarianism is then seen as a legitimate way for élites to manage crisis. Order is made the highest political good. Opponents of regimes are described as 'system wreckers': 'the interest in order of those at the top is given logical precedence over the interest in social justice of those below' (Sandbrook, 1976, pp. 80–1). Supposedly value-free, scientific models of political development end up leaving a strong ideological message (Cammack, 1997).

Unilinearity

The fallacy of placing societies on a continuum between traditional and modern, along which all societies progress during their histories, led to the proposition that the new states appearing on the international scene as a result of political independence, particularly after the Second World War (the phase of liberation from colonialism with which this school of thought was most concerned), were replicating the European experience from the sixteenth to the nineteenth century.

This formulation understates a very fundamental difference: that the history of the advanced societies does not include colonization by more powerful countries. This makes it impossible to think of a unilinear developmental process. The new states of the world were structured by the old in a way which does not apply to the histories of countries whose own development was made possible by their exploitation of pre-industrial and pre-capitalist societies (Pratt, 1973). The West's development was built, some would say, on the active *underdevelopment* of weaker societies and economies (see Chapter 3).

Unilinear models of change are too teleological. There can be no preordained path to development for all societies. Cultures and traditions vary too much from one society to another, and the process of modernization varies from one time period to another. Furthermore, defining development in terms of direction rather than content means that anything that happens must be seen as part of the process of development. The concept loses utility as it loses precision and specific content (Kothari, 1968; Huntington, 1971).

Thus modernization theory can be accused of denying underdeveloped countries their own histories, ignoring the connections between these histories and the histories of developed countries, overlooking the fact that penetration by foreign influences had not produced development or led to 'take off', and misrepresenting the histories of today's developed countries as not having benefited from the exploitation of today's underdeveloped societies (Frank, 1972b)

Underestimating the significance of such historical factors was compounded by a lack of consideration of continuing relationships with the powerful economies of the West. Continuities from colonialism that call the significance of political independence into question were ignored, especially economic and military aid programmes, interventions by international financial organizations such as the World Bank, and investments by multinational corporations (Pratt, 1973).

In 1987 Almond attempted to rebut the charge that developmentalism's theory of change was unilinear, arguing that developmentalists had always recognized that new states might develop authoritarian rather than democratic, pluralist tendencies. He also claimed that the school never neglected international influences on domestic politics. However, it is noticeable that he restricts his refutation of the uniliniarity charge to an awareness of authoritarianism. He does not attempt to answer the criticism that modernization theorists ignored the implications of colonialism and continuing economic dependency for the current autonomy of Third World countries. His lively critique of dependency theory does not dispel doubts that modernization theory can provide a framework for understanding the unique relationships between rich and poor countries, or if it did it was only after the impact of dependency theory had been felt. He reminds us that in 1970 he himself argued explicitly 'against the simple diffusionist notion of unilinearity in the early 1960s'. However, the interaction of economics and politics which Almond insists was always a feature of comparative studies of political development, such as the political consequences of industrialization or the distributional effects of economic growth, does not encompass the factors which critics regarded as significant and distinctive of Third World status (Almond, 1987, p. 449).

Ethnocentricity

Modernization theory may thus be criticized for its ethnocentricity, judging progress by reference to Western, and largely Anglo-American, values and institutions. It is difficult to avoid the conclusion that the modernization theorists' perspective on change was determined as much by ideological leanings as by rigorous scientific investigation. Modernization theory is heavily marked by 'widespread complacency towards American society, and the expansion of American political, military and economic interests throughout the world', so constituting a form of cultural imperialism (Tipps, 1973, pp. 207–10).

Functionalist approaches to political development also appear ethnocentric, when a developed political system looks very much like Anglo-American pluralist democracy. The end-state appears to be the system of government in the country producing the major exponents of the theory (Holt and Turner, 1966). There is nothing wrong *per se* in advocating a functionalist view of politics, such as the separation of powers, to which Almond's output functions clearly correspond. A distinction between the input side of the political equation, conceptualized in terms of socialization, recruitment, interest articulation and aggregation, and communication; and the output functions of rule making, application and adjudication, is useful (Varma, 1980). It asserts the relationship between the mechanisms for public participation and those for liberal government. The input functions imply mass participation on the basis of political equality in a modern society. However, such advocacy is a far cry from a science of political change.

Change and causality

In biology the analysis of function is related to the analysis of causality. In sociology and political science the move from description to causality was never really achieved. So the claim of functionalism to be a *theory* has been seriously questioned. It has been acknowledged as an elaborate description and classification, able to describe the social practice which we find strange and difficult to comprehend. But as explanation of causality functionalism suffers from the fact that it is tautological – no explanation can be disproved because things are defined in relation to themselves. A practice is said to persist because it contributes to the maintenance of society. Its persistence is taken to prove that the society is motivated to maintain itself. If the practice ceases this has to be taken as indicative that it was no longer functional to society's maintenance. Statements about the causes and consequences of social and political practices are merely true by definition, not proved by explanation (Dowse, 1966).

Originally developmentalists offered no theory of change. Huntington (1971) points out that *The Politics of the Developing Areas*, for example, does not deal with development. It, and similarly inspired works, employs concepts to compare systems presumed to be at different stages of development. But there is no explanation of a dynamic process. Later work, such as that by

Almond and Powell (1966) and Pye (1966) identified the key changes that occur as a society becomes more developed politically, associating political development with greater political equality, governmental capacity and institutional differentiation; subsystem autonomy, cultural secularization and structural differentiation (Almond and Powell, 1966); rationalization, national integration, democratization and mobilization (Huntington, 1965). Even then, however, 'the stress was on the elaboration of models of different types of political system, not different types of change from one system to another' (Huntington, 1971, p. 307).

The problem was that political development was taken as given. Meanings had then to be attached to the concept – hence, a proliferation of definitions and conceptual entropy. No account was given of the forces that must, for developmentalism to work, drive societies along the development path. The lack of agreement on what political development actually meant made it impossible to posit a *theory* of change (Eckstein, 1982; Cammack, 1997).

When the shortcomings of political development theory in solving the problem of explaining political change were eventually acknowledged, theorists abandoned the attempt to predict the direction of change, concentrating instead on relationships between specific variables indicative of development identified by different theorists as particularly significant. For example, Huntington focussed on the causes of political stability in any society, however 'developed', claiming the key variables to be levels of political participation and political institutionalization (Huntington, 1965, 1968). Other theorists of change also focussed on the destabilizing effects of developments within the political system. The central question became: what type of change in one component of a political system (culture, structures, groups, leadership, policies and so on) can be related to change or its absence in other components?

Unfortunately functionalism does not provide explanations of causes of change so much as definitions of key concepts, political function, structure, system and culture. The difficulty which some of the contributors to *The Politics of the Developing Areas* had in fitting the categories and concepts to traditional society in the regions that they analysed from a functionalist perspective supports the critical opinion that political development theory was only able to describe the current situation, not explain how it had come about.

Biological analogies

The analogy with biological organisms further undermined functionalism, being insufficiently close to provide valid explanations of social and political phenomena. It is very difficult to talk about the normal or pathological functioning of society, in the way that we can about organisms, without making massive value judgements. Societies can change their structures. Organisms do not. It is not possible to examine the numerous instances of the same social function as it is with biological organisms. The analogy thus leads social explanation up a cul-de-sac. It does not provide the opportunity for theoretical explanation that the assumed parallel between natural and social science appears to offer.

Definitions

Modernization theory is over-ambitious in its attempt to incorporate all social change since the seventeenth century. Consequently the key concepts are too vague and open-ended, often reducing theoretical propositions to tautologies. Modernization theory proceeds by way of assumptions about change based on the prior definition of concepts. Concepts take the place of facts (Tipps, 1973; Varma, 1980).

Furthermore, the definitions of functionalism are flawed. 'System' is defined in terms of what a system does. So a political system which does not perform the functions which such systems are defined as performing ceases by definition to be a political system. Again the explanatory power is reduced to a tautology. Any statement about the political system is either true by definition because that particular system is doing what all political systems do, or is not about political systems at all. The same is true of 'structure'. When structures are perceived and qualified by their salient functions – when the question is not what a structure is but what it is for – it is not possible to distinguish between structure and function and thus provide accurate descriptions of the former (Sartori, 1970).

The term 'function' is equally problematic. The word is used in different ways without the differences being fully acknowledged. 'Function' can mean maintaining something: for example, the function of the political system is to integrate society and allow it to adapt. Function can also mean merely a task, such as when the 'function' of a political organization is to articulate an interest. The functionalist literature tends to switch from the more mundane meaning to the almost mathematical meaning of function as the result or consequence of some other factor in the social equation.

The concept of 'boundary' is also controversial. If political systems could not be clearly differentiated from the economic and the social as, say, in China or the Soviet Union, it was heavily value-laden to say that they were, as a consequence, less developed than a society where state and economy operate in their own self-contained spheres. It may or may not be justifiable to prefer such separation, or *laissez-faire*, but it is not a scientific stance to say that a more modern society creates clear boundaries between polity and economy. That begins to look like a subterfuge for saying that societies where there is heavy state involvement in the economy are backward. This leaves aside the fallacy of assuming capitalist societies themselves demarcate between politics and economics. In fact, in all societies people move from one system to the other by virtue of the different roles which they perform. The boundaries are blurred even if we wish to distinguish between societies where polity and economy are closely integrated because of public ownership, state planning, or collectivization, and societies where that is less so. To insist on an analytical boundary being drawn between the processes of politics and those of social integration and adaptation, or between the political system on the one hand, and churches, economies, schools, kinship, lineages and age sets on the other, either leaves non-boundary systems non-political systems; or makes statements about political systems true by definition and untestable empirically (Holt and Turner, 1966).

Changes of emphasis

The pessimism about Third World politics that set in after what was perceived to be the failures of the United Nation's first Development Decade, together with American support for authoritarianism abroad (especially in Latin America) when directed towards the containment of revolutionary forces and the preservation of order (Higgott, 1983), led to subtle changes of emphasis in modernization theory. Three such changes can be distinguished.

First, the possibility of regression as well as progression was recognized. For example, it should not be inferred from developmental concepts such as 'structural differentiation' and 'cultural secularization' that trends in such directions are inevitable. Development theory's commitment to progress excluded the possibility that political systems might 'decay' (Huntington, 1965).

The second significant reorientation was towards an emphasis on political stability and social order. Political development theory had always been concerned to some extent with threats to stability such as mass participation. The political modernization literature became increasingly concerned with factors associated with the maintenance of regimes, élites and political order, as well as with restrictions on the capability of systems of government to produce decisions, policies and interventions that can be enforced successfully. This change of emphasis was particularly damaging for some of the evolutionary assumptions of functionalist political theory (O'Brien, 1972; Cammack, 1997).

The third change was a stronger emphasis on political integration, another dimension of political stability and social order. The problem of producing a political consensus in the face of cultural diversity was growing. New states encountered many obstacles to the creation of a sufficiently widespread sense of loyalty and obligation to the nation and its government: parochial loyalties; incomplete governmental control of its territory; conflicting values of elites and masses; and a lack of organizational ability for collective purposes. This was seen as the problem of nation-building or creating loyalty and commitment (Weiner, 1965; Wriggins, 1966).

Conclusion

Functionalist modernization theory raised the questions and identified the issues which remain central to an understanding of Third World politics, many of which remain unresolved: what effect does the lack of effective political institutions have; which types of political change are consistent with stability and 'integration'; what are the relationships between political norms, structures and behaviour; how do new patterns of political authority emerge from old ones; and how do governmental processes select and transform political demands into public policies? (Apter and Rosberg, 1994).

However, the attempt to establish a rigorous mode of analysis and unifying theory of political development was eventually abandoned. The pressures were too many for it to bear. Dependency theory, derived substantially from a critique of modernization theory, gained in popularity. Definitions of 'development' proliferated, reflecting a fragmentation of interests into specialized studies of institutions, areas and processes. Disillusionment with the lack of political development in many parts of the Third World made earlier theorizing appear 'naively optimistic'. Eventually, 'as the new and developing nations encountered difficulties and turned largely to authoritarian and military regimes, the optimism and hopefulness faded, and interest, productivity and creativity abated' (Almond, 1987, p. 444).

3

The Politics of Neo-Colonialism and Dependency

Constitutional independence

The two decades following the Second World War saw the final and most dramatic wave of independence sweep across the European empires in Asia, the Middle East and Africa, either as a result of more or less peaceful negotiations between the leaders of the nationalist movements and the European powers, or as the outcome of wars of liberation. What Michael Barratt Brown called 'one of the great transformations in modern history' occurred when all but a few million of the 780 million people living in the colonial possessions of the imperial powers 'freed themselves from subject status' (Barratt Brown, 1963, pp. 189–90).

Politically it was assumed that indigenous governments, representing the interests of local people rather than alien groups, would have sovereign state power at their disposal. Their relationships with the governments of other sovereign states would be those of independent nation states entering into treaties and agreements within the framework of international law. Economically it was assumed that following independence the process of 'diffusion' would continue as capital, technology and expertise spread. Foreign aid and investment would increase the productive capacity of the less developed economy (Rosen and Jones, 1979; Mack and Leaver, 1979).

However, a very different perception of the relationship between sovereign states is conveyed by the term 'neo-colonialism', originally coined by mainly Third World leaders who found that the achievement of constitutional independence and sovereignty did not give total freedom to the governments of the newly formed nation-states. Political autonomy was found to be something of a facade behind which lurked the continuing presence of powerful Western financial and economic interests. The end of colonial government was not seen by leaders such as Nkwame Nkrumah, the First Prime Minister of Ghana and author of a book entitled *Neo-colonialism: the Last Stage of Imperialism*, as ending economic colonialism.

The core of the neo-colonialist argument is that a distinction between political and economic freedom misses the point that there can be no real political independence while economic dependency remains. Economic colonialism has serious political consequences. So political autonomy had not really been achieved with the formal and constitutional ending of colonial government. Supposedly independent societies and their sovereign governments were found to be lacking control of their economies (Berman, 1974). The expression 'neo-colonialism' tries to encapsulate the idea that economic power and the political power that flows from it still reside elsewhere even when 'independence' has been achieved (O'Connor, 1970). But those subtle and indirect forms of domination had, as their root cause, the economies bequeathed by the colonial powers at the time of constitutional independence.

The new rulers of the former colonies found that the major proportion of the resources available to them was controlled from metropolitan centres that hitherto had ruled their countries directly. Independence appeared largely symbolic. For Nkrumah:

> the essence of neo-colonialism is that the state which is subject to it is, in theory, independent and has all the outward trappings of international sovereignty. In reality its economic system *and thus its political policy* is directed from outside (Nkrumah, 1965, p. ix, emphasis added).

According to Julius Nyerere, the first President of Tanzania, his country achieved 'political independence only' in 1961. It attained neither economic power nor economic independence:

> We gained the political power to decide what to do; we lacked the economic and administrative power which would have given us freedom in those decisions. . . . A nation's real freedom depends on its capacity to do things, not on the legal rights conferred by its internationally recognised sovereignty (Nyerere, 1973, p. 263).

The politics of neo-colonialism

In dependency theory, as will be shown later, there is the view that imperialism had created economies that had been and still are positively and actively *underdeveloped* by dominant economies. Neo-colonialism as an interpretation of post-colonial history did not express itself in those terms. It did, however, recognize a failure on the part of colonialism to develop the economies of the colonized territories beyond the small but important sectors needed by the European economies and for which colonial rule was imposed. The post-colonial economy was characterized by a high level of dependence on foreign loans, technology, foreign investment, and foreign aid which together often 'decapitalized' the host economy through a net outflow of capital, with more being extracted in excess profits than being invested locally (Rosen and Jones, 1979). For example, Latin America was a net exporter of capital in the form of profits and interest throughout the 1980's, contributing to economic stagnation and declining living standards, with average per capita income shrinking by 11 per cent, and the number in poverty increasing by 60 million to 196 million, or 46 per cent of the total population (Robinson, 1999).

The *political* manifestations of foreign economic involvement proved difficult to describe in concrete terms, except for those for whom politics was merely an epiphenomenon of the economic. One reason for this was that much contemporary political science accepted the constitutional formalities as accurate representations of reality. Another was that the economy was seen as a completely separate sphere or system of action. The economic power of the decolonizing state and the political influence this conferred were not considered. Liberal political science, represented most potently by the functionalists, acknowledged that the formation of new states had been profoundly influenced by the existence of old ones but did not allow that conclusion to lead to 'the logical question of how precisely an old state might influence the formation of a new one' (Bretton, 1973, pp. 22–4).

Even if this is thought too harsh a judgement, it will nevertheless probably be accepted that political science had largely concerned itself with institution-building during the decolonization process and the 'preparations' for independence in those colonies where the relationships between nationalists and the imperial powers could be described as such, involving more or less peaceful diplomacy and negotiation rather than wars of liberation. Thereafter politics was seen as the concern of an internally and externally sovereign state. Conflicts with other sovereign states, including the former colonial powers, were interpreted as matters of international law and diplomacy and left to the specialists in those fields. The political aspects of international economic relations were overlooked.

Yet even the political scientists and political economists who recognized the continuing economic dependency of post-colonial states rarely demonstrated how the mechanisms of the internal political consequences operated. The nature of the economic linkages could easily be described and disputed over, but the domestic political effects were left to be inferred from them. The uneven distribution of primary resources among new states was said to have a greater effect on governmental orientations than internal interests. The power of foreign interests could even be measured by 'the ratio of export–import trade to overall GDP of the host country'. Mining concerns were said to constitute 'rival governments' (Bretton, 1973, pp. 25–6, 205). General policy constraints on post-colonial governments were noted, such as limitations on monetary policy by the high propensity to import (Hymer, 1982). In Africa, for example, 'The international power and influence flow is indeed so massive, concerning as it does the major share of the national resources available to the new rulers, that in many instances it is not possible to determine where national prerogatives end and foreign ones begin' (Bretton, 1973, p. 22). Integration into colonial economic blocs further strengthened external influences on the room to manoeuvre of domestic governments and indeed domestic economic interests.

The political power of external interests

It was, however, possible to identify neo-colonialists as an organized interest, an interest having political significance internally but mainly externally oriented economically and carrying more political weight than economically marginal local groups. Foreign corporations, banks and trading houses were well positioned to exert influence and counter nationalistic economic pressures. The commanding heights of the economy were largely in the hands of foreign firms. In the immediate post-independence years indigenous small-scale capital entrepreneurs had nothing like the same influence as the multinationals. Companies such as Unilever, the Firestone Corporation or United Fruit dominated the economies of the new states.

Organizations representing external interests were able successfully to contain the range of policy and ideological choices open to governments within limits acceptable to themselves (Berman, 1974). Multinationals could inhibit development planning by limiting the government's tax raising capacity through transfer pricing and the movement of production from one country to another (Sutcliffe, 1972; Hymer, 1982). Foreign owners and managers of foreign capital received special advantages. In francophone Africa, for example, '*la presence francaise*' meant the complete penetration of public life by such interests and their pressure groups. In Kenya, European organizations representing the agriculture-based industries exerted great influence on policy-making because of dependence for competitiveness on European involvement. In the 1960s the foreign owners of the greater part of non-agricultural capital were also represented locally by 'a substantial bureaucracy employed by the branches of foreign firms . . . mainly themselves foreigners', although increasingly including Kenyan Africans. As this ownership spread, so the political power of foreign capital increased (though in the interest of nationalist economic ideology and rhetoric it had to be ritually humiliated: Leys, 1975, p. 174).

In Senegal and the Ivory Coast the influence of French interests on government boards, chambers of commerce and informal meetings of businessmen exceeded the power of parliaments, cabinets and political parties

(Bretton, 1973). After independence, in the Ivory Coast, French private interests were dominant in the commodities which formed the basis of the economy (coffee, cocoa and cotton). Manufacturing and processing were mainly in foreign hands, and governments had to obtain the approval of big foreign firms with the equipment, trade outlets, capital, and skills for groundnut shelling, cotton ginning and cocoa cleaning before formulating any policies towards indigenous producers.

Nkrumah understood well the 'rights' and privileges that could be demanded by foreign interests as a result of their economic power: land concessions, prospecting rights, exemptions from customs duties and taxes, and privileges in the cultural sphere: 'that Western information services be exclusive; and that those from socialist countries be excluded'. So, for example, agreements for economic cooperation offered by the USA often included the demand that the United States Information Agency ('a top intelligence arm of the US imperialists') be granted preferential rights to disseminate information (Nkrumah, 1965, pp. 246–50). Cultural neo-colonialism also rested on the dependence of newly independent states on Western ideas and methods in education, administration and the professions (Berman, 1974). The top executives of the subsidiaries of multinationals, the largest corporations in the country of operations, were influential in the social and cultural life of the host country as well as in its politics. Governments dependent on the information coming from such sources were unable to work out their own solutions to the problems, such as poverty, which were of no particular interest to foreigners (Baran, 1957; Hymer, 1982).

The anti-colonialists of the post-independence era found neo-colonialism to be operating in diverse ways other than legitimate pressure group activity. Nkrumah described how neo-colonialists 'slip past our guard' through military bases, advisers, media propaganda, evangelism, and CIA subversion. Military dependence on the former colonial powers for arms, training, advisers and basic military doctrine has been seen as one of the most visible aspects of neo-colonialism. The success or failure of a *coup d'état* was often dependent on the level of external encouragement. In Africa the 'metropolitan centres, especially France, have assumed the role of arbiters of the survival of particular regimes' (Berman, 1974, pp. 6–7). France's neo-colonial role continued into the 1990s in Rwanda, Zaire, Gabon and Togo.

Comprador elites

Other important political features of neo-colonialism are the common interests of local elites and external organizations, whether they be foreign governments, multinational corporations or international agencies. Merchants, 'expanding and thriving within the orbit of foreign capital', formed a 'comprador element' of the native bourgeoisie which, together with 'native industrial monopolists', acted as 'stalwart defenders of the established order'. Large landowners not only benefitted from foreign capital but also found outlets for their produce, employment opportunities for members of their families, and rising land values in the neo-imperial connection (Baran, 1957, pp. 194–5).

The multinationals affect the class structure and power distribution in less developed countries by creating dependent classes of local merchants, financiers and privileged sections of the labour force – 'satellite classes whose interests are tied to the *dependencia* syndrome' (Rosen and Jones, 1979, p. 254; Schuurman, 1993). Under neo-colonialism the imperial power is represented by 'collaborative classes within post-colonial society, some more dependent on foreign interests than others'. The following distinctions were identified:

> Large-scale industrialists involved in production for the local market and with a powerful presence in the state are more likely to be *associate power-sharers* with imperial interests. Import–exporters tied to foreign markets, shipping and credits are likely to be *dependent power-sharers*. Joint ventures, in which industrialists produce for foreign markets, drawing on foreign technology, capital and management, and with little direct representation in the state, are likely to be *subordinate* collaborators (Petras, 1981, p. 18).

Indigenous elites, the most important being the bureaucracy and indigenous management cadres employed by foreign companies, develop an interest in maintaining economic arrangements in which foreigners hold a major stake. The close contacts between members of the national politico-administrative elite and external organizations then 'makes the distinction between domestic and international affairs meaningless' (Berman, 1974, p. 9). The 'mutuality of interest' across national boundaries between national economic elites and the senior management of transnational corporations and banks produced a 'transnational class formation' of an international oligarchy or 'corporate international bourgeoisie' with local and international 'wings' which ensured that public policy supported the interests of international capital (Becker and Sklar, 1987).

The foreigners are usually the dominant partners because of their superior resources, information and negotiating skills compared with national governments. With the possible exception of the military, governments, labour organizations and most non-business institutions and associations are 'far behind' multinationals in terms of financial, technological and administrative strength (Hymer, 1982). While foreign interests are thus included in the policy process, indigenous interests not represented by the elite are excluded. Institutions for representation and participation (parties, local governments, trade unions, youth organizations) have been left powerless relative to the bureaucracy.

Dependent economic development also often required the demobilization by repressive governments of the popular forces which had formed movements for independence. Non-popular, pro-Western regimes, often resting on alliances between the military and indigenous propertied classes, were the political prerequisites of economic growth (McMichael et al., 1974).

Aid dependency

Another source of external influence on public policy is official aid, which increasingly has been linked to 'conditionalities'. Aid is used as a lever to determine domestic government policy. Donors can withdraw vital aid if the neo-colonial governments fail to adopt policies favouring the interests of the donor government or firms based in the donor economy. In this way the donor government secures strategic and diplomatic advantages, as in 1983 when the United States Congress made economic assistance to developing countries conditional upon support for American foreign policy. Economic interests that the donor represents secure a profitable policy environment. Special loans from a multilateral agency such as the International Monetary Fund or the World Bank come with conditions attached, such as a requirement to cut public expenditure programmes, particularly food subsidies and social services. Implementing them can lead to political unrest.

Other conditions on which bilateral aid is given have included the award of contracts to firms in the donor country and the purchase of arms. The 'war on terror' launched by the USA in 2001 has increased the amount of military aid available to countries identified as fighting terrorism, including the Philippines, Pakistan, Indonesia, Saudi Arabia, and Egypt, regardless of human rights concerns. Thus donors continue to allocate substantial amounts of aid for strategic and commercial reasons, despite the ending of the Cold War.

Aid also affects the power structure of neo-colonial society. It increases the power of those in command of the state apparatus relative to any opposition. The power of the bureaucracy is enhanced by aid, this being the channel through which aid flows. Technical assistance programmes to national defence and police forces strengthen these sections of the political elite. Much of the aid from developed countries is in the form of military assistance which has affected the distribution of political power in neo-colonial society. Food aid distorts the neo-colonial economy and society by enabling recipient governments to avoid land reforms and changes in methods of agricultural production which would reduce external dependency and the power of the landed classes. Aid empowers the state at the expense of free markets and increases the power of ruling groups at the expense of the people generally. Aid has also biased development towards urban rather than rural society (Bauer, 1971; Lipton, 1977; Mack and Leaver, 1979).

Most donors require public services to be privatized, despite the threat of increased poverty that this brings. Privatization has meant massive price increases unrestrained by regulatory bodies, forcing poor families to reduce spending on food and put school-aged children out to work. The increased cost of services has driven people into poverty in Vietnam, Bangladesh, China and Cambodia. Services are often not supplied to poor communities which are not profitable. Allowing the private sector to supply profitable areas undermines the revenues of the public services left to cope with unprofitable communities. Privatization also drains staff from public services, especially in health care, again benefiting affluent members of society (Hilary, 2004).

Debt relief has become a major objective of international aid, especially, since 1996, for the most heavily indebted poor countries. International indebtedness remains on a large scale and for some poor countries, particularly in Africa, at an unsustainable level even after rescheduling agreements. The cost for developing countries of servicing debt, both as a percentage of GDP and a percentage of exports rose in most regions of the Third world during the 1990s (see Table 3.1). In 2005 the total external

Table 3.1   *Debt servicing 1990–2005*

Region	% of GDP			% of exports of goods and services		
	1990	*1999*	*2005[1]*	*1990*	*1999*	*2005[2]*
Arab states	5.5	3.6	2.5	14.7	11.4	8.5
East Asia	3.8	5.2	3.0	15.7	15.8	2.6
Latin America	4.0	8.1	..	23.6	41.6	22.9
South Asia	2.6	2.8	..	20.0	16.6	5.4
Sub-Saharan Africa	3.9	4.6	..	19.7	14.3	5.8
Developing countries	4.4	5.8	4.6	18.7	22.3	13.0
Least developed countries	2.7	2.8	2.3	15.5	13.0	7.0

NOTES: [1] Figures for Arab states and East Asia are for 2003.
[2] Figures for Arab states, East Asia, and Sub-Saharan Africa are for 2004.
SOURCES: UNDP, 2001, Table 15, p.194; 2005, Table 19, p. 283; UNDP, 2006, Table 18, p. 347; UNDP, 2007, Table 18, p. 293.

Table 3.2   *Aid as a percentage of GDP, 1990–2005*

Region	1990	2000	2005
Developing countries	1.4	0.5	1.1
East Asia	0.8	0.3	0.3
Latin America	0.4	0.2	0.3
Middle East and N. Africa	2.0	0.8	3.9
South Asia	1.3	0.8	0.9
Sub-Saharan Africa	5.8	4.1	5.5

SOURCES: UNDP, 2001, Table 15, p.194; World Bank, 2001a, Table 4.3, p. 89; World Bank, 2007b, Table 6.11, p. 350.

debt of developing countries stood at US$2,800.4 billion, but had fallen as a percentage of GDP and exports. Debt relief also comes with strings attached. For example, the IMF and World Bank's Heavily Indebted Poor Countries Initiative requires 'sound' economic policies, the adoption of a poverty reduction strategy, and economic adjustment and reform programmes to maintain macro-economic stability. These requirements are not always compatible.

Budgetary restraints coupled with public scepticism about the effectiveness of aid in donor countries led to a 25 per cent fall in the volume of aid in the 1990s. Aid to countries judged to have poor policy environments fell particularly sharply. As a percentage of developing countries' GDP, aid fell from 1.4 per cent in 1990 to 0.5 per cent in 2000, rising to 1.1 per cent in 2005 (see Table 3.2). Despite conditionalities, more aid is required in some regions, notably Africa, where the economic growth needed to reduce poverty cannot be achieved by domestic savings and private investment.

Ideas about neo-colonialism and dependency provide inadequate guidance to the political consequences for Third World societies of aid and other economic factors. However, while the emphasis in aid policy now tends to be on requiring recipient countries to feel 'ownership' of projects and programmes and responsibility for their success, aid still comes with conditions attached. These now recognize the threats posed by economic reforms and restructuring and aim for laudable objectives such as poverty relief and good governance. But developing countries still need to demonstrate that they provide an environment of policy and institutions that is conducive to reform. The latest doctrine on aid is that it should support reforms that originate from domestic political pressures. In the past aid has not been very successful in stimulating donor-specified reforms. Recognition that aid is likely to be more effective and sustainable if a recipient country's government feels committed to the project now informs aid policy, but governments still know what donors expect and require.

The independent state and political forces

The view that formal political independence had not substantially modified the relations of domination and exploitation between the capitalist imperialist powers and the new states of the Third World received a major challenge in the early 1970s from the British Marxist Bill Warren (1973, 1980). While not denying that imperialism persisted 'as a system of inequality, domination and exploitation' (1973, p. 4), Warren argued that the term 'neo-colonialism' obscured the role played by the achievement of formal sovereignty and its consequences. The post-war achievement of independence, together with other socio-political and economic trends, had created the conditions for significant capitalist industrialization. These trends included collaboration between imperialist and Third World governments to suppress anti-capitalist movements.

The inevitable inequalities associated with fast growth had sometimes been politically destabilizing. However, political independence, far from being a sham, was a significant change in the internal politics of former colonies, mainly because it provided a focus for the domestic state management of economic processes. The newly independent state became the focal point of economic development. Formal independence gave Third World states 'institutional control' over their domestic economies. The powers to establish central banks and parastatals, enforce export and import currency controls, and implement taxation and public spending 'stem directly from independence' and affect far more than industrialization, especially the reinforcement of capitalist social relations of production, commodity production in agriculture, and economic restructuring 'along lines more suitable to a successful indigenous capitalism' (1973, p. 13). The state exercised powers to direct investment and channel external capital whether from aid, multinationals or foreign countries, and controlled the development of capitalist relations and modes of production. This led to it becoming a significant actor in the national political system and not totally subject to external political forces.

Politically, independence and formal sovereignty produced states which were significant actors in national political systems and the focal points of economic development. Third world states, and the elites which controlled them, often successfully negotiated with foreign investors over profit levels, wages, rents, pricing policies, volumes of output, transportation needs, sources of supply, taxes on multinationals, export policies and other interventions in the domestic economy. Third World states had shown themselves capable of taking controlling action against foreign firms located in their territories, including nationalization, the acquisition of majority shareholdings, joint ventures and service contracts. Independence provided opportunities for the national bourgeoisie, liberal reformers, democratic socialists, communists or military populists to alter relationships with rich countries. Independent governments could enter into alliances and trade agreements that were not open to them before, strengthening their bargaining positions in international economic relations (Cohen, 1973). The bargaining power of newly independent countries was further increased by collective organizations such as OPEC and the Andean Pact.

Some newly industrialized countries (NICs) confirmed the significance of the state in autonomous national economic development and of the national bourgeoisie in using that state apparatus in order to promote high rates of growth along capitalist lines. The NICs have been classified among the most *dirigiste* regimes with state intervention at all levels in support of private capital. They are among the most planned and some would say corporatist economies. In supporting private capital the state has interfered with the free operation of market forces by the suppression of organized labour, the lowering of wages, and the weakening of political opposition to government policies. Foreign investment has been welcomed. Protected enclaves have been provided, such as free trade zones for high growth activities in which enterprises qualify for tax relief and enjoy a docile labour force, and where import tariffs and export licences are easily available. All this has been provided on behalf of what appears to be a dominant property-owning class.

So the NICs require us to think again about neo-colonialism. Their recent histories strongly suggest that not everything is determined by the international division of labour, and that political leaders can exploit, within limits, commercial links (to diversify trade), domestic assets (or even liabilities, such as debt), and a range of external sources of aid and loans (Seers, 1981).

What the concept of 'neo-colonialism' had achieved, in Warren's view, was to indicate that newly-independent governments could not *immediately* exert their bargaining power, because of skills shortages and delays in establishing effective state institutions and representation on international bodies. It had also provided ideological support for, and international acceptance of, 'Third World bourgeois nationalism' – 'a fundamental ideological condition for the creation of modern nation-states out of states previously characterized by feudal particularism, religious and communal division, and all varieties of patriarchal backwardness' (1980, p. 185; see also Twitchett, 1965, p. 319).

Warren's thesis on the political consequences of independence was criticized for exaggerating the significance of popular pressures released by independence, and of omitting any analysis of the social forces exerting pressures on government or the linkages between ruling groups and external interests (McMichael et al., 1974). But the main issue dividing Warren from his critics is the consequences of capitalist industrialization and growth for different classes within Third World societies. Warren's critics were anxious to establish that development usually meant the political repression and economic exploitation of workers and peasants. He was accused of failing to distinguish the period of popular mobilization leading to national independence, from the post-independent *demobilization* of such forces to enable dependent industrialization to take place in countries such as India, Algeria, Indonesia, Nigeria and Kenya. Non-popular, pro-imperialist regimes, often resting on alliances between the military and propertied classes, have been the prerequisites of industrial growth (McMichael et al., 1974, p. 94).

Warren did not deny this – as a Marxist he was hardly likely to. His conviction, however, was that growth and development were based on increasingly autonomous, nationalistic, political leadership and that this produced conditions for the development of capitalism *significantly* different from those preceding formal independence. Capitalist forces might have been exploitative (must have been, in fact) but at least they were national. National classes and their political representatives acted autonomously towards subordinate classes and foreign interests. The importance for Marxists of Warren's conclusion about national independence and the power of the new national bourgeoisies was that it identified the fundamental division as between classes, not nations (Brewer, 1980). His critics maintained that these classes and their regimes continued to be the instruments of foreign capital, and that as a consequence the economic record was not as good as Warren made it out to be, let alone the political and social record for those whom capitalism exploits.

New ruling groups, often petty bourgeois in nature, could mobilize themselves. The absence of a fully formed national bourgeoisie has been compensated for by a state apparatus which has assumed the role of a bourgeois ruling class. So Third World societies had acquired their own indigenous ruling class, not in the form of a private property-owning bourgeoisie but in the form of a public property-directing state apparatus, particularly the bureaucracy. Conditions increasingly existed for the formation of a national bourgeoisie and therefore the forms of control, management and politics that such a class requires. The state became a focal point of political pressure of an urban petit-bourgeoisie demanding higher standards of living and consumption, all of which encouraged manufacturing and industrialization. In Kenya, for example, a class of agrarian capitalists was able to use its strong representation in the state apparatus to increase the rate of indigenous capital accumulation through policies on trade licensing, monopolies, state finance capital, private credit and state capitalist enterprise (Leys, 1978). Independence also encouraged the development of social movements which gave added momentum to economic development. Popular, diffuse indigenous pressures for higher living standards were stimulated, a major internal influence sustaining industrialization policies.

Dependency theory

The neo-colonialist model of post-colonial politics was prompted by concern with the real, rather than symbolic, significance of independence from a colonial power. However, continuing economic relationships between poor and rich countries were not placed in a broad theoretical framework to produce an interpretation of the continuity between imperialism and independence. This was not achieved until the idea of neo-colonialism was incorporated into a theory about an international system of economic subordination that had a very strong impact on countries long after their independence. This is generally referred to as dependency theory.

Dependency theory had its roots in the crisis of American liberalism in the late 1960s (particularly associated with the war in Vietnam), the failure of many Third World societies to move in prescribed directions, and doubts about the credibility of social science's claims to be neutral and value-free. Other influences included the Cuban revolution, de-Stalinization and Maoism. It was in part a critical response to modernization theory's assumption that 'backwardness' was the result of the isolation of less developed countries from the rest of the world, rather than their exploitation by more advanced countries under various forms of imperialism (Phillips, 1977; Leys, 1977; Higgott, 1983). The major contributors to this new paradigm in the study of development were Latin American Marxist economists such as Dos Santos, Cardoso, Sunkel and Faletto, non-Marxist Latin American economists such as Furtado and Prebisch, and North American neo-Marxists such as Bodenheimer, Petras, Magdoff and A.G.Frank (Foster-Carter, 1976). Dependency theory originated in the analysis of Latin American countries where independence had been achieved in the early- or mid-nineteenth century but where problems of foreign economic exploitation persisted, similar to those found in countries that were still colonies or had only recently achieved independence.

Dependency theory adds the idea of peripherality or satellite status to the concept of neo-colonialism. This was achieved in two phases. The first was concerned with dependency as a function of primary production, with poor countries having to rely on a small number of primary products for their export earnings. The second phase began as a critique of international trade theory and an explanation of why import substitution was needed. It then explained the failure of this strategy by reference to the structures introduced by industrialization (Philip, 1990).

Import substitution had political dimensions. First, it was assumed that greater economic sovereignty would follow. Secondly, (and here there are echoes of modernization theory) it was predicted that industrialization would weaken traditional society. Manufacturing activities need different pattern variables to traditional societies. In Latin America this would mean that the status and power of the traditional landed oligarchy would be undermined. If this almost feudalistic stratum could be weakened the way to greater democracy would be paved. Thirdly, industrialization would start to make a real impact on the extreme inequalities found in Latin American societies, and contribute to the integration of the rural masses into the main activities of society. The rural masses, formerly isolated on plantations and *haciendas*, would become closely incorporated into society through new economic opportunities and improved standards of living. This would then contribute to the reinforcement of political stability. When the rural masses were marginalized by semi-feudal forces dominating the rural areas, political stability was always at risk.

Integration would produce not only stability but greater democracy. The state would gain legitimacy by its association with the industrialization process and by contributing to social and political equality as well as economic efficiency. National sentiment would be strengthened, especially for rural people hitherto allied economically and politically with rural oligarchies – economic and religious – rather than the state. Thus a secular goal for the import substitution strategy was political integration into a liberal democratic society (Dos Santos, 1973).

The second phase of dependency theory was prompted by the apparent failure of this strategy to solve the problem of dependency or to produce the intended political outcomes. By the end of the 1960s import substitution had increased dependency, but now upon foreign capital goods – machine tools, plant and technology.

Income distribution became more, not less, unequal. Inequality developed a new dimension, that between the rural and urban areas. People displaced from the land were not being absorbed into new industrial activities and thereby integrated into the social fabric, largely because the new industries were capital rather than labour intensive. New forms of marginalization were created in the slum populations gathered on the fringes of the major urban and industrial centres. Instead of integration into a modern economy, disparities in social and spatial terms and new forms of marginalization were brought into being as a growing proportion of the populations found themselves without jobs, education, political influence, security or proper shelter. Such people were politically highly volatile and therefore not committed to political stability. Their exclusion from politics did not engender consensus towards the state.

The state, it was argued, had become subservient to the multinational companies that controlled the industrialization process. Greater sovereignty had not been achieved. Politics became more authoritarian and repressive, rather than liberal democratic and pluralist, as governments tried to cope with the social strains brought about by the industrializing process. Managing the industrial labour-force as well as the marginalized masses seemed to require military dictatorship rather than pluralist democracy.

The elements of dependency theory

There are five main strands in dependency theory: the idea of a hierarchy of states; the concept of 'underdevelopment'; a view about the nature of capitalism; propositions concerning 'disarticulation'; and the effect of economic dependency of the structure of political power.

Hierarchy finds its expression in 'centre-periphery' or 'metropolitan-satellite' models of relations between the great world centres of capital and the economies that are dependent upon them. A hierarchy of centres and peripheries is said to connect all levels of exploitation between one country and another and within the countries of the periphery. There is a steady extraction of surplus through the different levels in the hierarchy: from peasant to landlord; from landlord to local merchant; merchant to subsidiary of a multinational; subsidiary to headquarters of the MNC; headquarters to the major financial institutions of the West. Mining, commercial, agricultural and even military centres within the peripheral satellites constitute 'micro-metropolises' in relation to their hinterlands of small towns, mines and *latifundia* which themselves relate in the same way to isolated workers. Similar relations of exploitation link industrial firms to the suppliers of components; large merchants and financiers to small traders and moneylenders; and city merchants and landowners to small rural producers and consumers (Frank, 1966, 1969a).

A satellite within this hierarchical structure will only experience development when its ties to the metropolis are weak: 'no country which has been firmly tied to the metropolis as a satellite through incorporation into the world capitalist system has achieved the rank of an economically developed country' (Frank, 1969a, p. 11). In Latin America the periods of autonomous industrialization have occurred historically during periods when trade and investment ties with Europe were loosened by European wars and economic recessions. The same applies, according to Frank, to relatively isolated regions within peripheral societies: the less integrated into the world mercantilist and then capitalist systems, the greater the growth of manufacturing and exports. The least developed and most 'feudal-seeming' regions are those which had the closest ties to the metropolis in the past. The incorporation of a satellite into the metropolitan-led hierarchy chokes off development, making it more difficult for industrialization and sustained development to take place.

Industrialization did not produce national or independent development, with an accumulation of capital under national control, self-sustaining economic growth, increased employment and growing levels of income, consumption and welfare (Bernstein, 1982). Rather, it was accompanied by increased foreign control. The peripheral economy is characterized by firms and sectors which are not highly integrated among themselves but which are linked into networks centering on the developed capitalist world.

Underdevelopment refers to a continuing relationship of exploitation where at any one level in the chain the full economic surplus is not available for reinvestment. It is removed, ultimately accumulating in the metropolitan centres (Frank, 1969a; Dos Santos, 1973). Far from experiencing development as a result of ties with metropolitan centres (which is what modernization theory tells us occurs), such ties hold the peripheral economy and society back.

Consequently, backwardness arises from the subordination of poor countries to the development of today's rich countries. Underdevelopment could not be explained in terms of an earlier stage on the path to modernity. The circumstances under which advanced countries progressed cannot be repeated: 'The now developed countries were never *under*developed, though they may have been *un*developed' (Frank, 1966, p. 18). Dependency is a continuing relationship, not confined to an imperialist past but continuing in the neo-imperialist present. Formal political control is not necessary for a relationship of dependency and exploitation to be maintained through structures of foreign capital intervention.

A controversy within dependency theory concerned the impact of *capitalism* on a 'peripheral' society. Frank argued that once an unbroken chain is created between rich and poor countries a complete and total capitalist system is brought into existence. Societies that become integrated into hierarchies of core-periphery relations are not backward in the sense of having pre-capitalist relations of production. Rather they become part of the capitalist system and, in the case of Latin America, had been since the sixteenth century when the mercantilist economies of Spain and Portugal had implanted the seeds of capitalism. Peripheral societies are part of an extended system of capitalist relations.

It was thus a myth to claim that the problems of peripheral countries could be attributed to the retention of pre-capitalist economic and political relationship in a 'dual' society of progressive and traditional economies, namely feudal forms of political authority and economic structure (Frank, 1969b). The so-called feudalistic institutions were as much the product of capitalist development as the more obviously modernized capitalist sectors.

This was to interpret capitalism in terms of trade and exchange rather than relations of production. Incorporating a society into a network of world trade was sufficient for it to be designated capitalist. Chile and other Latin American countries have been plagued by an 'open, dependent, capitalist export economy' since the sixteenth century (Frank, 1969b, p. 5). This of course has implications for the analysis of the political situations in such countries. The political relationships that we associate with capitalism – namely liberal democracy based on the institutions of private property, freedom of contract, and political rights – should have accompanied the incorporation of those societies into a capitalist world system.

This understanding of capitalism is controversial. It is generally thought that capitalism exists more in terms of the relations of production rather than exchange – private property, free wage labour, and freedom of contract (Laclau, 1971; Taylor, 1979). These features were absent in many of the societies on the periphery. It was possible for the goods that were traded and exchanged to be produced under pre-capitalist relations of production. Social relations of production underpinning structures of political authority need not necessarily be capitalist at all for a rich country to be interested in what is produced. Just because the commodities emerging from a Latin American *hacienda* find their way into other parts of the international economy does not means that they were produced through capitalist relations of production. Relations were often highly feudalistic, involving peasant production on tenancies closely controlled by landlords, a control that extends far beyond what is bought by the payment of a wage. Dependency often sustained the production of goods through feudalistic tenancies, bonded labour, controls over the movement of the population, and other non-capitalist controls exercised at the point of production. The penetration of foreign capital should not be confused with the installation of capitalist relations of production or indeed the political forms of the capitalist state (Brewer, 1980). Political analysis is not helped by the association of capitalism with relations of *exchange*.

Many Third World societies thus had the remnants of pre-capitalist political authority, particularly in the rural areas. Landed oligarchies dominated the local peasantries in ways that are inconsistent with capitalist forms of political authority. Feudalism was not the 'myth' that some assumed it to be and the remnants of feudalism were among those factors that made it difficult for democratic government to survive. Political equality and the political freedoms that are the necessary corollary of economic freedom are incompatible with the power of such landed oligarchies.

The concept of *disarticulation* attempts to distinguish between forms of international dependency. One developed capitalist economy may be dependent upon another. Therefore it may be thought that dependency is not peculiar to poor countries and weak economies. The UK economy is dependent on the American economy in terms of foreign investment, foreign ownership of economic resources and the interventions of US-based multinationals. Increasingly there is a similar dependency on Japan. Dependency theorists, however, argued that there is an important difference between that kind of dependency and the dependency experienced in the Third World (Amin, 1982).

When there are two developed economies with a degree of inter-penetration of capital between them the advanced nation remains an independent centre of capital accumulation. This has consequences for the structure of political forces in that society. When, however, a peripheral society experiences dependency a distinctive form of capitalism is produced. The poor society's economy is conditioned by the expansion of the stronger economies in ways which are quite different to the relationships between two developed economies. In particular, the conditioning or 'disarticulation' of the poor economy discourages internal growth by transferring the benefits of growth abroad (Frank, 1972a; Roxborough, 1979).

Politically this has an effect on class structure. It produces a dominant class of merchants not engaged in production, which is primarily in the hands of foreign enterprises. The emergence of an industrial bourgeoisie is blocked. So the emergence of the political institutions upon which a domestic bourgeoisie thrives, those of the liberal democratic state, is blocked too. The nature of dependency has a profound impact on the development of the state and political forces within it. The idea of disarticulation suggests that the capitalist state in its democratic form requires a certain kind of ruling class, one whose interests will be protected by such a state. If it does not have such a unified ruling class because of external dependency, the political consequences will be some kind of authoritarian regime.

The whole class structure of peripheral society is determined by the position of that society in the international division of labour – whether the country has been predominantly an agricultural export economy with a rural-based oligarchy, an enclave economy based on the extraction of natural resources, or an import substitution economy with an industrial and financial bourgeoisie. None of these ruling classes have a vested interest in the reproduction of a working class through better health, housing and education because there is a surplus of labour in excess of industry's needs created by a combination of stagnating agriculture, population growth and capital intensive industrialization (Hein and Stenzel, 1979).

The *structure of political power* is also affected by economic dependency. The ruling classes of the Third World (merchants, landowners, financiers, industrial capitalists and state bureaucrats) are seen as junior partners within the structure of international capital. These 'clientele classes' have a vested interest in the existing international system and perform domestic political and economic functions on behalf of foreign interests. They enjoy a privileged, dominant and 'hegemonic' position within society 'based largely on economic, political or military support from abroad' (Bodenheimer, 1971, p. 163). The policies of governments reflect the vested interests of the ruling class in the continuation of dependency.

In Brazil, for example, groups 'expressing the interests and modes of organization of international capitalism' gained disproportionate influence over policy-makers. An ideological as well as economic affinity between the holders of economic power and the 'anti-populist' sectors of the military and technocracy enabled the latter to gain in influence not only in modernizing the administration, but also in the repressive functions of the state, culminating in the *coup d'état* of 1964. Other sections of the ruling class declined in power including agrarian, merchant and some industrial interests, the traditional bureaucratic component of the middle class, and career politicians, while organized sections of the working class were successfully marginalized.

Changes in the relative power position of different élites and classes were expressed through the accumulation process, requiring that 'the instruments of pressure and defense available to the popular classes be dismantled' so that wage levels could be kept low. This included unions and political organizations through which wage earners had defended their interests during the populist period. In allowing the military to repress the working class, parts of the bourgeoisie lost control of the political process, especially the party system, elections, press freedom, and liberal education (Cardoso, 1973, pp. 146–59).

Different 'patterns of dependence' accounted for shifts in the relative power of different classes. Moving beyond import substitution in an attempt to reduce dependency meant moving away from a stage of development that was 'significantly controlled by the local bourgeoisie' (Cardoso, 1973, p. 157). The role of international monopolies became comprehensive, including the remaining areas of primary exports, the private manufacturing sector, and even public enterprises such as the state oil monopoly PETROBRAS. The political consequence of this economic realignment was an autocratic, developmentalist, military-bureaucratic regime.

Dependency and economic performance

It is difficult to fit the impressive growth in per capita incomes achieved by a number of dependent economies into dependency theory. In some regions, development requires more, not less, foreign capital (Emmanuel, 1974, 1976). Nor has the introduction of capitalism necessarily held countries back economically. For example, in Zambia, Saudi-Arabia and Sri

Lanka the capitalist sectors have developed, when foreign investment has been used to produce for world capitalist markets. In some African countries, too, capitalism 'has accomplished more than dependency theory allows' (Leys, 1996, p. 121). What has held back development is lack of know-how, enterprise, capital and pre-capitalist social and political traditions (Nove, 1974). Relations between centre and periphery are non zero-sum games, so 'economic relations with the metropolitan centre may act as an enormously powerful engine of growth in the periphery' (Cohen, 1973, p. 217). Foreign capital, even with a net outflow, can add to the total of domestic capital by the multiplier effect of investment-generated local payments such as wages, taxes and purchases of local supplies (Ray, 1973). Developing countries can also reduce their dependency by using their bargaining strength derived from the developed economies' dependence on them (Philip, 1990).

Such criticisms have received some support from comparative research. An analysis of data on 30 tropical African countries in the middle and late 1960s found measures of dependency unrelated to economic performance variables. In the mid-1960s African countries with high ratios of exports and imports to GNP and high levels of foreign capital had the best economic records. However, when this research made a distinction between 'market dependency' (a generalized feature of the international capitalist system) and 'economic power dependency' (meaning an economy is conditioned by the decisions of individuals, firms and agencies in metropolitan centres) it found the latter negatively related to economic performance (McGowan, 1976; McGowan and Smith, 1978).

Dependency and class

A further weakness of dependency theory is the over-generalized treatment of social classes. The absence of a sound analysis, of the class content of the metropolitan-satellite 'chain', means that the qualities of the different social relations within it are left unspecified. The analysis of class in dependency theory is insufficiently dynamic. Dependency theorists did not examine changes in class relationships within the periphery which could influence relationships with external interests. For example, the emergence of new classes can cause 'shifts in peripheral economic activity and relations with the metropolis', as when metropolitan interests are 'displaced' from the agro-mineral sector by national social forces such as peasant and industrial labour movements or the petty bourgeoisie (Petras, 1975, p. 305). However, this line of criticism may understate the importance of the transition from dependence on primary products to dependence on multi-national corporate investment.

Leys claims that Kenya is an example of the emergence of an independent, indigenous, capital-accumulating bourgeoisie under conditions where, according to dependency theory, it could not. He argues against assuming *a priori* that an independent local capitalist class cannot develop, and in favour of analyzing the factors that stimulate or inhibit its development. Among the former are the scope for rural capitalism, the significance of the informal sector, and global capitalism. Among the latter are ethnic conflict, state administrative capacity, and parasitic political leadership (Leys, 1996).

Dependency theory's revolutionary socialist solution to the problem of dependence does not carry conviction in the absence of a structural analysis that demonstrates there are classes or movements on which a revolution could be based. There is very little analysis of oppression, exploitation or class-based organizations. The failure to explain underdevelopment by reference to the interplay of political, social and economic forces thus exposes dependency theory to the charge that it is a-historical (Leys, 1977).

The weakness of the class analysis springs in part from a conflation of spatial entities and social classes. Relations between classes, such as landlords and peasants, are presented as comparable to relations between geographical tiers in the metropolitan satellite hierarchy. Relations of exploitation among classes are identified with transfers of value between spatial regions. The implication is that an exploiting class at one stage in the centre-periphery hierarchy is exploited by the class at the next higher stage. Such an assumption provides no basis for an analysis of the political behaviour of different socio-economic groups when 'the real relation of exploitation is a direct wage relation between the workers and the corporation as a unit of capital' (Brewer, 1980, p. 173).

Dependency theory leaves much work still to be done on the problem of societies that are supposedly capitalist yet find it so difficult to sustain the institutions and forms of state that we associate with the development of capitalism. However, the concept of 'disarticulation' takes us a bit further than saying that if the propertied classes do not like what is happening under parliamentary government they do not hesitate to support military intervention; or that there is a contradiction between the material inequalities of capitalism and the political equality of democracy. But that contradiction is an inadequate explanation in many Third World countries where there is no fully-developed working class.

Levels of generality

Dependency theory operates at too high a level of generality and conceptual imprecision for it to be refutable at the macro-level or applicable at the micro-level (Higgott, 1983; Leys, 1996). It is too static and unhistorical to explain successfully the distinctive elements of economic and political development in backward countries, and the mechanisms of social reproduction, modes of social transformation, and modes of politics. Operating at such a high level of generality makes it difficult to focus on the specifics of a particular country at a particular moment in history and how important they have been to development prospects (Philip, 1990). Past politics and policy instruments in particular receive only cursory treatment (O'Brien, 1975). Factors such as the size of a developing country's population, its ethnic or linguistic composition, its degree of self sufficiency in natural resources particularly energy, its physical location in relation to countries better endowed in terms of population, technology or military threats – make a great deal of difference to the prospects for development but tend to be overlooked by dependency theory. They cannot be described merely as features of world capitalism or the chain or hierarchy of metropolitan-periphery relationships. As factors affecting the room for manoeuvre which governments have they would not disappear if the international capitalist system did not exist. So any explanation which overlooks such details must be deficient (Seers, 1981).

The function of the state in Third World societies cannot be reduced to external, international economic influences. Legacies of authoritarian government, ideologies of corporatism and populist nationalism, patterns of patron-client relations, the aggregation of local interests, the internal evolution of social and political forces – all produce variable styles of state action that are not wholly externally induced (Long, 1977; Smith, 1979). Hence the importance of considering the evidence supporting different theories of the Third World state (see Chapter 4).

Hierarchy

Dependency theory has also been criticized for restricting the idea of a hierarchy of domination or influence to relations between rich and poor countries. Critics have denied that there are qualitative as well as quantitative differences between rich and poor countries which make their dependency distinctive in international terms. Dominance, dependence, influence and the inter-penetration and internationalization of capital apply just as much at the core or centre of the world capitalist system as at the periphery (Lall, 1975; Kay, 1975; Bernstein, 1979). Brewer refers to 'interdependence' and 'dominance' because 'dependence' implies that some countries are economically independent, which is not the case (Brewer, 1980, p. 178).

Dependency theory's argument is that in the core economies cultural, legal and political institutions are the product of indigenous development in the way that they are not in peripheral and particularly ex-colonial societies. Here institutions have developed from those originally imposed from outside. The class structure of dependent societies is also more a reflection of external economic interests than of the distribution of material resources and interests within the country (Larrain, 1989). What is significant in Third World dependency is the representation in some general sense of external foreign interests rather than a class structure – and political configurations representing it – which are contained purely within the borders of that country.

But does this provide a firm analytic base for distinguishing dependent from non-dependent politics? Class relations in poor countries, where the rich benefit from mutual interests with the rich in rich countries, seem comparable to class relations in developed countries. So perhaps all societies are in the pyramid of social, political and economic dominance with the apex occupied by the most powerful capitalist country and the bottom by the poorest countries. It is difficult to find some special dividing line horizontally which separates dependent from independent economies and societies.

The political significance of independence

It is easier to judge the economic analysis underpinning neo-colonialism and dependency interpretations of post-colonial history than to evaluate their contributions to an understanding of Third World politics. The main problem for students of Third World politics is that dependency theory does not make a systematic attempt to demonstrate the political consequences of dependency. It was predominantly an explanation of economic relations, leaving political relationships to be derived from them. It has a distinct tendency to see the state as epiphenomenal – that there is nothing to be explained in terms of the state, social classes and movements, politics and ideology other than as derivatives of the economy and without an independent role of their own. The state is merely a consequence of relationships and power structures that lie elsewhere, namely in the economy (Leys, 1977; Goulbourne, 1979; Hoogvelt, 1982).

Empirical tests of dependency theory have produced conflicting results as regards political consequences. Analysis of cross-sectional aggregate socio-economic and political variables for 20 Latin American states in the 1960s found the *greater* the dependency, the higher the level of political participation, the better the government's democratic performance and the less military intervention is likely, though the greater the level of civil strife. But a study of Africa in the 1960s found that dependence and inequality were related – in line with hypotheses derived from dependency theory (McGowan, 1976; McGowan and Smith, 1978; Vengroff, 1977). A difficulty with this type of test is the operationalization of concepts. The serious limitations of aggregate data techniques are shown by some of the indicators used to measure aspects of a 'dependent' economy and society – the level of unionization and voting turnout as measures of class structure, for example (Kaufman et al., 1974).

Dependency and democratization

Since 1980 the integration of poor countries in the global economy has taken a new turn. The spread of formal, or procedural, democracy has freed an often vibrant civil society to mobilize disadvantaged and marginalized sections of society into different forms of political activism, including electoral politics. Yet inequality and poverty have grown in most regions of the Third World, and especially Latin America. The opportunities created by democratization for lower class mobilization and political pressure have been negated by the economic forces of global capitalism, to such an extent that developing (and, indeed, developed) societies have become even more dominated by the interests of capital.

Globalization has strengthened the political power of international capital and its local representatives. Neo-liberal policies have been designed to integrate national economies into the global by enabling international capital to be fully mobile. Deregulation and privatization have removed the state from key areas of economic decision-making: 'the state defers to the market as the sole organizing power in the economic and social sphere'. However, the state retains its power over labour, with laws ensuring labour 'flexibility', reductions in real wages, the withdrawal of the social wage through the privatization of health care and education, the neglect of human rights, controls over political activism, and 'a transfer of income from labour to capital' (Robinson, 1999, pp. 44, 49). While the more strident forms of authoritarianism that characterized earlier forms of economic dependency may have largely disappeared, economic globalization having forced the dismantling of dictatorships, market forces have effectively countered the formal political rights of the non-propertied classes.

Consequently even the centre-left regimes in Brazil, Argentina, Uruguay and Bolivia, elected with the expectation that their anti-poverty rhetoric would be put into operation, have benefited capital over labour. The power of employers over workers has been increased, wage controls have been imposed, and social programmes have been cut. Privatization has been extended and agribusinesses subsidized. Land redistribution policies have been abandoned, while multinational corporations have been encouraged to exploit natural resources (especially in Bolivia). The state regularly resorts to violence against political protest: 'the great majority of Latin Americans – workers, peasants, the unemployed and the poor – have suffered grave consequences as a result of the support given to "centre-left" parties and coalitions by movements to which they belong' (Petras, 2006: 290).

Structures of socio-economic power remain intact and reflected in the class nature of public policy. Government ministers have strong ties with international and domestic capital and financial institutions – banks, the World Bank, and IMF. These currently dominant capitalist interests are confronted by trade unions, mass movements in urban areas, landless agricultural workers, poor peasants and Indian militants. In Colombia the Revolutionary Armed Forces have yet to be defeated. Yet it is often easy to co-opt the leaders of popular movements and economic organizations with lucrative government posts (Petras, 2006). The populism of ostensibly left-leaning politicians has proved to be a veneer covering the inevitable disparities in political power under global capitalism.

Conclusion

The critique of neo-colonialist explanations and dependency theory can be summarized as a doubt that dependence can be causally related to underdevelopment. Dependence is either so general that it fails to have any explanatory value in the context of poor societies, or it arbitrarily selects certain features of international capitalism to produce a definition of dependence. Those features similarly do not allow the important distinctions between rich and poor, developed and underdeveloped, independent and dependent to be made in the way that dependency theory wants to.

Nevertheless, dependency theory served an important function in the analysis of development, especially in Latin America (Larrain, 1989). Its emphasis on the weak and relatively dependent position of the less advanced economies of the world was timely and a necessary corrective of much development theorizing at the time, especially ideas about unilinear economic development and 'dual economies' (Luton, 1976). It called attention to the ideological implications of pluralistic and structural-functional development theorizing, challenging the conventional wisdom that economic development in Latin America is inevitably consistent with US interests (Ray, 1973, p. 6). Its 'militant critique' of a highly ideological developmentalism that ignored social classes and treated the state as an instrument of popular will or the public interest, showed that underdevelopment was not a 'primal' or 'original' condition. Dependency theory 'stimulated the empirical study of institutional and structural mechanisms of underdevelopment' such as multinationals, fiscal policies, capital expenditures and aid programmes (Leys, 1977, p. 93). It showed that capital does not necessarily break down non-capitalist modes of production, but can bolster 'archaic political and economic forms' through alliances with pre-capitalist social forces.

Neo-colonialism and dependency arise in large part from the need felt by developing countries for investment capital that cannot be sourced locally. Foreign exchange crises caused by the fluctuating value of primary products and insufficient domestic savings can only be averted by borrowing, foreign investment and aid. The modern and dynamic sector of the economy consequently falls increasingly under the control of multinational corporations. It is therefore significant that foreign investment in developing countries rose, between 2005 and 2006, by 21 per cent to US$379 billion, giving MNCs, the main source of foreign direct investment, a growing role in the economic development of poor countries.

The political consequences of this growing economic presence affects the state in the Third World which, as will be shown in the next chapter, facilitates globalization by creating the conditions which enable international capital to remain a major force in domestic politics. Consequently, Western states continue to exploit their advantages and power over Third World economies, mainly through 'global' corporations with national roots.

4

The State and Politics in the Third World

Controversies

The different attempts to explain the nature of Third World politics in terms of encounters with richer countries make reference to the form of the state and the configuration of political interests sometimes articulated by the state and sometimes suppressed by it. There are contrasting theoretical perspectives to assist understanding of the state in the Third World. The nature of the state – the institutions through which legitimate power (political authority) is exercised and enforced – is central to the study of politics in any country. Third World conditions produce additional reasons why the analysis of the state is necessary for an understanding of politics in developing countries.

First, there is the legacy of colonialism which social scientists of very different ideological points of departure have recognized to be a formative influence on the contemporary state in developing countries. The key question posed here is whether the post-colonial state can develop the attributes of a pluralist political system or a distinctive relationship to new class formations. The next two sections of this chapter present these contrasting interpretations of the state in post-colonial society.

Secondly, there is a controversy between the proponents of society-centred and state-centred approaches to the state, the former presenting the state as an arena for the resolution of conflicts between private interests, the latter regarding the state as an independent force with its own policy agenda (Nordlinger, 1987). The conviction that the state must be 'brought back' to politics will be assessed in this chapter, together with the claim that in so doing the socio-economic context of politics is in danger of neglect.

Thirdly, there is a controversy about whether the forces of globalization have rendered the state obsolete or at least transformed state power. This forms the latest stage in a long debate about whether states in the Third World are capable of governing, why some have been so much more successful than others in bringing about development, and why seemingly strong state structures frequently fail to implement policies and programmes.

Fourthly, Third World states have generally presented a picture of acute political instability, with frequent violations of the rules of the political game in the replacement of governments, the transformation of regimes and the behaviour of individual actors, whether they be corrupt public officials or unconstitutional political movements. Theoretical explanations of political instability in the Third World deserve and must await a separate chapter.

The pluralist political system

We have seen that political developmentalists preferred the language of the political system to that of the state, encouraging us to think of the institutions and processes at the centre of government in politically neutral terms (Coleman, 1960). Following the ideas of the German sociologist Max Weber, the functionalist saw the state or the political system as a set of social relationships for converting, through the use of legitimate physical compulsion, demands and supports into outputs – decisions, statutes, laws, regulations, investments and so on. Government is a neutral set of arrangements consisting of political institutions and recognized procedures for interpreting political demands, resolving political conflicts, and producing outputs that satisfy those demands.

From this perspective the state is perceived as an arena in which conflicting interests compete for scarce resources. It is a means of managing competition, so that the state is recognized as a legitimate way to settle such disputes. The pluralist view of the political system sees its governmental functions as neutral in relation to the interests of different groups in society. It may be likened to an umpire, administering impartially the rules of the game without bias in favour of any particular player. The pluralist view of the state sees modern society as divided into competing elements which nevertheless find a kind of equilibrium. None is persistently more dominant than any other. None gets its way to the exclusion of others to a disproportionate extent. In this respect pluralists are building upon traditional ideas of liberal democracy and the role of the state, though rather than focus on the individual as the unit of analysis they are focussing on groups. They see society as consisting not of atomized individuals – the egotistical rational person seeking their own interests in a society which the state has a duty to preserve – but of groups and associations. Only by cooperating with similarly placed and like-minded people can individual interests be protected. Complex modern societies produce such associations for the articulation of political interests.

Pluralism finds equilibrium in the power of different groups, partly because of cross-cutting loyalties. No group will have an interest in pushing its demands excessively to the exclusion of other groups in society because individuals are members of a multiplicity of groups and associations. As producers our demands for higher incomes from wages will not be pushed to an excessive degree because we are also consumers who have to pay the price of those increased costs of production. Attachments and loyalties cut across other groups as well. There is not only a balance of competing forces but there is also multiple membership of different and sometimes overlapping groups. This serves to reduce the extremism of the demands of interest groups.

In the context of poor and developing societies the pluralist view of the state assumes that as pre-capitalist social structures and economic arrangements are replaced by capitalism and industrialization so the authoritarian political institutions associated with the pre-capitalist era, especially feudalism, will also be swept aside. They will be replaced by the institutions of the liberal democratic state, perhaps in the form of a parliamentary democracy in which interests are protected by freely-formed associations, freely competing electoral alliances, and freely articulated ideas about public policy preserved and protected by civil and political rights such as freedom of speech and association, universal suffrage, and freedom of the press (Carnoy, 1984).

Such an approach to the state is also likely to see a sharp distinction between society and polity. It does not reveal how much state intervention there will be. Those on the extreme Right of the liberal democratic spectrum of ideas will reduce the role of the state to the minimum. Those at the social democratic end will allow a considerable role for the state. But the extent of intervention will be an outcome of the interaction between competing groups. It will be the result of the success that some groups have in protecting their interests via publicly funded state interventions as opposed to the success that other groups have in protecting their interests by maintaining levels of state activity, public expenditure and taxation to a minimum, thereby maximizing the level of private incomes. But even though there might be considerable state intervention, even including elements of public ownership, polity and economy are seen as separate and independent spheres of social action.

Another feature of the pluralist state is to play down the significance of class divisions in society. Liberal democratic and pluralist assumptions about society are that it may be disaggregated along occupational, gender, ethnic, or religious lines, but not into classes. Class may be used as a summation of some of those other more significant factors indicating occupation, income and lifestyle. But class is not seen as an identity around which people form alliances in order to compete for scarce resources politically. If a concentration of power is found, as in some undeveloped political systems, it is assigned to particular groups or élites, such as the executive and bureaucracy in a tutelary democracy, the military in a modernizing oligarchy, or a dynasty in a traditional oligarchy (Almond, 1960). But a notion of class that involves mutual antagonism and irreconcilable economic and political interests is rejected. So there is no sense in the pluralist model of the state of diametrically opposed interests, one gaining only if another suffers.

This view of the state, though not particularly well-articulated, was adopted by some of the imperial powers in their attempts – often hesitant, partial and delayed – to prepare colonies for independence. These were the assumptions of the constitution-builders when independence seemed inevitable and even desirable. They were also the assumptions of many within colonial society who collaborated with the processes of constitutional design. The leaders of some nationalist movements had similar views about the nature of the state. Many had, after all, been educated in the prisons and universities of the British Empire. Where they departed from it was less in the direction of Marxism than in the direction of some indigenous modification such as African socialism or the traditions of Indian village communities. Nationalist leaders such as Nyerere and Gandhi harkened back to what they regarded as a golden era preceding European intervention and while not being so romantic as to think that the clock could be turned back, nevertheless advocated values which had been lost and which could be retrieved to the advantage of a society that would henceforth be developing according to its own prescription.

Historically, the post-colonial state has been far from neutral in its dealing with society, and socio-economic groups have been far from equally empowered in their dealing with the state. The state in the Third World has rarely, if ever, developed as a politically neutral institution. Under some circumstances it has been able to maintain a degree of autonomy from social classes and other social divisions (see below). But normally the state has been discriminatory, on either ethnic or class grounds.

The Third World state has frequently fallen under the control of élites from dominant ethnic groups. State power has then been used to promote the political and economic interests of those groups at the expense of others. For example, in Sudan the Islamic government has favoured the Arab people of the north against the African communities of the south of the country. Discrimination against the Christian and animist communities led to 40 years of civil war leaving an estimated two million people dead. In Kenya, the post-colonial government has been dominated by the Kikuyu people, leading to communal violence whenever elections in an otherwise stable democracy are suspected of having been rigged. Successive governments have allocated the Kikuyu land regarded by the Kalenjin and Masai as historically theirs, especially in the Rift Valley. Land is extensively used for the purposes of patronage in a political system in which elites exploit ethnic identities for political purposes, and to enable the political elite to amass wealth. Since 1971 the government of Malaysia has implemented policies amounting to positive discrimination in favour of Malays, and against the ethnic Chinese, in business, education, and the civil service. The Malays, who constitute 60 per cent of the population, are dominant politically, while much economic power is held by members of the Chinese community.

Even where the post-colonial state has been weak, as throughout most of Sub-Saharan Africa, it has not acted impartially. Rather, political elites have used state resources and patronage to benefit themselves and the communities they represent. Governance is dominated by prebendalism, under which state offices are exploited as 'benefices' of the office-holders. Legitimacy is bought by sharing the spoils with designated communities. The state 'lacks the autonomy from society that makes it an instrument of collective action. Instead it tends to respond to community pressures and demands that undermine its authority as a public institution' (Hyden, 2006, p. 65).

Nor is the Third World state neutral in class terms. Capitalism in all its forms, including its current global stage, requires the exploitation of labour. For example, in Latin America's capitalist states the law operates in favour of the economically powerful, mainly by allowing them to break it with impunity. Powerful economic interests are able to flout the laws on taxation, money-laundering, child labour, slave labour and drug-trafficking. Law enforcement agencies combine violations of the rule of law with actions to protect the rich from 'dangerous elements' amongst the poor and underprivileged. Consequently 'Political democracy, which now prevails across the continent, has not created a truly civil democracy where the rights of the citizen are scrupulously observed' (Munck, 2003, p. 69). Material, as distinct from legal, inequality results from the state's enforcement of neo-liberal economic restructuring, which everywhere adversely affects the poor and increases the share of national income taken by the rich.

Consequently, social movements, trade unions and other organizations representing the poor and underprivileged, find themselves engaged in struggles against the state, rather than other organized economic interests with the state as neutral arbiter. The neo-liberal agenda requires the state to protect and promote property rights, deregulate labour markets in favour of employers, and weaken trade unions: 'Historic rights and victories won by labour are being replaced and eliminated from the world of production' (Antunes, 2003, p. 235).

In the Third World (as elsewhere) the power to influence governments is never equally distributed. So another precondition of democratic pluralism is missing. This inequality may result from restrictions on freedom of association imposed by the regime, or from a maldistribution of resources needed if social and economic interests are to be empowered.

In the first category are found countries where constitutional guarantees are absent or routinely violated in practice. In Burma, freedom of association is not protected by the Constitution. Only pro-junta organizations, into which the government has mobilized people, are permitted to be active in politics. Independent trade unions are illegal. In Iran the Constitution permits the formation of political associations provided they do not violate 'the criteria of Islam or the basis of the Islamic republic' (Article 26). This enables the government to turn a blind eye to attacks by paramilitary groups on dissidents. There are no free and independent trade unions, and workers are denied the right to strike. Freedom of expression is compromised by censorship and the prosecution of journalists for comments critical of the regime. In Algeria, the government has withheld formal authorization from NGOs that have been critical of government policies. Human rights groups have faced harassment from the authorities. A number of Third World governments have used the post-September 11, 2001 'war on terror' as an excuse to criminalize the opposition and clamp down on civil society, including ethnic-based associations in Nigeria and community groups demonized as Western agents in Namibia, South Africa and Uganda (Howell et al., 2006, p. 15).

In most poor countries civil society has not developed in a way which gives all interests an equal opportunity to influence governments. In an era of global capitalism, the interests represented by business and industrial associations are dominant, forming as they do part of the ideological consensus on neo-liberal economic restructuring, which gives them greater access to government than other groups. They also have greater financial resources and greater sanctions to bring to bear on governments than workers, peasants and the poor (Kamat, 2004).

The post-colonial state

The pluralist view of the state has been challenged by approaches which focused on the state as a potentially autonomous and dominant actor in the political process. A need was seen to 'bring the state back in' to political analysis. This was not only a reaction against modernization theory which replaced the state by a concept of the political system in which governments mechanically converted demands into policy 'outputs'. There was also dissatisfaction with economistic interpretations of the state as epiphenomenon, giving economic and property relations such a determining significance that other institutions – political, legal, cultural and ideological – become merely a reflection of them. Such economic reductionism was found in dependency theory, with its implication that the dominant class in a peripheral society could only play a *comprador* role.

Marxism has provided a useful analytical framework for the analysis of the Third World state. However, if we turn to Marxism for a view of the state, we find not one but five (Jessop, 1977; Ziemann and Lanzendorfer, 1977). First, there is the idea of the state as a kind of *parasite*, particularly through a privileged, bureaucratic caste. The state extracts resources from society not for purposes of social reproduction, but to sustain an élite. Governments become parasitical when officials and politicians use their powers to accumulate wealth for themselves or members of their families. This has been an all-too familiar feature of post-colonial politics, especially in Africa. Political leaders have granted themselves permits, licenses and loans which give them access to capital, foreign exchange, land, contracts and business opportunities. Simple embezzlement of state revenues is another method. For example, between 1999 and 2007 the Nigerian Government paid US$50 million to over 30 non-existent companies. It has been estimated that Nigeria lost US$380 billion to corruption of various kinds between independence in 1960 and 1999.

In Pakistan, corruption is said to be 'a way of life', and nourished by cultural norms. It has become institutionalized in many government agencies, especially Public Works, Water and Power, Customs, Revenue and Police. Corruption's effect on economic and political development is highly corrosive. It damages incomes, human rights, allocative efficiency, the quality of government programmes, accountability, and transparency (Islam, 2004).

Secondly, there is the idea of the state as *epiphenomenon*, when economic and property relations are given such a determining significance that other institutions – political, legal, cultural and ideological – are merely a reflection of them and entirely explained by their dependence on prevailing economic relations. An epiphenomenal view of the state finds evidence for the power of different classes in the structure of economic relations and the policies pursued by governments. The state is 'a moment of class power relations' as well as a set of political institutions. Under globalization, the nation state functions as 'a particular constellation of class forces and relations bound up with capitalist globalization and the rise of a transnational capitalist class'. Nation states 'advance the agenda' of global capital. Power shifts from national classes to those 'whose interests lie in global circuits of accumulation'. Government programmes to restructure economies in favour of exports, private markets, and the free movement of capital are 'an essential requisite for the activity of transnational capital'. A 'political restructuring' follows, redistributing power in society and state towards the interests of transnational capital and its local allies (Robinson, 2001, pp. 165–85). In Central America, for example, 'the tremendous structural power that accrues under the global economy to the transnational elite and their local counterparts has shifted the terms of struggle between dominant and subordinate groups', exacerbating the concentration of economic resources in the élite and the pauperization of the masses (Robinson,1998, p. 493).

Thirdly, there is the idea of the state as an instrument of *class domination*, an executive committee for managing the affairs of the whole bourgeoisie. This comes close to being a view of the state as a neutral instrument which can be controlled equally effectively by any class which achieves a position of economic dominance. The state is not pluralistic in the sense of being a neutral arbiter, but is a set of institutions existing independently of social forces and which at different stages in history will be controlled in the interest of a dominant economic class, whether it be the landed aristocracy in a feudal economy or the industrial bourgeoisie of early capitalism.

The class structure of post-colonial society has not always lent itself to analysis in terms of capitalist class domination through the institutions of the state. Most societies emerging from colonialism did not have an industrial working class or indigenous bourgeoisie. The dominant class was likely to be bureaucratic rather than capitalist. The landed classes tended to be feudal rather than capitalist. The rural masses were divided between landless labourers and peasants, with frequent movements between the two groups. Foreign capital had also to be accommodated in the class structure.

However, as economic development has taken place, class conflict has formed a more familiar pattern. As post-colonial élites have accepted, or been forced to accept, a neo-liberal approach to the state, the state's role under capitalism of preserving the dominance of the middle classes has emerged in a purer form. Following the 1997–98 financial crisis in East Asia, the powers of the state have been rolled back, and class conflict under democratic political arrangements has had to be managed. Foremost here has been the coalition of business élites and the state in the control of labour. For example, in Thailand trade unions have been repressed, minimum wage legislation has been left un-enforced, and food staples in the urban areas have been subsidized. Education expenditure has been biased in favour of primary and tertiary education and against secondary, a pattern which is 'understandable from a political standpoint: mass education at the primary level extends government control and helps to instill a national identity, and good university education is necessary for the children of the elite' (Jansen, 2001, p. 361). The private sector has been released from government regulation, and the state has limited itself to investment in physical infrastructure, especially roads and irrigation, though over-concentrated in the Bangkok region. While poverty has declined, gains from economic growth have not been evenly distributed, leaving Thailand with the highest level of inequality in East Asia.

Fourthly, there is the notion of the state as a factor of *cohesion*, where the state is involved in regulating struggles between antagonistic classes and using both repression and concession to moderate and manage those conflicts while sustaining the economic and political dominance of the most powerful economic class and preserving the social relationships which a capitalist economy requires. Here the state operates through a combination of repression and concession. Zimbabwe under the Zimbabwe African National Union – Patriotic Front (ZANU-PF) government of Robert Mugabe provides examples of most forms of repression at the disposal of the state. Whole communities can be targeted when ethnicity is a basis of political opposition, as in Matabeleland in the early 1980s, when an estimated 30,000 people died as Mugabe tried to eliminate tribal enemies and political rivals. Next, incumbent governments can intimidate voters by allowing supporters to attack opponents, as happened in 2008 in Zimbabwe when many people were killed and injured in the run up to Presidential elections, mainly supporters of the Movement for Democratic Change (MDC). The Zimbabwe government has also unleashed attacks on critical journalists and lawyers representing opposition activists, as in 2007 during a demonstration by the Law Society of Zimbabwe. Neighbourhoods harbouring opposition can be erased, as happened in the notorious Operation Murambatsvina of July 2005 when the police bulldozed informal markets and dwellings in Harare's central business district and wealthy suburbs. Some 700,000 people lost their homes or livelihoods.

Civil society can be intimidated, as when police in Zimbabwe beat and tortured civic leaders attending a prayer meeting in August 2007 led by the Save Zimbabwe coalition and the MDC. Opponents of a government or regime can be imprisoned or placed under house arrest, as in the case of Aung San Suu Kyi, the leader of Burma's democratic opposition who has spent most of the past 18 years under house arrest. Harassment through the courts can also be effective in limiting opposition, as in Singapore where opposition leaders are frequently sued for libel, sometimes facing bankruptcy as a result. Governments may give tacit support, or turn a blind eye, to the use of private paramilitary groups against the opposition. The government of Zimbabwe has used the so-called war veterans to intimidate, injure, and kill farmers and farm workers who objected to the illegal seizure of land. In Colombia, the military has been accused of supporting paramilitary groups in a 'dirty war' against human rights activists and civilians sympathetic to leftist rebels.

The alternative to repression when managing crisis in the capitalist state is the award of concessions to those most adversely affected by the economic system. These include subsidies to food, education and health care. The poverty reduction strategies required of Third World governments as a condition attached to aid from the World Bank and IMF can be seen as safety nets to accompany the neo-liberal economic restructuring required by international capital, and a means of pre-empting political protest and dissent. For example, the Bolivian Emergency Social Fund was created to counter resistance to the economic 'shock therapy' of the New Economic Programme (Wober, 2004).

The Bonapartist state: Pakistan

The idea of the state being a factor of cohesion, managing and manipulating class struggles without fundamentally damaging the economic system that preserves the dominance of a particular economic class, is close to the idea of the state as something that can stand aloof from the immediate interests of even the dominant economic class in society for a longer-term aim – that of moderating class conflict and preserving the social and economic system. Bonapartism is a model of the state that is not merely the product of a dominant class and an instrument to be wielded by which ever socio-economic group is dominant. It is not simply an executive committee of the bourgeoisie. The state is, rather, almost autonomous and able to free itself to a degree from civil society, not to manage it neutrally in the interests of all sections, but in the long term interests of a bourgeois class against the irreconcilable interests of other classes.

This interpretation seemed to some social scientists examining the post-colonial state to be enormously perceptive and resonant. Post-colonial society appeared to have a number of competing bourgeois factions whose conflicts needed to be managed in the long-term interest of capitalist growth and the social institutions upon which such development depended, in particular private property and the right of accumulation.

For example, when Pakistan succumbed to military rule in 1958 the relationship between class and state in post-colonial society gave the state *relative autonomy* from class control. The state in Pakistan in the 1950s was not merely a set of institutions controlled by a dominant class. Its autonomy was not complete because it was not totally neutral or independent of all class forces. The state was neither autonomous in the pluralist sense, nor was it the prisoner of a single dominant class (Alavi, 1972, 1990).

To support the idea of the state as *relatively* autonomous there has to be an accompanying analysis of class. The specific circumstances of the propertied classes in Pakistan meant that three could be identified: a national bourgeoisie whose interests centred on the ownership and control of industrial capital; an indigenous landed class dominant in the agricultural sector and consisting of a relatively small number of wealthy and powerful rural families owning large tracts of cultivatable land; and a metropolitan bourgeoisie. While the significance of a national bourgeoisie can be readily appreciated because they are actively present in the economy and polity, the metropolitan bourgeoisie is much less visible or tangible. The interests of these three propertied classes were found to be competing but not contradictory. They were in competition with each other for the resources which were under the control of the state.

The state essentially performed a function of mediation between conflicting propertied classes. Their interests were not contradictory since they all had in common one essential value, the preservation of private property in the social relations of production. But they had clearly competing interests. A particular kind of state was most appropriate for this mediating role, one that could free itself to a degree from the direct control of a faction of the bourgeoisie. Such a state needed a 'bureaucratic-military oligarchy', a regime that would be sufficiently removed from the immediate interests of any one of those three classes to be able to exercise independent power and manage conflict provided it did not challenge their common interest in private ownership of the means of production. So whereas the national bourgeoisie in a developed capitalist society, or the metropolitan bourgeoisie in a colony, could establish their dominance, this was not possible in post-colonial conditions where 'none of the three propertied classes exclusively dominates the state apparatus or subordinates the other two. This specific historical situation confers on the bureaucratic-military oligarchy in a post-colonial society a *relatively autonomous* role' (Alavi, 1972).

The Bonapartist state: Tanzania

This model of state autonomy was inspired by a particular country at a particular period in its history. It did not always fit the post-colonial situation in other countries. Imperialism and the penetration of foreign capital had been less intrusive in some regions than in South Asia. The internal social structure was consequently very different at the time of independence. In Tanzania, for example, the ethnic composition of society was relatively untouched by European intervention. It consisted of a large number of small groups with no pattern of inter-ethnic dominance. One group in the region of Mount Kilimanjaro, the Chagga, had benefited from the introduction of cash crops. A class of relatively rich peasant cultivators developed, but not a class of large landowners receiving part of their wealth in rents. Some of the richer peasant producers became petty-capitalist investing in other activities such as local trade, but the extent to which this constituted any kind of new socio-economic class was very limited.

The relations of production within the different societies that made up Tanzania were communal, based on settlements consisting of kin-groups, and lacking landlords or employers of landless labour. The relationships between producers were those of kinship and ethnicity. Population density was relatively low. Land was readily available. Some societies, notably the Masai, were pasturalist. By the time of independence a class structure, brought about by the combination of indigenous economy and foreign intervention, hardly existed. Rural people produced goods on the basis of small-scale communities with land held in common. Land could not be alienated and accumulated. Rights to occupancy and cultivation alone were attached to individuals and families. There was a relatively small basis for a landed oligarchy or an industrial or commercial middle class, the last being mainly Asian in origin. An embryonic working class was also beginning to emerge at the time of independence based on textiles, motor transport and tobacco processing.

The most powerful African class in the process of formation was a petty-bourgeoisie of teachers, civil servants, prosperous traders and farmers. The East African colonial state had subordinated pre-capitalist, though non-feudal, social formations to the needs of colonial capitalism. This pre-capitalist agriculture had moved towards commercialization without 'quasi-feudal stopovers' and the indigenous bourgeoisie was confined to mainly Asian traders (Shivji, 1973, 1976; Saul, 1974).

Thus class conditions in Tanzania differed considerably from those in Pakistan. It is correspondingly more difficult to think of the state as having to mediate between well-articulated class interests, including those owning capital and those with only their own labour, as well as divisions within the capital-owning classes, including capital located outside the country. The metropolitan bourgeoisie, most notably represented by multinational corporations, was much more powerful than indigenous classes. The post-colonial East African state had nevertheless not become international capital's 'executive committee'. It retained a measure of autonomy because of its role in the production process and strategic position within the economy. The growing level of state intervention in the economy, with the state as the country's major employer and the main vehicle for social mobility for those able to obtain educational qualifications, again appeared to parallel the Pakistan situation. The state was a means to economic power, rather than an instrument of an already dominant economic class. Class formation takes time, and African experience confirms that in the interim the state can independently act in a mediatory role and affect the process of class formation by the success or failure of its policies, for example in protecting local firms from foreign competition (Kasfir, 1983, p. 8).

State autonomy was sometimes a temporary feature of the immediate post-independence period, quickly giving way to control by a dominant class. In Kenya, for example, the dominant class following independence was the metropolitan bourgeoisie. This was the interest that the post-colonial state articulated. The state in such a peripheral economy supported metropolitan capital against its main rival, a newly emerging property-owning middle class. The struggle did not have to be mediated. It had been won by metropolitan capital. The state performed municipal functions on its behalf. Domination of the mass of the population by foreign capital required the existence of domestic class interests, in this case the petty-bourgeoisie, allied to foreign capital through joint interests. State power was not relatively autonomous but rather protected the dominant classes through policies to subsidize the petty-bourgeoisie and subdue the unions by means of clientelism, ideological domination and official repression (Leys, 1975).

In India too, the over-developed state was a temporary phenomenon. As society became more complex and the private sector grew stronger and more diversified so the political institutions representing classes in society became stronger and the bureaucracy took on a more subservient role. A significant bourgeoisie emerged which, despite the presence of foreign capital, captured control of the state (Wood, 1977).

An overdeveloped bureaucratic state

Another distinctively post-colonial feature of this theory of state structure is the idea of an overdeveloped bureaucratic state apparatus. Two factors in particular contributed to this phenomenon. First, colonialism produces a distorted state structure. Certain institutions which had been particularly significant for colonial government and which had a relatively long history had been highly developed, namely the bureaucracy, the military and the police. A central feature of colonial government was a heavy reliance on these institutions. Colonialism required a state structure which would enable control to be exercised over all indigenous classes. This state apparatus had to be bureaucratic. The bureaucratic-military nature of the colonial state represented an overdeveloped state.

The Indian subcontinent had probably had the longest history of democratic development of any part of the empire, but even here the bureaucratic state apparatus was overdeveloped. This would be more the case in countries where there had been virtually no experience of parliamentary and representative government before independence. In territories where nothing had been done to prepare for democratic self-government the distortion was even greater. Experience of parliamentary government prior to independence varied enormously. Even where it was considerable the bureaucracy still emerged with prestige, power and status, monopolizing the knowledge and expertise required for running a government and developing a society. Government was the main source of employment for professional people and the highly educated. It absorbed the supply of technical expertise. For example, long practice in the mobilization and organization of people for political ends through the Congress movement in India still did not produce a capacity to control a highly developed administrative system in the years immediately following independence.

Colonialism in Tanganyika had also left a relatively highly developed bureaucracy, although one that had not been extensively penetrated by Africans. Africans were only recruited into positions of influence in meaningful numbers on the eve of independence, when it was essential to replace expatriate officialdom with local people. The colonial state was paternalistic rather than mediatory. The state apparatus, particularly in its bureaucratic form, was more overdeveloped in relation to civil society and the private sector where capitalism either in agriculture or industry had hardly begun to emerge.

Secondly, this bureaucratization was intensified by the disproportionate involvement of the state in managing the post-colonial economy. Where the private sector is small, where the market as a basis for the arrangement of production and distribution is weak, and where the economic activity of the state is significant, the state becomes the key economic actor. It is the major employer. It plays a prominent role in managing the flow of international finance from aid, loans and foreign investment. The state becomes the source of capital. It controls its use. An extensive state apparatus supports economic development, even when it is in the form of an emerging capitalist system. Public sector management, state marketing and rationing of scarce foreign exchange and consumer goods, state ownership, the provision of an infrastructure of communications, energy supply and transportation, the creation of a legal structure for commercial transactions, maintaining political stability to create confidence among investors – all are the responsibility of the state and contribute to bureaucratic overdevelopment.

Bureaucratic control over economy and civil society was extensive everywhere following independence. Some countries, such as Tanzania, had single party regimes. In addition to the state bureaucracy there was a party bureaucracy, adding to the overdevelopment of the state apparatus. The party's own hierarchy of officials corresponded to the hierarchies of state officials in the structure of administration. However, this system was somewhat paradoxical. Appointed state officials were powerful. But a party bureaucracy could constitute a counter-balance to the state bureaucracy and its colonial inheritance in terms of structures, processes of decision-making, status and prestige. Party bureaucracies, arguably representing a democratic check on state bureaucracy, complicate the picture of the relationship between bureaucracy and other political institutions. To the extent that the two bureaucracies are highly integrated, however, especially when civil servants are appointed on the basis of partisan criteria, the distinction between the two organizations can become completely blurred. If a provincial commissioner (a civil servant) only occupies that office because the correct partisan credentials are held, to what extent are such officials a different species of bureaucrat as far as the ordinary citizen is concerned?

The bureaucracy could also be central to the career opportunities of the small middle class, as in Mali where it became the focus of political competition. In the absence of other fully developed institutions political pressure and lobbying was directed towards the bureaucracy which became the arena in which political conflict was fought out (Meillasoux, 1970).

The high-performing Asian economies have also managed economic development to varying degrees through bureaucratic and technocratic means rather than through liberal democratic politics, with the state's technocratic elite operating autonomously from civil society and seeking 'bureaucratically determined goals' (Jones, 1997, p. 199). The bureaucracy was insulated from 'growth-compromising pressures' from agricultural interests and weak commercial and industrial classes. A meritocratic bureaucracy provided stability, a capacity for strategic planning, and competent, coherent administration. There was, however, successful 'collaborative linkaging' with economic interests, allowing the bureaucracy to mobilize resources for developmental aims (Weiss and Hobson, 1995, pp. 162–8).

The bureaucratic-authoritarian state

In Latin America the persistence of military regimes in relatively advanced societies with long experience of independence led to 'bureaucratic-authoritarian' politics. The historical sequence typified by Brazil, Argentina, Chile, Uruguay and Mexico through the 1960s and 1970s moved from rule by oligarchies of powerful families, through populist politics and on to bureaucratic-authoritarianism.

Contrary to the theory that economic development encourages more pluralistic and democratic politics, Latin America became more authoritarian. Higher levels of industrialization and growing GNP per capita were linked to retreats from democratic competitive politics. It is useful to compare the bureaucratic-authoritarian model with that of the relatively autonomous post-colonial state, because of the claim that as societies develop economically and socially the latter model becomes less viable. Latin America seems to present evidence of bureaucratic-authoritarianism accompanying and even growing as societies become more economically advanced.

In dependent economies the process of modernization did not lead to the gradual enrichment of mass politics, but to the collapse of political systems in which the working classes and lower-middle classes were important participants in, and beneficiaries of, the dominant coalitions. Populist politics, notably in Argentina under Perón, produced movements that sought mass support, but to maintain an élite rather than promote an ideological position This is a form of politics from which the masses can acquire influence and benefits. The important question is why populism so often degenerated into repressive authoritarianism, often of a military character, together with a regressive redistribution of wealth in favour of the economically privileged.

Comparison of Brazil, Argentina, Chile, Uruguay and Mexico identified an underlying common historical sequence starting with oligarchical political systems in which power, both economic and political, is held by a small number of families. This is then followed by a phase of populist politics eventually degenerating into bureaucratic-authoritarianism (O'Donnell 1979). Three factors in 'constellation' are said to account for the stage reached by any particular country: regime, coalition and policies. By *regime* is meant the existence of civil rights, freedoms, electoral competition, and organized interests – compared with repression, intimidation, gerrymandering, ballot-rigging and the other practices which undermine and destroy the democratic process. *Coalition* refers to the class and sectoral composition of the dominant political group. *Policies* refer to the distribution of resources among different classes and sectors of the economy. Each constellation is seen as the result of relationships between three key aspects of socio-economic modernization: levels of industrialization; levels of political activism among the lower classes (or 'popular sector'); and the growth of technocratic occupations in both the public and private sectors. Constellations of regime, coalition and policies reflect constellations of levels of industrialization, activism and technocracy.

Bureaucratic-authoritarianism is characterized by a *regime* in which electoral competition is eliminated and other forms of political participation are closely controlled by the authorities; a *coalition* of high level military and civil technocrats working with representatives of foreign capital; and a *policy* of promoting advanced industrialization.

The particular development identified here as more significant than others is the greatly increased role of technocrats in society. Technocrats do not have a great deal of time for democracy. Participation, consensus-building, negotiation, and compromise all run counter to the values of the technocrat. Democracy is seen as an obstacle to economic growth. The bureaucracy and the military are identified in Latin America as being the main repositories of such technocracy on the state side, forming a natural coalition with the technocrats leading the private sector. Managers and engineers, rather than shareholders, are the dominant influences in industry. A new professionalism within the military supports technocratic views of the economy and society generally. Problems are seen as needing solutions that can only be provided by those with the training and qualifications. Democracy gives way to the power of those with knowledge. This line of analysis touches upon other interpretations of military intervention in Third World politics. A coalition between civil and military officials seems natural, not just because they have the same paymaster but also because they espouse the same technocratic approaches to politics.

According to this perspective, the origins of bureaucratic-authoritarianism lie in the need for governments to satisfy the demands of national entrepreneurs and the indigenous middle class, while at the same time enacting policies in support of foreign capital. Different countries have had different degrees of success in handling this contradiction. Brazil was better than Argentina at integrating the national bourgeoisie after establishing political and economic stability to ensure large injections of foreign capital. The case of Chile shows that the pre-*coup* crisis and post-*coup* repression in the 1970s were so extreme that there was great difficulty in attracting foreign investment.

Bureaucratic-authoritarianism is not exclusively associated with later phases of industrial modernization in Latin America. There are other regimes where it seems equally likely that the phenomenon has appeared at different phases of industrial development. Certainly the 'regime' and 'coalition' features of bureaucratic-authoritarianism have been experienced in other regions of the Third World. What may be distinctive about the Latin American case is the association with a particular policy – that of promoting advanced industrialization. Further refinement of the concepts would make it possible to identify whether one type of policy is a necessary condition for a bureaucratic-authoritarian state, or whether certain kinds of regime and coalition are consistent with other policies for the distribution of resources within a society. In the case of Latin America, interaction between regimes and policy changes seems to cut across the BA/non-BA distinction (Collier, 1979). The possible explanations of the rise of authoritarianism are many and varied. Not all confirm the 'deepening of industrialization' hypothesis, or the preceding strength of the 'popular' sector.

State-society dialectics

Inquiry into the Third World state needs to consider an ambitious attempt to produce a comparative framework designed to encompass states in all regions of the world, whatever their level of wealth, industrialization or economic development. Here the state was to be 'brought back in' as part of a dialectical relationship with a political environment that shapes state action and structure as well as being affected by them (Evans et al., 1985).

Tendencies towards autonomous state action vary according to the type of state structures available to support such interventions. Some states are better placed than others constitutionally, politically and culturally. Bureaucracies vary in levels of centralization and integration. Constitutional powers vary in their degree of dispersal among sub-national governments. Administrative agencies differ in the degree of penetration by organized interests. State executives vary in their level of power over representative legislatures. Organizational structures are themselves the consequence of past state policies which vary from country to country.

States will also vary in the extent of their capacity to implement their policies. Capacity is affected by such factors as: an ability to control the state's territory; the availability of human and financial resources; and the organizational instruments available for the achievement of the state's objectives. The quality of such factors will not necessarily be spread evenly across all policy areas. The fact that historically and comparatively states are found to have different capacities in different policy areas warns against the categorization of states as either 'strong' or 'weak'.

The capacity of a state to intervene internationally or domestically also depends on the state's relationships with the social, economic and political environment. Capacity is affected by relationships between state authorities and domestic socio-economic groups. For example, military success depends upon effective fiscal capacity which in turn requires a willingness on the part of key sections of the population to be taxed. In the domestic arena, successful state interventions, such as in pursuit of economic objectives, equally depend on relationships with economic interests. The successful pursuit of industrialization in a developing country, for example, may depend upon the state achieving autonomy from agrarian interests, as in Taiwan.

The capacity of states is more or less balanced by the capacities of organized sections of civil society and the international economy. Analysis of the state thus requires a method of inquiry that is *relational*. Effective policy implementation may be as dependent on networks of support as much as on the state's own instruments of intervention. State and society consists of actors in complementary as well as conflicting relationships.

Hence the importance of recognizing that states affect the development of the political process. States are powerful and autonomous organizational actors, capable of shaping society as well as being shaped by it. Such recognition must extend to modern and emerging democracies, and not just totalitarian and authoritarian states, where the primacy of the state as an actor in control of social and economic development is more obvious.

Through its administrative, legal and coercive systems the state structures its relationships with civil society as well as relations within civil society. First, state structures affect the political culture – on society's perceptions and judgements of political rules, roles and processes, rather than just being the product of cultural differences in political life.

Secondly, state structures affect the way collective action is mobilized for political ends and the formation of political groups and movements. The configuration of interests and interest groups in a society reflects the composition of state interventions in society and economy. The state's organization, patterns of intervention in economic and social life, and public policies determine which group interests are activated, which social cleavages are politicized, and which political demands are pressed. Political identities and attempts to capture control of parts of the state apparatus are responses to state intervention. For example, working class political orientations have historically been affected by the timing of democratization in relation to industrialization; by the administrative structure of the state; and by legal conditions bearing on working class organizations such as trade unions. States may induce different forms and levels of corporatism which influence the way sectional interests are defended. Social movements reflect in part variations in constitutional, legal and coercive state apparatuses. Economic intervention by bureaucratic authoritarian regimes in Latin America affected social resistance by reducing the state's capacity to dominate civil society. Shrinking the public sector can undermine social forces behind political opposition.

Thirdly, the structure of the state is related to the way in which political interests are mediated by political parties. For example, the extent to which the state bureaucracy is free from partisan control determines how far it can be used as a source of political patronage and therefore how far political parties need to secure electoral support by promising the spoils of office or by offering ideologically coherent programmes capable of securing majority support within the electorate. State administrative structures also influence party organization and styles. Variations in relationships between the state administration and party organization also affect the kinds of issues that regularly appear on the political agenda: collective versus divisible benefits, for example.

Fourthly, the political expression of class interests is never wholly economically determined. This is because the ability of classes to achieve consciousness, mobilization and representation is affected by the structures and activities of states. For example, working class activism has historically been conditioned by the nature of the state and in particular the extent to which state and society are sharply differentiated, and the extent to which workers are incorporated into a political system based on locally-rooted political parties wielding patronage. The political capacity of dominant socio-economic classes is also a function of state structures, such as decentralized forms of administration or parliamentary forms of political decision-making, and not simply an extension of class interest.

However, an autonomous state does not automatically mean a reduction in the power of all social groups. The game is not zero-sum. State autonomy and the power of socio-economic groups and interests can increase or decrease together. For example, transnational corporations have stimulated a capacity for autonomous state action on economic issues. Similarly, a reduced state capacity to intervene in the economy may be deliberately selected by state élites in order to protect other state capacities, such as in the area of control and repression, and thus reduce the expression of grievances by economically disadvantaged groups.

However, strong state interventions are likely to encourage interest groups to mobilize to exert pressure on policy makers or even colonize parts of the state apparatus. State autonomy and group power may increase simultaneously, but only temporarily as newly mobilized and empowered groups exert influence and reduce the scope and possibly capacity for further state interventions, at least in that particular policy area. We are thus presented with the intriguing conclusion that state intervention in the economy provides an environment supportive of working class mobilization and participation in policy-making.

The thrust of this theory is that political analysis needs to recognize a dialectical relationship between state and society. In activating group identities, politicizing some social conflicts and not others, and selecting social identities on which political conflict is based, the state influences the meanings and methods of politics for different groups and classes. The state is not solely the product of social cleavages and interests. Sectional interests and classes seek to influence the state. But the way they do so, and their capacity to do so, depends on the state structures with which they interact.

Globalization and the nation state

It has been argued that the forces of globalization are increasingly rendering the state obsolete. Thus debates about the nature of the state become redundant. How convincing is this stance?

There is by no means consensus on what 'globalization' means (the fate of many terms that are mere buzz-words means that no discussion of current affairs dares omit them, treating them as scientific concepts), but the term tries to capture aspects of international relations which must be delineated if the argument about the contemporary relevance of the state is to be assessed.

Economically, globalization refers to an accelerating process of international transactions in the form of trade, investment and capital flows. For example, in developing countries the share of international trade in total output increased from 10 per cent in 1987 to 17 per cent in 1997. Over the same period the world's flow of foreign direct investment more than tripled, from US$192 billion to US$610 billion. Capital flows to developing countries also increased sharply in the 1990s, though concentrated on a small number of countries designated as 'emerging markets'. Such trends have been fostered by technological developments in transportation and communications.

Globalization has social and cultural dimensions, too. Cultural uniformity is encouraged by increased travel and migration, and the media networks of rich Western countries. Global communications networks have far-reaching consequences for businesses, governments, educational institutions, voluntary bodies and community groups. Social globalization is reflected in the illicit trade in drugs, laundered money, weapons and women. Civil conflicts threatening political stability are fuelled by the global traffic in weapons and mercenaries. Global markets put huge pressure on the environment.

The nation state is said to be undermined by these forces. National policies for economic development, employment, social protection and fiscal objectives are made redundant by mobile capital, global markets, and transnational industrial production. Nation states are rapidly being reduced to a 'municipal' role in the global system, providing the required infrastructure, physical and legal, for international capital (Hirst and Thompson, 1999). Transnational networks of production, trade and finance relegate national governments to 'transmission belts' for global capital. World market forces are more powerful than state actions both domestically and in the international arena, so that while state *intervention* may have increased, the state's *effectiveness* in providing what markets do not – security, financial stability, law and order, and public goods such as infrastructure – has declined (Strange, 1996).

Global capital imposes a discipline on states, leaving governments only with policy choices that are consistent with a free market. The welfare state is ruled out. National sovereignty has been displaced by global and regional institutions (e.g. free markets and free trade) and organizations such as the IMF, the World Trade Organization, the Association of South East Asian Nations, Asia-Pacific Economic Co-operation, and the Southern Cone Common Market. Forms of international co-operation between states have proliferated (to deal with crime, terrorism, migration and capital flows) and the number of international agreements (treaties, charters and covenants) has grown enormously. Global governance and politics is not only conducted through international organizations, but also through international NGOs, social movements and pressure groups, such as Greenpeace, the International Confederation of Free Trade Unions, the World Muslim Congress, the International Red Cross, and the Catholic Fund for International Development (Held et al., 1999).

Such conclusions for the nation state are only convincing if the significance of globalization is exaggerated and the need for the state underestimated.

The picture of globalization as a completely supranational economy is false. The economic world is still made up of national economies in which most companies are embedded, subject to national regulations and benefiting from state power which provides stability and security in financial markets, free trade, and the protection of commercial rights, albeit within the context of growing international trade and investment (Hirst and Thompson, 1999, pp. 270–4). Indeed, the state is a key facilitator of globalization by creating the conditions under which international capital is a major force in the domestic politics of contemporary states. The fact that policies change under the influence of domestic and international pressures found within the global economy does not distinguish the state from earlier incarnations (Bisley, 2007).

Support for the international order has to be managed at the national level through the institutions of the state. Powerful nation states are required if international regulatory regimes, trading blocs, agencies, economic policies and treaties are to be effective. Nation states represent societies on international agencies and regulatory bodies, supporting international decisions with national laws and policies. Only through nation states will such agencies be endowed with legitimacy by, and accountability to, those societies (Hirst and Thompson, 1999). National governments are becoming *more* important in promoting and regulating international trade and investment. National institutions, government strategies, and position in the international system allow states to mediate and resist the effects of globalization. The fact that pressure for the establishment of international treaties and conventions may come from international, non-governmental sources, such as human rights activists (most of which are *nationally* based) or the 'will of the international community' does not mean that states no longer have to consent to international law (Held et al., 1999, pp. 6–14, 63).

A growth in the scale of international relationships in which states are engaged does not necessarily diminish the power of states to decide when it is in their interests to participate in activities which have formed part of the context of sovereign statehood for centuries (Krasner, 1995). It is wrong to confuse a changing world with which states have to cope with a diminution of state power. States have always had to respond to changing economic, military, technological, ecological and cultural developments. It is also debatable how far it is anything new for states to be subjected to the threats which 'mobile capital' is able to pose. Has it really required globalization to generate 'powerful pressures on states to develop market-friendly policies, including low public deficits and expenditure, especially on social goods. . . . [threatening] welfare budgets, taxation levels and other government policies' (Held and McGrew, 2000, p. 13)? This has always been the experience of states that have to accommodate capitalism.

Nor is economic interdependence new, and is arguably less significant for national governments than it was in the nineteenth century. Western states are as involved in the exploitation of their advantages and power over Third World economies as at any time in the past, mainly through 'global' corporations with national roots. 'Global governance' is a euphemism for an international system in which national governments, especially Western, are the main actors. The international economy may restrict policy choices by national governments in some policy sectors, but it expands them in others. The demise of the state from globalization only becomes a convincing idea if one accepts a false conception of statehood as 'an absolute, indivisible, territorially exclusive and zero-sum form of public power' (Held et al., 1999:, pp. 6–9).

A continuing need for the state also arises from the threats to livelihoods from globalization, especially in developing countries. While trade increases incomes on average, it does not guarantee that inequalities will not increase and poverty remain. Trade liberalization also produces 'adjustment' costs as labour and capital shift to export industries. Global competition has led to a growth in 'flexible' (i.e. precarious) employment conditions. Only states can provide safety nets to protect vulnerable people or manage the political conflict and crime caused by poverty (Hirst and Thompson, 1999). The costs of economic adjustments also need to be moderated by retraining policies, health care, and macroeconomic policies that produce economic stability. Social policies are needed to protect people not only in the context of changing labour markets, but also of declining cultural diversity and the damage done to public services by deliberate reductions in state resources. This calls for policies that invest in skills, promote job-creation, strengthen workers' rights, generate tax revenues, improve the efficiency of tax administration, reduce military spending, and support culture and the arts. The state is also needed to remove barriers in developing countries excluding people from the benefits of information technology, through policies for group access, training, and adapting technology to local skills (UNDP, 1999).

The state also has the leading role to play in environmental protection. Environmental degradation and pollution is more a consequence of economic growth, whether or not generated by globalization. However, in so far as globalization stimulates economic growth, whether this entails pollution depends on environmental policies pursued by national governments, such as the removal of subsidies from environmentally harmful activities, transparent environmental regulation, and information and education about environmental problems (e.g. the public disclosure of factory pollution, as in Indonesia and the Philippines).

The state is needed to provide a legal and fiscal context that encourages economic development. The rule of law is necessary to provide social and economic security and the enforcement of economic obligations (Hirst and Thompson, 1999). Government policies protecting property rights are needed to attract capital investment, a problem for the poorest developing countries being their *exclusion* from a global order which denies them investment and a reasonable share of world trade. Capital market flows are very volatile and can create financial crises as in East Asia in 1997–98. Reducing the risks of such crises and their consequences for incomes, social unrest and crime requires national institutions and policies, such as strong legal and regulatory regimes for the financial sector.

Consequently, economic globalization gives rise to a need for a strong state. Weak states, such as those throughout much of Africa, lacking the rule of law, honest and accountable government, policy-making capacity, and efficient public services, can neither absorb the benefits of globalization nor manage its negative consequences: 'African economic growth and development in the era of globalisation are hamstrung by weak states' (Lawson, 2003, p. 39). The costs of globalization – lost livelihoods, depressed wages, and unemployment – need to be managed by policies that are of some benefit to the losers: redistribution, social safety nets, and progressive taxation. The developmental states of Asia also demonstrate that while global economic structures were important for their success, state capabilities were more important. It is also widely recognized, even among the advocates of neo-liberal economic policies, such as the World Bank, that effective states are needed if markets are to function properly and democracy is to amount to more than a procedural formality (Batley, 2002).

Even if the assertions about overwhelming globalization are accepted, it does not follow that the state is powerless to moderate the effects of international economic forces. What is significant is that states vary hugely in their *capacity* to do so. And capacity is not a function of globalization. Such capacity – to respond to economic change by mobilizing investment, increasing manufactured exports, and co-ordinating technological innovation – is the key variable in the analysis of the state in a global economy (Weiss, 1998).

Conclusion

The literature on the post-colonial state aids understanding of the factors identified by dependency theorists as being central to the nature of the state in the Third World, in particular the role of the bourgeoisie and its level of development. Foreign capital is part of the class structure of the peripheral state. However, it does more than compete with the national bourgeoisie. It affects the rate and direction of its development. Indigenous classes do not develop autonomously. They are distorted by the presence of foreign capital which is not merely another class in competition with indigenous classes but actually affects the formation and coherence of indigenous classes and strengthens the mediatory role of the state.

However, a single model of the post-colonial, relatively autonomous and bureaucratically oligarchic state cannot be applied everywhere. The range of historical conditions in the Third World is too great.

There is also scope for confusion regarding the concept of 'overdevelopment'. This concept is applied to the state in relation to civil society and its class structure, overdevelopment arising from the state's original need to protect the interests of imperial capital against indigenous economic interests or classes. But it is also applied to internal state structures, with the bureaucracy being overdeveloped in relation to other political institutions. The connection between the two seemingly separate propositions lies in the argument that the power of the bureaucracy *within* the state enables the state to maintain a degree of autonomy from any class in civil society even after independence from the imperial power. The institutions that would allow classes in society to control or even colonize the state apparatus, and to dominate the bureaucracy, are insufficiently powerful.

It might also be asked why, particularly when there were no strong indigenous classes to be subdued, an *overdeveloped* state should be needed. The colonial state at the time of independence in East Africa did not appear to be particularly strong in terms of civil and military personnel or percentage of national income taken by government revenues and expenditure, let alone overdeveloped. The post colonial state was typically smaller, relative to population and size of the economy, than advanced capitalist countries and less involved in the ownership of productive forces or interventions in social life (Leys, 1976; Ziemann and Lanzendorfer, 1977; Crow, 1990).

'Bureaucratic authoritarianism' is a fair description of Latin America's militarized regimes, provided that the differences in the regimes and their economic policies are also recognized. Further conceptual refinement is needed in each factor of a 'constellation' – regime, coalition and policy – in order to appreciate the degree and nature of differences between bureaucratic authoritarianism and other types of state (Collier, 1979). As an analytical model it declined in significance in the 1980s as civilian politics was restored, competitive party systems established and economic liberalism enforced (Cammack, et al., 1993).

The dialectical approach brings to the fore important interrelationships between state and civil society. But it does not distinguish itself sufficiently from other approaches to politics which also understand that the state is structured by its environment, that states are actors in the international arena, that strategically placed elites are capable under some circumstances of taking control by military force, that state elites, especially professional bureaucrats, make contributions to foreign and domestic public policy that are more influential than those made by political parties and pressure groups, and that autonomous state action is motivated in part by the desire of state élites to reinforce their power and prerogatives.

There is also a danger that the state will be reified when construed as an autonomous actor influencing and being influenced by international and domestic contexts. However, the theory does suggest some potentially fruitful lines of further inquiry in its interpretation of the impact of state intervention on the mobilization of political interests and the form that such mobilization might take. Critiques which attempt to restore socio-economic factors as the determinants of politics (such as Migdal et al., 1994) not only need to show how their approach differs. They also have to avoid confusing state powerlessness with state incompetence. The damaging consequences of economic mismanagement do not indicate a loss of power on the part of state authorities so much as demonstrate the dreadful influence of powerful but venal and incompetent state leadership.

While it is debatable how far nation states have ever not had to share power or contend with forces cutting across national boundaries, there is no doubt that the international economic and governmental system is more complex, 'influencing institutional agendas' and changing the balance between national, regional and international legal frameworks (Held et al., 1999, p. 81). However, the nation state remains at the centre of these complexities and takes the lead in managing their domestic and international consequences.

The concept of globalization may also provide states and governments with a convenient myth with which to discipline society to meet what is presented as the inevitable, impersonal and unalterable requirements of the global marketplace (Held and McGrew, 2000). If governments cave in under pressure from multinational corporations over investment rights, environmental regulation, or food production, it is because they choose to favour corporate interests, not because they are subject to the natural laws of some global order. And if international governance is needed to deal with the international costs of globalization, such as the growing inequality between countries, the international threats from civil conflicts occasioned by financial volatility, or global crime, hopefully it can move towards more representative, democratic and transparent bodies than the currently dominant agencies – the IMF, World Bank and World Trade Organization.

5

Political Parties and Party Systems

Mass mobilization

Political parties are the most important institutions of political mobilization in the context of mass politics. Whatever the nature of a civilian regime – whether based on the principles and institutions of liberal parliamentary politics, monopolistic forms of political leadership, or on some interpretation of Marxism-Leninism – political parties reflect the fact that government is no longer the prerogative of an hereditary élite or alien oligarchy, but rests to some degree on the support or mobilization of the masses. Parties emerge whenever the notion of political power comes to include the idea that 'the mass public must participate or be controlled' (LaPalombara and Weiner, 1966, p. 3).

A party may mobilize and control support through ideological devices or even repression, but it has to be managed so that power can be captured and the legitimacy of constitutional office secured. The objectives of parties may be many and varied, seeking revolutionary change or maintaining the status quo, but they all require the mobilization of mass support. Parties accommodate demands for greater political participation and, in various ways including repression and patronage, help manage the conflict that such mass participation in politics inevitably produces. Political parties are both a consequence of a process of political change and a cause of further change by increasing a society's capacity to cope with crises of integration, participation and distribution (LaPalombara and Weiner, 1966).

Defining a political party is difficult, especially in the Third World, because of the immense variety that is found. A satisfactory definition is that parties are associations formally organized with the explicit and declared purpose of acquiring and/or maintaining legal control, either singly or in coalition or electoral competition with other similar associations, over the personnel and the policy of the government of an actual or prospective sovereign state (Coleman and Rosberg, 1964, p. 2).

It is easier to classify what Third World parties do than provide a definition that will encompass all manifestations of them. Classification is also
easier than explanation of change in party system and organization, two
issues to be explored later. The main classifications to be used by political
science have been based on functions, ideology and organization.
Typologies have also been formed from a combination of these factors.

The role of political parties

Political parties in developing countries perform a number of roles
(Coleman and Rosberg, 1964; LaPalombara and Weiner, 1966; Randall,
1988; Cammack et al., 1993). Firstly, they can in some circumstances
endow regimes with legitimacy by providing ideologies, leadership or
opportunities for political participation, or a combination of all three. By
providing a means of peaceful political succession within a competitive
party system they legitimize the authority of government based on mass
participation and representation (Yanai, 1999). In competitive situations
parties permit a degree of rotation of power among the different élites
which they sustain.

Secondly, they can act as a *medium for political recruitment*, perhaps
simultaneously creating opportunities for upward social mobility. In developing countries political parties provide the most important civilian route
into a political career. Within certain ideological perspectives parties
perform a different kind of recruitment role. They mobilize people into
self-help projects at the local level in an attempt to supplement government
interventions under conditions of extreme scarcity of resources. Such
mobilization is often associated with the socialization function referred to
below, as local party organs attempt to spread the party's doctrine among
the masses.

Thirdly, parties provide opportunities for *the formation of coalitions* of
powerful political interests to sustain a government. This is what the functionalists refer to as interest aggregation, a function of parties which is more
important in competitive systems when electoral and legislative majorities
have to be formed by the broadening of political support. Such coalition
formation can assist in the process of political integration if parties are
successful in drawing support from across regions to which people feel an
attachment greater than that to the nation state. In Nigeria such importance
is attached to the potentially destructive force of regionally or ethnically-
based political mobilization that parties are required by law to draw their
membership from across the country (Oyediran and Agbaje, 1991).This
indicates that parties can, under some circumstances, impede political integration by aggregating primarily ethnic and regional interests.

Parties also act as the *conduits of upward pressure* from the rank and file membership, affiliated organizations representing special interests such as women, youth or trade unions, and, if they are forced to compete for office through the ballot box, the electorate. Some parties have represented traditional oligarchies as in parts of West Africa, for example, where oligarchs adapted the modern institution of the party to their own political ends. In a constitutional arrangement that assigns one person one vote even an aristocracy has to obtain mass support. It has the advantage of being able to trade on the traditional allegiances of naturally deferential societies within the wider context of more egalitarian principles. Other parties have been based on the demands of the professional classes such as teachers, lawyers and low ranking officialdom. Ethnicity is often a parallel defining factor limiting membership and cutting across occupational and economic interests. Often, rather than act as conduits of influence from below, parties give political élites the machinery through which to manipulate ethnic, religious, linguistic and regional identities in order to secure power (Manning, 2005).

Parties also contribute to *political socialization*, affecting the attitudes of party members and the wider public on such maters as the management of the economy, national identity and the legitimacy of government. By giving participants a vested interest in the continuation of party politics, it is hoped that parties contribute to the consolidation of democracy (Gunther and Diamond, 2001). However, socialization can include attitudes and beliefs that are inimical to democracy, such as hatred for supporters of the opposition, as in Kenya, following multiparty elections in 1992 and 1996, and Zimbabwe in 2008. In India, the RSS (Rashtriya Swayamsevak Sangh) which gave birth to the Hindu Nationalist Bharatiya Janata Party (BJP) has much in common with fascist parties. Such socialization can lead to violence, which then becomes part of the party's heritage into which subsequent cohorts are socialized.

In theory political parties should also be major *influences on public policy* as a result of devising programmes to attract a workable aggregation of interests or through the application of official ideology to current problems. In the past, however, in Third World countries parties have usually had a minimal impact on public policy and even more rarely exercised any effective supervision of policy implementation (Randall, 1988). Policy options are, after all, often restricted by dependence upon foreign aid which comes with conditions attached, notably neo-liberal economic restructuring.

However, there is growing evidence, especially from newly democratizing polities, that parties are relevant to policy outcomes. For example, parties are crucial to strategies designed to reduce poverty by the empowerment of the poor. Experience in some of the states in India and parts of

Latin America suggests strongly that the opportunity to elect pro-poor parties to office makes a significance difference to the strength of public policies designed to alleviate poverty, especially if the parties are unified rather than fragmented, and with a coherent ideology and programme (Moore and Putzel, 1999, 9–11).

The type of party system also helps explain whether or not governments will target social spending on the poor. Party systems that allow leaders to secure office despite narrow electoral support are unlikely to initiate poverty alleviation programmes. In democracies with a small number of parties and stable party systems, such as Costa Rica and Sri Lanka, politicians seek broad electoral alliances, including links with pro-poor non-governmental organizations. In democracies with fragmented systems, such as Brazil and Thailand, with unstable support for a large number of parties that are based on individual leadership rather than programmes, parties respond to narrow interests, a lack of incentives to provide poverty alleviation programmes, and the vetoes of coalition partners. Even elected authoritarian regimes, as in Mexico until 2000, where elections are held regularly, but where one party dominates in a virtual one-party system, have incentives to respond to the needs of the rural poor if confronted by a pro-poor opposition movement, a loss of urban support, a loss of credibility as a developmental regime, or demands for democratization. However, such programmes are also more likely to be instruments of social control than empowerment (Niles, 1999).

Finally political parties have been seen as necessary for *political stability*. Stability depends on a society being able to absorb the increasing level of political participation by the new social forces generated by modernization. Parties offer the principal institutional means of organizing that participation in constructive and legitimate ways, especially if the parties are created before the level of participation gets too high. A combination of high levels of participation and strong party organization provides a defence against anomic politics and violence. The risk of military intervention, for example, increases if political parties are too weak. So 'the stability of a modernising political system depends on the strength of its political parties. A party, in turn, is strong to the extent that it has institutionalised mass support' (Huntington, 1968, p. 408).

Party ideology

Inevitably, given their appeal to certain class interests, the ideological positions of Third World parties have often resembled those of their First and Second World counterparts. Western ideologies have been adapted to provide a common framework of values for very heterogeneous societies and to strengthen national integration. Both socialism and communism have been deployed in the Third World for such aims. But they have been adapted to the particular context in which they are to be a guide to action. Special versions have been developed, such as Tanzania's African socialism which purports to draw on traditional communal values as well as European ideas about equality. Chinese Marxism-Leninism has also developed its own distinctive qualities.

Where capitalism has developed over a prolonged period as in the relatively lengthy post-independence histories of Latin American countries, parties most clearly reflect class interests in their ideological stances. Conservative parties are supported in Argentina, Colombia and Equador by coalitions of landlords and the Catholic Church. Liberal parties are supported by coalitions of urban business interests. They compete for the support of workers and peasants with socialist and communist parties (where these are not proscribed). Some parties have been nationalistic and, to a limited extent, ethnically-based. Most European ideologies have been represented in Latin American politics at one time or another.

In most parts of the Third World, however, ideological developments and the political organizations based on them have been distinctive in a number of important respects. Firstly, the ideologies of Third World political parties have often been derived more from religion than from materialistic ideologies of the West which were expected to take a hold in many post-colonial societies. Examples are the Hindu communal parties in India, the Moslem party in Indonesia, and the Islamic party in Libya. The development of Islamic political ideologies is increasingly significant in many regions of the Third World.

Secondly, some parties have developed to defend the distinct way of life of different ethnic communities, for example Malays, Chinese and Indians in Malaysia. Ideologies reflect the culture of these distinctive communities rather than class interests. In India caste may provide the foundation for a political party as in the case of the Bahujan Samaj Party representing Untouchables. This party was successful in state elections in 1993, forming part of the coalition government in India's most populous state, Uttar Pradesh. The party aims to promote social justice for India's most oppressed and deprived people. Since 40 per cent of Indians belong to lower castes, this is a very significant political development. Elsewhere, however, and especially in Africa, the tendency of political parties to reflect ethnicity and regional consciousness, rather than identities that cut across such cleavages and unite people on a national scale, has been a cause of their weakness and the weakness of governments built on such party competition (Diamond, 1988).

Ethnicity as a basis for party organization and support in countries such as Zambia, Kenya and the Democratic Republic of Congo (formerly Zaire) was encouraged by part of the colonial heritage, namely the absence of any other significant identity by which to mobilize people into electoral politics. This type of mobilization was then consolidated by political leaders who used ethnic discrimination and patronage to secure support. Where ethnicity has been less significant as a focus of political identity, the party system has been more genuinely competitive and therefore democratic (Carey, 2002).

Thirdly, political parties in the Third World are frequently populist. This is a style of leadership rather than an ideology. It seeks to mobilize people regardless of class by denying the significance of class and of any class-based ideology. Populism tries to mobilize all interests under a single conception of the national interest. It rejects the idea that groups have irrec-oncilable interests. Political leaders such as Sekou Toure of Guinea claimed that though their societies might be divided into occupational, age and other groups, all shared a common interest represented by a particular party and its leadership. Society is presented as 'cellularized' into factions whose common interests outweigh their particular and possibly conflicting interests as illiterates or intellectuals, young or old, producers or consumers, men or women, peasants or urbanites, bureaucrats or clients.

Populism is thus a way of presenting a view of society that stresses homogeneity rather than diversity. In order to appeal to all interests in soci-ety, populist parties and leaders define special interests in ways that make them ultimately reconcilable. Issues associated with particular interests, or which are divisive, are, where possible, avoided. Leaders specifically aim to prevent the development of a consciousness of conflicting interests. The methods used include building support on the basis of rewards rather than ideological conviction, and expressing contradictory policy objectives incoherently. Populism is inevitably conservative since it seeks to prevent alternative perspectives to the status quo developing.

Social diversity is not regarded as a barrier to the identification of a more important common interest. In some countries the structure of post-colo-nial society lent some support to this way of viewing the political world, particularly those that appeared to be devoid of significant class distinc-tions simply because economic underdevelopment had prevented classes from emerging fully. Congress in India must rank as one of the most successful populist parties. It attracts support from very different sections of society whose interests might appear to be incompatible. It has proved able to manage an alliance between different kinds of class structure, those of the rural and urban areas, even when such stratification has been over-laid with linguistic, ethnic, communal and religious differences.

There have been two dominant preoccupations in the analysis of Third World parties. One concerns the development and survival of party systems and in particular the emergence of single party systems. The other concerns the survival of parties as institutions.

Party systems

Observations of the tendency in the early 1960s for single-party systems to emerge in Africa led Coleman and Rosberg to produce a typology of parties based on a combination of ideological, participative and organisational variables. This enabled them to contrast a 'pragmatic pluralist' pattern with a 'revolutionary-centralizing' pattern. Pragmatic pluralist parties were those that generally tolerated the persistence of traditional politics, only partially and intermittently tried to mobilize support, and assimilated group interests to a limited extent. Revolutionary-centralizing parties in contrast espoused a modernizing ideology, were highly committed to mass political participation, and developed monolithic and centralized organisations.

This classification was used to explain the level of success achieved by African countries in solving the problem of national integration, both in the sense of 'transcending the élite-mass gap' and in the sense of territorial integration. However, it proved difficult to develop a theory of successful political integration as distinct from identifying integration as a function that parties can perform, especially in the single-party system of government. Coleman and Rosberg were able to go little further than stating that 'In all but a few of Africa's new states the primary structure . . . for coping with the myriad parochial and ethnic pressures is the national political party, the single or dominant party currently governing the state' (Coleman and Rosberg, 1964, p. 691).

A similar combination of regime and ideology is employed by LaPalombara and Weiner in their classification of parties in developing countries. They distinguish firstly between competitive and non-competitive systems and then two dimensions along which parties differ within each system. *Competitive systems* are associated with large and/or ethnically fragmented countries such as India, Nigeria, Malaysia and Sri Lanka. One dimension of such a system ranges from 'hegemonic', where one party dominates for a long period, to 'turnover', where change in the party of government is frequent. The other dimension refers to parties themselves rather than regimes, and distinguishes between ideological and pragmatic parties. The hope is that this typology will have theoretical value in so far as 'the particular combination of hegemony or turnover, ideology or pragmatism that a party pattern manifests may tell us something about how the parties relate to social, economic and political development' (LaPalombara and Weiner, 1966, p. 37). The typology was also useful if one was interested in the ability of parties to manage conflict effectively: 'in competitive systems the ideological-hegemonic and the ideological-turnover systems are less able to cope (short of repressive measures) with conflicts than either pragmatic-turnover or pragmatic-hegemonic systems' (p. 418). Another hypothesis offered is that any drive for hegemonic control is likely to be made by parties with a strong ideological position.

Party control in a *non-competitive system* is by definition likely to be hegemonic rather than 'turnover'. Combinations of hegemonic party systems and the ideological variable produce three main types of single-party system. The one-party authoritarian system (such as Mali, Ghana and South Vietnam in the 1960s) treats opposition as a threat to revolutionary or nationalistic objectives. The one-party pluralist system is characterized by a pluralistic party organization and a pragmatic ideology, as in Mexico's Institutional Revolutionary Party. The one-party totalitarian system has the state itself as an instrument of the party whose objective is social and economic transformation, as in China, Vietnam and North Korea.

Single party systems

In some cases party systems in the Third World have resembled their Western counterparts, offering a degree of electoral choice, legitimate political opposition, and accountability to the interests ranged in support of them electorally. Others have resembled the democratic centralism of the former Soviet Union and Eastern bloc. In some countries multiparty politics has survived more or less intact since independence, as in India. Elsewhere it has appeared intermittently, as in Nigeria. But the Third World has produced important variants of its own, most notably the single party system in the context of parliamentary government and capitalist economy, as in Kenya until 1991. Single party regimes in the context of capitalism prove that this form of economy often requires the negation of liberal democracy rather than guaranteeing it.

With the emergence of independent states whose institutions were based on Western models of government it was assumed that parties would become the main institutions for the political mobilization of different sections of society, aggregating different interests into workable coalitions that could constitute majorities, sustain governments, and provide for the alternation of governments at regular intervals (Kilson, 1963). This alternation is often regarded as the crux of a modern democracy. Political development in the pre- and post-colonial era had seen the emergence of parties based on the nationalist movements that fought for independence. The Indian Congress is a classic case of an organization with a long pre-independence history. In some colonies more than one nationalist movement emerged to develop into parties, especially in Africa where nationalist movements often represented different tribal groupings each with its own ideas about the ending of colonialism. This again lent support to the expectation that this was the origin of multiparty systems of government.

The emergence of single party systems of government was thus a distinct departure from the expectations of the constitution-builders on the eve of independence. Consequently, considerable effort has been made to uncover convincing explanations for what was often regarded as deviations from the normal developmental path.

Firstly, it has been argued that an 'aura of nationalist *legitimacy*' achieved by a single nationalist organization at the moment of independence as a result of being seen as the victor over imperialism led to overwhelming electoral support (Kilson, 1963, p. 266). Such an achievement was taken as evidence that the organization could continue to reflect the common interests of all sections of society. Popular support then enabled the dominant party to make it unlawful for other parties to exist so that a single-party state is established *de jure* as well as *de facto*. Not all single-party regimes outlaw other parties, but when they do not it has been very common for them to put obstacles other than the law in the way of effectively organized opposition.

Secondly, the single party tendency was said to reflect the *autocratic* form of government which was the new state's inheritance both from colonialism and traditional government. Pluralism and multi-party democracy are not inherited from the past. Rather, autocracy is the dominant aspect of political history. The situation that party leaders confronted at independence had been formed by the autocratic power of the departing colonialists, a culture supported by, in the case of African societies at least, elements that were predisposed towards more authoritarian forms of government (Coleman and Rosberg, 1964). Multiparty democracy was too alien an importation for it to survive in the local political culture, traditions and history. Perceptions of tradition and what was appropriate for a particular society combined with the colonial legacy, such as a centralized administrative apparatus, paternalism and electoral systems, to give unfettered control to a party that has not necessarily gained a plurality of the votes. Where the legacy was different, a plurality of parties stood a better chance of survival (Randall, 1988).

Thirdly, the political culture of the new indigenous leadership was *elitist* – governments were believed to possess a monopoly of wisdom and legitimacy. Since there were few if any other social or political organizations that could compete with the concentration of professional knowledge that existed within government it was difficult to dispute this claim.

Fourthly, the leadership culture was also *statist*. The state was regarded as the modernizer and agent of development. Multiparty democracy was often perceived as a luxury that could not be afforded. The immense problems confronting the governments of new states meant that discontinuities in the pursuit of public goals were an indulgence. However, research has failed to reveal evidence which consistently supports the view that the absence of party competition is better for policy outcomes, such as economic development and social equality (Sirowy and Inkeles, 1991).

The leadership was also *nationalist*, emphasizing national unity as the paramount goal, condemning any sub national sentiment to tribe, religion, region or other centres of political attachment and loyalty as destructive of national integration. Political leaders in new states undoubtedly encountered many separatist tendencies. The need for political order made the single party system attractive. Some Western political scientists discussed single party systems approvingly as well as descriptively and analytically. Huntington noted the relative success of communist states in providing political order, seeing it as derived from the priority given to 'the conscious act of political organization'. A strong party could assimilate the social forces generated by modernization that would otherwise threaten political stability. Huntington could find no stable multiparty system in any modernizing country. Single parties seemed better able to institutionalize and regularize political conflict and competition than parties in a multiparty system.

Another factor is that political office is not readily relinquished, least of all in the Third World context. The *rewards of political office* in the context of underdevelopment are so great that there must always be a temptation to manipulate politics to exclude the organized opposition. This goes further than mere corruption, serious though this problem is. The problem is rather that the state, being the main engine of economic development, is something that those who aspire to benefit socially and economically from such development need to control. An emerging bourgeoisie cannot look to other sources of capital. Production, trade and commerce all depend upon capital channelled through the state which also controls licences, the law governing the labour force, and access to foreign exchange, import licences and export permits. The state is an organization which has to be captured by any group that wishes to accumulate economic resources. Political power and political careers bring huge rewards that are not lightly conceded to opponents.

It was also believed that the *classless* nature of some Third World societies removed the need for more than one party. Tanzanian society, for example, was composed of a number of more or less equally balanced ethnic groups without any major forms of social and economic stratification. So it was thought too homogenous to need more than one party to represent interests effectively.

Not all new states came into existence on the basis of a preparation for independence in a Western European constitutional mould. The preparation for independence in Algeria, Indo-China, Angola and Mozambique was rather different. *Marxist-Leninist ideology* has played its part. Such an ideology, perhaps having its origin in mobilization for a war of liberation, identifies party with state and nation. Anything outside the party, and certainly anything that opposes it, is almost treasonable by definition. An organization founded to wage war under such ideological motivation would have an automatic propensity to form the sole leadership in the context of post-war civilian politics.

Acceptance of single-party government was made easier by apparently *democratic tendencies* within some sole parties. It appeared as if some parties could sustain democratic decision-making within the party sufficient to compensate for the lack of choice between parties. Intra-party democracy could perhaps allow for just as much or just as little discussion of alternatives as inter-party democracy. Tanzania has often been cited as a case in point. During its single party regime Tanzania's one legal political party, the Chama Cha Mapinduzi (CCM), was democratically organized, with the national conference electing delegates to the national executive council which in turn elected the central committee. For parliamentary elections the party selected two candidates for each constituency, sometimes from a large number of nominations – 85 in one constituency in 1990, for example. Seats were vigorously contested in a carefully regulated campaign. It was not uncommon for incumbents, including ministers, to be defeated.

Consequently, some political leaders in the Third World claimed, not without some justification, that the policy choices offered by, say, Democrats and Republicans in the USA were no greater than the choices being made within the mass organizations of sole parties and between the candidates that those parties sponsored in parliamentary elections. Different factions within a single party could also compete for political office.

Finally, following independence in many new states, the political leadership argued that *traditional society* had its own forms of democratic decision-making that could be adapted to contemporary conditions without needing more than one political party. Leaders such as Julius Nyerere of Tanzania and Leopold Senghor of Senegal claimed that traditional African decision-making was based on consensus, unity and egalitarianism, claims on which historical research has thrown some doubt (Hodder-Williams, 1984; Riley, 1991). Pre-colonial African village communities were said to have had 'a sense in which basic political democracy functioned. . . . The tribal elders might make the decisions, but they would be decisions that reflected the consensus' (Nursey-Bray, 1983, pp. 97–8). A more convincing explanation for the appeal to a pre-colonial Golden Age might be that it was necessary for political leaders to distance themselves from the institutions and values associated with the colonizers.

Political leaders might also find it advantageous to distance themselves from the ethnic conflict and discrimination associated with many multi-party systems in the Third World. For example, between 1986 and 2006, when the first multiparty elections in 25 years were held, Uganda was governed by a National Resistance Movement (NRM). This was known as a 'no-party system', under which other parties were allowed to exist but not to contest elections. The NRM leadership associated multiparty politics with ethnic exclusion and political instability. By making all citizens members of the Movement, it was hoped to generate ideas about policies that would be judged on their merits. A combination of intra-organizational democracy and restrictions on alternative political organizations, made the Ugandan system a 'hegemonic party-state', with leaders of the Movement occupying all important political offices, rather than a dominant party system such as characterized much of the post-colonial history of Mexico and Taiwan (Carbone, 2003).

The development of an alternative form of democracy to that of Western liberalism appears more natural still when it is recognized that for much of the post-independence period Third World countries lacked the two vital conditions, one economic and one political, which preceded liberal revolutions in the seventeenth and eighteenth centuries in the West: the availability of capitalist enterprise, finance and skills; and a loyalty to the nation rather than an ethnic community. It was therefore to be expected that there would be 'a painful, long period of accumulation of capital and of productive skill. . . . A pre-political or pre-national people has to be brought to a political and national consciousness. This puts a premium on the mass movement with strong ideological leadership' (Macpherson, 1966, p. 27).

In recent years international influences and democratization movements have encouraged an acceptance of multiparty politics. Aid donors have added political pluralism, 'good governance', democracy and respect for human rights to their list of conditions attached to international development assistance. For example, in 1990 President Mitterrand of France warned African leaders at the sixteenth Franco-African Congress that 'France will link its contribution to efforts designed to lead to greater liberty and democracy'. In 1991 the British Minister for Overseas Development announced that British aid policy would require recipient governments to move towards pluralism, the rule of law, democracy and respect for human rights. Multilateral aid agencies such as the World Bank have added to the pressures demanding 'good government' in return for aid (Williams and Young, 1994, p. 84).

Such pressure combined in the early 1990s with the influence of the momentous events in Eastern Europe and the Soviet Union on domestic political groups demanding political reforms and especially an end to the single party regime. Competitive party politics have emerged in a number of countries as a consequence, most notably Nepal, Angola, Ghana, the Ivory Coast and Zambia. However, resistance to multipartyism has been strong. The one-party state continues to be defended by reference to the threat of tribal factionalism (Zimbabwe), the need to concentrate on economic development (Tanzania), and the lack of readiness for democracy among the people (Kenya). Elsewhere the former sole party remains in power thanks to vote-rigging.

The governments of some former single party regimes have held on to power by whatever means necessary following the introduction of competitive elections. Uganda's first multi-party elections in 25 years were won by the incumbent President though declared flawed by international observers. Zimbabwe's ZANU-PF party holds on to power by throwing every type of obstacle at the opposition Movement for Democratic Change (MDC), ranging from interference with the judiciary and mass media, through vote rigging, to the violent intimidation of suspected opposition supporters. Failure to release the results of the 2008 presidential election, and the decision to hold a run-off election without proof that this was necessary, unleashed gangs of armed Zanu-PF supporters bent on 'punishing' opposition supporters, many of whom were identifiable because the secret ballot had been violated, with physical assaults, torture, arson and murder. Violent intimidation of opposition supporters reached such a pitch that in 2008 the opposition candidate for the presidency pulled out of the second round in an attempt to quell the bloodshed.

The demise of party government

A more alarming tendency has been for parliamentary and party politics to collapse altogether under the impact of political crises. Party systems have often given way to military rule. Both single and multi-party regimes seem to have fared equally badly in terms of the political stability which they were able to secure. It is difficult to find any pattern in the decay of party systems. Single party-systems sometimes survived, as in Kenya or Tanzania, when others succumbed to military *coups*, as in Ghana. Multiparty systems have sometimes survived, notably in India, but elsewhere they have not (for example in Pakistan or Nigeria). Between 1960 and 1969 of the 15 multi-party states in Africa ten had experienced military intervention. Of the 20 single-party states, 11 had had *coups*.

It is not surprising that some commentators started to write-off party-systems generally as a total failure. This is reflected in the general downplaying of the political significance of Third World parties (see Randall, 1988). Yet in some countries party government has survived for a very long time. The continuity of some Third World party systems is now greater than in Eastern Europe. There is no shortage of examples of countries with long histories of party government. There are also examples of the military being instrumental in the reinstatement of parties, albeit to legitimize the military's role in politics.

There are no obvious explanations for the survival of party government.

Economic growth, which might be expected to increase prosperity and therefore a sense of satisfaction with the regime, does not guarantee the survival of party systems, although the World Bank pointed out in 1989 that the African countries with the best economic records (Botswana and Mauritius) had parliamentary democracies. Support for this conclusion was seen to be provided by Gambia which has had multiparty democracy since independence in 1965 despite a GNP per head of only $US240 and an average life expectancy of 43 years in 1989 (Riley, 1991) but which succumbed to the military in 1994.

Alternatively it might be hypothesized that social structure might offer an explanation in that stratification based on class seems to provide a better basis for competitive politics than vertical cleavages based on race, language or religion. However, social factors such as class and related indicators of stratification such as urbanization and literacy do not appear to be systematically related to patterns of party politics (Randall, 1988).

It is more difficult to account for the stability of a party system than to explain variations between systems. Explanations of the latter include the legacy of colonialism, the time that parties have to take root and become established (India and Jamaica are examples of countries in which political parties have long histories), and whether independence was won by war or negotiation, the former method leading to the creation of the 'party-army' of national liberation such as the FLN in Algeria which had great difficulty in transforming itself into a civilian political movement after the French withdrew.

Party systems and democratization

It is clear from the role played by political parties that their significance for the process of democratization is immense. The success of democratization is in part dependent on the existence of institutionalized parties and party systems of government. The consolidation of democracy is widely regarded as conditional upon the institutionalization of regular electoral competition between parties which can adapt to new constitutional rules. Parties have been crucial to opposition to authoritarian rule, when they mainly had the characteristics of social movements (for example, the African National Congress before majority rule in South Africa). Such political movements need to 'institutionalize' themselves in readiness for the establishment of electoral competition (Ware, 1996).

The concept of party system 'institutionalization' has been developed by Mainwaring and Scully (1995) using Latin American data to compare prospects for democratic consolidation in different countries. 'Institutionalization' was deemed to be found when:

- the rules governing party competition are commonly observed, widely understood and confidently anticipated;
- there is stability in the number of parties competing for office;
- parties are strongly rooted in society, affecting political preferences, attracting stable electoral support and demonstrating continuity in ideological terms;
- political elites recognize the legitimacy of electoral competition as the route to office; and
- party organizations exist independently of powerful leaders, with well-resourced nationwide organizations and well-established internal procedures for recruitment to party offices.

The more party systems are characterized by these qualities, the more institutionalized they are – the fewer the qualities, the more 'inchoate' the system.

Latin American democratization supports the hypothesis that an institutionalized system encourages moderation, coalition building and compromise, while 'inchoate' systems pose risks for democracy of unpredictability, complexity, weak legislatures, personalism and fragile legitimacy. Institutionalized party systems mean party organizers have a vested interest in party competition and party discipline makes government effective. Citizens support parties rather than demagogues. Interests are pursued through elections as policies and programmes are compared and assessed. Conflicts are more easily mediated and managed. Political competition is restricted to democratic processes and political accountability is effective. Participation can be channelled and consent expressed (Mainwaring and Scully, 1995).

While an institutionalized party system may not be a sufficient condition for the consolidation of democracy, it would seem to be a necessary one. However, in the 'third wave' of democracy the party systems in poorer countries tend to be inchoate. Consequently their democracies are characterized by personalism, weak accountability, electoral volatility, uncertainty and, most significant for democratic consolidation, low legitimacy conferred on both parties and party systems (Mainwaring, 1998). Extending the analysis of the effects of party system institutionalization to Africa, Kuenzi and Lambright found wide variation in the level of institutionalization, but with the majority of countries falling into the 'inchoate' category. They also found evidence of a virtuous circle: an institutionalized party system is a 'requisite for democratic government', but the more experience a country has of democracy the higher the level of party system institutionalization (Kuenzi and Lambright, 2001, p. 463).

Partisan loyalty is necessary for party institutionalization and stability. But such attachments are being weakened in new democracies as well as established ones by the mass media and organized interests. This 'dealignment' was confirmed by a comparative study of electoral systems conducted in 2003. Only six Third World countries were included among the countries examined, so the results have to be treated with caution by those interested in the institutionalization of parties in developing countries. But the most significant finding was that as opportunities for participation in democratic elections increase, partisan attachments are likely to become stronger (Dalton and Weldon, 2007). It is important to add that partisanship must be associated with parties that accept free and fair competitive elections as a means of forming governments.

There is, however, a political development that may work against such a trend. In new democracies party attachments are of declining importance to political élites who can mobilize electoral support through the mass media. There are fewer incentives for political élites today to build strong partisan loyalties and organizations than in the early democracies, when élites were dependent on parties to win elections. In the older democracies, parties created new citizens by extending the franchise and affiliating to organized interests such as trade unions, whereas in newer democracies 'parties have been less central in the struggle to expand citizenship, and they never had the far-reaching social functions or fostered the strong identities that they did in the early democracies' (Mainwaring and Zoco, 2007, p. 166). Electoral volatility (measured by the turnover of support from one party to others from one election to the next) ensues, which has worrying implications for democratic stability if party attachment is necessary for party institutionalization.

Another controversy about party systems and democratization has focused on the number of parties in the system, comparing the stability of two-party competition with a multiparty system. A multiparty system is thought to be less stable. Huntington, for example, predicted that in the long-term two-party and dominant-party systems were more likely than single or multiparty systems to produce political stability because they provide a form of party competition that is more effective is assimilating new groups into the political system. Single parties find it difficult to incorporate the new social and economic interests created by modernization without coercion and therefore instability. In the multiparty system, the assimilation of new social forces into politics can only be done by increasing the number of parties: 'The two-party system . . . most effectively institutionalises and moderates the polarisation which gives rise to the development of party politics in the first place' (Huntington, 1968, p. 432).

However, a preference for a two-party system may simply reflect Eurocentric and Anglo-American biases, a confusion of governmental with regime instability, and an assumption that party politics is dominated by a single Left–Right dimension, when in Third World countries other dimensions of conflict, such as ethnicity and religion, are superimposed. A multiplicity of parties provides for the representation of all interests, encouraging lawful political participation and reducing incentives to engage in political violence. This controversy remains unresolved, though one comparative study of Third World democratization found only 'weak and fragmentary' support for the hypothesis that democratic consolidation was more likely under a multi than a two-party system (Power and Gasiorowski, 1997; see also Lijphart, 1984). This is encouraging in view of the propensity for countries emerging from authoritarianism to spawn a multiplicity of political parties. For example, the small state of East Timor, with a population of 850,000 fielded no fewer than 13 political parties to contest the first elections to an 88-seat assembly following separation from Indonesia.

The survival of parties as organizations

We have seen that one element in the institutionalization of party systems of government is the strength of parties as organizations. Strong parties are adaptable (e.g. in shifting from opposition to government), complex, autonomous (e.g. from narrow socio-economic interests), and coherent (Dix, 1992). Comparing Korea, Taiwan and 12 Latin American countries Stockton found that democracy requires strong parties as well as institutionalized party systems (Stockton, 2001). Consequently, the sustaining organizational characteristics of parties have become a topic of scientific interest. This is a very difficult task because it is hard to know whether something that a party does to its internal organization is crucial to its long-term existence.

Analysis of parties in French-speaking West Africa in the early 1960s led to a distinction between 'mass' and 'patron' parties. This was based on differences in organizational structure (particularly at the local level), size of membership (including its social composition), finances, functions, methods and patterns of authority. All such organizational factors reflected the way in which party leaders related to the rest of the population. Mass parties, such as the Democratic Parties of the Ivory Coast and Guinea or the Union Soudanaise, sought the adherence of all individuals, whereas patron parties such as Niger's Union Nigerienne 'usually terminated their structure simply with the adherence of influential notables or patrons'. Patron parties were weakly organized, undisciplined, and with little direct membership participation. Local patrons were relied upon to reach the local community. The individual was of interest to patron parties 'only insofar as he happened to be included in the franchise, provided candidates for election and the minimum machinery for bringing the voter to the polls'

(Morgenthau, 1964, pp. 336–41). Mass parties in contrast had extensive organizations, performed the function of 'social integration' through their mass membership, and were interested in all aspects of their members' lives, not just their voting choices. Organizational strength thus requires a mass membership. Parties become stronger the more they can institutionalize mass support and develop a complex organization linked to socio-economic bodies such as trade unions.

At one time ensuring survival required an elaborate internal apparatus to mobilize society, and penetrate it through a mass membership involved in a local as well as a central organization. Parties could then create a sense of national legitimacy and become successful instruments of political recruitment. Parties survived because they had firm grass roots. Where parties failed to create machinery for transmitting interests, opinions and needs upwards to the policy-making élite, and only created channels of communication and coercion downwards from the leadership to the masses, they experienced difficulty surviving. A local organization had significance beyond organizational structure and embraced a whole approach to the management of society and economy as well as political education, indoctrination and control. The Muslim Brotherhood survives in the hostile environment of Egyptian politics with an effective organization at grassroots level of at least 750,000 members each contributing 7 per cent of their earnings to party funds.

While developing an ideology and communicating it is crucial to creating a sense of legitimacy, recent trends indicate a significant shift in the relationship between party leaderships and their mass memberships. In Latin America, party organization has changed in respect of relations with affiliated bodies. These have become less important for mobilization and financial support than the mass media and external funding. In India, too, Congress has an elaborate organizational structure not only at grass roots level, but also at state, provincial and district levels, with a high level of internal democracy. However, as in Latin America, party organization and grass-roots political activity have been neglected in favour of 'increasing reliance on the electronic media, advertising and whirlwind campaigning' (Sridharan and Varshney, 2001, p. 221). This is not to imply that grass-root organization can safely be abandoned. Latin American experience shows that 'virtually all electorally successful parties . . . have learned to cultivate clientelistic ties at the grass roots' (Coppedge, 2001, p. 176).

Organizational survival also depends on making the party leadership representative of a broad range of interests (Randall, 1988). For example, the United National Independence Party in Zambia was successful in making the leadership representative of a wide range of social élites. There also has to be a balanced membership. Activists who sustain the organization through membership drives, fund raising, candidate selection, voter mobilization and party debate have to be balanced with professional experts in different policy fields. There must also be a balance between nominal members and party activists, and between collegial leadership and a willingness to remove leaders who are out of touch with members and the electorate. A balance has also to be struck between the principle of open membership to whoever supports the party's ideals and objectives, and a rule of restricted access, either to avoid capture by interests that would narrow the party's electoral appeal, or to ensure effective action in government or opposition (Graham, 1993).

Leaders that identify themselves with the party rather than using it as a means to office elsewhere such as in the government bureaucracy are also required (Huntington, 1968). Huntington is here referring to the loss to political parties when scarce talent is drawn off into other loyalties. He is not denying that parties should seek office for their leaders when they compete for positions in legislatures, executives and other parts of the state whose personnel are recruited by electoral competition.

The strength of party organization is also dependent upon consistency – in ideological position, discipline (among members and elected representatives), patterns of internal organization, rules of leadership succession, and methods of mass mobilization. A weakness of the Kuomintang (KMT) in Taiwan was its lack of a routine method for organizing leadership succession, making the cohesion of the party vulnerable during any change in the leadership. Organizational reform became unavoidable when the party was defeated in 2000 by the Democratic Progressive Party, especially new procedures for the election of party chairman and central committee, leaving the party strong despite its loss of office (and access to patronage) and the transition to multiparty democracy (Chu, 2001).

The volatile party systems of Latin America, in which fewer than 20 per cent of the 1,200 parties competing in twentieth century elections survived more than one election, suggest another explanation for party survival: adaptation to the political environment. Party survival may be a function of 'political Darwinism' when adaptability to changes in the environment (urbanization, rising crime, regime change, inflation, growing inequality, economic decline, economic liberalization and so on) proves impossible for all but the fittest. The survivors are those that cope with economic stresses, and provide organizational alternatives to those that have failed, for example the strong party discipline of Brazil's Workers' Party in contrast to the anarchy within the Partido de Movimento Democratico Brasiliero. Strength of party identification among voters appears to be another crucial variable in this explanation of party survival (Coppedge, 2001).

Autonomy from 'founding personalities' is also needed, as well as significant financial and human resources, including professional staff

(Mainwaring, 1998; Stockton, 2001). Funding and institutional autonomy, including freeing the party from domination from the civil bureaucracy or military, are also important organizational features (Randall, 1988). It has to be noted that India's Congress Party, with considerable bureaucratic infiltration, seems to be the exception to this.

In poor countries, there are few resources to sustain political parties, other than what can be obtained from public office. Thus foreign support may be necessary for a new party to survive, especially if its natural constituency is among the poor. For example, the Ugandan Democratic Party depends for its survival on overseas support which it receives via an NGO, the Foundation for African Development, which is funded by the German Konrad Adenauer Foundation (Carbone, 2003).

Factionalism and clientelism

The strength of party organization in the Third World has frequently been dependent upon the distribution of patronage and the allocation of state resources and positions within the military and bureaucracy. The distribution of rewards to supporters and clients on a personalized basis can be crucial for the survival of a political party.

Clientelism represents a rational form of behaviour for people under conditions of inequality and when parties need the support of regional, ethnic and personal factions (Clapham, 1982). Eisenstadt and Roniger identify nine 'core analytical characteristics' of the social interactions and exchanges involved in patron–client relations:

- they are particularistic and diffuse;
- resources are exchanged, both economic and political (support, votes, protection, solidarity);
- resources are exchanged as a 'package', not separately;
- the relationship is strongly unconditional and long-term;
- there is a varying amount of solidarity in the relationship;
- it is based on informal and not necessarily legal understandings;
- patron–client relations are entered into voluntarily;
- the vertical nature of patron–client relations undermines horizontal solidarities, especially of clients; and
- the relationship is based on strong inequality and power difference (Eisenstadt and Roniger, 1981, pp. 276–7).

Political and economic changes, particularly the development of the state and the spread of capitalism have fundamentally altered the nature of patronage. Patron–client relations increasingly take the form of brokerage and mediation between clients in their dealings with government and the market (Powell, 1970; Lemarchand, 1981; Kurer, 1997).

Clientelism has become a key component of the electoral process in many Third World countries. Political parties are compelled to recruit from among local patrons and brokers in order to secure the political support of their clients. The links between leaders and followers in party factions are therefore highly personalized. Special interests pursue their objectives through such links with the political authorities. Party leaders offer support and protection to those who accept and support their leadership. Identity with a leader will cut across conflicting interests, so that the leaders of factions have to mediate between the groups who support them. In India, for example, political parties and notably Congress have had to incorporate many different kinds of loyalty – those based on caste, landlord–tenant relations, language, tribe and religion.

However, within parties different interests are often expressed through factionalism which can have highly variable consequences for the durability of political parties. Factionalism refers to informal aspect of party organization. It is an inevitable consequence of alliances and coalitions between leaders and followers that have no ideological foundation but which are designed to secure electoral support. Relationships between leaders of factions and their followers are based on a range of social and economic conditions, such as feudalistic tenure systems (when a landowner can guarantee electoral support from tenants because of their economic dependency), cultural loyalties and other traditional obligations. Alternatively the factional linkage may be tribal, linguistic or caste based.

Factionalism leads to a segmentary form of party politics. The internal structures of factions are very much alike and political relations within them are always transactional, instrumental and dependent. Factionalism is stimulated by the rewards which are accessible to those in political office. Class interests and conflicts are overlaid by the common interest of patron and client. Factional conflict is about obtaining a broader basis of followers, so the outcome of conflict does not change the social structure.

If a leader fails to mediate successfully between different economic interests, his faction may split. If the split runs the length of the party, factional conflict may lead to a new party being formed. The conflicts between factions are not ideological. They are conflicts over resources, over influence at key points in the decision making structure of party and government, and over the ability to gain enough followers to win office so that patronage can be extended and the size and power of the faction can be increased. Success breeds success in a system of patronage. Leaders who win office can be expected to use their powers of patronage to enlarge their faction, drawing others into their sphere of influence. Leaders can then seek higher office, greater patronage and an enlarged following. Factional politics within parties and patron–client relationships produce a distinctive image for Third World parties.

A successful party thus has to contain centrifugal forces and contend with factors that encourage factionalism and undermine party unity, such as caste or communalism in India. India's Janata Party has failed to develop a cohesive organization because of caste conflict and the geographical and cultural divisions between people of the same caste (ironically for a party whose aim is an egalitarian reform of the caste system) (Bjorkman and Mathur, 1996; Sridharan and Varshney, 2001). Another such factor is the electoral system, as the case of Uruguay demonstrates (Morgenstern, 2001). Clientelism is only likely to decline in significance when parties form along ideological lines, mobilizing political support on the basis of horizontal rather than vertical linkages (e.g. class rather than kinship). The significance of clientelism in politics is also reduced by the bureaucratic allocation of public services on the basis of legal entitlements. The development of a universalistic political culture, and institutions of civil society through which citizens can pursue their individual rights and entitlements, also provide alternatives to clientelism (Roniger, 1994a, 1994b).

Conclusion

The question of survival of party government and representative politics leads on to considerations of political stability and democratization. The 'problem' of political instability is primarily seen in terms of the demise of party politics, especially of the competitive type. Not surprisingly the attention that has been paid to political instability in the Third World has focussed particularly on the supplantment, usually by the military, of a civilian form of government based on a system of parties. Consequently, military intervention, political stability and the process of democratization are the subjects of later chapters.

6

Bureaucracy and Political Power

The challenge of bureaucracy

Bureaucracies are important institutions in all political systems. Public officials cannot be thought of as merely the neutral implementers of the political decisions of others. In the Third World the bureaucracy has come to be regarded in some circumstances as the most powerful political institution. We have already touched upon ways in which the bureaucracy is so regarded. Theories of the post-colonial state have employed the concept of a bureaucratic oligarchy, clearly implying that government is in the hands of the paid officials of the state.

This chapter distinguishes between different concepts of bureaucracy and shows that all are contained in the analyses, which have been carried out, of the role of the bureaucracy in Third World societies and states. Sources of bureaucratic power are categorized, as well as bureaucratic features which have been taken to be signs of the emergence of a new kind of ruling class. Bureaucracy also implies a certain kind of rationality in the context of the official allocation of scarce resources, requiring consideration of the concept of 'access'.

Some indication of the significance of bureaucracy in developing countries is gained from the scale of public employment. State employment accounts for a higher percentage of the non-agricultural labour force than in developed countries. During the 1970s and 1980s the growth rate of public employment was higher in developing countries (Rowat, 1990). Nevertheless by the end of the 1990s government employment as a percentage of the population was smaller than in OECD countries and, with the exception of the Middle East, accounted for a smaller proportion of total employment. The share of public employment in total employment varies greatly from one country to another (Hammouya, 1999; McCourt, 2000). In all regions of the Third World, however, public sector wages take up a larger proportion of government budgets than in developed countries (see Table 6.1).

Table 6.1   *Government employment in the mid-1990s*

Region	Government employment as % of population	Government employment as % of total employment	Wages as % of government spending
Sub-Saharan Africa	2.0	6.6	35.3
Asia	2.6	6.3	22.4
Latin America and Caribbean	3.0	8.9	27.1
Middle East and North Africa	3.9	17.5	34.8
OECD	7.7	17.2	12.2

SOURCE: McCourt, 2000, Table 1, p. 6.

Part of the explanation for the growth in the size of public bureaucracies in developing countries lies in the demands that have been made on governments to stimulate development by providing a social and economic infrastructure and engaging directly in production. After independence, state bureaucracies were seen as promoters of social and economic change through planned development programmes (Jain, 1992). Even when the ideology has been predominantly capitalist and free-market, the state has intervened to support private capital. In the NICs of South East Asia and Latin America, the state and the bureaucracy have been highly interventionist. In the Philippines the civil service continues to expand, despite efforts to trim the bureaucracy. Between 1960 and 1997 the bureaucracy grew faster than the population. In 1970 there was one civil servant for every 90 Filipinos. In 2001 the ratio was 1:50. One in five employees works for the government. A combination of presidential patronage and a wide range of policy objectives in health, education, housing, security, environment, law and order, and support to economic sectors explain the growth. Some 10,000 senior staff are presidential nominees (Robles, 2008). In Tanzania, instead of reducing the size of the bureaucracy, the public service reform programme started in 2000 has accompanied an increase in the numbers of government agencies and personnel (Mamuya, 2008).

Consequently, controlling the bureaucracy is one of the main challenges facing political leaders, especially in new democracies where the machinery of accountability is usually weak. It is made doubly difficult by dependence on the bureaucracy, an inescapable feature of political life for incoming politicians; however sound their popular support and democratic credentials.

Concepts of bureaucracy

One of the problems when studying bureaucracy is that the term carries different connotations for different people. These will appear as we examine the way in which political science has integrated the study of bureaucracy into the analysis of Third World politics. A number of different definitions have been attached to the term. This conceptual ambiguity can, however, be put to good use. If we remind ourselves of the different meanings of bureaucracy, we can explore its full significance as a political force, a significance which extends well beyond the implementation of public policy.

'Bureaucracy' is sometimes used simply to refer to government administrative agencies staffed by public servants. It is synonymous with public administration, consisting of organizations set up as part of the modern state to carry out the policies of decision-makers. The state needs specialized institutions for implementing public policy and employs large numbers of people who make it their career to serve the state in a professional capacity. The bureaucracy thus refers to the public services and the organizations into which they are structured. It is a category of governmental personnel and offices that are filled in a particular way. It tells us no more about the way those organizations function or about the political power that the bureaucracy might exercise either over the formulation of public policies or their mode and even degree of implementation.

Within democratic theory it is assumed that this bureaucracy will be both accountable to those who have been elected to govern; and politically neutral and independent in the advice they give ministers and other political leaders. This enables them to serve which ever set of party leaders forms a government following competitive elections. Accountability is especially difficult under the political conditions typically found throughout the Third World. Whether the aim is to curb unacceptable personal behaviour (such as corruption or nepotism) or improve performance (by checking on probity and efficiency), accountability requires legislative oversight, transparency and judicial review. How effective such mechanisms will be depends on the historical legacies of colonialism, the effectiveness of political opposition, and the level of judicial development, as the experiences of Southeast Asian countries demonstrate (Fritzen, 2007).

Bureaucratic neutrality has been undermined by patronage and the political leadership's demand for partisan loyalty and affiliation. Single party regimes have required bureaucrats to be card-carrying party members. Military juntas have encouraged and rewarded political bias. Civil service jobs are used as rewards for services rendered. For example, in Eritrea those who fought for independence from Ethiopia have been given civil service posts, especially at the higher levels. These personnel have recently been targeted under administrative reforms because their appointment 'has not always been in keeping with the specific technical qualifications or administrative capabilities of the ex-combatants' (Soeters and Tessema, 2004, p. 624). In Cambodia the bureaucracy has been highly politicized by a combination of political appointments and pressure on officials to identify themselves with the ruling party. In Latin America and the Caribbean most government jobs 'are assigned on the basis of political party affiliation, social class, ethnic group, nepotism or family connections' (Meacham, 1999, p. 282). Such departures from the democratic model of public administration, under which staff should be recruited solely on merit can, and in Africa has, produced administrative systems that are inflated, inefficient, ineffective, dishonest and, of course, politically biased (Adamolekun, 2002; Fritzen, 2007).

The concept of bureaucracy also identifies a particular kind of organizational structure in which people are recruited into positions of authority in a special way. Bureaucracy is a rational means for the performance of collective tasks, especially those requiring large-scale organization. This clearly implies that some organizations may be more bureaucratic than others. Insofar as they are, they have clearly distinguishable features. They have clear lines of command from one level of a hierarchy to another. Recruitment to positions or offices within a bureaucracy is on the basis of merit demonstrated by the acquisition of relevant qualifications or success in a competitive entry test. Officials are dependent on a salary. They do not own the means of administration. They cannot take personal possession of a share of any revenues that they might be empowered to collect. Officials are merely paid a salary in return for their services to the state.

This reinforces the demarcation of official jurisdictions. There is a clear division of labour within a bureaucratic organization. It is divided into different offices to which attach certain clear-cut powers – regular, stable and precisely defined authority. This is sometimes represented graphically in an organigram or organizational chart set out as a pyramid of offices. The officials occupying such offices have clearly defined powers laid down in abstract rules. Their authority will be closely prescribed by those rules. They will be engaged in applying general rules to specific cases. This is a particular feature of government bureaucracies and especially those bureaucrats who encounter members of the public on a face-to-face level. They deal with the public as claimants, people who feel they are entitled to something that the state has to allocate, and that they fall within the category that the state has defined as being in need of, and entitled to, some benefit. The task of the bureaucrat is to make the allocation in a fair, impersonal and impartial way, treating like cases alike and having regard for nothing other than the factors that the regulations deem to be relevant. The bureaucrat is interested in nothing about a claimant other than what the regulations define as significant for arriving at a decision. If, for example, the official works for a small farmers development programme which defines entitlement in terms of size of land-holding, all the official needs to know is how much land the applicant occupies. All other aspects of the claimant's life – age, gender, race, tribe, caste, language, family size, place of origin – are irrelevant unless the law brings one or more of them into the calculation.

In the Third World cultural values have inflicted numerous departures from a model of bureaucracy which should in theory provide efficient policy implementation and fairness for the individual citizen. Third World bureaucracies have been marred by 'bureaupathologies', especially goal displacement (when following routine procedures is given precedence over the aims of the policy), disdain for the needs of clients, powerful opposition to change, and preoccupation with official status. Many such defects can be explained by cultural norms. In East and Southeast Asia, for example, these norms include family obligations, superstition, fear of losing 'face', exaggerated respect for authority, rank and qualifications, discrimination against women, and the need to avoid conflict in decision-making (Turner and Halligan, 1999).

This brings us to another meaning of bureaucracy and one which most readily occurs to the ordinary person if they use the term. That is inaccessible administration, rigid decision-making bound up in 'red tape', and insensitivity to personal circumstances and needs as defined by the applicant rather than the bureaucracy. These are the 'dysfunctional' or 'pathological' traits of bureaucracy. Rational organization and procedures deteriorate into inefficiency. In particular, 'strict adherence to regulations' induces 'timidity, conservatism and technicism' as well as conflict with clients (Merton, 1952, p. 367). Bureaucracy becomes an end in itself and thus self-defeating. It becomes characterized by buck-passing, red tape, rigidity, inflexibility, excessive impersonality, oversecretiveness, unwillingness to delegate, and reluctance to exercise discretion (Heady, 1959). Such bureaucrats are perceived as being unconcerned with personal problems, limiting their attention to narrowly defined circumstances that rules happen to define as significant. Bureaucrats are caught within a double-bind. If they do not administer the rules rigidly in order to avoid appearing to be inflexible and inhuman, they will be accused of abusing their power, exercising too much discretion, and moving outside their circumscribed jurisdiction; if they apply the rules rigorously, they will be accused of being bureaupathological. The bureaucrat treads a difficult path between those two alternatives.

Finally, 'bureaucracy' can also mean a form of rule, a category of governmental system along with democracy or aristocracy. It can mean government by officials rather than government by the people, a single person or a hereditary class. In many Third World societies that is precisely the kind of government that is in place, a kind of government that in many ways is very reminiscent of colonial government, which was also government by appointed officials, both military and civil. In such regimes, exemplified by military oligarchies and dictatorships, the bureaucracy is not merely a powerful political force within the political process. Government is virtually coterminous with the bureaucracy, which may also take on some of the characteristics of a ruling class as well as a ruling stratum. Bureaucratic government is a pattern represented by Thailand which until relatively recently was ruled by a military-bureaucratic alliance under which politics was largely a matter of internal bureaucratic conflicts (Fritzen, 2007).

The political power of bureaucracy

A major theoretical issue concerns the political power of the bureaucracy and how this may be conceptualized. Ideological and methodological choices have been important here. Functionalists and Marxists have both had distinctive things to say about the bureaucracy in the Third World. What they chose to focus upon and the way they have interpreted the role of the bureaucracy has depended very much upon their wider views and theories of society and the state.

One source of political power is *knowledge*. In the Third World, bureaucracies are often said to monopolize the knowledge and expertise relevant to government. The concentration of technical, professional and administrative expertise within the bureaucracy is unrivalled. Even when there is strong parliamentary government and virile political parties and other centres of political power, and when the bureaucrats have a constitutional role which only permits them to advise the political executive, they do so from positions of great influence. In many developing countries there are no political institutions which can compete with the bureaucracy in terms of a monopoly of technical and professional expertise. In addition, the majority of professionals have for many years been employed in the public sector and public services. This again limits the availability of countervailing forces that can present political leaders with alternative plans, policy advice and techniques of implementation to those put up by government officials. Development planning has consequently tended to be highly centralized, technocratic and of the 'top down' variety, where the experts at the top make the decisions about what the masses need in terms of programmes of development, whether in health care, agriculture, education or other areas of planned development. This feature of bureaucracy reflects the concept of a specially recruited group appointed on the basis of merit to produce rational and efficient methods of working. A system of recruitment that admits only those that can demonstrate the required level of expertise and competence is bound to produce organizations which lay politicians find difficult to dominate.

Even when the dominant ideology demands a reduction in the role of the state, bureaucratic expertise remains crucial in the search for solutions to the problems which continue to beset Third World countries: 'More than ever before, it should assist the policy-makers in crafting alternatives to contemporary development policy and, particularly, to the ongoing "poverty reduction" schemes' (Balogun, 2002, p. 541).

Bureaucratic power also arises from *dependency*. Effective administration is a necessary if not sufficient condition for planned change in developing countries (Abernethy, 1971). Insofar as the state has been at the forefront of planning change in economy and society through programmes of investment, education, family planning, nutrition, sanitation and the like, it has been dependent for the success of those plans upon a powerful and effective administration. It is one thing for a government to legislate on, say, land reform. The subsequent implementation requires thousands of land-titles to be registered, compensations to be settled and paid, and disputes to be processed and adjudicated upon. Without officialdom, nothing is properly implemented. What the politicians might win through electoral support or force of arms has to be consolidated by administrative proceedings and by the multitude of development programmes formulated by governments in the Third World. Dependence on the bureaucracy applies not only to the implementation of social and economic policy, but also to administrative reforms and political transitions (Balogun, 2002).

A third source of bureaucratic power is the social esteem and *status* enjoyed by senior bureaucrats. This may originate from a number of different sources – the public's acknowledgement of the impartiality of the public service, or of its professional expertise; and the legacy of colonialism when, particularly in the rural areas, officials stood at the apex of the power structure. When post-colonial officials inherited the offices, pay scales and perks of the colonial expatriates, they also inherited their prestige and standing in the community. When also there are few other opportunities for educated people to find employment, posts in the public service become the goal of the technocratic élite. For many years the private sector could not offer the opportunities which government service could and still does in many societies of the Third World.

Employment in the national government also offers the tempting possibility of secondment to an international bureaucracy of a UN agency such as the FAO, UNDP or WHO, with the World Bank, the IMF or even a regional organization such as the OAS or the ECLA. The universal values that are disseminated through such movements and contacts further enhance the élite status of bureaucrats in their own countries. This may lead to a bureaucracy that performs a kind of hegemonic role disseminating an ideology and a particular view of the state and its role in development. In the functionalist literature this has been especially identified as aimed at national integration through the enunciation of universalistic, Westernized and modern values. Bureaucrats were identified as pulling countries along the path to progress. They not only influence the policy choices of governments but also the way people outside government perceive the role of the state in development.

A fourth factor was alluded to in the earlier discussion of the post-colonial state. This is the *relative* power of the bureaucracy as a political institution *vis-à-vis* others (Wallis, 1989, pp. 24–30). This perception is common to both Marxist and functionalist political science. The functionalist position was first put most persuasively by Riggs (1963). A very similar line of argument appears in Alavi's neo-Marxist analysis of Pakistan and Bangladesh. Both schools of thought emphasize that one colonial legacy was the retarded development of political institutions that might have held the bureaucracy accountable. Colonialism developed bureaucracies at the expense of other institutions. It was more interested in the power of officials in relation to society than in the power of representative assemblies, political parties, pressure groups and other organizations representative of different sections of society and expected to evolve into institutions capable of controlling the bureaucratic apparatus of the state.

Colonialism left behind a well-organized bureaucracy that new governments had to staff with their own people, often in the context of a great shortage of qualified indigenous manpower. Crash programmes of training were launched to produce people capable of replacing the expatriates who were not invited to stay on and assist the newly independent governments to function. New states thus inherited bureaucracies that were prestigious, well organized and with a strong sense of corporate identity, and other political institutions lacking the same power and legitimacy. As party organizations became stronger, this situation changed. As mass parties threw up leaders not dependent upon the bureaucracy but on mass support at elections, and the longer that parliamentary institutions had to establish themselves, the stronger techniques for controlling the bureaucracy grew. The more that groups outside the state, in business, agriculture, the labour movement, and the professions developed and produced their own organizations, the more the bureaucracy was further held accountable to other groups of policy-makers.

However, the political power of the bureaucracy is not necessarily matched by administrative competence. It frequently has to work with inadequate information, particularly statistical. The fact that it monopolizes policy-relevant knowledge does not mean that it will have the quantity of skilled manpower for the tasks allotted to it. It may also be reluctant for political reasons to complete projects started under the preceding political leadership (Milne, 1972). Riggs argued long ago that the greater the political power of the bureaucracy, the weaker the incentives for effective administration and the more ineffectual the bureaucracy. He also claimed that *efficiency* varied inversely with the weight of bureaucratic power, largely as a result of the imbalance between bureaucracies and other political institutions and the consequent preoccupation among bureaucrats with furthering their bureaucratic interests rather than serving political masters (Riggs, 1964). The administrative capacity of Third World states is of current concern to international agencies such as the World Bank which are trying to redefine the role of the state in economic and social development.

Riggs also found historical and contemporary evidence to support the conclusion that bureaucratic power and expansion had adverse consequences for the development of political systems. The merit system, represented most strongly by bureaucratic recruitment methods, undermines one of the strongest supports of an emergent party system, namely the 'spoils' of office. Bureaucratic centralism and control of local governments weaken the educative effects of political participation. The bureaucratic mobilization of interest groups weakens centres of autonomous political pressure. Parliamentary legislative institutions cannot thrive on a foundation of weak parties, pressure groups and popular participation. Bureaucracies rather than parliaments control revenue raising, expenditure and policy initiatives. Bureaucratic 'formalism', whereby laws are enacted but not implemented, further undermines representative institutions. The judicial system, lacking popular support, can be exploited by the bureaucracy to assist its abuse of power. Consequently, 'too rapid expansion of the bureaucracy when the political system lags behind tends to inhibit the development of effective politics . . . separate political institutions have a better chance to grow if bureaucratic institutions are relatively weak' (Riggs, 1963, p. 126).

Thus a bureaucracy can positively discourage the development of institutions which can ensure accountability and function as alternative policy-making bodies. The development process of different political institutions such as bureaucracies and parties are not separate and unrelated. In effect the bureaucracy creates political vacuums for it to fill itself (Heeger, 1973, pp. 605–6).

The functionalists conceptualized this institutional imbalance as 'multi-functionality', arguing that in transitional societies political structures have not become as specialized as they would ultimately when society had become fully modern. The functionalist idea of political modernity included a bureaucracy fully specialized in rule application. In advanced societies as defined by the functionalists, power resides with the people and public servants are there to give advice and obey orders. Transitional society has political structures that have not become fully specialized, but are multifunctional. It becomes logically possible for bureaucratic structures to perform all the input and output functions of the political system and be as much concerned with the function of rule-*making* as rule-*application* (Almond, 1960). However, there was always difficulty in fitting the behaviour of Third World bureaucrats into the functionalist taxonomy (Smith, 1988).

Marxist social theorists have adopted a different approach to bureaucratic overdevelopment. A study of Mali found a 'crisis of colonialism' which had brought about independence before any viable political structures other than the bureaucracy had had a chance to develop (Meillasoux, 1970). Alavi's analysis of Pakistan and Bangladesh also refers to the overdevelopment of the bureaucracy relative to other political institutions. Once freed from direct metropolitan control, this oligarchy was able to extend its dominant power in society, assume a new economic role, proliferate bureaucratic controls and public agencies, manipulate the facade of parliamentary government, and eventually even seize power from the democratic regime.

Experience elsewhere indicated the need for qualifications to this depiction of the bureaucracy. In Kenya, for example, the bureaucracy was divided into different branches and strata. Civil servants did not always have identical interests to the managers of state-owned enterprises and the latter were 'especially exposed to the bourgeois values embodied in the technology, management practices, "efficiency" ideology, etc. of the firms they take over'. Career bureaucrats also needed to be distinguished from party officials inserted into the civil administration, particularly in terms of their respective class linkages (Leys, 1976, p. 44).

Other authorities have qualified the post-colonial model by seeing it as a passing phase and one that in some Third World societies has been left behind – notably in India, where the colonial administration was overdeveloped and had enormous prestige supported by a complex ideology of racial superiority, paternalism, and tolerance of those indigenous institutions deemed to be compatible with metropolitan interests. But after independence a fairly well established Indian middle class increasingly articulated its interests through the formal institutions of political democracy. Administrative behaviour in post-colonial India has become increasingly bureaucratic and instrumental 'as a response to the emergence of legislatures, political parties, and new forms of class differentiation which together have functioned to undermine the autonomy of the state administrative apparatus' (Wood, 1977, p. 307). In particular, a class of capitalist farmers had emerged as dominant in the formation of agrarian policies. The establishment of democratic institutions meant a loss of authority, power and status for the bureaucracy. When class interests sought to oppose reforms by undermining administrative authority, the bureaucracy retreated into ideologies of professionalism, instrumentalism and neutrality.

Bureaucratic stability, or the *continuity* of the bureaucratic élite compared with other political élites, is another source of power. Governments come and go, *coups* bring about changes of regime, but the bureaucracy remains. Other élites come to be dependent on it: 'it seldom occurs to the men leading a *coup* to throw the administrators out' (Abernethy, 1971, p. 95). In the case of Pakistan, it seems that the bureaucracy had been in control from the very inception of 'military' rule (Alavi, 1990). The same applied to Africa: 'In countries like Togo, Nigeria, Ghana, Sierra Leone, Liberia and the former Zaire, it was to the civil service that the military juntas turned when embarking on the difficult challenge of "suspending" the constitution, dissolving parliament, and ruling by decree' (Balogun, 2002, p. 547). Under conditions of political instability the continuity of the bureaucracy enhances its power. It is impossible to dispense with it as an institution and often extremely difficult to replace its personnel with those who have the ideological commitment needed by the leaders of a new government or regime, especially if administrative expertise is monopolized by the old guard.

Bureaucracy and access

Bureaucratic power is also related to the *administrative allocation* of scarce state resources to meet politically defined needs among different sections of the population – for income support, employment, land, agricultural inputs, food, health care, education, credit, shelter, and other public provision that has to be bureaucratically administered.

If we recall the different meanings attached to bureaucracy, and in particular bureaucracy as a certain kind of rationality, we find that in the context of the bureaucratic allocation of scarce resources rationality takes on a special political significance. High levels of need, particularly among the poorer sections of society but also among other sections, such as private capital, mean that the bureaucracy has to allocate scarce resources according to politically determined categories of need. The market is not left to make such allocations, it is done through official action.

For example, if the poor are deemed to be in need – of an income, work, land, health care, agricultural inputs, food, education and so on – because they lack the resources to obtain from the market what is required to maintain life at a certain officially designated standard, bureaucratic allocations have to be made. In the case of income, steps may be taken to create jobs such as a public works programme into which will be recruited labour from a target group whose need has been officially identified and which the public intervention has been set up to meet. Or the need may be identified as land so that people can support themselves. The policy might then be a land-reform programme which allocates land to the landless. The need might be for shelter which cannot be demanded in the private housing sector. Similarly the private market for education may be beyond the reach of certain categories of people who are politically defined as 'needing' educational provision. Health care is in a similar category.

Such allocations affect other client groups. Particular categories of agricultural or industrial producers might be identified as having a need for inputs which should increase levels of productivity. A potentially productive group may be unable to obtain credit in the financial markets because of the lack of secure collateral or ability to repay at the market rate of interest, so the state provides loans at a subsidized rate. The need for increased productivity may be seen in terms of physical inputs such as fertilizer, seeds or equipment, which again will be allocated by the state.

A wide range of state interventions aimed at particular groups of beneficiaries is virtually synonymous with development planning in many parts of the Third World. Those state interventions should be managed bureaucratically by officials acting according to the Weberian model of public service. Rules and regulations will be applied to specific cases. Entitlements to public benefits are created for specified groups. In theory, the intended beneficiaries will be able to identify themselves as such, will be informed of their newly defined rights, and will be able to comprehend the way bureaucratic organizations arrive at final decisions in individual cases. Officials correspondingly behave according to norms which structure the decision-making process, seeking relevant information to test whether specified conditions have been met. The conditions may be numerous and complex. Nevertheless, a claim can still be systematically examined to see whether a claimant falls into the category of eligibility or not.

For many people there is no problem in understanding the way public organizations plan such expenditure and interventions, and the way they make decisions about its allocation. There may be political interference with the process of administrative allocation, leading to deviation from the bureaucratic norm. Allocations may not then be made impartially and according to the rules. It is a highly politicized process, but for the more Westernized and educated sections of society the processes of decision-making are comprehensible. However, for other sections of society in poor, agricultural economies that are in the process of change, bureaucratic methods of decision-making are difficult to adjust to.

In a peasant community such bureaucratization may appear very alien; this is not because people lack intelligence, are irrational or are too backward. It is because bureaucratic rationality does not coincide with peasant rationality. The behaviour of the bureaucrat, who can only deal with information that is relevant to the case that falls within his jurisdiction, may appear very strange in the context of rural society in many parts of the world. To dismiss information about a person's current situation as irrelevant is difficult for a person to accept when they are part of a community in which aspects of different lives interact. People do not see themselves as standing in a single-stranded relationship with others, but in multistranded relationships (Wood, 1977). A money-lender rather than an agriculture extension officer may be approached for credit, but the relationship with the money-lender will be very different from that with a government official. The multistranded relationships of peasant communities combine debt, kinship, tenancy, employment, reciprocity, political factionalism and patronage. A bureaucrat treating like cases alike and focusing exclusively on officially selected aspects of an individual's circumstances is using a peculiarly Westernized form of rationality that rich and educated farmers in the community may be able to appreciate and co-operate with. But poor, illiterate, uneducated and *dependent* members of the community, at whom the programmes of public expenditure may have been specifically and deliberately targeted, may find the process difficult to adapt to. A bureaucrat cannot be approached in a multistranded way. Other aspects of an individual's economic and family circumstances which are currently all-pervading will be defined as irrelevant to the bureaucrat. Needs will have been defined in terms of officially selected attributes of a person's existence. The claimant, on the other hand, will not want to present a case. He will want to present a story about the integrated parts of his whole existence.

Bureaucrats perhaps should not be surprised to discover that their programmes do not have the impact which the policy-makers hoped for. Resources provided by officialdom are often used to satisfy what the beneficiaries regard as more pressing needs (Wood, 1977). Nor should they be surprised that the intended beneficiaries do not come forward and claim their rights. Entering a government programme may be risky if it involves disengaging from the traditional obligations of the community. If the bureaucratic allocation fails to work as intended, and if one has withdrawn from community structures, no longer seeking the protection, assistance and reciprocity of local relationships, the consequences could be disastrous. A position of dependency and even exploitation may be preferred to the position of recipient of a state programme.

The bureaupathologies referred to earlier create other problems for those who cannot avoid contact with administrative agencies. In India, a bureaucratic culture infected with formalism, delays (despite overstaffing), corruption, and arbitrary discretion disfigures relations between officials and their publics to such an extent that agents are employed to pursue cases through the bureaucracy by claimants wishing to avoid face-to-face contact with officials. Clearly such a system puts the poor at a further disadvantage when seeking access.

Pressures on officials, including corruption, may mean that the resources to be allocated are not received by the target group but instead find their way to other destinations. Administrative officials may to a certain extent be at the mercy of political pressures to benefit local élites at the expense of target groups identified by government programmes. Bureaucrats need to be able to demonstrate success. They can use their discretion to allocate resources to those who can produce the results, say in terms of agricultural output, that can be translated into the levels of administrative performance that will satisfy superiors: for example, farmers who have experience of modern agricultural techniques and commercial transactions. Since it is the capitalistic, rationally economic, literate and market-oriented *farmer* who corresponds to the model of behaviour on which bureaucratically administered programmes are predicated, such programmes will inevitably favour him rather than the survival-oriented, indebted, dependent, marginal and vulnerable poor peasant. In this way bias is introduced into much development planning that directs state interventions at particular groups of beneficiaries (Wood, 1977, 1984).

A ruling class

Bureaucracies may become more than just political institutions. They may form a new kind of class, and a ruling class at that. There are a number of reasons why this conclusion has been reached for some Third World states.

Firstly, some developing countries have had what has been called a bureaucratic mode of production. The bureaucracy controls and manages the means of production through the state. It provides the necessary organization. It proliferates opportunities for bureaucratic careers by the creation of public bodies needing public managers – marketing boards, development corporations and other parastatal organizations and their subsidiaries (Hirschmann, 1981). It articulates an ideology of state ownership and planning. It organizes the means of its own reproduction by passing on to the offspring of bureaucrats disproportionately advantageous opportunities to obtain the qualifications needed for entry into bureaucratic occupations and therefore the new class.

For example, the post-independence bureaucracy in Mali used its access to political power to acquire some of the characteristics of a social class. It controlled the infrastructure of the economy and the means of repression, using them to maintain its dominance, particularly in its conflict with weak indigenous social classes, notably the landed aristocracy and the petty-bourgeois class of traders. Above all it created a nationalized sector of the economy which under the label of socialism enabled the economy to be brought under bureaucratic control.

Tanzania is another case. The ideology of African Socialism justified public ownership and bureaucratic management and direction of, at the very least, the commanding heights of the economy. The state controlled most of the economic surplus created rather than leaving it to be privately appropriated. Surplus extraction was through state institutions. The bureaucracy thus acted in relation to the means of production in a way analogous to a *property-owning* ruling class. The bureaucracy not only managed the means of production through state-owned enterprises, but also controlled the different prices of the factors of production to ensure that direct producers generated a surplus which the bureaucracy then accumulated and deployed. Removing the rights of workers to strike, imposing other government controls on trade unions, enforcing statutory wage ceilings, engaging in manpower planning, taking control of agricultural marketing, and controlling the prices paid to agricultural producers, were all part of the bureaucracy's control over the means of production and the surplus created. The weak social classes allowed a 'ruling clique' to become a 'bureaucratic bourgeoisie' consisting of ministers, senior civil servants, high military and police officers and high-level party bureaucrats. This 'bureaucratic bourgeoisie' developed from being essentially politico-administrative with a regulative role in the economy to being 'dominant actors in the economy': 'political power and control over property now came to rest in the same class' (Shivji, 1976, p. 85).

Secondly, the expertise which the bureaucracy has can be seen as another factor of production, in addition to land, labour and capital. The bureaucracy supplies the organizations necessary and the managerial, scientific and technical knowledge required. It takes over that legacy of colonialism in which the bureaucracy dominated embryonic indigenous classes. The bureaucracy monopolizes organization and all its attributes necessary for the management of the economy. It articulates an ideology in support of this. Any mode of production requires a set of ideas to justify control of the surplus by the ruling element in society. In Tanzania the ideology has been African Socialism (Stein, 1985), but different brands of socialism have been articulated by leaders in other parts of the Third World: Mali's version of socialism has similarly acted as a justification for state-directed development.

There are, then, bureaucratic features which have been taken to be signs of the emergence of a new kind of ruling class. The fact that ownership resides with society and not the bureaucracy is taken to be a legalistic fiction. Control is what matters, as indeed has been said about capitalism – that the managers not the owners of corporate assets are the power-holders. The accumulation of personal wealth is made possible by a career in the bureaucracy. The salaries enjoyed by the upper ranks in many African states, their easy access to credit, and their control over permits, licences and tenders, have enabled them to acquire urban and rural real estate and business ventures (Hirschmann, 1981).

However, the class interests of the state bureaucracy do not necessarily describe the class character of the state. For example, the dominant class in African society in the 1970s was the *foreign* bourgeoisie. Any class interests which the personnel of the state might have had were only reflected in state policy in a secondary way (Leys, 1976). Senior members of the bureaucracy might be able to embourgeoise themselves through the opportunities to acquire property made available by their official positions, siphoning off 'a large part of the economic surplus that is generated in society to accumulate wealth for themselves' (Alavi, 1990, p. 23) and even enjoy substantial social mobility for themselves and their families as a result, but this alone does not amount to evidence of the emergence of a new class structure.

Reducing bureaucracy

The role of bureaucracies in the politics of developing countries is increasingly affected by the principles of economic liberalization and New Public Management (NPM). Under conditionalities imposed by multilateral agencies such as the World Bank, the IMF, UNDP and the Asian Development Bank, and with the support of powerful bilateral donors such as the USA's Agency for International Development, some Third World governments have been obliged to undergo structural adjustment programmes. Others, such as China and Thailand, have embraced such reforms autonomously (Worthley and Tsao, 1999; Bowornwathana, 2000).

These have included reducing the size of the public sector through the privatization of state-owned enterprises. The same international agencies have also required and supported administrative reforms according to the principles of NPM. The results of these policies for the role of bureaucracies in the politics of Third World states have been mixed, and by no means all in the direction of securing greater democratic control over public officials (Turner and Hulme, 1997; Hughes, 1998).

On the face of it a programme of privatization would seem inevitably to reduce the power of bureaucrats simply by taking the production of goods and services out of their hands and selling them off to the private sector. There is then much less for bureaucrats to manage. However, no sooner had Third World states been instructed to privatize than they were advised to regulate. As part of its discovery that the state must after all play a central role in developing a country, the World Bank revealed that 'governments are learning that market reforms and fast-changing technology pose their own regulatory challenges. States cannot abandon regulation' (World Bank, 1997, p. 61).

Depending on local administrative capabilities, states need officials to enforce rules that support competitive markets, protect the environment, foster industrial innovation, prevent the abuse of monopoly powers, enlighten consumers and workers (e.g. about health and safety risks in production or consumption), safeguard the health of the financial system (e.g. by regulating banking), and protect savers and borrowers from 'information asymmetry'. Regulation has to be performed by public administrators, and regulators need discretionary power to respond flexibly to changing circumstances. Once again the public interest and welfare are heavily dependent upon the competence and integrity of public officials.

The importance of public services to vulnerable people has also been rediscovered. Services giving the poor access to health care, education, clean water, sanitation and other vital resources have become part of a new 'poverty agenda' advocated by aid donors and some progressive governments (Smith, 2007).

Nevertheless, the NPM approach to administrative reform also has among its aims a reduction in the size of the bureaucracy. A central requirement of NPM is to make greater use of the private sector by contracting out to private firms activities that were once performed 'in-house', in the expectation that competition will ensure reduced costs and therefore greater efficiency. Governments then become more concerned with 'enabling' the supply of services than with their direct production.

Governments have also been urged to de-bureaucratize by delegating to the 'Third Sector' of non-governmental organizations (NGOs), consisting of non-commercial organizations such as business associations, youth groups, women's organizations, voluntary bodies, community associations, religious foundations, professional bodies, and autonomous organizations providing economic and social services such as agricultural extension, vocational training, social welfare, irrigation and credit. 'Third Sector' organizations often fill gaps left by inadequate state provision.

NGOs are preferred to bureaucratic provision because they are presumed to offer better access to services, and to respond more flexibly to the needs of individual clients. Their altruism may motivate them to work in areas which civil servants and other professionals try to avoid, such as remote rural localities. Democratization in parts of the Third World, especially Latin America, has created political space for NGOs to develop. In some new democracies, NGOs have been set up by the state.

Relationships between the state and NGOs include contracts, service agreements, grants, subsidies, tax exemptions, and accommodation. Contractual arrangements with NGOs have been recorded in the policy areas of agricultural extension (Uganda and Mozambique), rural water supply and sanitation (Bolivia and Chile), tube well installation for landless irrigation groups (in Bangladesh), training home visitors in child health for the Ministry of Health in Brazil, forest conservation in Nepal, the distribution of government-subsidized food in Mexico, child health and family planning in Haiti, and therapy under India's national tuberculosis programme.

State-NGO relations depend on the level of pluralism in the political system, the state's capacity to provide services itself, and how NGOs see their own political roles. NGOs usually engage in advocacy and pressure group activity. The more radical the NGO, the less favourably will it be viewed by governments. Relationships range from equal partners at one extreme to virtual absorption into the bureaucracy at the other.

The potential political advantages for governments of contracts with Third Sector organizations, in addition to reducing bureaucracy, include demonstrating a commitment to accountability, participation, and reducing political patronage. A further attraction is that NGOs can easily be discarded when politically necessary.

The benefits to the non-governmental sector include access to funds (especially from aid donors), a heightened profile, and opportunities to influence public policy. But there are also potential costs. Civic organizations risk becoming professionalized, bureaucratized and dependent, rather than voluntary, creative and autonomous. Co-operation with governments may strike at the independence of voluntary bodies, especially the freedom to campaign politically as pressure groups. Government agencies may force NGOs into a 'responsible' mode by defining politically acceptable behaviour, leading to a loss of credibility among client groups. Contracts may require conformity to government objectives rather than objectives defined by NGOs. Governments are likely to be interested in NGOs as service providers, rather than as sources of new ideas about public policies. Indeed, states often impose a restrictive environment of laws, taxes, controls, bureaucratic resistance, and even political repression on civic organizations and other parts of the Third Sector. Conflicts are particularly likely when state officials are closely allied socially and politically to local economic elites, but then have to collaborate with NGOs attempting to extend the economic and political opportunities of the poor and other disadvantaged groups.

Some NPM principles point to an increase in the autonomy and therefore power of public officials in both their enabling and service providing roles. It is recommended that new public managers should be given greater discretion to use the resources at their disposal. While they may be judged against performance standards that have been made more explicit and quantifiable than in the past, their accountability to political leaders would be weakened. Furthermore, the constraints of the public service ethic would be abandoned in favour of private sector management techniques and practices, particularly in relation to personnel management. NPM also discards the unrealistic distinction between politics and administration, acknowledging that public managers will inevitably decide on policy issues of political significance.

While there are obvious public benefits to be derived from any greater efficiency and effectiveness in the provision of public services and functions achieved by the employment of better managers, an emphasis on achievements rather than budgetary inputs, the use of effective incentives within public bodies, and greater concern for the economical use of public resources, it is far less obvious that such reforms weaken the power of officials *vis-à-vis* political leaders. Public officials become more like the equals of politicians than their servants. The requirement under NPM that officials be responsive to the needs of their clients actually increases their political power by acknowledging their right to decide what needs to meet and how to meet them. They will not be responding to sovereign consumers in the manner of competing private forms.

Under NPM the actions of public officials may become more transparent, making it easier for the public to judge the wisdom of government policies. But the politicians' control of their bureaucrats will have been weakened. It is by no means clear that administrative reforms inspired by NPM will ensure as much accountability of public officials to elected representatives as more traditional methods of public administration, especially under Third World conditions where legislatures are weak and client groups poorly organized. In Tanzania, for example, public sector reforms designed to improve efficiency, strengthen motivation, and reduce corruption, have increasingly shielded decision-makers from public scrutiny and parliamentary control, 'since the majority of the members of parliament belong to the ruling party, and have by and large refrained from voting for stricter government accountability' (Mamuya, 2008, p. 280).

The practice of the new dogma in public management also affects the balance of power within civil society. Redefining the citizen as 'customer' or 'client' – an approach adopted by many countries in Asia, Africa and Latin America – implies a monetary transaction and exchange rather than a public duty to provide a service to those entitled to receive it. Charging for services makes essential services such as education and health care less affordable to low-income groups. Divestment and 'downsizing' of public services and social expenditure reduces the capacity of the state to serve the basic needs of citizens for health, education, and shelter, services which are critical to the living standards of the poor (Haque, 1999).

Partnerships with the private sector give corporate élites a privileged relationship to bureaucrats compared with those sections of society dependent on public services financed through taxation. The loss of a 'democratic tradition of ethical standards' requiring accountability, the representation of minorities and women, impartiality, and responsiveness, in favour of market values, productivity, competition and profitability, means that 'the normative criteria or rationales for public policies and administrative decisions are likely to be based on market driven criteria rather than the opinions and expectations of citizens'. The role of bureaucracy as the facilitator, regulator and co-ordinator of private sector contractors makes it more difficult to create a culture of public service in the public interest (Haque, 1999). Attempts to create an entrepreneurial culture in the public service turn public accountability into 'formalistic irritants'. Managerial autonomy weakens 'important institutional and legal safeguards in areas of vital concern to vulnerable segments of the population', especially the rule of law, and encourages 'the abuse of power, corruption and arbitrariness' (Argyriades, 2007: xxvi, 16).

Despite the strength of the advocacy in its favour, public management reform may encounter contextual and cultural obstacles that are difficult to overcome. In Ghana, for example, reform has been impeded by poor communications, low levels of literacy, ethnic diversity, regional imbalances, and politicization of the civil service. Changing the practice of public management has proved incompatible with cultural values, including trust in traditional indigenous political institutions, gender biases, ethnic obligations, and distinctive approaches to community life and collective action. In Southeast Asia, the introduction of NPM has encountered obstacles in the form of state structures inherited from authoritarianism, whether military (Thailand) or communist (Vietnam); the persistence of patronage and patron–client relations (Philippines); the weakness of the private sector; politicized civil services (Laos), ethnic discrimination (Malaysia); and the reluctance of politicians and bureaucrats to relinquish power. There is also fear that NPM has an adverse effect on the poor and weakens the state's capacity to manage financial crises. The precepts of New Public Management also conflict with the fatalism, paternalism and nepotism found in many Third World bureaucracies (Haruna, 2003; Soeters and Tessema, 2004; Haque, 2007).

Conclusion

Bureaucracy as a form of government stands in stark contrast to the concept of a neutral administrative instrument. The former rests on a perception of bureaucracy as being able to exercise power in its own right, either relative to other political institutions of parliamentary democracy or party government, or as a consequence of having usurped them in alliance with the military, or as having emerged as a new kind of politically *and* economically dominant class. The latter model must form part of the democratization process that is currently underway in many Third World countries. To secure bureaucracy's place in a democratic regime requires institutions capable of ensuring recruitment on the basis of merit rather than patronage, nepotism or corruption; transparency in the administration of public policy; and accountability for maladministration and incompetence. Most developing countries are still a long way from enjoying effective scrutiny of bureaucracy by legislatures, courts and civil society, and are under pressure for the international development community to reform in ways which are unlikely to redress the imbalance in political power.

7

Military Intervention in Politics

Introduction

Direct military intervention in the politics of Third World countries has been a depressingly regular occurrence since the high-water mark of post-war independence. Between 1960 and 1980 three-quarters of Latin American states experienced *coups*, as did half of the Third World Asian states and over half of the African states (Clapham, 1985; Woddis, 1977). The 1980s saw the trend continue strongly. Not a year passed without there being a *coup* or an attempted *coup* in some part of the Third World (World Bank, 1991). Despite the wave of democratization in the 1990s there have been *coups* or attempted *coups* in Chad (1990), Togo (1991), Peru, Sierra Leone, Venezuela and Haiti (1992), Guatemala and Nigeria (1993), Gambia (1994), Pakistan (1999), Venezuela (2001), and Chad again in 2008. Between 1990 and 2003, 11 African states attempting to democratize experienced no fewer than 26 instances of military intervention, including successful coups, failed coup attempts, and military rebellions (Clark, 2007).

In the independence era expectations were very different (Wells, 1974; Charlton, 1981). Military intervention in politics, including the *coup d'état*, was nothing new in historical terms, but that it should become such a remarkably common occurrence in Third World states surprised and dismayed many national politicians and outside observers, including Western social scientists who had shared the view that the military was unlikely to be a threat to civilian regimes. In the late 1950s and early 1960s many social scientists were fairly confident that though the military might be a problem in Latin America, conditions were so different in other regions of the world that it was unlikely to be so there. It was widely believed that there was little chance in the newly independent states of the world that the military would play anything other than the constitutional role of professional servants of the state. Yet no sooner had the complacency been expressed than events were to prove such optimistic predictions false. In one African state after another civilian government succumbed to the military, and in other parts of the Third World military support became a necessary condition of regime survival even if the military did not take over complete and direct power.

The question as to why the military became the political force that it did in so many newly independent African and Latin American countries and remained a dominant force in Latin America, despite longer histories of independence and higher levels of economic development, is of more than just academic interest. With fragile democracies being created in all regions of the Third World, sometimes following prolonged periods of military rule, it becomes of paramount importance to understand the conditions which relate to military intervention and therefore threaten the consolidation of democracy. Attention has focused in particular on the *coup d'état* and how, often with apparent ease (First, 1972), the military is able to supplant civilian regimes. This is the problem with which this chapter is concerned in order to establish when a threat to a new democracy might emerge and what conditions are necessary to increase the likelihood that the armed forces will remain loyal to civilian political leadership and amenable to its direction.

No single explanation has achieved total acceptance, as might be expected with such a complex phenomenon occurring in such widely differing societies. Many of the explanations produced of military intervention have dwelt more on why the preceding civilian regimes were so fragile and unstable, almost taking it for granted that if a civilian regime collapses in less developed societies the military will inevitably be the successor. In the context of underdevelopment this is not an altogether unwarranted assumption. In some circumstances of political instability the military has represented 'the only effectively organised element capable of competing for political power and formulating public policy' (Pye, 1966, p. 283). Other explanations, however, have looked at the political advantages which the military enjoy under such conditions.

Explaining military intervention

Much of the research that has been done on the military in Third World politics has been from a macro and quantitative standpoint. Here the literature is based on statistical analysis of a large number of countries which are ranked by variables that measure levels of instability or military intervention. These are then correlated with socio-economic factors that seem likely to have explanatory value. A good example is a study of 31 countries in Sub-Saharan Africa in 1970 which related, through multivariate analysis, social and economic variables to military *coups* in order to explain why some African countries had experienced them and others had not. Population size and growth rate, urbanization, literacy, mass-media availability, GNP per capita, economic growth rate, and measures of 'centrality' (the geographical concentration of political and economic life) were taken as relevant indicators of social and economic conditions that might be thought *a priori* to be related to the likelihood of military intervention. Indicators of the size of the military and police force, and of defence expenditure, were used to establish the significance of organizational characteristics in military intervention. The level of loans from the USA was taken as indicative of external influence on vulnerability to the *coup d'état*. The results were disappointingly inconclusive. Even combining all the independent variables only explained 56 per cent of the variation in *coup* activity. The final explanatory model produced owed more to case studies than statistical analysis (Wells, 1974).

This is fairly typical of the problems that are encountered when making quantitative statistical analyses to explain and predict military *coups* (Jackman, 1986; Johnson et al., 1986; O'Kane, 1986). First there is the question of which states should be included in the analysis. Were colonies 'states'? Should they have been included in the populations at risk from military intervention as they have been in some analyses? Statistical explanations require the rule of *ceteris paribus* to be satisfied, so the cases compared have to have things other than military intervention equal. With nation-states 'other things' are hardly ever 'equal'. Grouping together 'Black African states', for example, could be said to produce heterogeneity rather than homogeneity. Aggregating a meaningfully comparable collection of countries produces problems, the solutions to which do not repay the effort put into finding them.

The second source of doubt about such analysis is how far the specific measurable variables chosen represent dependent and independent factors such as social mobilization, characteristics of the military itself, degrees of political development, international economic dependence and so on. For example, how well do 'voter turnout' or 'degree of multipartyism' represent 'political development' as an independent variable? How satisfactory is the total of US loans and credit in a single year as an indicator of the external influences that might encourage a military take-over? The weak conceptual foundation of much multivariate analysis can result in unjustifiable conclusions being drawn from the statistical results.

Thirdly, measures used as dependent and independent variables should cover the same time periods, otherwise temporal variation introduces problems of 'simultaneity bias'. How, for example, can it reasonably be claimed that 'party fractionalization' in 1975 caused *coups* starting 15 years earlier, especially when the military commonly banish political parties and therefore determine themselves the level of pluralism (or 'fractionalization') in the political system?

Fourthly, there are tautological pitfalls that await the quantitative analyst, when some part of what is to be explained is contained within the definition of the *explicandum* (the explanatory or independent variable). An example is when 'increased military expenditure' is used as an independent variable but has resulted from military domination of the state, the dependent variable that is to be explained by expenditure on the military. The same problem is found in the attempt discussed later to explain military *coups* by reference to the level of the political culture in a society, when political culture is defined by reference to a lack of consensus, evidence for which is found in the failure of the civilian system to withstand military supplantment.

The use of doubtful indicators of the variables under consideration and the unwillingness of researchers to replicate each others' methods in different regions undoubtedly account for, along with the problems of correlational analysis already mentioned, the widespread dissatisfaction with this mode of analysis. However, it would be wrong to be too dismissive, either on the grounds that there are no identifiable patterns of military intervention – that it is totally random – or that statistical comparisons and correlations force the use of indicators of political, social and economic development that are of doubtful validity. Quantitative analysis generates interesting hypotheses. The fact that so far they have produced nothing more conclusive and leave us still needing a convincing theory – and are probably incapable of meeting these needs – possibly explains some of the frustration and irritation which they engender.

Forms of intervention

The main focus of academic interest has been supplantment – the act of taking political control by force and replacing civilian institutions with military leadership forming a self-appointed junta with absolute power unconstrained by any civilian political institutions. Government is then by decree. Constitutional niceties such as parliamentary procedures, popular consent, or political representation are ignored, because elected assemblies are dissolved immediately upon taking power, elections are suspended, and political parties are abolished. Some constitutional principles might be observed if it is judged necessary to obtain a modicum of legitimacy, such as leaving the judiciary intact and with the power to declare on the legality of some administrative decisions. But supplantment may be defined as the substitution of a civilian regime by a military one by means of armed coercion.

An example is Burma, where a military junta is still in power. Political power was first seized by the military in 1962. The federal constitution was abolished. Parliament was dissolved. Political activists and ethnic minority leaders opposing the junta were imprisoned, and student protesters were massacred. Existing political parties were banned and the army created a new political party, the Burmese Socialist Programme Party whose membership included 80 per cent of the armed forces. A new Constitution was introduced in 1974 under which an elected parliament was reinstated, but only one candidate, approved by the BSSP, was allowed to 'contest' each constituency. The BSSP lasted until 1988 when the junta assumed responsibility for all aspects of government. Independent media were closed down. The senior officers formed a Revolutionary Council and ruled by decree (Smith, 2002).

Supplantment is by no means the only role which the military can perform. It is an important organized interest or pressure group in all states. It is one of the best endowed organizations in terms of access to the state apparatus. The military leadership is always incorporated into the machinery of government through various consultative and executive arrangements such as defence councils, advisory committees, and the close working relationships between top political, bureaucratic and military personnel. In no system of government should the political importance of the military be underestimated. A key question about the military in politics is how far it has values that extend beyond decisions about how best to defend a country and wage war, to those which express not only a corporate interest in good pay, good conditions, and the highest level of weapons technology but also a sense of how society should be organized.

Furthermore, in its normal constitutional role the military is very difficult to subject to democratic control and accountability because it is so easy for it to surround itself with secrecy and so avoid parliamentary and other forms of scrutiny. This secrecy commonly extends far beyond what it is necessary to keep from potential or actual foreign aggressors, to include detailed financing of expensive projects for which the taxpayer has to pay.

Another form of intervention is when the military displaces one civilian regime and replaces it with another. A refusal to act as the instrument of the government against its opponents is one way in which the military can bring about a change of government (Woddis, 1977). In any revolution control of the army is a vital factor.

This was clearly the case in Iran in 1979. The Shah's regime finally collapsed when the military declared itself 'neutral' as regards the conflict between revolutionary fighters and parts of the military supportive of the revolution, especially within the air force, and troops loyal to the Shah, especially the Imperial Guard. The Chief of Staff declared that the armed forces must not interfere in politics, thereby ruling out a military *coup* to restore order. Supporters of the revolution had penetrated the rank and file of the military to such an extent that the revolutionaries were well supplied with arms. The order from the High Council of the Armed Forces to military units to return to barracks recognized the reality of popular support for the revolution.

Whether a new regime has control of the army and can use military power against remnants of the *ancien régime* is a critical factor determining the outcome of a period of revolutionary upheaval. Changes of government resulting from the military switching its allegiance from one group of political leaders to another can also occur and have frequently done so in recent Latin American history. The military is often the power behind the throne. For example, in Ecuador the military ruled from 1972 to 1978, but has intervened on several occasions since to change the civilian government, most recently in 2000 when the military responded to economic crisis, corruption and instability by replacing the elected president with someone of their choosing (Danapoulos and Zirker, 2006). Clear examples of this are also found in South East Asia, where in both Indonesia and Thailand the military has long been the final arbiter in political conflict. In Thailand the military, when not directly in control, operates behind the scenes influencing electoral choices and party policy. During the elections in 2007 organized by the military following a coup in 2006, the media were censored, freedom of speech restricted, and martial law used to stifle dissent in areas supportive of the deposed Prime Minister.

Similarly in Burma the junta has consolidated its hold on politics in readiness for any return to civilian rule by building up its political base as well as by measures to limit protest. A youth movement has been created, the Union Solidarity and Development Association, whose members are required to swear allegiance to the junta and are then given special privileges and used to intimidate opposition groups. In 2003 another militia, the Swan Arr Shin (SAS) was formed to harass the opposition, including the notoriously violent attack on an NLD motorcade in May 2003 when 70 activists were beaten to death. The junta doubled the size of the armed forces between 1990 and 2003, all of whom enjoy subsidized housing, food and transportation. A quarter of a million poor urbanites have been dispersed from the centre of Rangoon to make political protest more difficult to mobilize. Opportunities for student protests have been minimized by splitting the University of Rangoon into three campuses miles from the centre with access routes easily controlled by the army. The military have also integrated themselves more strongly into the economy, especially with the formation in 1990 of the Union of Myanmar Economic Holdings, a company backed by the armed forces (and reputedly using forced labour on construction sites: Smith, 2002)

When military regimes hand power back to civilian politicians, it is often to people of their own choosing in a constitution of their own design. For example, in 2005 the Burmese junta convened a National Convention to write a new constitution. Representatives of the major pro-democracy organizations were excluded, enabling a constitution to be drafted which excluded the leader of the democratic opposition National League for Democracy, Aung San Suu Kyi, from electoral politics, reserved a quarter of the seats in both houses of parliament for the military, and required three-quarters of parliamentarians to support any amendment, enabling the military to veto any change it does not like. The president was empowered to transfer legislative, executive and judicial powers to the military if a 'sufficient reason' to declare a state of emergency was identified.

Military leaders, including those who have conspired in the past to stage a *coup*, have often turned themselves into politicians, creating new political parties, and competing for political office. Venezuela's President Chavaz, a ringleader of the first of two *coups* in 1992, is a case in point (Baburkin et al., 1999). Civilian politics in developing countries is often a veneer behind which lies military power that is ready to take full control.

The *coup d'état*

Most military *coups* fall into one of four categories (Huntington, 1968). First there is the governmental or *guardian coup* – for example, Pakistan in 1999. The military's role is one of guardianship in the sense that the new regime leaves the prevailing economic system intact, brings about little fundamental change in government policy, and bases its right to rule on the claim that its task is to provide a period of stability before handing power back to civilians. The leadership of the government is changed, but not the social or political structure. An 'arbitrator army' accepts the existing social order, creates no independent political organization, and expresses an intention to return to barracks once the civilian disputes are settled or an alternative and acceptable regime is established (Perlmutter, 1971).

The first Burmese coup in 1962 has many of the hallmarks of a guardian coup, following the promotion of Buddhism by the government as a state religion, separatist tensions and civil war. The Sudanese Islamic coup of 1989 was designed to prevent the signing of a peace treaty with the southern secessionists that would have allowed the Dinka and Nuer Christians and animists to be governed by secular rather than Sharia laws. The coup in Thailand in 2006 also falls into this category, with the military deposing the Prime Minister, suspending the Constitution, and dissolving parliament while accusing the government of corruption, electoral irregularities and human rights abuses (which the military junta proceeded to emulate).

The *veto coup* occurs when the military supplants a civilian government that is committed to radical social and economic reform that will be to the cost of the wealthier classes in society. Examples are Chile in 1973, and Haiti in 1991 when the army ousted President Aristide, Haiti's first democratically elected President who, because of his liberationist theology and reformist programme, was idolized by the poor and hated by the rich and their military allies.

A sub-set of the 'veto' *coup* is the *anticipatory veto*, when the military intervene to pre-empt power passing to a revolutionary or radical government as distinct from the overthrow of an existing progressive and reformist government. Ajub Khan's *coup* in Pakistan in 1958 may be seen as one to pre-empt the electoral success of a left-wing party (Woddis, 1977). Similarly in Algeria in 1991, when the Islamic Salvation Front, with a programme of social change, won twice as many votes as its nearest rival in the first of two ballots and the military cancelled the second round, appointed a 'High State Council', and embarked on repression of the fundamentalist movement.

Burma in 1990 is another example. Having placed leaders of the democratic opposition in detention or under house arrest, the junta held parliamentary elections. However, the National League for Democracy (NLD) still won 392 of the 485 seats. The junta annulled the results of the poll, despite a commitment in 1988 to recognize a new government formed by whichever party won the election. The junta, or State Law and Order Restoration Council (SLORC) as it was then known, decreed that the People's Assembly could only draft a new constitution to be approved in a referendum. SLORC also confirmed that it retained legislative, executive and judicial powers.

An anticipatory *coup* may even be encouraged by the incumbent civilian government if it fears it is about to lose power through the ballot box. In Zimbabwe the government party Zanu-PF indicated it would welcome military intervention if it lost the 2002 general election. In 2008 senior police and military officers warned the presidential electorate that they would not allow Robert Mugabe to be beaten. Opposition candidates were told that any victory on their part would not be recognized, amounting to what the Movement for Democratic Change (MDC) saw as a *coup* threat. The military's intrusion into the electoral process was mainly motivated by fear that an MDC government would not secure them immunity from prosecution for criminal acts and human rights abuses.

Finally, in a *reforming coup* the military seeks to change the social order and place state and society on a new ideological foundation. Three subtypes can be distinguished within the military intervention which rejects the existing order, challenges its legitimacy and creates its own political organization to legitimize and maximize military control over the state: (i) the anti-traditionalist, radical reformer (for example, Argentina, 1945–55); (ii) the anti-traditionalist, anti-radical reformer (for example, Nasser's Egypt); and (iii) the anti-traditional, republican reformer (for example, Turkey under Ataturk) (Perlmutter, 1971).

This does not mean that the political motives of a country's armed forces will necessary fall into one category only. In the 1980s the Venezuelan military contained adherents of the Bolivarian Revolutionary Movement, with radical ideological leaning and which staged a failed *coup* in 1992. It also contained a more moderate faction concerned with the corruption and incompetence of politicians, but without a radical or ideological agenda, which also attempted to lead a *coup* later in the same year (Baburkin et al., 1999). In 1999 the coup in Pakistan was prompted by economic and political crises at home, conflict with India abroad, and governmental corruption within the civilian regime, giving the military an excuse to intervene in the name of national stability, unity, integrity and sovereignty. But there was also an element of self-preservation in the military's motives, after the government attempted to alter the command structure of the armed forces in response to failures in the disputed area of Kashmir.

Social mobility and military intervention

One explanation of military intervention focuses on the destabilizing effects of social mobility. As societies become more open and fluid, people can use the opportunities provided by new economic activities and institutions to change their status in society. Wealth, education and skills confer status on groups that in traditional society had lacked such opportunities. Social mobilization is followed by political mobilization as the new socio-economic interests brought into existence as a result of modernization, particularly in the economy, seek effective means of expression within the political system. Such political mobilization will be encouraged by the democratic milieu and participative ethos of post-colonial society.

The social mobility following the spread of industrialization and its associated developments in education, urbanization, mass communications, and the commercialization of all sectors of economic life increases the rate of political participation and mobilization and places intolerable burdens of conflict management on civilian regimes. The division of society into more complex groups and structures has to be politically articulated through unions, voluntary associations, political parties, professional bodies, trade associations, industrial organizations and chambers of commerce. These are rarely sufficiently developed for the task. Political resources become spread over a larger number of actors than in traditional societies where a privileged minority has command of political decision-making. In modern society power becomes more dispersed, at least in principle if not in practice. Expectations of a more equal dispersal of power are aroused. This is reflected in the right to vote and to share in the selection of political leaders. Such participation needs institutions through which it can operate in a structured and ordered way. Procedures and organizations have to be created through which political demands can be expressed effectively and decisions can be made which will be regarded as legitimate and binding.

Processes of government represent the latter kind of organization. Parties and pressure groups represent the former, required for people to protect and promote their interests effectively.

The propensity for military intervention will be reduced, the more such institutionalization occurs (Huntington, 1968; Perlmutter, 1971). The higher the levels of social mobilization, the higher the levels of political participation. If this is accompanied by the development of organizations through which political participation can be channelled, the population will develop a commitment to their civilian institutions and regime. They will see them as an effective means of obtaining access to power and the resources that follow from it. The military will not find themselves in an environment conducive to their intervention, over and above that of a technical and professional élite in whose hands a major function of the state rests – that of national defence.

There is a related technological argument. Social mobility results from changes in the level of economic development. This not only increases the wealth and political significance of a wide range of groups with an interest in preserving civilian forms of government. It also increases the technological complexity of government and puts it beyond the grasp of the military.

One problem with this theory is that it is of too high a level of generality, trying to provide a framework that can encompass all instances of military intervention. As soon as one tries to apply it to specific countries, all sorts of exceptions and variations begin to appear (Dowse, 1969; Philip, 1984). The other is that social mobility might explain political instability, but not why the military is the only solution.

The hypothesis that rapid social change will lead to political violence and military intervention has received support from some comparative studies but not others. For example, Putnam found negligible correlations between military intervention in Latin America and political participation and the strength of parties and pressure groups. This led him to conclude that Huntington was mistaken in thinking that stable civilian rule depends on strong political institutions. He also found that countries sharing the same level of economic development were less prone to military intervention if more socially mobilized. If two countries are equal in their levels of social mobility and one has had more economic development, it will be more likely to experience a *coup* (Putnam, 1967).

Jackman carried out a similar type of analysis, using African data from 1960 to 1975, but came to rather different conclusions: notably that social mobilization did have a destabilizing effect and that political participation, when measured by electoral turnout, decreases the probability of *coups*, suggesting the conclusion that 'political mobilization in the form of higher levels of mass electoral participation may reflect a higher degree of acceptance of conventional non-violent processes of élite succession' (Jackman,

1978, p. 1274). Johnson et al. (1986) also found party competition, espe-cially between mass parties with nationwide rather than ethnic or regional support, to be strong protection against military intervention.

The military and the middle class

Social explanations of military intervention have sometimes had a class dimension. The more developed the indigenous middle class, the stronger the political foundation of civilian democracy. The middle class is seen by modernization theorists as a stabilizing force but one which in the early stages of development is 'small, weak, ineffective, divided and therefore politically impotent'. The economic and political interests of a fragmented middle class diverge, thereby encouraging 'praetorianism' or a potential for the military to dominate the political system (Perlmutter, 1971, p. 309).

The lack of alternatives to the military when social cohesion breaks down may be explained by reference to divisions within all sectors of soci-ety, including the middle class. Praetorianism occurs when the middle class is too weak to defend democratic civilian institutions. But it can equally happen when it is large, growing and more cohesive, as in Latin America where 'military intervention assures the middle class of power if and when they fail to come to power by electoral means' (Perlmutter, 1971, p. 309). This is consistent with Huntington's view that in societies that are too underdeveloped to have produced a middle class the military will be a radi-cal force (trying to abolish feudalism), but that when a middle class has developed, the military will side with it as a conservative force (Huntington, 1968; Jackman, 1986). Unfortunately, attempts to prove this quantitatively have failed, throwing serious doubt on the proposition that the effects of military government change systematically as countries become wealthier.

It might be assumed that a new middle class will have a vested interest in civilian government which represents their interests rather than those of the classes of the pre-industrial era. Putnam (1967) tested this hypothesis with data from Latin America and found that economic development was correlated with social mobility and moderately positively correlated with military intervention. Nevertheless, the development of a middle-class produced obstacles to military intervention.

An alternative interpretation of the significance of class development is to see it as a source of fragility in civilian institutions. The key development is not that there is a new middle class, but that there can be conflict between factions within the middle class particularly under conditions of depend-ency and underdevelopment. Such conflict has often preceded the *coups* that have been staged in the Third World. The very category of a 'guardian' *coup* reflects awareness of this possibility. This may be accounted for by the centrality of political power to the needs and interests of the middle class in less developed societies, when capital comes largely from state sources. If sections of the middle class feel disadvantaged by the operation of the political system, they may support its overthrow by a military that is allied to their interests.

If the political consensus and ideological foundation of the system are weak, as was often the case in the immediate post-independence period, when the remnants of pre-capitalist social relations such as forms of feudalism remained in rural areas, support for modern, democratic, civilian institutions can be fragile. The rules of politics are not firmly established in such a context. If one middle-class faction attempts to secure a permanent monopoly of power and therefore of the limited resources available for the generation of wealth, there is a strong temptation for other factions to resort to extra-constitutional means to gain power. This is the classic Bonapartist scenario where the pure form of bourgeois rule through liberal democratic institutions is impossible to sustain during crisis, and where other classes become increasingly difficult to manage and incorporate into the social order, again because of a weak ideological base.

The 'crisis of hegemony' in post-colonial societies to which a form of Bonapartism responds includes conflicts between tribes and regions as well as interests founded on pre-capitalist, capitalist and comprador class structures. Military intervention often represents a way of managing such conflict rather than a way of profoundly changing the power structure of society. In many instances *coups* just 'speed the circulation of élites and the realignment of factions of the ruling classes more often than they bring about fundamental change in the organization of state power and its allocation between (rather than within) social classes' (Luckham, 1991, p. 368).

However, Latin American experience suggests a number of reasons why the middle class might not feel that its interests are best served by military dictatorship. If it is fragmented, the military may deny political power to newly emerging factions of the bourgeoisie. Repression of the workers may reduce the profits derived from mass consumption and disrupt production. The state under the military may encroach upon the private sector. The intellectual element of the bourgeoisie may have a different ideological position from that of a military dictatorship. Bourgeois politicians resent being ousted from power, and foreign aid and investment may be dependent on showing a democratic face to the world (Therborn, 1979).

Military intervention is further related to class by providing opportunities for military embourgeoisement or upward social mobility on the part of the armed forces themselves. Take, for example, the 1971 *coup* in Uganda. One interpretation was that the *coup* reflected the interests of the army as a marginalized group subordinate to a post-independence élite based on

Westernized educational attainment and the use of English as a *lingua franca*. This excluded the armed forces from élite status because army personnel operated in the vernacular Swahili. The *coup* therefore provided an opportunity for social mobility of an uneducated *lumpen militariat*. Thus, without altering the class basis of political power, the *coup* produced a realignment of ruling groups and an opportunity for upward mobility for groups not prominent under the previous civilian regime because they were drawn from underprivileged sections of society or regions of the country that had not been a major source of political recruitment for leadership positions. Other examples from Africa would include the 'middle belt' tribes of Nigeria, and the northerners of Togo. Political power for a minority group, especially one with an ethnic identity, has often 'flowed from the barrel of a gun' (First, 1972, p. 435; Lloyd, 1973).

Embourgeoisement may take an even more literal form when the senior ranks of the military use their political power after a successful *coup* to enrich themselves with wealth and property. Members of the armed forces can rise from petty-bourgeois status, with social origins among rich peasants, technocrats, intellectuals, state bureaucracy, industrial management and small-scale private capitalists, into the new bourgeoisie through the accumulation of wealth from commissions, corruption, land acquisition and speculation, trade and rents (Woddis, 1977).

Economic development and military intervention

An economic explanation of military intervention argues that it is encouraged by a lack of economic development. When civilian governments are perceived as having failed to modernize the economy via industrialization, they run the risk of being ousted by frustrated sections of the modernizing élite that are out of office. Evidence to support this is offered by a study of military intervention in Sub-Saharan Africa between 1956 and 1984, which found that the lower the economic growth and level of industrial employment, the higher the incidence of military intervention in politics. However, as the authors recognize, causation is unlikely to run in one direction: the political instability caused by *coups* hinders economic development. 'We are left with the image of a vicious circle in which economic stagnation and decline lead to military interventions, which themselves in turn usually produce more economic uncertainty and stagnation' (McGowan and Johnson, 1984, p. 659).

Economic underdevelopment can work in other ways to encourage *coups*. Dependence on primary export products whose world prices can fluctuate wildly produces economic instability because a lack of a diversified economy means there are no alternative goods and services to offset those fluctuations. This is conducive to *coups*, because it produces problems which can be blamed on governments. When a very high proportion of tax revenues come from the export of a single commodity, the terms of trade have an immediate impact on the ability of a government to develop the economy and provide for the welfare of society. Government inevitably is the focus of attention when the value of the country's commodities falls in world markets. So in a country which has a high level of specialization because of the nature of its exports and a high level of dependence of its economy on those export revenues, the probability of a successful *coup* is increased (O'Kane, 1981).

There will always, however, be factors which will reduce the likelihood of a *coup*. Firstly there is the proximity of independence. *Coups* are more likely the longer a country is independent, giving governments time to demonstrate an inability to cope. Secondly, there is the experience of military intervention – what might be called internal contagion. Once a *coup* has occurred, there is likely to be another. A country with no experience of the *coup d'état* is less likely to have one than a country where one has already taken place. Here the military gain skills in domestic coercion, popular support for government is discouraged by experience under the military, and subsequent periods of civilian rule become increasing difficult to sustain. Thirdly, the presence of foreign troops is an obstacle. They would not be present with the approval of the domestic government in the first place if there was any chance of them being sympathetic to military take-over. Even though there is evidence of foreign powers encouraging rather than hindering *coups*, the presence of foreign troops invited in by the civilian government will deter interventions by the local military. The absence of these three conditions removes the obstacles to military supplantment and increases the probability of a *coup* (O'Kane, 1981).

A methodological problem here is to know how recent is 'recent'. Nigeria had 5 years of civilian government before it succumbed to its first military *coup*. It did not need long for civilian government to reveal its inability to cope with the tensions and conflicts of an underdeveloped economy and an ethnically divided society.

The political culture

The most influential political explanation of military intervention relates it to the level of the political culture. Finer (1962) classified political cultures as mature, developed, low and minimal in a descending scale of modernity. Each level is related to the propensity of the military to intervene, and to different kinds of military intervention. A mature political culture is one in which the military are an important force in defence policy-making, but

have no wider role ascribed to them by social values, attitudes and expectations. A sense of legitimacy supporting the civilian regime is widespread.
At the other end of the scale are found countries with 'minimal' political
cultures, where the legitimacy of civilian government is almost totally
lacking. Such countries are likely to experience the most extreme form of
military intervention, the *coup d'état*.

Low levels of political culture and a weak sense of political obligation
are found predominantly in the Third World. Here there is a lack of confidence that political demands will be heard, and a lack of trust in other
groups which might gain power. Because political values and beliefs do not
coincide with the presuppositions upon which the regime is built, there
may well be widespread popular support for direct military intervention.
The destruction of democracy and the rise of authoritarianism may be
tolerable in societies that do not feel that the form of civilian government
which they have is the best that could have been devised (Finer, 1962)

This sounds tautological. A low level of political culture is defined as a
lack of consensus. It is defined by reference to what it is supposed to
explain. Rather than offering an explanation of a lack of political consensus, the concept of political culture offers a statement that is true by definition. There is further circularity in the argument, in that military
intervention is taken to be evidence of a low political culture because it is
evidence of the breakdown of consensus. So, military intervention is being
explained by reference to conditions which are represented by that intervention itself. Insofar as there is explanatory value in the theory of political
culture, it is more about how civilian governments fail than why the military should be the inevitable successor. Furthermore, the theory does not
explain why *coups* occur in some states with minimal political cultures but
not others (First, 1972). The only solution to this problem is to make intervention itself an indicator of the level of political culture, but this makes the
explanation even more tautologous.

Organizational factors

Knowledge of why the military have usurped power in so many states may
depend more on observations of the military itself than the socio-economic
context in which Third World governments find themselves. There has
been a long-standing debate between the supporters of an 'environmental'
approach to military intervention, emphasizing the influence of social and
economic factors on the propensity for intervention, and the 'organization-
alists' (Charlton, 1981). The organizational characteristics of the military
may be crucial to understanding military intervention, especially when the
socio-economic conditions of different countries, such as India and

Pakistan, look similar, yet their experience of military intervention has been so markedly different.

The military appears to have many political advantages over other organizations involved in politics. It has a clear chain of command, with a well-understood and rigorously observed set of superior–subordinate relationships. Decisions are obeyed, not debated until some consensus is reached. The military is well-organized for striking at civilian institutions. When the military intervenes, the leadership of the *coup* is often drawn not from the top-ranking officers but from the middle echelons of younger officers, perhaps because their senior officers are too closely associated with the civilian regime; or because that particular stratum of the officer corps is drawn from an ethnic group that feels disadvantaged by the way political power is being used. However, even if the decision to stage a *coup* is not taken by the most senior ranking officers, those who do lead the overthrow have at their disposal an organization that is likely to respond to their commands.

However, the organizational unity of the military in the Third World should not be exaggerated. It is often riven with factions based on age, education, rank, religion or tribe, reflecting divisions within the wider political community (Charlton, 1981). For example, in October 2001 Pakistan's military ruler, General Musharraf, felt it necessary to dismiss two of his most senior generals, regarded as hard line Islamists and leaders of a faction opposed to the President's pro-American policies. The military needs to be viewed as thoroughly integrated into society in this respect and not as a self-contained entity. It is also worth noting that when Putnam tried to test the importance of variations in organizational characteristics to the propensity for intervention, using Latin American data – a difficult feat given the availability of 'only a few gross characteristics of the armed forces' – he found a negative correlation between the size of the military establishment and the extent of military intervention. Of course, as with all such quantitative analysis, it is easy to reject the indicator used on the grounds that it is an unreliable proxy for the variable under investigation (Putnam, 1967, p. 110–11). However, a study of politics in 35 Black African states between 1960 and 1982 found that military 'cohesion' (a large and ethnically homogeneous armed forces) and political 'centrality' (its role in repression against the government's opponents and its share of public expenditure) to be positively related to military intervention, leading them to recommend strongly 'that variables specific to African military establishments must be considered in any search for the structural determinants of military intervention in African politics' (Johnson et al., 1986, p. 634).

The military also have a symbolic status which endows them with legitimacy should they intervene in the world of civilian politics. Without articulating this as part of a corporate philosophy or belief system, the military may symbolize something valuable to the rest of society. They may represent modernity because of their technological expertise, structures of authority and training. Symbolic status can also derive from successful performance. Shortly before the first military coup In Nigeria in 1966 the army had been involved in a UN peacekeeping force in the Congo in which it acquitted itself well, gained an international reputation for being well-disciplined and effective, and so brought credit to the country internationally.

The apparent modernity of the military, according to some developmentalists, is a major reason why the military is an obvious alternative to a democratic government that has failed to function effectively. Their rational structures, capable of relating means to ends and associated with rapid technological development and specialist skills, enable them to be viewed as 'possible saviours' where there is 'a sense of failure in the country' (Pye, 1971, pp. 278–83). However, as Mazrui has argued, though the military may be a modern organization in structural terms, in Africa, where soldiers are frequently recruited from the rural and less Westernized areas 'the attitudes of the soldiers to the wider society is probably more deeply conditioned by traditionalist sympathies than by the modern characteristics of a particular profession . . . the military as an organisation might in part be a carrier of scientificity, while the soldiers remain carriers of more primordial habits' (Mazrui, 1976, p. 251–2). Consequently the military, in Africa at least, may play a traditionalizing role.

The availability of modern weapons is clearly an organizational asset to the military, providing it with a near-monopoly of physical force. If the civilian regime lacks military support, but the idea of a military government lacks legitimacy, then the deciding factor will be the deployment of coercion. Communications too are vital in this kind of political intervention, particularly in a large country with many administrative centres. The military's communications system enables them to strike at different centres of government simultaneously and to co-ordinate their activities in the immediate disorderly aftermath of the *coup*. Such organizational advantages offset the political weaknesses of the military such as its lack of legitimacy and administrative expertise.

The professional culture of the military may be related to the intervention in politics. Professionalism can mean that the code of conduct within the military, into which recruits are trained and socialized, supports the supremacy of the civilian government. The professional soldier's duty is to obey the directives of the properly constituted civil authorities (Rapaport, 1962). Professionalism is made up from expertise, social responsibility and corporate loyalty. The more professional in this sense the military is, the more 'politically sterile and neutral' it will be (Huntington, 1957, p. 84).

However, military professionalism in some cultures can mean something quite different: that the army sees itself as having a duty to defend the state against forces that would undermine its integrity, even though such forces might be the civilian politicians (Finer, 1962). If the politicians appear to be weakening the nation and making it vulnerable to external forces, economic as well as military, the army might give priority to the defence of society's basic values. The military is then not a neutral instrument of the government of the day, but rather an instrument of the nation, whose interest is capable of interpretation by the military itself. If the military contains within its corporate culture such a set of attitudes, it might provide sufficient justification for direct intervention in politics, especially since there will almost certainly be sections within civil society that will approve of the military taking such responsibility. Military involvement in politics may have a powerful ideological foundation such as nationalism, *dirigism*, a moral code and 'a deep distrust of organized civilian politics' (Janowitz, 1970, p. 145).

Two myths underpin the military's acceptance of responsibility for the nation's core values, the integrity of the state and political order. One is that without the military the nation would not have been formed or survived. The other is the belief that the military are more competent at managing affairs than civilian politicians (Koonings and Kruijt, 2002). Neither claim is supportable as a general proposition, though there have been occasions when the military has played a major role in creating a new state, such as in the struggle against colonialism. But the latter claim is rarely defensible. Many military regimes have proved as corrupt and incompetent as their predecessors. Burma, for instance, was by 1987 transformed by the military junta from a prosperous economy to one of the world's poorest, such that the government had to apply to the UN for the status of a Least Developed Nation.

Foreign influence

Finally, external involvement by a foreign power has sometimes been crucial in the decision of the military to stage a *coup d'état*. For example, the USA supported the Chilean military in overthrowing the Allende regime. The USA also played a role in the failed *coup* against President Chavez of Venezuela in April 2001.

Continuity of links with developed countries through military aid, training and equipment has also strengthened national armies in the Third World relative to the civilian authorities. The influence of foreign support, through clandestine military, security and intelligence agencies such as the USA's CIA, has been critical in a number of Third World *coups*. Through 'covert operations' involving political advice, subsidies to political organizations and individuals, propaganda, training, economic interventions, paramilitary support to domestic groups, and infiltration and co-option of local agents and allies in trade unions, corporations, political parties, the media and the military itself, foreign influence has penetrated deeply into Third World societies (Woddis, 1977).

In recent years, with most Western governments supporting democratiza tion in the Third World (and Eastern Europe), foreign influence has tended to be exerted to stave off the *coup d'état*, and leading Western powers have made it clear they will not recognize or deal with a military regime, to the extent that 'restraining factors would appear to have been responsible for drastically diminishing the incidence and effect of military intervention over the past decade' (Danapoulos and Zirker, 2006). Coup attempts in Guatemala, Paraguay and Ecuador have been foiled in this way. France has supported civilian governments thwarting military intervention in Cameroon, Côte d'Ivoire, Gabon and Senegal. In 2008 the American government warned the Thai military to respect civilian rule and refrain from intervening in politics during a period of anti-government protests. However, it is always possible that the USA will feel that security concerns make authoritarianism accept- able, as in the case of America's support for the recent military regime in Pakistan which was committed to restraining Islamic terrorism.

Alternatively, foreign influence has been defined in terms of 'contagion' (First, 1972). There have been times when it appeared as if some states experienced *coups* because neighbouring states had shown how easily it could be done, and what advantages accrued to the armed forces as a result. There is some evidence from West Africa that military commanders did 'learn' from the experience of their counterparts in other countries how to take power, and about the financial attractions of it, lessons which entered into their calculations about whether and when to intervene. However, this argument cannot be taken too far in general explanatory terms, since the logic of it would be that there would be no end to military intervention as it spread like wildfire from one state to another. Neither Putnam for Latin America nor Wells for Africa found empirical evidence to confirm the contagion hypothesis (Putnam, 1967; Wells, 1974). There are clearly effec- tive barriers to contagion.

External influences also include the international context in which domestic conflict and insecurity occur. When Third World countries were at the periphery of the Cold War or at the centre of regional conflicts, the strength and significance of the armed forces, concerned with both national security and national pride, were enhanced and their motivation to inter- vene strengthened (Luckham, 1991).

The military and democratization

A major concern during democratization, especially after a period of mili- tary rule, is how to ensure that the military remain loyal to civilian political leadership. Experience of democratic transitions suggest a number of hypotheses about the conditions necessary to restrict the power of the military during the consolidation of democracy in order to establish civil–military relations consistent with democratic government.

Firstly, it is necessary to demobilize the military and reintegrate those not needed by a professional army into society. This is particularly important when armed insurgency has been part of the transition to democracy, as in Zimbabwe, South Africa and Mozambique (Griffiths, 1996). The challenge here is starkly revealed by the case of Afghanistan where some 700,000 people are estimated to be armed, when a standing army needs about 200,000 and when most militias owe allegiance to tribal warlords rather than the state. Integrating rebel militias into the country's armed forces is one way to bring them under government control, as well as providing employment to a potentially volatile group. A combination of integration into the military with alternative opportunities for civil employment can be successful, as in Mali, where demobilization in 1996 at the end of the civil war between Taureg separatists. The government was assisted by a United Nations trust fund enabling 7,000 Taureg rebels to be incorporated into the regular army and other government bodies.

Secondly, civilian political control over the military must be institutionalized by organizational changes. Professionalism in the armed forces has to be strengthened by improvements to the management of military establishments, and changes in senior military personnel. Privileges which are not appropriate for a military which is subordinate to civilian control may need to be removed, such as special banks, welfare systems and economic organizations.

Political mechanisms which hold the military accountable to civil control and establish civilian control of defence policy need to be made more effective, such as by strengthening parliamentary supervision, ensuring civilian control of defence ministries, and giving legislatures authority to control defence spending and endorse senior appointments in all the security services. The military has also to be brought under the Rule of Law. An imbalance between civilian and military institutions, which in Latin America 'contributes to military perceptions that they are better organized, better trained, more cohesive and more patriotic than civilian political leaders' has to be corrected (Fitch, 1998, p. 159). The right incentives to induce the military to accept subordination to civilian leadership have to be chosen. Military attitudes have to be reoriented away from a guardian role and towards loyalty to civilian political leaders. Any duplication of roles between the military and civilian politicians must be minimized, for example by ending the military's role in internal security, environmental protection, development projects, and the war against narcotics trafficking (though the earthquake in the Sichuan province of

China in 2008 showed how indispensible the military can be in relief work following a disaster). The military leadership must be restricted to an advisory role in defence policy. Equally, political leaders have to agree not to draw the armed forces into conflict resolution and recognize that military leaders have a legitimate role in defence policy-making. Politicians need to be able to communicate on equal terms with the military on defence matters and demands for military expenditure, a capacity that has been conspicuously lacking among legislators in developing countries (Frazer, 1995; Huntington, 1995, pp. 9–10; Fitch, 1998; Bland, 1999; de Kadt, 2002).

Thirdly, keeping the military under civilian control requires extensive public support for democracy and hostility to military rule, perhaps fuelled by recollections of past authoritarianism, as in Venezuela in 1992 (Baburkin et al., 1999). Unfortunately not all sections of society are hostile to military intervention. Many sections of the middle class in Chile supported the 1973 coup, feeling that their privileges were threatened by the Allende regime. There is no guarantee that during the consolidation of democracy such support for the military will not resurface. Support for the military may come from technocrats in the bureaucracy, who have been closely associated with military governments in Latin America; and political parties which originated as offshoots of the army, as in Eritrea and Ethiopia (de Kadt, 2002; Koonings and Kruijt, 2002).

Comparison of different levels of military intervention in liberalizing African states since 1990 suggests strongly that intervention is less likely, the stronger the democratic legitimacy of the civilian regime in the minds of the public. Economic or political crises may prompt military intervention even when successful elections and peaceful transitions from one government to another make it appear as if democracy is being consolidated. But in general 'liberalizing states which enjoy relatively high levels of public legitimacy do not experience military interventions' (Clark, 2007, p. 149). Regional alliances supporting civilian political supremacy can also help, as in southern Africa in 1994 when South Africa, Botswana and Zimbabwe helped reverse the *coup* in Lesotho (Frazer, 1995). The Brazilian case also supports the theory that removing social support from a politicized military is necessary for the consolidation of democracy. In Brazil 'the military never made any political move without the support of important social groups' (Castron, 2002, p. 108), so a broadening of support for democratic politics, and a decline in civilian social support for military intervention, reduce the risk of a *coup d'état*.

The timing of reforms to civil–military relations is also important. Movement towards reform should start in the transition to democracy when negotiations are being conducted between officials and political leaders who are committed to change. This will go some way towards guarding against the new regime acquiring an inheritance of disloyal and disaffected military personnel (Frazer, 1995).

The extent to which the conditions for reform are achievable is affected by a number of factors. Past patterns of civil–military relations (e.g. the extent to which the armed forces have been politicized or a lively civil society allowed to exist), and threats posed by democratization to the sectional interests of the military (e.g. the scale of cuts to the military budget proposed by the new civilian government) will be important. Popular support for democracy may be fragile and political parties that have not created a disillusioned populace needed. There may need to be 'ethnic balance' in the social composition of the armed forces, though there may be costs if ethnic representation means foregoing the benefits of recruitment solely on merit: there are risks in turning the military into an equal opportunities institution (Fayemi, 2002). The effect of military reorganization during democratization on the policy goals of the new government, such as whether the military is assisting in the control of drug trafficking, may also be important for the establishment of democratic civil–military relations (Griffiths, 1996). It is not easy to find new missions for the military which do not undermine their professionalism and exclusion from politics, such as UN peacekeeping rather than combating crime.

The new civilian regime may have to compromise on demands for military leaders to be brought to justice for their crimes (Rouquie, 1986). The military will continue to have much political influence, especially if during the transition it has been able to negotiate immunity from prosecution for human rights violations (Fitch, 1998). Equally, removing immunity may prompt an adverse reaction from the military. Hence the concern in Argentina in 2001 when the courts struck down as unconstitutional the immunity laws which had protected military officers from prosecution for human rights abuses during the military regime of 1976 to 1983. The immunity laws had been passed after Argentina's return to democracy in 1983 was followed by uprisings by military officers who feared prosecution under the new democratic regime. While welcomed by human rights groups, the annulments were recognized as a potential threat at a time when the economy was in crisis. Nevertheless in 2005 the Supreme Court confirmed the ruling which had already been upheld by the federal Court of Buenos Aires in 2001.

Political developments confronting the new civilian government will also be significant. Of particular importance are factors which distract governments from the reform of civil–military relations, such as hyperinflation and other economic crises which undermine public confidence in the civilian authorities. Excluding the military from civilian governmental roles may be made difficult by confrontations with revolutionary movements and/or organized crime (as in Colombia) that make it difficult to avoid using the military in policing activities.

There has nevertheless been some success in newly democratizing countries in reforming civil–military relations. Norms of military professionalism and civilian control have become more widely diffused and accepted. Military leaders have learned that attempts to govern have been destructive for the armed forces. Civilian politicians recognize that their interests lie in a professionalized, a-political military. Popular support for an end to excessive military budgets, abuses of human rights and military involvement in economic enterprises has grown. *Coup* attempts might occur, but are less likely to be successful in newly democratized countries with a reasonable level of economic development. Huntington was even prepared to specify the cut-off points: 'Countries with per capita GNPs of $1,000 or more do not have successful *coups*; countries with per capita GNPs of $3,000 or more do not have *coup* attempts' (1995, p. 15).

Conclusion

Many of the factors associated with military intervention, particularly social and economic variables, have also figured in attempts to understand the context of political instability within which military *coups* may occur. Military intervention is by no means the only form of political instability. Communal violence, separatist movements and ethnic conflicts can escalate into civil war and create prolonged instability. This more general and widespread picture of instability is the subject of a later chapter. The present chapter has identified the circumstances surrounding military interventions in Third World politics in order to explore how successful explanations of the phenomenon have been. An understanding of military intervention is particularly important when it undermines democracy either by the *coup d'état* or by refusing to reinstate democratic politics in response to widespread popular demand. There are implications for public policies and governmental strategies if it can be shown that the propensity for military intervention is related to the level of political institutionalization, economic development, political participation, economic specialization, the development of mass political parties, the centrality of the state in the process of capital accumulation and the development of a middle class, or the professional culture of the military itself.

8

Nationalism and the Politics of Secession

Introduction

In most regions of the Third World there are political movements campaigning, in many cases through armed struggle, for political self-determination on behalf of minority groups. In the Western Sahara, Polisario fights for liberation from Morocco. In Western Somalia the Liberation Front aims to restore the Ethiopian Ogaden to Somalia. The Kurds of Turkey, Iran, Iraq and Syria seek an independent and united Kurdistan. The National Resistance Council in Iran aims to establish an autonomous Baluchistan. In India there are movements for autonomy among the Sikhs, Nagas, Mizos and Tripuras as well as in Kashmir. The Shanti Bahini of Bangladesh seek autonomy for the Chittagong tribes. In Burma the programme of the Federal National Democratic Front includes a federal union based on self-determination for the Shan, Karen, Mon, Arakan and Kachin peoples. The Karen National Union has been fighting for independence since 1948. The Tamil minority in Sri Lanka have been engaged in a civil war since 1983 with the objective of forming a separate state in the north of the island. Indonesia has movements struggling for independence in West Papua and Acheh. In the Philippines the Moro National Liberation Front seeks independence of the Muslim Moros in the south. There has been a strong ethnic revival since 1960 and a corresponding growth of interest among social scientists (Brown, 1989).

Such organizations should be distinguished from revolutionary movements seeking to overthrow the incumbent regime. Secessionist movements do not want to overthrow national governments: they want to withdraw from their jurisdiction. This, from the perspective of the centre, may appear very revolutionary; and the movement itself may have a revolutionary agenda in addition to independence, though this is not inevitable. Only in Latin America are revolutionary movements almost exclusively concerned with a different kind of independence – that of a whole country from repression by an authoritarian regime. Separatism in Latin America is largely an aspect of nineteenth-century history (Anderson et al., 1974).

Few secessionist movements are likely to be successful in achieving full independence for the people they represent, but it is unlikely that they will give up the struggle and disband. They may, however, be crushed by the superior military might of the national government – as in Nigeria, Zaire and the Sudan. Occasionally, however, a separatist movement succeeds, as in the case of the violent separation of East Pakistan to form the state of Bangladesh, the secession of Somaliland from Somalia in 1991, the secession of Eritrea from Ethiopia in 1993, and East Timor's independence from Indonesia celebrated in 2002. Military conflict often marks the passage from integration to autonomy, as with the birth of Bangladesh.

This chapter examines the demand for independence on the part of ethnic or national minorities. Three theories of separatism are examined: political integration, internal colonialism and 'balance of advantage'. It is suggested that explanations of nationalism and secession need a class dimension because of the social stratification found within cultural minorities, the petty-bourgeois leadership of ethnic secessionist movements, and the significance for the outcome of nationalism of the reaction of the dominant class in the 'core' community to nationalist political mobilization.

The political movements fighting for separation often do so in the name of nationalism. Their aim is secession, though other organizations and factions may be prepared to negotiate for less than full separation. Before examining the causes of ethnic separatism, the main aim of this chapter, it is necessary to clarify some of the terms that are central to the analysis.

Secession

'Secession' may be defined as the formal separation of a region from a nation-state of which it formerly constituted an integral part. The region may already have experienced considerable decentralization of power. Secession, however, is not further decentralization but complete separation so that the breakaway region becomes a state in its own right, with its own constitution and recognized as such in international law. Normally secessionist movements aim at autonomy rather than integration with a neighbouring country. Such autonomy does not necessarily mean that all political and economic links with the 'parent' state will be severed. Economic relationships are particularly likely to persist, especially in the form of trade.

The central authorities of the parent state may attempt to contain secessionist tendencies by offering various concessions, such as constitutional autonomy which stops well short of separation (Brass, 1991). There is some evidence that a measure of devolution or federalism, rather than encouraging secession by increasing the resources and identity of regional minorities, actually reduces separatist demands by increasing the power of moderate nationalist leaders. The case of Bougainville in Papua New Guinea supports the view that democratic provincial devolution based on effective and accountable provincial government, strengthens relations with the state, and resolves grievances, preventing rather than promoting secession (Ghai, 2000). In the Tamil area of India, Tamil nationalism abandoned separatist demands after Tamil nationalist political parties gained representation in the federal parliament. Tamil nationalism now only seeks 'adequate representation in power-sharing and maintenance of cultural identity' (Oommen, 2006, p. 445). By making concessions to ethnic minorities Thailand has been able to de-radicalize Malay-Muslim separatism (Brown, 2006).

National governments may be assisted in their negotiation of a compromise by nationalist factions that are prepared to accept less than complete political independence. Surveys of political attitudes mainly, it has to be admitted, in developed countries, have revealed that significant numbers and often majorities within the ethnic groups concerned are prepared to accept constitutional autonomy rather than separation for their country – a finding that almost certainly applies to developing countries. However, surveys also show that even among those who do not favour separation and who reject violence as a means to that end, there are many who sympathize with those engaged in violent resistance – explaining 'how guerrilla struggles have been maintained for years in the face of overwhelming odds' (Connor, 1988, p. 216).

The demands of separatist movements may be significantly modified over a period of time, so that national independence is displaced by lesser objectives, such as the creation of a new territorial unit within a federation, official recognition of a language and symbolic distinctions. Equally, modest demands can escalate under pressure of events, such as East Pakistan's progression from linguistic equality to autonomy in a loose federation and from there to secession (Wright, 1976). Different ethnic groups vary in their demands. In South Asia, for example, some have demanded reforms within existing state structures, such as affirmative action policies. Others have called for the restructuring of the regime, including devolution and provincial autonomy. Still others agitate for the restructuring of the state through secession and irredentist change (Phadnis and Ganguly, 2001). In Palestine the nationalist movement is divided between those who support the creation of a sovereign state consisting of the occupied territories, and those wishing to transform Israel from a Jewish state to a democracy for all its citizens, regardless of religion and ethnicity. But the ultimate goal of secessionists is the creation of a new nation-state (Farsoun and Aruri, 2006). Decentralization is unlikely to provide a lasting solution if there is widespread support within the affected region for the secessionist cause, and there is likely to be widespread support if the secessionist movement is founded on a sense of nationalism within the aspirant state.

Responses to secession

Ethnic demands are partly a function of the state's orientation to them, such as the imposition of 'nationality' under the Ethiopian constitution (Ghai, 2000). Though the Bengalis of East Pakistan had long been conscious of their cultural distinctiveness, and had found it necessary to assert this from time to time in the face of assimilationist policies (notably the one-language issue of 1950–52), it was not until their gains through the democratic process had been vetoed by the central authorities that they were driven towards secession. Until then their programme had been for reforms within the state of Pakistan (such as the Six Point Programme which called for a confederal constitution, fiscal devolution, and separate trading and commercial relations with foreign countries). Secessionist demands were precipitated more by the intransigence of the central authorities than by spontaneous articulation.

Responses to nationalism and separatism have ranged from genocide to expulsion, assimilation, language policies, quotas in political and bureaucratic élites, revenue allocation formulae, positive discrimination, cultural autonomy and political decentralization (Coakley, 1993). In South Asia, governmental responses to secessionist movements have included military action, police restrictions, constitutional obstacles, electoral manipulation, economic subsidies, policy concessions (such as job quotas, the co-option of separatist leaders and language rights), constitutional accommodation and, in principle only, the granting of autonomy (Wright, 1976; Phadnis and Ganguly, 2001).

Repression is always part of the state's response to separatism, often accompanied by attempts at forced assimilation and the suppression of language and culture, as in Sudan's attempt to Arabize and Islamize the Africans of southern Sudan and Darfur (Neuberger, 2006). An alternative strategy is to dilute the dominant ethnic group, as in Tibet, where the Chinese government has encouraged the mass immigration of Han Chinese while dispersing ethnic Tibetans to other parts of China. According to the Tibetan government in exile, this has made Tibetans a minority in their own homeland (and accounts for the violence against Han Chinese in Lhasa in March 2008), though official census data show Tibetans making up over 90 per cent of the population of the Tibetan Autonomous Region (Misra, 2000).

It is unusual for national governments to approve the breaking away from the nation-state of a distinctive region, especially if part of that region's distinctiveness is its endowment with valuable natural or other economic resources. Demands for independence are revolutionary from the perspective of the centre (Connor, 1973; Clay, 1989) and history teaches us that 'attempts at secession are generally seen by governmental leaders as a threat to the authority of their regime which is so intolerable that it is worth spilling blood to prevent it' (Birch, 1978, p. 340). In South East Asia, for instance, responses to separatism prove conclusively that 'the nation-state clings above all to territory' (McVey, 1984, p. 13). In 1994 Morocco's King Hassan threatened a return to war if the people of the Western Sahara voted for independence in any referendum which the UN might organize. The people of East Timor suffered hugely at the hands of the Indonesian military and local militias allied to it when they attempted (successfully in the end) to secede. Since 2003 the Sudanese government has used its own armed forces, security and intelligence services, and an unofficial militia known as 'Janjaweed', mobilized by members of the ruling party, former military officers and leaders of nomadic tribes, to commit 'crimes against humanity and war crimes on a massive scale' against insurgents in Darfur. The 'ethnic cleansing' of Sudan's western region has entailed air strikes against civilians, summary executions, rape, torture, and the destruction of property, bringing about a collapsed economy and the loss of over 3 million livelihoods (HRW, 2005, p. 1). Ethiopia's response to the rebellion by ethnic Somalis in the Ogaden currently includes extra-judicial killings, rape, torture, forced migration, the destruction of villages, public executions and the slaughter of livestock (HRW, 2008). The Burmese army takes the view that if Karen fighters are in a locality then its civilians can be killed and villages burnt. Hostility to secession is particularly strong among African governments, where arbitrary colonial boundaries have fuelled disaffection on the part of minority groups. Hence the involvement of Tanzania and Sudan, both facing secessionist demands, in the African Union's military action against the Anjouan separatists of the Comoros federation:

> the fact is that during the last three decades it has been far easier for a country to achieve formal independence from ex-colonial power than for a minority to obtain a measure of (effective) autonomy within a Third World state. The reaction of demands of every kind has been almost universally negative. (Chaliand, 1980, p. 9)

Nationalism

Nationalism, which may extract concessions in the form of political decentralization of various kinds, including federalism, has become increasingly widespread in recent decades. It has been argued that it, rather than ideology built on class, was 'the dominant political passion' of the second half of the twentieth century (Payne, 1975, p. 249), though it may now have been overtaken by religion.

Nationalism presupposes some cultural distinctiveness on the part of the inhabitants of a particular region. Nationalism in the context of colonialism is a relatively straightforward concept, but nationalism among minorities indicates cultural identity and uniqueness, often strengthened by linguistic distinctiveness, that unites a particular population and which may inspire a nationalist movement. Crucial to this sense of identity and the demand for autonomy to which it can lead is a belief that the group once enjoyed self-government. Tibet is a case in point.

Although the Chinese government claims Tibet is an integral part of China, and just one of its Autonomous Regions, Tibetans claim that they have always been an independent nation, despite periods of Chinese intervention, until China's invasion in 1950 which reduced them to the status of a colony (Government of Tibet in Exile, 1996). Tibet for them extends beyond the Tibetan Autonomous Region to include neighbouring provinces with Tibetan populations. The historical relationships between Tibet and Mongul, Manchu and Chinese rulers, upon which China bases its claim are, in the eyes of Tibetan separatists, not just part of distant history and irrelevant to the current situation; they did not imply integration of the Tibetan state into the Chinese state. According to the International Commission of Jurists, Tibet between 1913 and 1950 exhibited the conditions for statehood normally demanded by international law. Although no country has recognized Tibetan sovereignty, the Tibetans claim that recognition has been implicit in the actions of foreign countries, such as maintaining diplomatic missions, referring to Tibet in international debates (for example, at the UN) as an independent country illegally occupied by China, and recognizing the Tibetan people's right to self-determination (for example, by the UN in 1961 and a conference of international lawyers in 1993).

What constitutes a 'nation', which may seek the status of a nation-state, is a question that has occupied the minds of political theorists for many decades. One view is that ethnic groups simply become nations when they develop ideas about obtaining political self-determination (Phadnis and Ganguly, 2001). But generally it is thought that a sense of nationhood will be based on some combination of religion, language, customs, institutions, mythology, folklore, culture, history and race, though it should not be assumed that each type of identity will have the same effect on political behaviour (Connor, 1988; Clay, 1989; Kellas, 1991). None, however, is sufficient in itself to define a nation, not even language (Smith, 1971). Economic and political features may also be considered necessary conditions of nationhood, in addition to cultural factors and group sentiment. A homeland territory and sense of collective history are also bases for national solidarity (Hechter, 2000). Smith lists the following seven features of a nation, and distinguishes 'tribes' and ethnic groups as having some but not all of these:

- cultural differentiae;
- territorial contiguity with internal mobility;
- a relatively large population;
- external political relations;
- considerable group sentiment and loyalty;
- direct membership with equal citizenship rights; and
- vertical economic integration around a common system of labour.

Tribes have only the first and second characteristics. 'Ethnie' have the first five. Nations have all seven. Some post-colonial societies are collections of tribes and/or ethnie and therefore lack at least two of the seven features – cultural differentiae and group sentiment – because of the arbitrary nature of colonial boundaries (Smith, 1971, pp. 186–90, 2001). Groups supporting secessionist movements, though usually having a sense of cultural identity, are not universally distinct ethnically. Secessionist groups may be ethnically heterogeneous. Nationhood may be claimed, but whether this is justified raises many problems of subjective and objective definition (Symmons-Symonolewicz, 1965; Rustow, 1967; Snyder, 1976; Wood, 1981). The subjectivity is captured in the following definition of 'nation':

> a relatively large group of people who feel that they belong together by virtue of sharing one or many such traits as common language, religion or race, common history or tradition, common set of customs, and common destiny. As a matter of empirical observation, none of these traits may actually exist: the important point is that people believe they do. (Rejai and Enloe, 1969, p. 143)

A subjective belief that people constitute a nation that deserves political recognition is more important than the objective definitions of historians and social scientists (Eriksen, 1993).

Secessionist alienation arises from a perception of special bonds between people which distinguish them from other communities within the nation-state (Enloe, 1973). In South Asia, 'the sociological characteristics of the various provincial populations are at the heart of their demands for autonomy or secession. All of the movements have asserted the primacy of particular criteria of identification which render the populations minorities in the country as a whole even if majorities locally' (Wright, 1976, p. 8). In Kashmir and Nagaland the principal factor is religion, in Tamil Nadu, East

Bengal and Baluchistan, it is language. South Asian societies and cultures lend support to the belief that territory and language are key to a sense of nationhood, whereas in Xinjiang, a predominantly Moslem region in north-west China, religion is the basis of separatist agitation. Since 1990 separatism has increased, with religious and ethnic consciousness 'very closely linked . . . dedication to Islam is part and parcel of being Uygur' (the largest indigenous ethnic group in the region: Mackerass, 2001, p. 296).

The ethnic foundation for nationalism is important not only because it provides a criterion for defining a nation, but also because it is central to the debate about what causes separatism, and whether ethnicity is a sufficient or necessary condition for the existence of demands for political autonomy. The *primordialist* theory of nationalism sees nations as organic ethnic communities with distinct languages, cultures, physiognomies and home-lands. Nationalism occurs when such communities demand self-determination from a 'polyethnic' state. This view of nationalism is backed by the fact that 'ethnicity remains a powerful, explosive and often durable force', generating strong feeling of belonging, obligation and dignity. Its persistence in advanced industrial democracies shows it is not eroded by the forces of modernization (Smith, 1995, pp. 33–47). But it is equally clear that it would be wrong to think of ethnic attachments as unchanging in relation to political action. They are subject to economic and social changes, especially urbanization, industrialization and the spread of education, which may alter perceptions of the relationships between minority and majority (Ozkirimli, 2000).

In contrast, the *situationalist* theory of nationalism sees claims to nationhood as based on a sense of common interest and self-preservation among people confronted by a threat to their well-being from uneven economic development, 'internal colonialism' and other forms of discrimination. Ethnic characteristics become important in defining group identity when the circumstances (or situation) make it rational to act defensively. Activists are needed to mobilize ethnic consciousness as a basis for interest articulation.

Constructivist theory sees nationalism as an ideology wielded by political élites to legitimize their demands for power. Nationalist ideology consists of myths about community ancestry, history, culture and homeland to provide people with a sense of identity, an understanding of contemporary problems, and prescriptions for their solution (Brown, 2000).

These interpretations underpin some of the explanations that have been offered for political secession as a destabilizing force in Third World states. Unfortunately, any attempt to find a simple causal explanation of nationalism and separatism is probably doomed to failure by the sheer diversity of the phenomenon. The history of nationalism reveals wide differences in the size, cohesiveness and mobilization of ethnic communities, in the goals of nationalist movements, in the threats that they pose to existing states, in the economic contexts in which ethno-nationalism is found, and in the political methods chosen by nationalist movements (Zubaida, 1978; Kellas, 1991). An exhaustive review of the literature on nationalism in the Third World is well beyond the scope of this chapter. All that can be attempted is a critical look at the theoretical perspectives which seem to be of greatest value for understanding why part of a country might seek to break away.

Political integration

The theory of political integration attaches great weight to ethnicity in explaining separatism. In the Third World context this emphasizes the fact that new states were frequently the arbitrary creations of colonialism. They consisted of a multiplicity of ethnic groups bound together under colonial domination and a common administrative and economic system, after the European powers had divided their tropical dependencies among themselves with scant regard to existing social and political boundaries. Differences of caste, region and ethnicity were further exacerbated by the representation of these incorporated societies in racial and tribal categories, and by the unequal impact of colonial educational, economic and political experiments (Nafziger and Richter, 1976). The nationalism which subsequently drew such communities together was based solely on opposition to subjugation by an alien power. They were united (and often far from completely) only in their desire to throw off colonial domination. The state created by the achievement of independence 'preceded' nationalism, in that there was no other common identity than anti-colonialism. The nation-state was not built on a basis of common religious, cultural, linguistic or racial factors as it is when nationalism precedes the state (Kohn, 1945; Coleman, 1954).

If cultural pluralism and sub-national loyalties are not eroded by a diffusion of cultural values during the process of modernization separatist tendencies will develop. A 'crisis of integration' is therefore likely to occur after independence unless a sense of territorial nationality can be created by unifying independent social, cultural and political entities. National integration is at risk not only when a minority is threatened by a single numerically and politically dominant group (as in Sri Lanka); self-determination may also be demanded where there is a more 'balanced' pluralism of ethnic groups, as in India and Nigeria (Weiner, 1965). The *diffusionist* school of modernization theory argues that when countries modernize, cultures become diffused and sub-cultures lose their significance. Ethnic loyalties become superseded by loyalties to the wider state. There are four factors involved in this process: bureaucratic penetration; social mobilization; industrialization; and mass communication. In conjunction these developments produce cultural diffusion that may even extend beyond the boundaries of the nation-state.

Demands for self-determination by ethnic groups are viewed from this perspective as deviations from the path to modernity. The 'problem' for the post-colonial state is one of 'nation-building' – creating loyalties and attachments to the new nation-state which supersede the parochial loyalties evoked by traditional values. Secession may then reflect a failure to integrate at all (for example, during colonialism) or a process of disintegration after a relatively stable period of unity (Wood, 1981).

In common with the theories of modernization and development from which this concept of integration springs, it mystifies rather than illuminates the sources of political conflict which may lead to attempts at secession. Integration theory presents the 'crisis' of integration as a deviation from the functional process of political change. Political 'disintegration', of which secession is one form, is portrayed as the consequence of an incompatibility between traditional and modern values, rules and modes of behaviour (Phadnis and Ganguly, 2001). Failure to incorporate regions successfully into the state system is regarded as evidence of persistent parochial loyalties, often founded on tribal communality, which elevate the legitimacy of traditional community above that of the modern form of political association – the nation-state. The 'primordial' attachment to tradition is thus seen as an obstacle to development.

The 'integration' approach to the phenomenon of secession suffers from all the teleological and ethnocentric defects of modernization theory generally. Although it is true that political hostility to the inequalities of contemporary states may be reflected in an appeal to a sense of common identity and historical continuity, such 'parochialism' is itself the consequence of other factors rather than the prime mobilizer of political action. These other factors have to be understood. It is inadequate to dismiss them as failures on the part of disaffected sections of society to understand how to articulate political demands through an (essentially imaginary) egalitarian and pluralistic political system. To talk about national integration as if it is simply a question of minorities becoming aware that new nation-states are the modern form through which politics must be carried on, is not very helpful. It is necessary to analyse what lies behind ethnic unrest. Ethnicity cannot be regarded as a primordial 'given'. It is subject to a range of economic and political forces such as economic competition between regions, the manipulation of ethnic identity by ruling élites to divert attention from other forms of socio-economic conflict, and the attraction of communalism in the absence of other effective forms of political participation (Nafziger and Richter, 1976). One reason for turning to ethnically defined activism is despair at ever protecting one's interests through other forms of political association.

Furthermore, there is also evidence to support an interpretation of post-colonial history which sees ethnicity as supporting national integration. In West Africa, for example, ethnicity assists national integration in at least four ways. Firstly, it provides the social support needed during periods of social upheaval that cannot be provided by either the state or the extended family. Secondly, ethnic groups aid the process of re-socialization during periods of rapid social change by providing opportunities for a range of social and political contacts to be made. Thirdly, by offering opportunities for social mobility, ethnic groups help to prevent the formation of castes and so assist in the maintenance of a fluid stratification system. Finally, they are an important 'outlet for political tensions'. Such potentialities have to be recognized and set against the inevitably particularistic and separatist potential of ethnic sentiment (Wallerstein, 1960).

Internal colonialism

The concepts of uneven development and internal colonialism were largely developed with reference to the UK, and used to explain Celtic nationalism. But it is a theory that owes its origins to interpretations of Third World colonialism and dependency. It would seem to have considerable resonance as an approach to territorial economic and political differentiation in the post-colonial states of the Third World and the consequent demands for autonomy on the part of the groups experiencing discrimination and exploitation.

This thesis finds some plural societies divided into a 'core' community and one or more peripheral communities, exploited by the core from a position of primarily economic advantage. The economy of the periphery is usually highly specialized and thus more vulnerable to fluctuations in world markets than the economy of the core community. This core–periphery distinction is a function of capitalism which entails territorial as well as class inequalities and conflicts through a process of uneven development (Orridge, 1981). A cultural division of labour is created in the course of such development. Nationalism feeds on this cultural division of labour, a stratification system which links a person's life chances to cultural distinctions, thereby giving culture a political salience. People see a shared material interest in cultural terms. This is a necessary but not sufficient condition of group solidarity and collective action. Other conditions are necessary to encourage solidarity with a nationalist organization, namely a high level of dependence on a nationalist movement as a source of benefits, and the monitoring of members' 'compliance with the movement's goals and procedures' (Hechter, 1975, 1985).

The politics of the peripheral regions are controlled by the core. Influential positions in the state are disproportionately occupied by people from the core community. This applies to the central state apparatus as well as to its local aims in the minority areas. Political organizations seeking to represent the interests of minority cultures may be restricted or banned. The repressive instruments of the state may be used selectively to counter expressions of dissent by a nationalist group. Such repression has often been justified by means of a racist ideology.

In addition to such economic discrimination, the marginalization and exclusion of an ethnic or regional minority may take the form of cultural discrimination, by stereotyping the cultural group as backward, uncivilized, unreliable, inferior or dangerous. Such claims can easily become self-fulfilling prophecies when, because of economic and social discrimination, a disproportionately large number of people from the minority group are found to be suffering from unemployment, low incomes, poor health, bad housing, illiteracy, low life-expectancy, high crime rates, high rates of suicide and other indicators of social disadvantage. Discrimination may be more overt, as when minorities are denied the use of their own language in education, the media and local administration. Indirect measures include requiring that education, information and social advancement generally are only available to those using the official language ('Kendal', 1980). Discrimination may even involve attempts by the core group to deny any ethnic distinctiveness, as in the case of Turkish efforts to prove the Turkishness of the Kurds, or the Iranian government's claim that the Kurds are 'pure Iranians' (Bulloch and Morris, 1993). Discrimination may well escalate as regimes retaliate against the agitation of nationalist groups, involving forced migration and even attempted genocide.

The internal colonialism thesis would seem to fit some cases of secession, such as Bangladesh which, as East Pakistan, was economically exploited and politically marginalized by West Pakistan, especially following the abolition of representative government after the military *coup* in 1958, and the consequent dominance of a predominantly West Pakistani bureaucratic–military oligarchy (Jahan, 1973). The liberation movement was strengthened by the existence of a political movement, the Awami League, which had a powerful presence in national politics because of East Pakistan's large population and therefore strong representation in the national legislature. This power was resisted by Western Pakistani political factions. The national cause, on the other hand, was weakened by the costly logistical problems of controlling an area separated by a thousand miles of Indian territory, and by eventual Indian military support to the Bengalis.

In South-East Asia, too, separatism has been a minority response to domination by an 'ethnic core' of Thai, Burman, Lao and Malay communities, for example, as well as Javanese in Indonesia, Khmer in Cambodia, and Kinh in Vietnam. Discrimination against minorities has then been partly structural, arising from geographical, social and economic marginalization, and partly an object of government policy, involving the imposition of alien officials, fiscal regimes, education systems, and economic planning (as in Malaysia's New Economic Policy which disadvantaged the Indian and Chinese minorities: Brown, 2006).

The struggle to form an independent state of Palestine is in response to a unique form of settler colonialism that produced internal colonialism within the state of Israel. At the end of the First World War the former Ottoman Arab territory of Palestine was, along with other areas, placed under British administration by mandate from the League of Nations. Instead of being given its independence, Palestine was opened up under the Balfour Declaration of 1917 to large scale Jewish immigration. The British authorities then allowed the creation of Jewish social, economic and political organizations that developed into the nucleus of a 'state within a state'. Despite resistance from the Palestinians, the territory was handed over to the United Nations in 1947. The UN proposed dividing the area into two independent states, one Arab, one Jewish. The Jewish part claimed independence as Israel in 1948, having already occupied parts of the territory designated as Arab by the UN's partition plan.

Thus the Arabs of Palestine, accounting for two-thirds of the population, found themselves colonized by a state which, unlike other colonial powers, did not exist prior to its occupation of the colony. By 1967 the state of Israel covered the whole of Palestine. In 1974 the UN affirmed the right of the Arabs to self-determination. In 1993 interim arrangements for self-government were agreed for the two physically separate areas of Palestine assigned to the putative Arab state in 1947, the West Bank and Gaza Strip, which had remained under Israeli occupation. Elections were held to form a Palestinian Legislative Council (PLC), and to fill the office of President of the Palestinian Authority, an executive body responsible for an administrative organization. In 2000 the territories under Palestinian self-rule were reoccupied until 2005 when Israel withdrew from the Gaza Strip. Elections were held to the PLC in 2006, but there has yet to be agreement on the final status of the Palestinian territories (Farsoun and Aruri, 2006).

The internal colonialism thesis clearly provides a framework for explaining secession in some contexts. However, there are some problems with it as a general theory of nationalism and secession. The main difficulty, as has frequently been pointed out with reference to developed countries, is that there have been prosperous regions that have demanded political autonomy from the state, and many poor ones that have not (Orridge, 1981; Ozkirimli, 2000). It is arguable that Katanga (now Shaba) in the Congo, Bougainville in Papua New Guinea, and Biafra in Nigeria attempted to secede because of their relative wealth, based on their natural mineral resources, rather than their backwardness. The internal colonialism thesis is further weakened by the phenomenon of ethnic nationalism and separatism in regions yet to be extensively penetrated by capitalist development – the Kurds, Naga and Eritrea, for example (Smith, 1979).

Thus 'uneven development', producing overdeveloped peripheral regions within poor countries, is awkward to fit into the internal colonialism model. A 'power disparity' can develop, when an economically better off region with *de facto* power demands *de jure* equality within the state. For example, although the Kurdish areas of Turkey and Iran are among the least developed regions of those countries, Kurdistan in Iraq has been favoured by natural conditions and resources, notably oil. However, being rich in natural resources does not guard against exploitation. The Kurdish parts of Iraq have consistently received disproportionately small quantities of development expenditure, industrial projects and infrastructure, despite the fact that they contribute some 80 per cent of Iraqi oil production and over 53 per cent of state revenue (Vanley, 1980).

The attempt by Nigeria's Ibo-dominated Eastern Region to secede as Biafra in 1967 offers a further example of a relatively well-developed area seeking to break away. The Eastern Region had not suffered discrimination in either revenue allocation or economic investment. Politically the Ibos played a major role in national as well as regional politics from the earliest years of the independence movement. The discovery of oil in the region made secession look like an economically viable option, while the pogrom in retaliation for what Nigeria's other main ethnic groups perceived as an Ibo-inspired military coup in 1966 made secession politically and socially necessary. The concept of an independent Biafra did not emerge among Ibo leaders until after the army rank and file had mutinied and assassinated hundreds of Ibo officers and men and after pogroms in some largely Moslem northern cities raised the spectre of genocide.

Consequently it may be theorized that if a region combines 'ethnic potential' with an improved economic position (or a faltering core economy) it may become politically assertive (Gourevitch, 1979; Wood, 1981). Part of the 'faltering core' may be a failure to develop effective political bargaining, notably through national political parties. The development of powerful regional parties in Nigeria and Pakistan increased secessionist instability by focusing political conflict on regional rivalries. Competition for economic and political power after independence became increasingly regional in character. The regional orientation of political élites intensified regional identities, conflict and the subordination of national class differences to tribalism.

This still leaves a need for an explanation of nationalism in the context of 'even' development, such as the nationalism in East Africa, French Saharan Africa, and the West Indies which prevented workable federal amalgamations between more or less evenly developed territories. There is also the problem of why uneven development can exist without nationalist and secessionist movements, though this may be a puzzle more for the developed than the developing regions of the world.

Explaining ethnic secession may require a distinction between spatial and population disparities. 'Backward' populations (that is, with below average educational attainments, per capita incomes and non-agricultural employment opportunities) from 'backward' areas (that is, with low regional incomes per capita) have attempted secession soon after independence from a colonial power because of their inability to compete. The southern Sudanese are an example, while the Hausa of northern Nigeria might have been had it not been for their numerical size which endowed them with political power. An advanced group in a backward region is only likely to attempt secession as a last resort and as a result of discrimination and violence. The Tamils in Sri Lanka are such a case. An advanced group in an advanced region may attempt secession when it feels it is subsidizing the rest of the country, unless there are economic and political advantages of remaining part of the state (Horowitz, 1985). Such distinctions point to the significance of internal social divisions within minority groups, and their political and economic calculations, necessitating analysis it terms of élite and class interests (see below).

A possible answer to the question of why inter-ethnic inequality is not sufficient to produce nationalism, and why dominant groups sometimes become nationalistic, is relative deprivation, in the sense of aspirations to standards of living which have yet to be reached but to which the 'deprived' group feels it has a right (Hah and Martin, 1975). This idea has been criticized because it is not possible to specify and measure the level of relative deprivation needed to turn an ethnic group towards nationalism. The theory also accepts as evidence of relative deprivation the claims made by the nationalists themselves. And 'deprivation theory cannot explain the nationalism of privileged groups, such as that of Afrikaners in South Africa' (Brass, 1991). However, it is not clear why objective measures of relative deprivation should not be constructed to compare two ethnic groups in conflict about political autonomy; nor why the theory cannot be applied to the examples of relative privilege for which it was designed. So the theory of relative deprivation would appear to retain some heuristic value.

A further problem with the theory of internal colonialism is that it does not explain why *nationalism* should be the response to uneven development and internal, colonial-style exploitation rather than, say, a return to pre-modern politics or revolutionary class consciousness. Why should a deprived community aspire to become a nation-state? The theory of uneven development also requires a clearer definition of what constitutes unevenness than has so far been provided (Orridge, 1981, p. 187). Unless it is known how to identify the significant spatial variations between regions, it is impossible to test whether or not the theory applies to a particular country.

The lack of consistent correlation between peripheral economic status and nationalistic mobilization draws us back to the significance of ethnic identity, which some would argue is the main cause of nationalism. Cultural differences are perceived by the groups they define, while spatial economic differences may or may not be. Ethnicity would seem to be a necessary condition for separatism. But economic exploitation by the core community does not seem to be a necessary, let alone a sufficient, condition of nationalism. The roots of separatism must be sought in other than economic factors. People must see themselves as a distinct nation before they will contemplate independence (Polese, 1985). Yet ethnicity seems not to rank as a sufficient condition either. The history of nationalism clearly shows that:

> the objective existence or subjective perception of inequality is indispensible to justify nationalism, but it is not in itself an explanation for it. The only certainty is that every nationalist movement has always justified itself in terms of existing oppression or anticipated oppression by a rival group. (Brass, 1991, p. 43)

Not all 'objective' cultural groups are nationalistic. Group identity becomes important under external threat, especially from the state, through assimilationist policies, discrimination, environmental damage, and the expropriation of natural resources, for example (Brown, 1989; Clay, 1989). The claims of both Eritrea and Somaliland to self-determination were based on a 'consciousness of oppression' (Adam, 1994, p. 35). Hence the appeal of political integration theory, which concentrates on interpretations of ethnicity and the conflicting cultural values, particularly those relating to politics, of different ethnic groups.

The balance of advantage

This theory builds on the idea that communities weigh up the costs and benefits of integration and separation. It entails a cost–benefit perspective on nationalism, seeing ethnicity as an independent variable, producing identities and loyalties which persist over long periods, largely regardless of other factors (Birch, 1978). Therefore ethnicity should be treated as given and not explained in terms of political discrimination, economic exploitation or relative deprivation. Nationalism will be supported or opposed depending on whether people anticipate greater wealth, power and prestige from independence, or feel that their welfare depends on ties with the larger political unit (Hechter, 2000).

Take again the case of Biafra in 1967. Arguing that 'the probability of secession of a regional unit from a nation-state is dependent upon the expected costs and benefits to the region from the maintenance of the national unit and those of secession from it', Nafziger points out that 'the benefits of regional autonomy for the East increased relative to the benefits of continued membership of the federation as a result of the discovery and commercial exploitation of crude oil centred in the region in the late 1950s' (Nafziger, 1972, p. 185). However, oil did not prompt secession. It simply made it a viable strategy in the eyes of the Biafran leadership against the national level of government. The share of revenue from oil accruing to the East became a major source of political friction – especially after 1959, when a new revenue allocation system left the East with a fraction of its earlier oil revenues. Another major factor was the decision in 1967 to increase the number of states in the federation from 4 to 12. Dividing the Eastern Region into three states meant that the Ibos would be in a majority in only one with only one-sixth of the region's oil output. The Ibo heartland would be severed from the oil resources and landlocked.

The level of economic integration also affected the calculation. At the time of the Biafran secession the value of inter-regional trade was low. Indigenous firms tended to sell to local markets. Virtually no capital moved between regions. Ethnic conflict between 1965 and 1967 further discouraged economic integration. The cost of secession was therefore perceived to be less than the benefits of integration, especially when opportunities for economic advancement through migration, from which the Ibos had formerly benefited, were discouraged, first by policies of regionalization in employment and then by pogroms.

Political integration involves costs and benefits to minority communities. There will be a changing balance of advantage from time to time in being incorporated into a wider community, and the incorporation is unlikely to be total, contrary to the basic premise of the diffusionist school that ethnic loyalties will be superseded by loyalties to the wider political unit because of bureaucratic penetration, social mobilization, industrialization and mass communication. Ethnic groups resist the erosion of their cultural identity, even gaining 'psychic income' from pride and satisfaction with the assertion of an identity which compensates for a sense of inferiority and deprivation engendered by a dominant culture.

The case of the Kurds in Turkey may be cited here. In addition to banning the use of the Kurdish language in favour of Turkish in schools, and the displacement of Kurds to non-Kurdish areas, the Turkish government allowed living conditions in the Kurdish south-east to decline, contributing to a growing sense of Kurdish nationalism and eventual armed revolt. This case supports the observation that allegiances to the host state declines the more the members of distinctive ethnic groups perceive the costs of integration to exceed the benefits (Hechter et al., 2006).

Since the Second World War the balance of advantage between the small community and the large state has swung in favour of the former, firstly because 'changes in the international order have removed one of the main benefits to be derived from membership of a sizeable state', namely diplomatic and military security (Birch, 1978, p. 335). Free trade and regional defence alliances also reduce the benefits of integration in a large domestic market and a state with an expensive defence capability. A weakening economy in the larger unit may also increase the cost of integration (Hechter, 2000; Phadnis and Ganguly, 2001).

Secondly, the development of international organizations such as the EC, OECD and the IMF give small states access to markets, loans, employment and investment that make their small economies more viable than they would otherwise be. Thirdly, the impact of the mass media on minority cultures and languages has heightened consciousness of, and hostility to, cultural imperialism and homogenization.

Finally, political agitation for minorities is less costly than in the past. Rights are more readily demanded and conceded. Agitation and terrorism are easier and get instant world-wide publicity. National energy supplies are more vulnerable to sabotage. Hence a decline in the acceptability to minorities of piecemeal reforms and in the value attached to the benefits of integration in the wider nation-state.

This explanation sounds highly plausible in the context of developing regions of the world. There are problems associated with it, however. Firstly, it concentrates more on the relative ease with which the break can be made, rather than on the factors that prompt disillusionment among some ethnic minorities and not others with the existing territorial jurisdiction of the state. It implies that the demand for separation is constant, only awaiting an easing of the circumstances under which a new, small state can be born and survive. Yet the demand is clearly not constant, so the factors precipitating nationalist mobilization have to be identified. Separation will only appear a more rational choice than integration, giving the minority the 'maximum net advantage' and worth the high risks involved, when specific conditions exist, such as material inequalities, the exclusion of minority élites, the movement's organizational capacities and geopolitical support (Mitra, 1995).

Secondly, as an explanation it pays insufficient attention to the organizational requirements of a successful bid for independence and the variable political context in which it is made. The following organizational factors affect a nationalist movement's chances of political success: command of community resources; identification with the community represented; an ability to shape the identity of the group to be led; continuity in leadership; and exclusive or dominant representation of ethnic demands. The intensity and form of nationalist politics is also affected by contextual factors, especially the realignment of political and social forces (as when an organization based on class proves more attractive to members of an ethnic group than a nationalist body), the willingness of élites from dominant ethnic groups to share political power, and the availability of alternative political arenas, such as federalism (Brass, 1991).

Thirdly, it is important not to underestimate the ideological, governmental and repressive apparatus which the state can bring to bear on separatist movements. Impressive powers are available to central governments in dealing with separatist regions, in addition to the more obvious and risky strategies of military coercion and the withholding of public funds. Governments have the ability to conduct a census which defines social categories for the purpose of internal comparisons. They have the authority to define the issues and conflicts that are to be politically managed, and an internationally recognized right to negotiate with the separatists. They control taxation (and therefore redistribution), define economic strata, collect information and invest capital. Governments have the right to control internal migration which can 'alter drastically the ethnic composition of certain regions, usually diluting the indigenous populations and thus undermining possibly separatist tendencies' (Enloe, 1976).

Central governments can also call on diplomatic, administrative and political resources, blocking external sponsorship of separatist dissidents and exploiting divisions within regional communities. Sometimes they add foreign interference to the list of reasons for not conceding independence, as in the case of India's handling of the Kashmir crisis.

Finally, it should not be assumed that the international context is wholly supportive of aspirant nation-states. External intervention can take the form of moral support, such as publicizing human rights grievances, or material support such as economic and military aid. Such assistance will be dependent on the supporting state's strategic and other foreign policy objectives, its previous relationships with the 'parent' state, and the presence of ethnic kinsmen within the supporting state's own territory, affecting, for example, India's attitudes towards Tamil separatists in Sri Lanka (Phadnis and Ganguly, 2001). The attitudes of world powers and neighbouring states to Bangladesh and Biafra were important factors in the contrasting outcomes of these two instances of secession (Wood, 1981). External influences are usually critical to the outcome of independence struggles (Wright, 1976; Tinker, 1981). They were conclusive in the history of the short-lived Kurdish Republic of 1946 (Ghassemlou, 1980). While Eritrea's secession depended much more on the internal political situation than external support, its long-term viability is dependent on international co-operation (Adam, 1994). Concerned about oil supplies from Sudan, the government of the United States attempted in 2002 to broker an agreement between the Islamic Sudanese government and the southern secessionists which could lead to power sharing, the separation of state and religion in the south, a fairer allocation of oil revenues, an end to discrimination against non-Moslems, and consequently an end to one of Africa's longest civil wars.

But support from outside is a difficult commodity to acquire, even when ethnic groups straddle national frontiers. In South East Asia, for instance, there has been surprisingly little support for ethnic separatism from neighbouring states when ethnic minorities are located in frontier regions. Existing boundaries have been regarded as sacrosanct (McVey, 1984). Neighbouring states may be impressed by claims, such as Indonesia's with regard to the province of Aceh, that secession will cause regional instability and insecurity. Securing external support for nationalist movements is dependent on their ability to obtain foreign financial, diplomatic and political backing, as well as their skill at publicizing their demands among the international community, both governmental and non-governmental (Phadnis and Ganguly, 2001).

Élites and class

It is a mistake to expect all sections of an ethnic minority to arrive at the same conclusion after calculating the costs and benefits of integration. Cultural minorities are not homogeneous societies. Like all societies they are socially stratified. Different classes in a peripheral community will experience different costs and benefits from incorporation into a wider economy, society and polity. A major influence on the degree of mobilization of ethnic groups for nationalistic ends is the relationship between élites and classes in the core and peripheral communities. One of the ways in which national governments attempt to manage secessionist tendencies is through alliances and collaboration with élites within national or ethnic minorities. Central élites (which in Third World countries usually means bureaucrats, whether civil or military, partisan or professional) form alliances with local ethnic organizations to manage ethnic conflict, either by opposing or supporting local élites (Brass, 1991).

An economically dominant class within the minority community may be well-integrated into the wider state and economy. Brass found that 'locally powerful economic, religious and political élites find it to their advantage to co-operate with external authorities and adopt the language and culture of the dominant ethnic group in order to maintain or enhance their own power' (1991, p. 26). In the Kurdish region of Turkey, for example, the

Kurdish landed class and wealthy merchants have been integrated into the Turkish economy through trade and investment in urban property and small-scale industry in the major urban centres. Since the 1950s the Turkish authorities have needed less repression against the Kurds because the corruption and self-interest of the Kurdish ruling class achieve the government's aims for it ('Kendal', 1980). The newly emerging Kurdish bourgeoisie also co-exists with the Turkish economic and political élite, serving as a regional section of the Turkish commercial network and enjoying representation within the national political parties.

Nationalism is often a weapon which regional élites use in their competition for national political power. Appeals to ethnic loyalties to build and sustain political support may be a consequence of a struggle for power between ethnic élites, rather than a cause of mobilization on the part of minority groups. For example, Indonesian experience of separatist regionalism in the 1950s was not an assertion of primordial loyalties, but an attempt to consolidate political support. Eventually the regionalist movements in Sumatra and Sulawesi came to nothing because their ethnic foundations were insufficiently meaningful (McVey, 1984).

Similarly, in India provincial bourgeoisies have from time to time espoused nationalism in order to obtain powers which could be used to strengthen their position in relation to national bourgeoisies whose interests lay in an economic market and political state coterminous with the whole of India. In Nigeria, on the other hand, the reinforcement of political mobilization on the basis of ethnicity by politicians exploiting growing inter-ethnic competition was a major factor in the descent into civil war (Melsom and Wolpe, 1970; Oommen, 2006).

Thus ethnic conflict reflects competition between élites for 'political power, economic benefits and social status'. In modernizing societies the development of ethnic consciousness is heavily dependent upon industrialization, the spread of literacy, urbanization and the growth of government employment opportunities, and the new social classes which such developments produce. Conflict between élites over the distribution of resources and political power between ethnic groups precipitates nationalism. The potential for nationalism is not realized 'until some members from one ethnic group attempt to move into the economic niches occupied by the rival ethnic group' (Brass, 1991, p. 47). Secession is a strategy likely only to be adopted when minority élites have no chance of acquiring economic and political power within the existing state, and when there is a good chance of foreign support.

Separatism may be seen as a way of gaining access to power for excluded élites, especially when the state in developing countries has boundaries that are recent and artificial, few constitutional outlets for 'minority grievances', a lack of resources for helping poor regions, and a form of government that is prone to discrimination rather than conciliation (Smith, 1979, pp. 21–35). For example, the bureaucracy can be an arena of ethnic conflict when trained and educated people from minority groups ('ambitious and qualified professionals') find themselves excluded from bureaucratic occupations for which they are qualified as the supply of such professionals outstrips the capacity of bureaucracies to absorb them. The state bureaucracy can be particularly discriminatory when the state itself is dominated by a core community.

The case of secession by East Pakistan shows how responses to nationalist demands for self-determination will depend upon class interests in the rest of the country. The landowning class in the West felt threatened by the Eastern leadership's proposal to tax hitherto exempt agricultural incomes in order to provide development capital. The Western bourgeoisie had an interest in retaining the East as a market for their manufactured goods and as a source of foreign exchange earnings. At the same time, however, Western agriculture was becoming an increasingly profitable source of investment to them, and they were concerned about revolutionary stirrings in the East. It was mainly the bureaucratic–military oligarchy that opposed secession and used armed force in the attempt to prevent it. Punjabi bureaucrats resented the promotion of Bengalis as a response to pressure from a political movement seeking to redress the regional imbalance within senior ranks. Regional autonomy also threatened their control over resources. The army was even more directly threatened by regional autonomy, which would have deprived the central government, responsible for defence, of funds. The Awami League was committed to a substantial reduction in expenditure on the military. The army's hostility was further strengthened by its belief that Bengali nationalism had been engineered by India to destabilize Pakistan.

The case of East Pakistan and Bengali nationalism is particularly illuminating to the question of how different classes respond to regional disparities. In the 1960s the central government under President Ayub Khan decided to create an East Pakistani bourgeoisie to provide the President with a political base in the province and restrict the spread of socialist ideas. Educated Bengalis with useful contacts in the bureaucracy and political élite were given permits, licences, construction contracts, loans, official support and equity. However, this new Bengali bourgeoisie also benefited from the pressures created by Bengali nationalism, and so was inclined to be favourably disposed towards it. Greater economic autonomy for the East increased nationalism's appeal among Bengali industrialists and businessmen when they found themselves unable to compete with the stronger West Pakistan businesses. At the same time they were uncertain as to whether an independent East Bengal could continue to provide the support and protection that the government of Pakistan could offer (Jahan, 1973).

However, East Bengali separatism existed before the Bengali bour-geoisie was created. The class basis of the movement was mainly petty-bourgeois. The urban salaried classes believed economic independence would reduce prices by removing the power of West Pakistan cartels. Bengali bureaucrats looked forward to freedom from the central govern-ment's fiscal policies. The radical intelligentsia supported autonomy because they believed it would provide greater opportunity for economic reform in a region with few indigenous capitalists (Alavi, 1971).

Conclusion

Even if investigations are restricted to the Third World, the phenomenon with which this chapter has been concerned is far too complex and diverse for simple generalizations of a causal nature to be arrived at. Each situation is unique in what prompts nationalism, how central governments respond to nationalist demands, and what further political forces are mobilized as a reaction to such responses. Variations are found in the way states attempt to manage ethnic separatism, the basis on which minority élites are selected for collaboration and accommodation, and the influence of such co-option on the movements involved in the struggle for independence. The socio-economic make-up of the factions within ethnic communities and national-ist movements may generate a willingness to negotiate for less than complete separation. Nationalist movements also vary in terms of organi-zation, objectives and strategy (including the extent to which they are prepared to resort to violence).

Consequently, the outcomes of ethno-nationalism are affected by the kind of political agenda which a nationalist movement has, whether there is more than one, and what those agenda prescribe for the future gover-nance of the territory should independence be achieved.

9

Instability and Revolution

Introduction

The number and social cost of military *coups*, civil wars, communal conflicts and other manifestations of political instability in the Third World have been too great not to attract a great deal of attention in political science. Since 1945, both inter-state and intra-state conflict (the latter far more common) moved from the industrialized to the developing countries, a trend only slowed by the outbreak of conflict in the states of the former Soviet bloc following the demise of communist regimes (Singer, 1996).

This chapter examines the theoretical preconditions for political stability that have been formulated in terms of poverty, the rate of economic growth, the revolution of rising expectations, foreign influences, ethnicity, the political culture, inequality, crises of authority and political institutionalization. The theoretical or empirical weaknesses of these conclusions are identified. Problems with the concept of 'political stability' itself are addressed: its normative content, the question of whether the analysis is concerned with stable government whatever the type of regime or just stable *democratic* government, and the lack of a satisfactory operational definition of 'instability'.

The social and economic costs of political instability are enormous. More than 4 million people died as a result of violent conflicts in the 1990s, either directly from military action or indirectly from the destruction of food supplies and health facilities. Civil war causes GDP per capita to decline by some 2.2 per cent per year, the result of a loss of production from the destruction of transport networks, capital stock, physical capital, infrastructure and natural resources. Highly skilled workers are driven to emigrate. Then there is the 'culture of violence' that develops from the breakdown of government, the dislocation of civil society, the violation of human rights and the growth of corruption. Vigilante and paramilitary groups proliferate, either beyond the control of government or with its tacit support, as in Colombia and Sudan. Military expenditure increases at the expense of government spending on social services and economic development, in turn leading to further hardship, insecurity, and 'crowding out' of social expenditure to finance spending on law and order (Mohammed, 1999).

Conceptual difficulties

It is thus not surprising that considerable effort has been expended on explaining political instability in the Third World. But the concept of 'stability' is fraught with difficulties which need to be recognized before a proper evaluation of causal explanations can be made.

Firstly, 'stability' is a highly normative concept. What is instability for one person might well constitute the welcome overthrow of a detestable regime for another. (Many in the West welcomed instability in communist Eastern Europe and the Soviet Union.) The USA has long been actively engaged in destabilizing regimes that it does not like. One person's stability is another person's repression. It is not easy to exclude values from the analysis of political stability. Outside the Marxist tradition, instability is seen as deviancy, a slip on the path to progress. It is an aberration that has to be explained. In the Marxist tradition, instability is accepted as inevitable in the progression of history. Class conflict is an unavoidable stage in the movement of society towards its end-state. Crisis is the inevitable consequence of the contradictions of economic development.

Consequently some would argue that it is not possible to handle the concept in a scientific way at all. An analytical obsession with instability simply indicates a preference for the regime that is under threat. Understanding a particular type of political change, especially one that often entails violence, loss of life and severe economic dislocation, has to be based on an objective analysis of the conditions leading to such change. This is not easy when there are so many values at stake when political instability is experienced.

Secondly, there is the question of whether the analysis should be concerned with stable government or stable *democratic* government. Interest has not concentrated exclusively on the travails of democracy. Whereas the attention of political science focused on the preconditions of stable democracy in the 1950s and early 1960s, interest shifted in the 1960s and 1970s to a concern with political order, whether in democracies or other types of regime. In the 1970s US political science in particular concentrated more on the prerequisites of order and control, rather than pluralism and democracy, revealing a strong ideological impulse (Leys, 1982). Since 1980 attention has swung back to democratic stability.

Concern for the maintenance of regimes and élites, political order and stability in policy-making arose from changing political realities in the Third World, the pessimism which developed during the first Development Decade, and perceptions of continuing external influence over supposedly independent nation-states and sovereign governments. Attention concentrated on the policy-making capabilities of national élites, their ability to bargain with foreign interests, and the need for strong centralized government. Successful governmental interventions were seen to be obstructed by competition between national and local élites and passive traditionalism. High rates of growth were seen as requiring authoritarianism, democracies apparently having relatively poor economic records both in terms of growth and distribution (Higgott, 1983; Huntington, 1987). However, cross-national quantitative studies indicate that coercion provokes rather than deters political violence, especially if the repression is not total but permits some political mobilization by opposition groups (Muller and Seligson, 1987). So authoritarianism cannot guarantee stability.

Stability is still sometimes seen as an end in itself, if not regardless of the regime involved, then at least with grudging respect for what can be achieved with less than full democracy. Consider, for example, one reference to political restructuring in Malaysia, which has limited political competition and restricted freedom of expression: 'While this restructuring has levelled parliamentary democracy down to semi-democratic status, it has also brought considerable ethnic peace, political stability and socioeconomic prosperity' (Diamond, 1989, p. 2).

It has also to be recognized that stable democracy might be replaced by stable authoritarianism or even a stable regime which may not conform to some definitions of democracy, particularly those entailing multipartyism, but which would be regarded by few as authoritarian. The failure of democracy should not be equated with the breakdown of stable government. It may simply be that a particular definition of democracy determines the scale of the failure, as in one analysis of the 'failure' of democracy in Sub-Saharan Africa where, by the early 1970s, multi-party democracy had disappeared in all but Botswana, Gambia and Mauritius (Diamond, 1988).

Handling the concept of stability is made additionally difficult by the fact that it is often used in a way which fails to distinguish between countries that have experienced the overthrow of a democratic regime and its replacement with a stable but authoritarian one, and countries where there is constant civil disorder and change of regime. Much of the concern for the health of democracy over the past 30 years has been prompted by tendencies to 'drift away' from democratic standards rather than a drift into instability, though the two trends are usually closely related. Huntington fell into this trap when he cited 'going communist' as evidence that Cuba and the Indian State of Kerala were unstable (Huntington, 1965, p. 406).

Thirdly, there is the problem of finding a satisfactory operational definition of 'stability'. Various indicators have been employed, such as the turnover rate for chief executives, deaths from internal group violence per million population, and the total number of violent incidents (Russett,

1964). Attempts have been made to measure the aggression of groups within the political system, the longevity of governments, and the constitutionality of governmental acts (Hurwitz, 1973; Ake, 1974). None of these completely captures a sense of what is involved in political instability. Even when political structures change, it may not necessarily be destabilizing. A formulation of instability in terms of members of society deviating from 'the behaviour patterns that fall within the limits imposed by political role expectations' has the advantage of extending the types of events that are to be considered beyond the élite interactions which are conventionally regarded as indicators of political instability – *coups*, electoral violence, political assassinations and so on – as well as acknowledging that what is destabilizing to one political structure may not be to another. For example, a refusal of leaders to seek an electoral mandate may be destabilizing to a constitutional democracy, but not to a hereditary monarchy (Ake, 1974, 1975; Castles, 1974).

Some indicators of political instability appear unhelpful when their occurrence coincides with the persistence of regimes. There may be frequent and serious political violence, perhaps associated with communal identities as in India, yet the system of government survives. It may be that instability can only be understood in retrospect. But this can only be done if instability is defined as events leading to the collapse of a regime (as distinct from a government or policy). Indicators of political instability should be taken as important and costly events whose causes and consequences deserve to be understood regardless of whether they lead to the breakdown of a regime. So the violent transfer from one form of government (e.g. democracy) to another (e.g. military rule) is only one of the consequences of civil war, riots, communal or religious conflicts and other forms of unconstitutional behaviour.

Fourthly, there is the time factor. In addition to knowing what it is a country must remain free from, it is necessary to specify some time period during which it must remain free from destabilizing factors for it to be labelled stable. It is difficult to know how to decide objectively on the timing of instability, especially when a brief period of conflict can bring down one regime (e.g. the Marcos regime in the Philippines) while years of recurring political violence are accompanied by stable democracy (e.g. India).

Despite such difficulties, much effort has been made to explain political instability, broadly conceived as the failure of a system of government to persist over a prolonged period. These explanations will now be examined.

Affluence and poverty

Firstly, increasing affluence is said to improve the chance of stability, especially in countries with democratic regimes. Conversely, absolute poverty has been seen as a major cause of political instability. For example, in Asia 'people who live at the margin of subsistence are either indifferent or hostile to government . . . it remains true for most of the new Asian states that all-pervasive poverty undermines government of any kind' (Brecher, 1963, p. 623). Poor countries are thus more likely to suffer more political violence than rich ones. So as a country becomes richer and *per capita* incomes increase, political instability should be eased.

An example is the Niger delta area of Nigeria, where poverty is driving the insurgency and where little of the huge revenues generated by the exploitation of oil reserves by multinational corporations has found its way into local communities. The region remains poor and undeveloped, with high unemployment, discrimination, environmental damage and state repression of protests. Consequently the 'contradiction of wealth generation amidst poverty has generated anger, frustration and hostility to the state and multinational oil corporations' (Ikelegbe, 2001, p. 437).

However, there have been many poor and underdeveloped countries with *stable* political systems. What they have had in common is authoritarian rather than democratic regimes. In fact it seems that the poorer the dictatorship the more stable it is likely to be. It also seems feasible that political stability might cause affluence and economic growth rather than be the consequence of it. Some politically stable nations achieved stability before they achieved their affluence. Similarly, some totalitarian regimes have also been able to produce stability before economic development. There is empirical evidence from 110 countries showing that political instability causes macroeconomic decline (Gasiorowski, 1998).

Poverty and political stability can coexist because of the many constraints on effective political action by the poor in defence of their rights and interests. Even with the right to vote, the power of the ballot box is easily emasculated by electoral frauds of one kind or another. In poor societies votes can still easily be bought. Poverty also means that successful appeals to the judiciary against the economically powerful and their allies in the bureaucracy when they obstruct the implementation of government reforms are rarely made because of the social and financial costs involved.

Political mobilization of the poor is limited by their isolation as economic actors, such as peasants working their own land with their own labour in scattered fields. Similar experiences may be felt in some industrial situations, such as mining, where workers are isolated in industrial villages and provided with their needs at the point of employment. They may become unionized, and that may constitute an important basis for political agitation. But union activity may be restricted to concerns in the workplace rather than political issues that affect people in their other roles. In the informal sector of the urban economy households and units of production are also isolated. Separate producers act in isolation to acquire minimal levels of capital, confronting antagonistic social classes in isolation – landlords, merchants, money-lenders, bureaucrats, and wholesalers who can exploit and further weaken them because of clientelist relationships. Class, or even group, consciousness is difficult to create as a basis for political organization.

The poor are also in competition with each other, rather than sharing a common experience that forms a basis for a common sense of identity and exploitation (Wolfe, 1968; Harris, 1970). Poverty, far from acting to unify people, intensifies the competition for scarce resources – rights to land occupancy, land purchase or rent, employment, loans, and access to grazing, water and implements. The members of the informal sector are in competition for cheap items with which to trade. Such experiences do not lead to solidarity among such people. Solidarity is further undermined for those who have exchanged rural for urban poverty by the precariousness of their existence in shantytowns and the constant threat of eviction. Tribal attachments, encouraged by the competitiveness of urban life and employment, have been a major source of conflict among the rural and urban poor in Africa. Competition for jobs has been an especially potent force in exacerbating ethnic rivalries, and ethnic associations have been one way of providing mutual support and protection for immigrants into the urban areas (Post, 1972).

The daily grind of hard manual labour leaves little opportunity to take part in political activity. The intensity of this problem is especially great for women. Poor women in Third World societies have heavy domestic chores in addition to cultivating, marketing and engaging in wage labour. This may include carrying large quantities of water long distances to service the home. With energy consumed at such a rate and inadequately replenished by a poor diet, it is not easy to persuade people to spend what little free time they have travelling by foot to and from political meetings. The physical effort and malnourishment experienced by the poor cannot sustain political activism.

There are also great risks for the poor in political participation, especially alienating the people upon whom one is dependent – landlord, employer, money-lender and people of higher status (Migdal, 1974). These are all participants in the local political process whose interests may be threatened by successful political agitation by the poor. Relations of dependency support the poor through systems of reciprocal obligations within the traditional framework of the local community. Kinsmen will help in times of need and adversity. Kinship networks consist of rich and poor, making it difficult for poor people to engage in political activism which appears threatening to their own kin. Similarly political action may be seen as putting other members of the kinship group at risk, even though the objective is the improvement of conditions for people of that class. Kinship ties cut across class lines, further reducing political consciousness (Wolfe, 1968).

Political action also risks severe repression by the state. Awareness of growing inequalities may breed a degree of radicalism, but this is easily contained by state repression and by clientelist and populist modes of political incorporation 'which facilitate state control and regimentation' (Mouzelis, 1989, pp. 20–6).

The potential for political organization and communication on the part of the poor is further reduced by low levels of literacy and education, extreme parochialism, and respect for traditional authority, religion and custom. Access to the mass media is limited. It is also difficult to organize and unionize when there are substantial reserve armies of labour available to much better organized employers. Women may feel reluctant to join male-dominated organizations such as trade unions. Another factor inhibiting political organization, whether of workers or peasants, is that leadership needs to be drawn from people with education and experience outside the countryside and from the intelligentsia (Migdal, 1974; Shanin, 1982). In parts of Latin America the Roman Catholic clergy have provided badly needed leadership, organization and consciousness-raising.

Finally, the poor experience cultural subordination, sometimes originating in colonial racialism. Domination is exercised through ideological devices which confer subordinate status on exploited groups such as indigenous Latin Americans, untouchables and tribals in India, and women in most countries. An important task of such ideology is to instil the belief that subordination is natural and irreversible.

The rate of growth

An alternative hypothesis is that the *rate* of economic growth is crucial to political stability. The more rapid the rate of development, the more difficult it is to maintain stability (Huntington, 1968). Rapid economic growth produces social groups that find themselves left behind in the progress being made and excluded from the new economic opportunities. For example, peasant proprietors may be turned into a rural proletariat. Discontent arises from a loss of status and autonomy. Economic development produces opportunities for social mobility by releasing the bonds that positioned people in a social order. New economic roles create new opportunities for economic independence for individuals who in a traditional society would not expect to enjoy them. The unity and bonds of family, kin group and village community are undermined by these new roles and values.

Rapid economic development also means that mass movements seeking fundamental political change will be made up from people whose bonds to the established order are changing. Rapid economic growth increases the number of such *déclassés*: by changing the methods of production and the distribution of income, and by weakening the bonds of family, class, caste, tribe and guild. The *nouveaux riches* use their economic power to challenge the social and political order. The *nouveaux pauvres* resent their poverty, a particularly significant fact given that economic growth can significantly increase the number of losers. Rapid growth concentrates material gains in relatively few hands as prices increase faster than wages and technological change replaces people with machines. At such times, and especially in the early stages of industrialization, there are unlikely to be welfare arrangements to compensate for economic hardship. There will also be those who, though making some absolute gains from economic growth, find that their relative position has deteriorated, a further source of dissatisfaction and of contradiction between the structure of economic and political power. Furthermore, levels of consumption can decline with rapid economic growth. Standards of living may have to be reduced to produce the required rate of savings. Consequently 'it is economic stability – the absence of rapid economic growth or rapid economic decline – that should be regarded as conducive to social and political tranquility' (Olson, 1963, p. 550).

In moving from an economy based on agriculture to an economy based on manufacturing there is a shift of population from rural to urban areas. The expanding cities of the Third World harbour extremism and activism. Urban people are attracted to volatile forms of political expression. Urban political organizations provide opportunities for power, status and social mobility to otherwise underprivileged groups, so political activism becomes even more attractive. When cities are full of 'marginalized' people, the opportunity costs of political activism may be very low. With poverty, unemployment, inequalities of income, insecurity, bad working conditions and poor health, accompanied by a lack of governmental provision for the poor and by disparities in political power that exacerbate disparities in wealth, it is not surprising that the process of urbanization is thought to be a major cause of political instability in the Third World.

This convincing *a priori* reasoning has been queried in view of the growth rates in many Western countries since 1945 which have been higher than at any previous period in their histories without causing political instability (Castles, 1974). The fact that there are examples of countries which have experienced high rates of economic growth and political stability, in Europe and Scandinavia, suggests that there are other influences being felt in developing countries. If political stability and high rates of growth go hand in hand in advanced industrialized countries, it does not necessarily follow that this would be the case in poor agrarian societies. Research on

Central America found that rapid growth in agriculture together with industrialization reduced the relative and absolute living standards of the working class, who then revolted against their governments. Only when, as in Costa Rica and Honduras, governments responded with policies to reduce inequalities and increase the real value of wages, did popular protest subside. Where the state responded with repression (Nicaragua, El Salvador and Guatemala) 'opposition mobilization and unity increased and led to a broad, rebellious challenge to regime sovereignty' (Booth, 1991).

It is also possible that role confusion and disorientation can stimulate group identity and associational sentiments rather than cause hostility and alienation. Industrialization can be integrative, creating new foundations for social linkages, such as class. Social differentiation can eliminate sources of conflict and reduce tension. New forms of political participation can be supportive rather than destabilizing. The fact that economic modernization can generate instability does not mean that it necessarily will (Ake, 1974).

The revolution of rising expectations

A period of rapid economic growth can be followed by an economic downturn. Then there may be a 'revolution of rising expectations' meaning that if there is a set-back in prosperity after a period of rapidly rising economic growth, frustration would be experienced by people whose expectations are rising faster than can be satisfied by the economy. This frustration among people who are denied the increase in the standard of living which they had anticipated can be politically destabilizing, because of the ways in which their frustration is likely to be expressed. Marx's observation that we measure our desires and pleasures by social comparison and not by the objects that provide the satisfaction, and de Tocqueville's conclusion that 'Evils which are patiently endured when they seem inevitable become intolerable when once the idea of escape from them is suggested', leads to a largely psychological explanation of one particular kind of instability which postulates that: 'Revolutions are most likely to occur when a prolonged period of objective economic and social development is followed by a short period of sharp reversal' (Davies, 1972, pp. 136–7).

The reversal in economic circumstances produces anxiety and frustration as an intolerable gap opens up between what people expect and what they actually get. Rather than deprivation, a sudden decline in the opportunities to continue improving one's condition in line with expectations leads to revolution. A 'revolutionary state of mind' requires an expectation of improvements in the satisfaction of needs (for physical, social and

Figure 9.1   *Needs satisfaction and revolution*

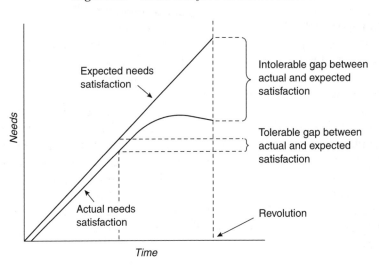

SOURCE: Davies (1972), p. 137.

political benefits) to be under 'a persistent, unrelenting threat'. The 'crucial factor' is the fear that 'ground gained over a long period of time will be quickly lost'. The relationship between *expectations* of needs satisfaction and their actual satisfaction can be demonstrated by a J curve (see Figure 9.1).

This theory explains the Egyptian revolution of 1952, after a series of strikes, peasant uprisings and urban riots was rounded off by a *coup d'état* by army officers. He points out that expectations of improvements began in 1922 with a grant of limited independence by the British, and continued with industrialization and an increase in exports following the Second World War. Expectations of continued progress were dashed between 1945 and 1951 by a collapse in the world demand for cotton, unemployment among a third of the work force, high inflation, humiliating defeat by the new state of Israel, government corruption and shortages of wheat and oil. The promises made by nationalist groups contribute to such problems when the anticipated benefits of independence failed to materialize (Davies, 1972). In 2008 Egypt again experienced riots and strikes in its larger cities following increases in basic food prices, threatening the livelihoods of people already close to the poverty line.

Other contemporary factors leading to perceptions of a widening gap between achieved and expected levels of welfare include environmental problems such as deforestation and land degradation leading to lower levels of economic output and the displacement of communities (Mohammed, 1999).

Foreign influences

Some explanations of instability emphasize the importance of foreign factors. In Latin America debt and dependency have destabilizing implications as they affect the legitimacy of governments by adversely affecting their economic performance. However, more overtly political factors act independently of such economic influences or mediate their impact. International demonstration and diffusion may be important, as in the case of the Cuban revolution within Latin America, military *coups* in neighbouring countries, or the attitude of the USA towards dictators and democracies. Aid is increasingly used as a weapon against political practices, albeit in the direction of democracy. External threats, real or perceived, to a country's security have fostered authoritarianism, militarization and curbs on civil liberties.

Foreign involvement can take the form of spillovers from crises in neighbouring states, as in the Democratic Republic of Congo where over a million Hutu refugees from Rwanda have imported the ethnic conflict that led to genocide in their own country. Alternatively, intervention may be orchestrated by powerful neighbouring governments, as with Syria's and Israel's incursions into Lebanon, especially if there are domestic political factions supported by foreign governments, such as Lebanon's Shia movement, Hizbullah. Foreign intervention in the name of 'the war on terror' currently fuels the border conflict between Eritrea and Ethiopia, with the USA supporting Ethiopia against Eritrea's Islamic government which is accused of links with al-Qaida.

Foreign intervention has often set out to destroy a whole regime, sometimes covertly, as with the USA's involvement in Chile in the early 1970s, and sometimes overtly, as with the USA's and Britain's invasion of Iraq in 2003 which destroyed the country's physical and administrative infrastructure and reduced politics to civil war, sectarian violence and infiltration of the security services and bureaucracy, and the prospect of new forms of authoritarianism.

Ethnicity

The destabilizing effect of economic and social modernization is related to the problems that many societies have had when loyalty to an ethnic group transcends loyalty to a new state. As we saw in Chapter 8, that problem is sometimes referred to as the crisis of integration or nation-building. Nation-building is sometimes seen as an ethical and psychological activity designed to reorientate people's loyalties towards a new political entity. But primordial attachments based on tribe, language, religion or race have been and still are enormously powerful in most regions of the Third World. They have been extremely divisive, and frequently lead to armed insurgency. Ethnic demands are currently the most important source of violent political conflict in the Third World, ranging from secession to equal rights, greater political participation, an end to economic and social discrimination, and the protection of cultural traditions (Horowitz, 1994; Gurr and Harff, 1994). India's democracy has been constantly threatened by communal conflict, especially between Hindus and Moslems.

Ethnic conflict has originated in historic antagonisms (for example, Sinhalese and Tamils in Sri Lanka), competition for scarce resources (especially employment), the disproportionate benefits from modernization enjoyed by some ethnic groups (for example, the Ibo in Nigeria), and exclusive ethnic occupational specialization and 'division of labour'. Colonial discrimination left legacies of ethnic hierarchies and disparities in material well-being (such as the Baganda in Uganda). Fears of political domination have been exacerbated by the exclusive right to rule claimed by some ethnic groups (such as the Pushtuns of Afghanistan) and by the designation of a single language as 'official' (as with Malay in Malaysia) (Horowitz, 1985). Political discrimination of one ethnic group by another led to civil war in Cote d'Ivoire in 2002. In Burundi a government dominated by the Tutsi minority and kept in power by military dictatorship led to 12 years of civil war with the majority Hutu population.

Whether ethnic diversity threatens political stability depends very much on how it is structured and managed. The type and extent of ethnic conflict is determined by the level of group cohesion (affected by the strength of grievance and the group's regional concentration), the strategies and tactics of leaders (particularly the use of violence), the type of political system confronted (its level of democracy), and external encouragement (Gurr and Harff, 1994). Ethnicity is reduced in significance when there are crosscutting identities rather than a correspondence between ethnic, religious, regional and linguistic cleavages. Combinations of ethnicity and religion have led to insurgencies in Cote d'Ivoire on the part of Moslem Dioulas and Senoufos, and in southern Thailand, where Moslem Malays resist integration into a predominantly Buddhist country. Instability is also more likely where there are a few large ethnic groups whose conflicts dominate politics, and less likely when there is a multiplicity of small ethnic groups – compare Nigeria and Tanzania in this regard.

The proposition that ethnic diversity makes a country more vulnerable to political instability has been tested empirically by quantitative analysis of 127 conflicts in 161 countries between 1945 and 1999. When civil war was taken as the indicator of instability it was found that neither ethnic pluralism nor state discrimination against minorities, whether religious or linguistic, made instability more likely. Rather, the presence of conditions favouring insurgency, whether inspired by communism, Islamic fundamentalism, or nationalism, increase the risk of civil war. Such conditions are weak and unstable government, topography, a large population, and familiarity with local conditions on the part of rebels (Feardon and Laitin, 2003).

These findings do not completely eliminate the role of ethnicity in political instability. Ethnic pluralism and discrimination may not be correlated with civil war but could still be causally related to other kinds of instability. The sample also included Eastern Europe, the former USSR, and two western countries. Per capita income was used as a proxy for governmental capability, and it was also acknowledged that 'ethnic diversity could still cause civil war indirectly, if it causes a low per capita income or a weak state' (Feardon and Laitin, 2003, p. 82) – per capita income being a strongly significant variable when examining vulnerability to civil war, with a drop of $1,000 raising vulnerability by 41 per cent.

The cultural pluralism which has been cited as almost a hallmark of political underdevelopment has often meant a lack of consensus about political values. There is then what is often regarded as a crisis of political culture.

The political culture

The political culture is usually defined as the way people evaluate and judge political acts and institutions (Diamond, 1993a). It is a system of beliefs, values and ideals about the way a system of government should function. Subject to some variations, 'political culture' refers to standards of evaluation about the rules of the political game. Some political scientists have limited the concept to values concerning the procedures of politics, and how political leaders should be selected, how they ought to behave, and how authoritative decisions ought to be made. Others add to this the scope of government action and the legitimacy of government intervention in certain areas of social and economic activity.

Cultural values will include the means for transferring power and the legitimate boundaries of the state. Nationalism and secession are the consequence of values about territorial boundaries and where they ought to be drawn. Ideas about personal political involvement, about who is entitled to participate, and about whether political action is likely to be effective within a given political system also form part of the political culture. Included too are attitudes towards other participants and their roles as political actors. A political culture may not endorse the involvement and participation of all sections of society. For example, women may be excluded.

Reservations have been expressed about the concept of political culture and explanations of change in terms of it. First, there is a problem of causality in assuming that certain types of political culture are conducive to the maintenance of certain sorts of political system, and that, if there is no congruence between culture and system, the system will change as a result of being undermined by a lack of consensus and legitimacy. Political culture must not be viewed too deterministically (Diamond, 1993b). There is a presupposition in much of the literature that the line of causality runs in this direction.

A further problem is that a good deal of the political instability which Third World countries have experienced would seem to coincide with widely shared values. The idea that the only way to protect one's own interests is to acquire and hold on to a monopoly of power to the complete exclusion where possible of other groups, has characterized the behaviour of many political movements in the post-independence era, as it did the behaviour of some of the fragmented nationalist movements fighting for independence. Because of the significance of the state in social and economic terms it has been the object of attention of political groups seeking to monopolize power, rather than share it in a spirit of trust with other groups. Such widely disseminated attitudes towards power have been very destabilizing.

So if some shared values are conducive to stability and others are not, the use of the concept of culture implying shared values as an explanation of stability no longer works. At the very least it becomes a circular argument: stability occurs if members of society share values conducive to stability. It depends what those shared values are. It is not enough to say that a society will be stable when a sufficiently large number of people share common values about how to conduct political affairs.

This is quite apart from the problem of how many are enough. In any particular society one is likely to find more than one set of beliefs about the role of government in society, the way it should be conducted, and the proper political roles of different sections of the community. This raises the question of what proportion of society there must be supporting one view of how government should be conducted before there can be said to be sufficient consensus to sustain a political system that corresponds to those shared values. How homogeneous does the culture have to be, and how widely shared?

Another difficulty arises if we assume that there is a crisis of legitimacy when some proportion of society feels that the rules of government lack moral authority and so dispute them, not seeing it as immoral to manipulate the constitution for its own ends. It is not easy to predict, simply by knowing that they believe some or all of those rules to lack moral worth, how far people will deviate from the established norms. People might believe that the rules do not deserve their moral approval without being prepared to break them. This is a universal dilemma in politics. A system can lose moral authority if it is proved easy to abuse. But acting contrary to some rules because others are being bent and broken may be more damaging than going along with the outcomes of the rules as they are presently being played.

If it is not possible to know how far people will deviate simply because they lack moral respect for government, it is equally impossible to know whether when they deviate it is because of that lack. In the Third World there is frequent flouting of the rules, with electoral malpractices very widespread. Does this signify a crisis of legitimacy? It does not always lead to instability, unless instability is defined as breaking the rules. So it again does not seem to be a very useful theoretical explanation to say that if consensus is lacking, there will be political instability.

Finally the concept of political culture implies that attitudes and feelings about politics reflect rational choices and high levels of awareness about what a political system means as far as individual interests are concerned. There is no place for the idea of false consciousness or hegemony. Yet what people believe to be in their interest in terms of structures of government may be ideas and values that are promulgated by socio-economic groups intent on maintaining their own domination. Alternative sets of values would undermine that dominance. Socialization may explain how political values are passed from one generation to another, but this is a generational process rather than as a class problem, whereby one generation passes on to another values that are contrary to their class interests. The idea of political power being in part expressed through false consciousness and an ability to gain acceptance of ways of organizing society has very wide implications throughout the study of politics. The political consciousness of specific groups in Third World societies is an important issue if we are to understand why so much deprivation, injustice and inequality is accepted in societies where such features are most severe. The political culture idea does not really tackle what must be regarded as an important dimension of political power.

Inequality

A proposition concerning political instability which can be traced back to Aristotle is that equality in society will secure peace and stability. This should be very relevant to the Third World where there are 'deep, cumulative social inequalities' (Diamond et al., 1990, p. 19; Pinkney, 1993).

While trends in inequality in the Third World do not follow any regional pattern, overall inequality has increased over the last 30 years, particularly because of increases in countries with large populations, such as China.

Table 9.1   *Percentage shares of income and consumption, poorest and richest 20 per cent of population, high and low income countries*

Low income	Lowest 20%	Highest 20%	High income	Lowest 20%	Highest 20%
Bolivia	1.5	63.0	Austria	8.6	37.8
Honduras	3.4	58.3	Belarus	8.5	38.3
Paraguay	2.4	61.9	Bulgaria	8.7	36.3
Sierra Leone	1.1	63.4	Czech Republic	10.3	35.9
Brazil	2.8	61.1	Finland	9.6	36.7
Central African Republic	2.0	65.0	Hungary	9.5	36.5
Guinea-Bissau	2.1	53.4	Japan	10.6	35.7
Nicaragua	2.2	49.3	Slovak Republic	8.8	34.8

SOURCE: Data taken from latest available survey year, World Bank, 2007b, Table 2.7, pp. 66–8.

The scale of the problem in developing countries is illustrated by a comparison of the percentage shares of income of the poorest and richest 20 per cent of the population in countries with the highest and lowest levels of inequality. The countries with the lowest inequality are not the richest in the world and those with the highest levels are not always the poorest. But none of the countries with low inequality is in the Third World.

Table 9.1 suggests that if inequality is a source of political instability, Third World countries are faced with a serious problem; but that relative equality can be associated with instability, too, though evidently mainly in countries in transition from communism to democracy.

A commonsense view suggests that if there are profound inequalities there will be resentment and discontent with a system of decision-making that is unable to redress the imbalance or is controlled by those intent on preserving the status quo. Maldistribution of income is likely to be a strong predictor of political violence, not least because it will be felt more strongly among the urban poor who are more able to mobilize collectively. Growing inequality in China led to 87,000 protests and riots in 2006 alone.

There is some evidence supporting a relationship between political instability in poor countries and material inequality, such as in land-holdings (Rueschmeyer et al., 1992). The poorest countries with unequal land distribution are less stable than countries that have inequalities in land but also have alternative sources of wealth and reasonable levels of income (Russett, 1964; Huntington, 1968). This relates to the economic backwardness argument: that poor countries cannot produce enough wealth to satisfy all needs, whereas richer countries satisfy basic needs and make the standard of living of the poorest reasonable and not too insecure.

However, other studies using political violence as an indicator of instability and land ownership as a measure of inequality have shown that while maldistribution of land ownership, including high levels of landlessness, have preceded revolutionary violence in Nicaragua and El Salvador, other countries in the same region (Cost Rica and Panama) with similar inequalities remained relatively non violent and stable. Agrarian inequality may not act independently but simply be part of inequality in the overall distribution of income (Muller and Seligson, 1987). How land inequality is measured is also an important consideration, since landlessness, rather than the distribution of land among the landed population, might be a better predictor of instability, since high levels of landlessness preceded political violence and even revolution in Mexico (1911), China (1941), Cuba (1959) and Bolivia (1952). However, extensive cross-national multivariate analysis has revealed the relationship between landlessness and political violence to be statistically insignificant (Muller et al., 1989).

The converse argument is that stable countries have relatively egalitarian distributions of income. But it has to be recognized that the hypothesis would seem to be falsified by inegalitarian societies that have nevertheless experienced considerable stability. India would be a case in point, frequently cited as a stable democracy, at least in Third World terms. It obviously depends on how stability is measured.

Evidently not all inequality is threatening to the status quo. Gender inequality is the most visible example of this. Discrimination against women in politics (and in other walks of life) is the defining characteristic of gender relations in the Third World (as in most other countries). Women's citizenship is limited. A study of 43 countries covering three-quarters of the world's population found that 'in no country do women have political status equal to men's' (Chowdhury and Nelson, 1994, p. 3). A contributory factor is that the management of the family and household falls disproportionately on women at the expense of political participation.

Women are grossly underrepresented in political institutions and organizations, especially political parties. Only in the Caribbean and the Seychelles do women occupy more than 20 per cent of ministerial posts at Cabinet level. The proportion is less than 5 per cent in Asia and the Pacific. In only 11 developing countries do women occupy 20 per cent or more of sub-ministerial positions in the executive branch. In all regions of the Third World women constitute no more than 15 per cent of national legislators on average. Table 9.2 shows that there are considerable disparities between countries in the same development category. But everywhere in the Third World the state is a 'gendered hierarchy' which excludes or marginalizes women by misogynist social and religious conventions which relegate women to the private sphere, especially in Islamic regimes (Whalen, 1996a). In China levels of women's political participation have actually fallen during recent economic and political reforms as women have been disadvantaged by the introduction of multi-candidate elections allowing discrimination in favour of men (Davin, 1996).

Table 9.2   *Women in parliament, selected countries*

Country	Parliamentary seats held in 2007(%)
Low income	16.1
Mozambique	34.8
Bangladesh	15.1
Lower middle income	16.3
Cuba	36.0
Morocco	10.5
Upper middle income	15.2
Argentina	35.0
Gabon	12.5
High income	22.7
Sweden	47.3
Kuwait	1.5

SOURCE: World Bank (2008), *Social Development*, http://go.worldbank.org/9HEOQTEM70

Even after periods of democratization in which women had been significant actors, cultures of patriarchy continue to exclude women from politics. The return to 'normality' usually entails restrictions on women's roles, especially in politics and government (Chowdhury and Nelson, 1994). Women in Latin America, for example, have been vulnerable to renewed exclusion after the transition to democracy, as the power of their social movements becomes displaced by male dominated political parties, and as governments focus on economic rather than the social objectives for which women campaigned – a 'remasculinization' of politics. Latin American history shows that even revolutionary states 'are as resistant as other states to the participation of women' (Craske, 1999, pp. 87, 161).

This is not to say that women have not been part of the campaigns to change politics fundamentally. They have played an important part in the movements for democracy, political reform, and resistance to authoritarianism, especially in Latin America, Taiwan and the Philippines, forming new social movements to protest, lobby and articulate political demands (Hensman, 1996). Women's organizations with feminist agendas have emerged in the 1980s and 1990s, such as the National Women's Lobby in Zambia and GABRIELA in the Philippines (Whalen, 1996b). The emergence of women in top political offices, such as the Presidencies of Chile and Argentina, may help improve the position of women in male dominated societies.

But much of women's political activism and organization (as distinct from self-help projects which sometimes alter the gender imbalance in local power networks – Jaquette, 2001) has not been directed at gender inequalities, backed perhaps by a feminist philosophy. It has been devoted to economic and social causes which are not gender specific and from which all would benefit, such as campaigning for human rights, food subsidies, employment protection and health care. The politics in which women engage has rarely placed equality (for example, through an extension of the suffrage) at the top of the agenda. Even when women have been involved in revolutionary movements which include women's emancipation in their agendas this has been 'limited and full of contradictions' (Whalen, 1996b, p. 90). Post revolutionary improvements to women's health, education and welfare can be accounted for more by improvements to the lives of the poor generally than by women's political activism.

Part of the explanation for this is that women do not constitute a homogenous group but are as divided as men in terms of class, religion and ethnicity. In Latin America, for example, 'women stress their class links rather than their gender identities' (Craske, 1999, p. 161).

Class conflict

From a Marxist perspective a theoretical explanation of instability would be in terms of class conflict. As classes develop within a capitalist economy and society, their interests become increasingly irreconcilable. The impoverishment of the labouring class is accompanied by its growth until eventually revolution becomes inevitable. But at least one of the problems with this line of thought in the Third World context is that if class consciousness is developing, it is in a unique way. It is less in terms of the ownership of the means of production and more in terms of political power. Those who control and manage the means of production, such as bureaucrats earning salaries, often confront a peasant society that has yet to develop class consciousness derived from its material position in society.

Then there is the problem alluded to earlier, that it is often the privileged members of society who indulge in destabilization. In the Third World conflict and crisis within the newly emerging middle class have been a source of political instability. In 2006 opposition to Thailand's Thai Rak Thai government was mounted by the urban middle class because of government policies favouring the rural poor, including affordable health care and cheap loans. A military coup briefly ended parliamentary government, and the middle class has again demonstrated against the democratically elected government. Factionalism, perhaps along ethnic lines, among the propertied classes and classes in charge of the state apparatus has often led to military *coups* or the illegal manipulation of political processes. Rather than peasants rising up against their oppressors, or workers revolting against their exploiters, sections of the middle class compete for control of the state, using methods that fall outside the law and the constitution.

A crisis of state authority

Third World states have often lacked the power to make their presence felt throughout society. They have experienced legal and administrative incapacity amounting to the collapse of state institutions. Bureaucracies might be overdeveloped in terms of political power but they are not necessarily effective in terms of administration. The state cannot deliver the services which taxpayers believe they are paying for; it cannot extract the resources from society that it needs to finance its activities; it cannot maintain law and order; it cannot police its territory effectively. The case of Uganda in the 1980s seems to support this kind of explanation. Too many areas were under the control of criminals, bandits and other groups which had no legitimate authority. There are other societies in which this is a problem. The Thai government does not control its northernmost provinces – they are under the control of drugs barons. In Colombia there has been virtual civil war between the state and organizations that want to remain outside the scope of the state's authority and the enforcement of its laws. The failure of 'new' states to extend effective political authority, maintain order and extract resources for the provision of public goods throughout their territories leads to crises, the erosion of legitimacy and security, and violent civil conflict in 'the already fragile post-colonial state' (Ayoob, 1996, p. 73; Migdal, 1996).

Somalia is an extreme example of state collapse. When the military regime of Mohamed Siyad Barre collapsed in 1991 with the withdrawal of foreign support, the Somali state totally lacked legitimacy. It was associated with the repressive personal rule of a dictator, militarism and clan-based patronage. The Somali bourgeoisie had been systematically destroyed, state terror had been unleashed against political opposition, and clan conflict had been deliberately intensified as 'loyal' clans were encouraged to wage war on 'rebel' clans, leaving a civil society in violent turmoil. State institutions 'were thrown into gridlock, jealousy, confusion and anarchy'.

Civil society was too divided to support state authority and political order, and unable to provide national leadership. Power was monopolized by clan warlords supported by heavily-armed militias who controlled society by extortion and violence, especially sexual violence against women. The warlords competed for control of the capital in a civil war which destroyed all institutions 'and records of central government'. Somalia reverted to the nineteenth century, with 'no internationally recognized polity; no national administration exercising real authority; no formal legal system; no banking and insurance services; no telephone and postal system; no public service; no educational and reliable health system; no police and public security services; no electricity or piped water systems; weak officials serving on a voluntary basis surrounded by disruptive, violent bands of armed youths' (Adam, 1995, pp. 72–8).

State incapacity springs from a number of sources. Colonialism weakened, fragmented or destroyed existing means of social control. State leaders have created organizations which compete with and threaten the power of the state's executive leadership. Strong societies have proved resistant to state domination through the power of chiefs, landlords, bosses, foreign corporations, rich peasants, clan leaders, castes, powerful families and 'strongmen' (Migdal, 1988).

This view of civil conflict and political instability may confuse cause with effect. The factors which are presented as the consequences of state failure, such as ethno-nationalism, social conflict, and external military intervention, can equally and possibly more convincingly be seen as causes of state incapacity and the collapse of hitherto effective states such as the Lebanon before the mid-1970s. This is not to deny that the collapse of state governance will exacerbate the social and economic forces that have worked to undermine it.

Furthermore, instability often results from the actions of those who control the coercive apparatus of the state rather than those who control extra-legal means of coercion, whether as criminal organizations or opposition groups. The military is the most obvious case in point. The crisis of authority comes because the coercive apparatus of the state turns against its civil masters, not because that apparatus is so weak that it cannot resist an external challenge to the state's authority. The strength of the state's coercive apparatus has been increased by Third World expenditure on arms. Such expenditure seems to be driven more by the political pressures which the armed forces in developing countries are able to exert than by security considerations. It tilts the balance of power and resources towards the military, blocks the development of 'strong and independent social and political institutions', and 'results in state institutions and elite groups being bent to the purposes of the institutions of organized violence' (Krause, 1996, p. 187). Thus the strong, rather than weak, state can be a source of instability.

Political institutionalization

Political institutions are important for stability in developing countries. An important political consequence of modernization in a pre-industrial society is a rapid increase in political mobilization and participation. If political instability is to be avoided, such participation needs to be matched by a corresponding level of institutional development. By and large this had not happened in developing countries. Violence and instability have been the consequence of political institutions developing more slowly than the rate at which new socio-economic groups were being politically mobilized. The lack of effective political institutions makes it impossible for demands to be channelled through effective and legitimate procedures (Huntington and Dominguez, 1975).

A problem with this explanation is that it contains a tautological element (Leys, 1982). 'Institutionalization' refers to a process through which conflict can be managed in a peaceful and structured way. It does not just mean the creation of organizations. The institutionalization argument seems tantamount to saying that if individuals and groups are prepared to participate in politics by playing according to the rules and abiding by the outcomes of so doing, there will be stability. An increase in participation leads to instability if political institutions cannot absorb it, but instability is the evidence that institutionalization is insufficiently developed. In other words, there will be stability when there is no instability. We are left needing an explanation of why people should behave in ways that are not constitutionally sanctioned.

Nevertheless, the view that political participation needs to be matched by institutional development if instability is to be averted is supported by comparative research into the 'coherence' or 'consistency' of different types of regime. Statistical analysis of quantitative measures of institutions and stability for a large number of regimes over the nineteenth and twentieth centuries confirms that political instability is a function of institutional consistency. A dictatorship with high levels of political participation is institutionally inconsistent, and consequently unstable. An autocratic regime will be stable if it prevents the development of institutions capable of challenging the power of the central executive. Similarly, a democracy will be stable if power is diffused, offering opportunities for power to a wide range of interests. Democratic institutions – elections, accountable government, channels of political participation – reinforce one another. Political instability occurs when institutions are inconsistent, that is, when there are elected bodies but restricted political participation. Institutionally inconsistent regimes are unstable not only because they are 'more prone to the expression of grievances, but also because they have weak institutions for addressing challenges to the authority of the regime' (Gates et al., 2006, p. 907).

A cross-national quantitative study of 141 severe political crises, including revolutionary wars, ethnic conflicts and anti-democratic coups between 1955 and 2003 also found that regime 'coherence' explained instability better than other variables such as ethnic pluralism, poverty, or economic performance. By asking 'what conditions enable a state to remain stable?' it was found that the risk of instability is lowest in full autocracies and full democracies, and highest in hybrid regimes, such as when there are competitive but not fully free elections, and political competition is dominated by particularistic groups (formed on the basis of religious or ethnic identity) which approach politics in a 'winner takes all' mentality. A lack of cross-cutting identities in political competition thus substantially increases the risk of political crisis (Goldstone et al., 2005). The factionalism found in the Lebanon, where exclusive rival communities based mainly on religion, many with their own militias, persistently block the development of stable democracy, would seem to fit this model.

Studies of this kind should only tentatively be applied to the contemporary Third World, because they include a large number of countries at different stages of economic development over a very long period. But it is interesting when quantitative analysis confirms what is suggested by contemporary events, as well as being supported by a study of coups, riots and political assassinations in 18 Latin American countries between 1971 and 2000 which found that the more democratic the country, the less the political instability (Blanco and Grier, 2007).

Revolution in the Third World

The ultimate manifestation of political instability is revolution. Revolution involves the replacement of a whole social order, and not just a political regime. Ideologies and new forms of organization are required. Solidarity is mobilized, mainly along class lines, but religion may be significant in raising class consciousness, as in the case of Islamic fundamentalism in Iran and Algeria. Existing social and political structures, particularly property relations, are defined as exploitative and oppressive and are challenged as such. The objective is an alternative form of society (Shanin, 1982).

In the first half of the twentieth century successful revolutions that were not instigated by foreign intervention took place in developing societies, 'peasant revolt being central to all of them' (Shanin, 1982, p. 321). Consequently, the analysis of such events has been largely dominated by a search for the conditions necessary for a peasant-based revolution. Historians and social scientists have asked why these should occur in some societies and not others which seem to be comparable in respect of the social and economic factors which *a priori* might be thought likely to lead to revolution (Goodwin and Skocpol, 1989).

Revolution is usually preceded by severe social dislocation, crisis within the political élite, a strengthening of class identity and militancy, and the emergence of an effective revolutionary organization (Shanin,

1982, p. 313). Crisis is commonly occasioned by fiscal problems, conflict between élites and élite alienation (especially when social mobility is restricted), and widespread grievances leading to popular support for change that can be mobilized against the regime. For example, in Iran, the regime had built up excessive debts and was unable to control inflation. The exclusion of the middle classes from power, government corruption, and repression alienated the religious élite and the merchant class. Population growth and urbanization outstripped economic opportunities, making society receptive to mobilization by nationalistic Islamic ideology. A coalition of traditional and Westernized élites led to the demise of the Shah's regime (Goldstone et al., 1991; Parsa, 2000).

The significance of crisis is affected by other features of the vulnerable state. 'Exclusive' states which restrict political power to individuals and dynasties, marginalize democratic procedures, exclude other élites from decision-making, and provide no opportunities for change are vulnerable. In times of crisis such states have to resort to repression and the external support of foreign powers, alienating moderate political opposition and extending the appeal of revolutionary action in the absence of alternative forms of politics. States that are highly interventionist economically (in terms of capital formation, ownership of assets, and economic regulation) are also vulnerable, since they attract criticism for economic as well as political failures. All aspects of society become politicized and all social classes are potential victims of state mismanagement (Parsa, 2000). Pre-revolutionary Iran, Nicaragua and the Philippines were all vulnerable because of the political exclusiveness of their regimes and their unsuccessful interventionism. External support from the USA and reliance on military repression failed to save them. Moderate opposition was weakened or eliminated in Iran and Nicaragua, which radicalized other social elements, especially students and the clergy. In the Philippines moderate political opponents were tolerated and able to limit the impact of revolutionary change to the political realm (thus not producing a *social* revolution).

Revolution usually begins with rebellions to redress parochial wrongs. This takes the form of extra-constitutional action, perhaps involving violence, when the rural or urban poor take direct action against the governmental authorities or local power-holders in an attempt to resist the intensification of exploitation through higher workloads, declining real wages, victimization of trade unionists, police harassment, loss of land, or the raising of rents and taxes. Here the political activism is short term. The objective is to redress a wrong. There is no long-term programme or ideology for fundamental change in social and economic relations.

What then turns rebellion into a revolutionary force? Firstly, an *ideology* is needed to redirect and focus political activism, though revolution is not always characterized by a single, coherent ideology – no single ideology united the entire population in Iran, the Philippines or Nicaragua, for example (Parsa, 2000). Secondly, outside *leadership* in the form of a coalition between peasants, intellectuals, students, professionals, clerics and industrial workers is needed to provide a forward looking revolutionary consciousness. This is confirmed by the cases of Vietnam, Iran, Cuba and Nicaragua (White, 1974; Goodwin and Skocpol 1989). Revolutionary leadership generally takes the form of an 'intelligentsia-in-arms', either as a military organization or a paramilitary political party.

Thirdly, revolution needs a *social exchange* between rebellious groups and a revolutionary organization. A rebellious community will seek to solve local problems with the benefits offered by revolutionary leaders as incentives to participate in revolutionary action. Revolutionary organizations, for their part, need to expand their power through recruitment within the community and by demonstrating that they can deliver what society needs, including substitutes for the socio-economic arrangements that are to be replaced by the revolution, such as marketing arrangements, land reforms, co-operatives, harvest labour, public utilities such as roads, communications and irrigation ditches, social services such as health care and education, and, most importantly, destruction of the power of corrupt officials, monopolistic merchants and landlords. Revolutionary organizations, such as parties and armies, also offer opportunities for social mobility. They must offer more than other political organizations because of the risks involved, not least that of severe retaliation by the state.

The Revolutionary Armed Forces of Colombia provide an interesting case of how such an exchange can work. While most revolutionary movements in Latin America between 1960 and 1992 found inspiration in some variant of Marxism, FARC developed its own 'Bolivarian' ideology. In practice this meant its aims were social protection for the lower classes, agrarian reform, greater equality and competent government. Consequently, FARC provides health, education, and public order functions in areas under its control, forming an alternative government, or even a parallel state. Being an 'alternative public manager' gave it wide appeal among a peasantry used to harsh working conditions, insecurity, state repression and violations of human rights, violence from right-wing paramilitary death squads, and under-investment by the state in social and economic development.

However, the maintenance of public order and protection against government forces also benefits the peasant coca growers and the criminals involved in the narcotics trade, on whom FARC levies taxes covering every stage of the business, estimated to be worth $300 million a year. Connections with drug traffickers also provide FARC with access to the international black market in arms, but also reduce its legitimacy in the eyes of the international community as well as within Colombia (Ortiz, 2002).

Fourthly, in the case of revolution in agrarian societies, the *class struc-ture* is significant for revolutionary potential. The poorest are likely to be the least revolutionary in the initial stages of class conflict because of extreme economic dependency. Those with a measure of independence and security, such as smallholders owning their own land and producing enough to be self-sufficient are more likely to be revolutionary when aggrieved by injustice. They are vulnerable to the changes brought about by commercialization – population growth, competition, the loss of rights to grazing land and water, falling prices, higher interest payments, and foreclosures – while remaining locked into traditional social structures of mutual aid between kin and neighbours.

Finally, revolution in agrarian societies is dependent on the threat to the peasantry from the *upper classes* and their response to the challenge of commercial agriculture. Explanations of revolution should not concentrate exclusively on the actions of the peasantry. Revolution is most likely when the aristocracy damages the interests of the peasantry as a class by exacting a larger surplus from it, but leaves it intact by failing to develop a suffi-ciently powerful commercial impulse in the countryside. When the commercial interest in rural life is sufficiently strong to destroy the peas-antry as a class, peasant-based revolution is less likely. Revolutions in predominantly agrarian societies have occurred when the landed classes by and large did not make a successful transition to the world of commerce and industry and did not destroy the prevailing social organization among the peasantry (Moore, 1973).

Conclusion

The focus in much of this chapter has been on the rural poor, the obstacles to their effective political participation, and the crises which precipitate extreme reactions against those who dominate them economically and politically. But many other factors have been related to political instability, though the direction of causality has not always been clear. None is suffi-cient in itself to explain the complexity of phenomenon. The significance of each factor will vary according to the circumstances of region, history, level of economic development, and place within the international system. It thus becomes important to know under what circumstances a factor such as economic inequality, rapid economic growth, or social differentiation is likely to lead to political instability.

One answer is when the expectations of political participants of appro-priate social, economic and political action are not met by changes in social organization. So if, for example, extreme inequalities in pre-industrial societies are found to be associated with political stability, contrary to the expectations of analysts, this can be explained by reference to the absence of egalitarianism from the dominant image of society. When that image is changed as a result of mass mobilization, inequality becomes less acceptable and political instability can result. Similarly, rapid economic growth in contemporary Western societies is not destabilizing because such changes have become institutionalized expectations of the dominant ideology (Castles, 1974).

The advantage of such a paradigm is that it provides a framework for understanding why supposedly causal factors operate under some circumstances but not others. In stressing the importance of the response to changes in society and economy by the dominant protagonists of current images it also helps to explain why a group or class that might be expected *a priori* to be violently dissatisfied with their lot expresses no political dissent likely to undermine political stability.

The finding that partial democracy, especially if accompanied by particularistic political groups in electoral competition, is likely to become unstable is particularly significant for processes of democratization, the subject of the next chapter. In the Third World the kind of political competition associated with instability is very common, as is income inequality and ethnic fragmentation, making any transition from authoritarianism fraught with danger.

10

Democratization in the Third World

Introduction: the 'third wave' and the Third World

Recent reforms in the direction of pluralist democracy and away from authoritarianism in the form of military rule, one-party systems, personal dictatorships and racial oligarchy have revived interest in how to identify the prerequisites of stable democracy. Identifying the necessary conditions for the survival of democratic regimes has long been a preoccupation of political science, but is particularly relevant today when so many attempts are being made to establish or restore liberal democracy in so many parts of the world. Developing countries have been caught up in the so-called 'third wave' of democratization, starting in Portugal in 1974 and sweeping across southern and eastern Europe and, to varying degrees, most regions of the Third World (Huntington, 1991; Pinkney, 1993).

This chapter covers theories of democratic transition and consolidation, and the contribution of economic and political factors to stable democracy: national affluence, with its implications for equality and class development; the political culture and the problem of the direction of causality; civil society as a counter-balance to the power of the state; the balance of power within democracies; and the importance of institutional development to democratic consolidation.

The latest wave of democratization that increased the proportion of countries in the world with some form of democratic government from 28 per cent in 1974 to 61 per cent in 1998 has included remarkable changes in the Third World. However, since 1980 the strength of democratization here has varied, with the strongest felt in Latin America. Asia too has experienced significant democratization. Sub-Saharan Africa has lagged behind with relatively weak attempts to democratize. The Middle East has seen very little effort to democratize (see Table 10.1). There are no true democracies or free societies in the Arab region and few free or democratic countries among states with a Muslim majority (Keratnyky, 2002).

The process of democratization has not been one of smooth progression.

Table 10.1 *Freedom: regional variations, 2007*

	Number of states rated:		
	Free	*Partly free*	*Not free*
Africa	11 (23%)	23 (48%)	14 (29%)
Asia and Pacific	16 (41%)	13 (33%)	10 (26%)
The Americas	25 (71%)	9 (26%)	1 (3%)
Middle East and North Africa	1 (6%)	6 (33%)	11 (61%)

NOTE: Freedom House divides countries into three broad categories on the basis of indicators of political rights (such as the right of all adults to vote) and civil liberties (such as freedom of assembly and demonstration): 'free', 'partly free' and 'not free'.
SOURCE: Freedom House (2008a), regional tables.

When new countries enter the ranks of newly democratizing states (for example, Mexico and Ghana in 2000), others suffer reversals in the form of *coups* (Ecuador and Fiji), or ethnic violence leading to the collapse of government (The Solomon Islands). While some developing countries register improvements in political rights and civil liberties, such as media freedoms in Peru, free and fair elections in Taiwan, and greater economic opportunities for women in Oman, others experience set-backs. There were 21 such reversals in 2007, including Bangladesh, where military rule was reintroduced and civil liberties curtailed; Kenya, due to electoral irregularities; and Egypt, following the suppression of freedom of association and restraints on the judiciary.

To account for the process of democratization and its set-backs, political science has drawn a broad distinction between the *transition* to democracy, or a particular kind of change and its historical antecedents and causes; and *consolidation*, or the conditions necessary for democratic regimes, especially those following a period of authoritarianism, to survive. Before examining attempts to generalize and theorize about these phases of democratization, a cautionary reference to the concept of democracy must be made.

Concepts of 'democracy'

In the study of Third World democratization, 'democracy' is usually defined in Western liberal terms. It requires a system of government to provide meaningful and extensive competition between individuals and groups, highly inclusive levels of political participation in the selection of leaders and policies, civil and political liberties sufficient to ensure such competition and participation, representative parliaments, the responsibility of government to parliament, regular free and fair elections, freedom of expression and association, and an extensive suffrage. Countries satisfy such criteria to differing degrees, and rules and principles may be contaminated by practice (Diamond et al., 1990; Rueschmeyer et al., 1992).

One of the reasons why understanding democratization is so difficult is the variability of regimes that are labelled democratic, and the nature of the democratic deficit found in so many. Regimes may be classified as new or restored democracies despite the circumvention by parliaments of presidential decrees (for example, Argentina), disregard of constitutional boundaries by the executive branch (for example, Taiwan), the award of veto powers to non-elected bodies such as the military (Chile and Thailand), and other deviations from the democratic ideal. Such variations make it problematic to relate democratization as a dependent variable to factors believed hypothetically to explain the process, especially consolidation (O'Donnell, 1998; Merkel, 1999).

The analysis of democratization is further complicated by the contested nature of the concept of democracy. Definitions often refer to the presence of different phenomena: procedures (such as the holding of free and fair elections); recognized human rights (such as freedom of association and speech); extensive participation; and material equality (because economic deprivation leads to political disempowerment). There are both formal and substantive conceptions of democracy. For some, democracy means 'meaningful political citizenship' (Grugel, 2002, p. 5). Analysis of democratization is affected by whatever view of democracy is held by the investigator.

The transition to democracy

Transitions from authoritarianism to democracy have been extremely varied, making it difficult to discern patterns that aid explanation. This complexity is sometimes compounded by confusion between the causes of authoritarian breakdown and the processes by which democratic replacements are introduced, as with a classification of the three 'routes' to democracy as: 'modernization', which stresses the economic prerequisites of democracy; 'structural', which focuses on the effects on authoritarianism of changes in class and power; and 'transition', which focuses on the bargaining between élites which negotiate the transition to democracy (Potter et al., 1997). Such confusions make it difficult to distinguish between the definition of a phase such as transition, and its causes. Furthermore, transition and consolidation are not always kept conceptually distinct, as when explanations of transition are used to test whether a democracy has become consolidated (see for example, Chadda, 2000). It has also proved difficult to distinguish between the causes of authoritarian breakdown and the form taken by the negotiation of change.

It helps to consider first what 'triggers' the end of authoritarianism and a movement towards a democratic alternative, though 'trigger' is perhaps not the best term when the causes of democratization may be long-term (such as a programme of industrialization), medium-term (an economic liberalization programme) or short-term (the calculations of political élites or popular struggles) (Luckham and White, 1996). The main causes of authoritarian breakdown are élite conflict, domestic crisis, and international pressure.

Élite conflict within authoritarian regimes has characterized all breakdowns, as coalitions begin to disintegrate under pressure from differences over aims, policies and survival strategies which have no means for consensual conflict resolution: 'the danger for authoritarian regimes is that the weakness of institutional procedures for resolving disputes creates significant potential for instability' (Gill, 2000, p. 32). The disunity preceding many transitions to democracy alerts opposition movements to the possibility of reform.

Internal crisis is another factor that often triggers the transition to democracy, such as economic recession or military failure (for example, Argentina's defeat in the Falklands/Malvinas war in 1983). The breakdown of authoritarian regimes has often followed economic crises brought about by poor economic management and international pressures (such as a steep rise in oil prices or a reduction in the availability of foreign loans). Policy adjustments, such as devaluation, to deal with the crisis then have adverse consequences for groups supporting the regime that have already been disadvantaged by the crisis itself. Declining domestic legitimacy then increases the cost of authoritarian power. Alternatively, the costs of democracy or the threat of revolution may be perceived by authoritarian governments to have receded (Gill, 2000).

External pressures may begin the demise of an authoritarian regime, such as the need to acquire international legitimacy or satisfy international expectations of political reform which may be made a condition of further development assistance from multilateral and bilateral aid agencies. Alternatively a foreign power may enforce democratization, as in Panama. The current wave of democratization originated in part as a response to intensified economic internationalization, the dominance of neo-liberal ideology, and the disintegration of the USSR (Przeworski, 1995). International pressures can act in support of domestic factors to cause the breakdown of an authoritarian regime – economic sanctions, trade embargoes, international ideological pressures, global recessions, 'contagion' (as in Latin America) and, rarely, military force. However, how such international factors affect democratizing regimes has depended on how domestic economic and political actors, institutions and structures were linked to global geopolitical forces (Gill, 2000).

Transition has frequently been initiated from above. Rather than being overthrown authoritarian regimes disintegrate. Authoritarianism has been ended by popular protest or revolutionary action in only a minority of cases. Transitions from above have been most likely to lead to democracy. Revolutions may overthrow authoritarian regimes, but rarely lead to democracy (Nicaragua being one exception to this rule). Reform efforts launched by mass movements usually encounter anti-democratic resistance from established élites. It has even been argued that mass participation and popular mobilization can harm the democratization process (Huntington, 1984; Weiner, 1987). In Latin America at least, democratization means the creation of 'pacts' between representatives of regime and opposition which guarantee some measure of protection for the interests involved, such as the military on the government side and trade unions among the opposition.

The dissolution of authoritarian regimes is commonly marked by liberalization, whereby repression is eased and the right of political association is recognized. Civil society is gradually 'resurrected'. Parties re-emerge (Mainwaring, 1992). But mainly transition is characterized by negotiations between representatives of the current regime and opposition forces to design the new system of government. Dominant élites may judge that a move towards democracy will be in their own interest, as in Mexico, leading them to concede to democratic reform. Alternatively they might have to retreat in the face of opposition pressure, a factor in Argentina's end to military rule. Opposition groups then take the lead in negotiating the end of authoritarianism. In most cases negotiation between representatives of the old regime and its opponents characterize transition (Huntington, 1991; Little, 1997). Latin American experience shows that successful transitions were usually negotiated by moderates on both sides who were willing to compromise in accommodating each other's interests (Peeler, 1998).

Negotiations and pacts have implications for the quality of the democracy created. For example, when transition requires pacts that protect the interests of groups and classes represented by authoritarian élites, the interests of those supporting greater participation, accountability and equity are unlikely to be dominant in the transition phase (Karl, 1996).

When the capacity for mass involvement in transition is understood it becomes evident that many of the political leaders involved in negotiating transition to democracy have popular power bases, and that their role cannot be understood in isolation from the sections of the populace they represent and to which they owe their position. However, the precise contribution which social forces and their leaders make towards the transition to democracy depends on the nature of the authoritarian regime to be changed, and the nature of the society within which it is located.

By distinguishing between different types of regime and different types of political society, it is possible to develop a theory of transition which combines information about both, regime and non-regime élites, the latter owing their power to their position in civil society. Regimes are either 'unitary' in the face of challenges, or 'segmentary', with different interests supporting the regime in conflict. Society is either 'atomized' (without independent groups and movements) or 'civil' – with independent organizations enabling interests to be articulated and a degree of popular control to be exercised. A political system's position in relation to these two dimensions determines its prospects for transition to democracy and the path that will be taken. A combination of unitary regime and atomized society makes democratization less likely, because the regime is better placed to deal with challenges to its power and society is unable to produce effective opposition. Conversely, a combination of segmentary regime and civil society offers better prospects for democratization. If a unitary regime confronts a strong civil society there is a likelihood of violence. Finally, the prospects for democracy are poor when a segmentary regime exists within an atomized society. Here authoritarian collapse is likely to be followed by further authoritarianism (Gill, 2000).

Negotiating the end of authoritarianism means attending to three main issues: the construction of a constitutional settlement; the dismantling of authoritarian government agencies;, and the abolition of laws unsuitable for democratic politics. The possibility of successful negotiation on these institutional reforms depends on five sets of factors (Pinkney, 1993). First, there is the type of authoritarian regime to be dismantled. For example, a caretaker military regime will be easier to remove than a radical or reforming one. One-party regimes present obstacles according to the level of integration of party, state and civil society. Secondly, negotiations will be affected by the ability of opposition groups to plan for democracy rather than just oppose authoritarianism. A third set of factors is the configuration of institutions and political structures under authoritarianism, and the extent to which parties, legislatures, constitutions and traditional political authority have survived during authoritarian rule.

Fourthly, transition depends on the changing orientations towards reform by key élites – cabinets, juntas, bureaucrats, military officers, and opposition leaders – and organizations representing sections within civil society (church leaders, trade unions, social movements). Such orientations determine whether democratization will be government élite-led, or driven by pressures from below and originating at grass-roots level or within the middle class.

Finally, there is the process of conflict resolution. Patterns have been found in the relationships between process and outcomes. The viability of new democratic regimes has been found to be strengthened by a process of transition characterized by gradual rather than rapid change, moderation rather than radicalism on the part of protagonists, consensus rather than conflict over the objectives of democratization, and a balance of power between negotiating groups. Such patterns, however, are far from fixed, and only tentative conclusions have been generated by observations of their detailed operation in specific cases.

Negotiations eventually lead to some form of provisional government while the institutional basis of democracy is put in place (especially a new constitution) and élites adjust their political behaviour to liberal democratic practices. Uncertainty inevitably surrounds the location of the boundary between the end of transition and the start of consolidation, not least because different analysts have different conceptions of democracy's key characteristics, and change is not always marked by some 'focal event' (Schedler, 2001).

Transitions have been highly variable processes, in terms of the sources of tension within authoritarian regimes, responses to pressures for political change by authoritarian leaders, the speed of transition, and the behaviour of élites, parties and civil society bodies. The structural conditions inherited by the transitional government also vary, providing the process of consolidation with 'structured contingencies' in the form of political institutions, informal interest groups, social polarization and relations between states and classes (Haynes, 2001, pp. 18–34).

The variability of transition

This depiction of transition has generated controversies. First, there has been a debate between those who emphasize the importance of conflict within the authoritarian élite, and those who stress the role of pressure from below or among opponents to authoritarianism. Those who explain transition by reference to the role of élites in negotiating the transition from authoritarianism, have been faulted for holding too narrow a view of democracy, ignoring the role of mass movements, and paying insufficient attention to structural factors, such as levels of economic development, which may account for both the decay of authoritarianism and subsequent obstacles to democratic consolidation (Grugel, 2002). Authoritarian regimes can be destabilized by public protest and industrial and political action by trade unions, even if the subsequent negotiations which design the new democratic regimes are dominated by members of different political and economic élites. Peru, Argentina, the Philippines and South Korea are cases in point, as well as some African states, where transitions have been predominantly brought about by mass protest in which church leaders, trade unions, professional groups, human rights campaigners, student and youth organizations and old guard politicians have been involved.

Some transitions in Africa have also originated in popular uprisings and demands for competitive elections and other democratic institutions, rather than pacts between élites (of which South Africa was a rare example) In Benin, for example, transition followed mass demonstrations against the authoritarian regime, and a new constitution was designed by representatives from grassroots organizations, trade unions, religious groups, the political opposition, and the old regime at a National conference in 1990. It depends on the nature of the authoritarian regime as to whether the democratic challenge comes from the mobilization of civil society or conflict within the regime (Diamond, 1997a; Haynes, 2003; Creevy et al., 2005).

Authoritarian regimes, single party more than military, mobilize the public through closely controlled activities – in trade unions, youth groups, business associations, cultural bodies and political parties. Political mobilization becomes a threat to the regime when it is organized by groups with a degree of autonomy from the regime. Such popular mobilization is usually stimulated by economic development or economic crisis (Gill, 2000). Popular participation through social movements such as women's groups (for example, the Mothers of the Plaza de Mayo in Argentina), labour unions (for example, the copper miners in Chile), community organizations and indigenous associations (such as the Zapatista movement in Chiapas, southern Mexico) were important in the struggle against authoritarianism (Grugel, 2002). The case of South Korea and some of the other 'Asian Tigers' also show how economic success can generate new élites and lead to social groups demanding more access to power and resources (Haggard, 1990).

Popular mobilization has, then, accompanied some successful transitions, and 'moderation' on the part of the working class has not proved essential for democratization which has occurred despite political extremism and violence (in Brazil, Chile, Ecuador, Peru, South Korea and the Philippines). This may be because authoritarian élites realize they have a choice between democratic reform and revolution, rather than between democracy and further repression. Similarly, moderate opposition leaders may be unified by the threatening presence of extremism (Bermeo, 1997).

So it should not be inferred from élite domination of negotiations during transition that the causes of authoritarian breakdown had nothing to do with popular pressure or civil society. Popular resistance to authoritarian regimes is common. And while élites may dominate the process of bargaining and pact-making, they represent non-élites – peasants, workers, campaigners, professionals – whose interests cannot be ignored and whose political activity is the subject of the bargaining process. There is also a danger when stressing the role of élites in the negotiation of political change that the process will be made to appear voluntaristic and unpredictable, making it very difficult to formulate a theory of transition (Gill, 2000).

Explanations of democratic transition in terms of power struggles within the ruling bloc or alliance may also be insufficiently dynamic to explain the shifting alliances between bureaucrats, the military, representatives of the property owning classes, labour, and other social entities. Such shifts arise from the inevitable uncertainty about the implications of the retreat from authoritarianism for different socio-economic interests (Przeworski, 1986).

A second controversy warns against assuming that transition is necessarily towards democracy. The majority of 'third wave' countries have not established properly functioning democracy, suffer from severe democratic deficits, and are not necessarily moving towards democracy. Voting has not deepened participation or strengthened accountability. In many cases democratization has been attempted in states which are weak and where state building has not been compatible with democratization. The extent to which civil and political rights are protected varies greatly. The rule of law is frequently undermined. The scale of poverty is such that it must be doubted whether large sections of the population in newly democratizing states enjoy full citizenship. In Africa elections have had little impact on the political order, pro-democracy movements are weak, and economic and political crises block change. In Latin America and Africa, participative democracy and political equality have been negated by persistent poverty, marginalization and exclusion of large sections of society. In Asia authoritarianism has become 'softened' rather than displaced by democracy. These defects should not be forced into the 'transition' model by the addition of adjectives like semi, formal, façade, pseudo, weak, partial, illiberal and virtual, because politics in these countries calls the whole paradigm into question. (Anglade, 1994; Carothers, 2002; Grugel, 2002).

Thus while electoral democracy might be widely established (with the possibility of alternating governments based on electoral choices), it has not always been accompanied by 'liberal' democracy and the protection of individual and group freedoms, pluralism, civilian control of the military, accountability, the rule of law, and judicial independence. In fact, while the number of electoral democracies has grown, levels of political and civil freedom have declined, leaving democracy that is 'shallow, illiberal and poorly institutionalized' (Diamond, 1997b, p. xv) .

A third issue is that comparative studies of transition have tended to concentrate on successful cases, neglecting what might be learnt from persistent authoritarianism. The Middle East, with its absence of any successful democratization, is instructive here. Authoritarian states have been sustained by a powerful coercive apparatus funded by rentier income from oil resources, electoral manipulation (including fraud and gerrymandering), a primordial relationship between the military and the political élite and Western support. At the same time, opposition is undermined by weak political parties, sectarian divisions, and an underdeveloped civil society. Low levels of political mobilization assist repression by lowering its political costs 'Consequently, strong popular mobilization against incumbent rulers are infrequent and until now readily suppressed' (Posusney, 2005, p. 16).

The transition model mainly tries to specify what undermines authoritarianism and what political action takes place as a new regime is negotiated. But the critiques do serve to show that part of the problem of democratic consolidation is that what is being consolidated in many cases is a regime that falls short of having full democratic credentials, and that this is likely to be the case so long as the state has to prevent political freedoms from encroaching on the economic interests of privileged groups.

The consolidation of democracy

The process of consolidating democracy entails strengthening democratic institutions (especially the rule of law and protection of civil rights), extending democratic processes, and preventing authoritarian reversals. Political institutions and civil society need to be infused with democratic practices, for example, by the empowerment of associations in civil society which increase popular participation and make it more difficult for élites to manipulate democratic institutions. Authoritarian political discourses need to be rejected, and authoritarian political actors need to be neutralized. 'Perverse institutions' should be abolished, such as tutelage by non-democratic élites (especially the military), restrictions on the scope of policy-making powers (for example, exclusion of the Chilean parliament from the defence budget), and forms of political recruitment which give some minority interest a disproportionate presence on law making bodies (O'Donnell, 1992; Valenzuela, 1992; Luckham and White, 1996). Latin America's experience of democratization reveals how persistent authoritarian legacies can be, especially weak and biased judiciaries, clientelism in public services, public toleration of illegal executive action (such as President Fujimori's closure of the national congress in 1992), and the survival or authoritarian organizations (such as Peronism in Argentina) (Philip, 2003).

Consolidation means that democracy has become routinized and internalized in political behaviour. No significant groups pursue unconstitutional, illegal, or undemocratic means to achieve their aims. Élites and the wider public accept democracy as the preferred means of governing and deciding on political succession. A democratic political culture has emerged in which trust, tolerance and compromise are the dominant political norms (Leftwich, 2000; Haynes, 2003).

What, then, are the prerequisites of such beliefs and behaviour? Explanations have variously stressed socio-economic variables, or political factors, including foreign intervention. The remaining sections of this chapter deal with explanations of consolidation in terms of these different sets of factors, recognizing that there are difficulties in applying predictions about consolidation derived from one region, such as Latin America, to another, such as Africa (Wiseman, 1996).

The economic preconditions of democratic consolidation

There is much evidence to support the conclusion that economic affluence and related social change are needed to improve the chance of democratic consolidation. Early studies found the stability of democratic government to be positively correlated with measures of affluence and economic modernization. Indicators of wealth such as per capita income, the percentage of the population owning motor cars, and the number of doctors, radios and telephones per thousand population, were combined with measures of industrialization such as the proportion of the population still engaged in agriculture, and measures of social development such as literacy rates, educational enrolments and levels of urbanization (Lipset, 1959, 1960).

The correlations were taken to show that affluence reduces lower-class discontent:

> only in a wealthy society in which relatively few citizens lived in real poverty could a situation exist in which the mass of the population could intelligently participate in politics and could develop the self-restraint necessary to avoid succumbing to the appeals of irresponsible demagogues. (Lipset, 1959, p. 71)

Levels of industrialization, urbanization and education were also found to be higher the more democratic the country. Economic development led to greater economic security and better education, both of which allow 'longer time perspectives and more complex and gradualist views of politics'. Increased wealth and education also contribute to pluralism 'by increasing the extent to which the lower strata are exposed to cross pressures which will reduce the intensity of their commitment to given ideologies and make them less receptive to supporting extremist ones'.

Economic development also enlarges the middle class, whose interest is in moderating conflict – which it is able to do by rewarding moderate political parties and penalizing extremist ones. Economic development affects other classes, too. The greater the wealth of the lower class, the less opportunity there is for the upper class to deny them their political rights. The wealthier a country, the less important it becomes if some redistribution takes place; losing political office becomes less significant and, therefore, non-democratic means of holding on to power become redundant. Growing national wealth proliferates, countervailing sources of power and opportunities for political participation, communication and recruitment, all of which are supportive of democracy.

Correlations do not necessarily indicate the direction of causality. Nevertheless, a large number of quantitative studies using multivariate analysis as well as cross-tabulations find a positive relationship between democracy and various indicators of socio-economic development. The finding of greatest significance for an understanding of political stability is that 'high levels of socio-economic development are associated with not only the presence but the stability of democracy'. Considering the different quantitative methods, time-spans and indicators used, 'this must rank as one of the most powerful and robust relationships in the study of comparative national development' (Diamond, 1992, p. 108). There are, inevitably, some exceptions to the rule, but extensive reviews of the literature make it safe to theorize that 'the more well-to-do the people of a country, on average, the more likely they will favour, achieve and maintain a democratic system' (Diamond, 1992, pp. 109–10; see also Rueschmeyer, 1991 and Rueschmeyer et al., 1992).

A study of 135 countries between 1950 and 1990 also found that democracy is more stable in more egalitarian societies. Democracies become more unstable as inequality in household incomes increases (Przeworski et al., 2000). Other comparative evidence also confirms the relationship between equality and stable democracy. A study of 33 countries between 1961 and 1980 found that the relationship between inequality of income and the *level* of democracy at a given point in time showed no causal effect. But when measures of democratic *stability* rather than level were correlated with income inequality, and the effect of economic development controlled, less-developed countries with democratic regimes and relatively low income inequality were found to experience regime stability (although countries with a relatively egalitarian distribution of income are not more likely to *inaugurate* democracy). So while income inequality is not incompatible with transition to democracy, it is with the stability of democracy. Continuing high inequality following the inauguration of democracy is likely to lead to a loss of legitimacy and breakdown of the regime (Muller, 1988). Furthermore, inequalities in land distribution are also less conducive to democracy than a more egalitarian social structure (Diamond and Linz, 1989).

There are some problems with this type of analysis, however. First, there is the role in supporting democracy ascribed to the new class structure of a developed economy. The middle classes might be expected to support democracy, but mainly because it legitimizes private property, and because they can 'manage' the democratic process to protect themselves against radicalism and redistribution through ideological control, state apparatuses, financial power, and the threat of capital 'flight'. The managerial middle class also supports democracy because through it they can protect their interests and become 'included' in politics (Moore, 1996).

In developing countries this class analysis can also exaggerate the interest which the lower classes will have in democracy. As well as weakening the power of the landed classes and giving rise to a new middle class, capitalist development also increases the power of the working class by creating the capacity for self-organization through urbanization, factory production, transportation and new forms of communication (Huber et al., 1993). But for democracy to be compatible with capitalism it may have to be limited and not founded on economic equality, social autonomy and citizenship. It will have to be designed to protect the rights of property-owning classes, not the rights of those with conflicting economic interests. Demands for the economic betterment of the working class are a threat to business interests. Procedural democracy is the most that can be expected under a capitalist economic system, not political reforms that would protect the social and economic interests of workers. The consolidation of democracy actually requires low levels of political participation, restricted rights of citizenship, a docile working class and an absence of many of the rights on which full democracy operates. This is why democracy in the Third World is likely to be tainted by clientelism, state repression and electoral manipulation (Cammack, 1997).

Secondly, quantitative studies of development and democracy actually tell little about the reasons why democracy breaks down, other than that there is likely to have been a drop in the level of some statistically significant socio-economic indicators. Such a mode of analysis cannot explain why a fall in, say, per capita income is likely to reduce the chances of democratic survival. For this a more qualitative and historical approach to individual countries needs to be taken (Potter, 1992).

Case studies, most notably by theorists of Latin American dependency, have often challenged the relationships which quantitative analysis purports to establish. Latin America shows no simple correlation between socio-economic development and democracy, with some relatively rich countries losing democracy (Argentina in 1930) and some relatively poor countries developing democratic institutions (for example, Chile in the first half of the nineteenth century). Often it has seemed that economic performance (that is, broadly distributed growth) has been more important for democracy than high levels of socio-economic development (per capita income or structure of production). Other case studies have, however, confirmed many of the hypotheses generated by quantitative analysis: that education strengthens commitment to democracy; that political violence is greatest in poor countries; and that the growth of a middle class is conducive to democracy (Diamond, 1992).

Asia also reveals that the relationship between development and democracy is by no means simple. The case of India shows that democracy is not necessarily incompatible with a low level of development. A high level of development might increase the demands and supports for democracy through increases in income, education, participation, the political consciousness of the middle class, pluralism or foreign contacts. Alternatively, it might be destabilizing by loosening traditional forms of authority, generating political demands from newly created political interests, and deepening ideological cleavages. Such developments can push authoritarian regimes in the direction of democracy, or present democracies with unmanageable problems. The consequences of development for democracy are very ambivalent (Diamond, 1989).

An explanation of how a relatively rich country might resist democratization is provided by a 'revenue bargaining' theory of democracy which divides states into 'coercion intensive' or 'capital intensive', depending on their sources of revenue. Where the state has no need to bargain with income earning classes and wealth creators in order to extract revenues, as in poor agricultural societies, oil-rich countries, or aid dependent states, it has no need of democracy: states freed from dependence on their subjects for revenue need not take too seriously any relationship of accountability with these subjects (Moore, 1996).

Political mediation

Despite the evidence suggesting democracy will only be sustained when the economic conditions and their associated structural changes in society are right, it would be wrong to think that socio-economic structures are all that matter. The 'autonomy of political factors' has to be recognized. How else can India's remarkable democratic history be explained, or authoritarianism in countries such as Argentina and Uruguay in the 1960s despite having the highest levels of GNP per capita and literacy in Latin America (Mainwaring, 1992)? It is thus possible for a state to be poor and free (for example, Benin and Bolivia) or prosperous and repressive (for example, Brunei and Libya). Politics are important to consolidation in many ways.

The process of socio-economic development may be supportive of democracy, but dependent on how élites respond to the new political demands generated by increased urbanization, industrialization, education and communications. After all, the middle class has not always opposed authoritarianism. Whether new groups are included in the political process

through institutional developments, especially political parties and organized interests, and given access to economic opportunities and rewards
(such as land, jobs, health care and consumer goods) are also relevant
mediating factors. So democracy has fared better in countries such as
Venezuela and Costa Rica, where the new social forces unleashed by development are accommodated within the political system, than in Brazil and
Peru where too often they have been excluded. The centrality of politics to
economic opportunity can be a fundamental cause of democratic breakdown (Diamond and Linz, 1989, p. 44).

Other intervening political variables include the speed at which democracy has been introduced. Thus in Latin America the abrupt and violent
seizure of independence followed by civil and foreign wars produced political turmoil in the nineteenth century that made progress towards any kind
of stable government very difficult to achieve. A long history of élite
competition is another political factor, significant in some Latin American
countries, and supporting the thesis that democracy is most likely to be
successful when political competition becomes institutionalized before the
expansion of the suffrage and other forms of political participation (Dahl,
1971). Democracy is likely to be more stable if based on a historical
sequence that establishes national identity first, followed by the creation of
legitimate state structures, followed by the extension of rights to political
participation to all members of society (Diamond and Linz, 1989).

The political culture

It has also been posited that there is a pattern of political attitudes that
supports democracy – a 'civic' or balanced culture 'in which political activity, involvement and rationality exist but are balanced by passivity, traditionally, and commitment to parochial values' (Almond and Verba, 1963, p.
30). Democratic consolidation also requires attitudes which recognize the
legitimacy of territorial and constitutional arrangements and a willingness
to accept the outcomes when the rules of political life (especially electoral
rules) have been adhered to (Leftwich, 2000).

The values and orientations found to be associated with the stability of
democracy are moderation, co-operation, bargaining and accommodation.
'Moderation' and 'accommodation' imply toleration, pragmatism, willingness to compromise and civility in political discourse. Time is often seen as
a critical variable here, producing (for example) a contrast between the
time available for India to acquire democratic values and have them
disseminated from élites to the masses, and the limited opportunity to
develop democratic values in Africa before independence (Diamond et al.,
1990; Diamond, 1993b).

There is much convincing evidence that a 'low' level of political culture can undermine democracy. A lack of commitment to democratic principles, procedures and beliefs on the part of African political élites, for example, has made it difficult to sustain democracy – even though some traditional values support consensus, moderation, consultation, the rule of law and controlled political authority. Similarly in Latin America democratic cultures have helped to maintain democracy and make it more difficult to consolidate and perpetuate authoritarian government, as in Uruguay in 1980 and Chile in 1988 where 'both the fact of the plebiscites and the ultimate popular rejections of the military at the polls reflected the continuing vitality of democratic culture' (Diamond, 1988, pp. 14–15).

However, there is no simple, deterministic link between political culture and democratic stability because experience of democracy is itself a powerful socializing influence. In Latin America democratic political cultures have been strengthened by the successful performance of democratic government in accommodating new interests, expanding the economy, developing education and securing the welfare of the lower classes. The legitimacy created by governmental success helps explain the strong correlation between the economic performance of democratic regimes in Latin America and their stability. Furthermore, studies of Asian society show that political cultures are often mixed, with countries having 'some significant values and orientations that press in a democratic direction and others that press in an authoritarian one' (Diamond, 1989, p. 17).

The relationship between the 'civic' culture and democracy implies that a set of values about political structures, individual political competence, and trust in other individuals and groups leads to stable democracy. But it could equally be argued that all such values could be a consequence of the experience of democratic government. When attitude surveys are carried out to determine what the predominant political culture is, all that may be revealed are the expectations that people have as the result of their experience of a political system. If there is the possibility that the political culture is not cause but consequence, it ceases to have theoretical significance for understanding change or the loss of critical levels of support for democracy.

The secret is knowing what creates the critical level of consensus. Democratic values are more likely to be preserved during great social change (such as when democracy is first introduced) if all major social groups are given some access to the political system early on, and the status of major pre-democratic institutions (for example, monarchy) is not threatened during the transition period. Legitimacy is also preserved by governmental effectiveness: efficient political and administrative decision-making which enable governments to meet the needs of the population. In many African states the squandering of resources by mismanagement, corruption, waste and greed has alienated support for democratically constituted regimes. It is no coincidence that Botswana is the most stable African democracy and has moved from being one of the poorest African countries to one of the richest in a decade and a half. A problem for many Third World countries is that they are locked into a vicious circle of low legitimacy and ineffective performance (Diamond et al., 1990).

The economic performance of democratic governments may be less important in deepening democratic values than political performance, or the level and quality of the democracy practiced. Feelings about corruption, political freedoms, and the trustworthiness of leaders all have an impact on attitudes about the way democracy works, and the greater the level of satisfaction with this, the stronger the democracy (Diamond, 1998). Public responses to the economic crisis of 1997–98 in Thailand, South Korea, Indonesia and Malaysia show that people were inclined to blame authoritarian tendencies rather than democratic politics for economic mismanagement. While not necessarily *deepening* democratization where it had occurred, the crisis did not undermine it. Although there is a long way to go before democracy is consolidated in these countries, the dominant public response to the crisis was a demand for social welfare policies that required a change of government rather than a change of regime (Freedman, 2006).

Research has also revealed strong statistical relationships between per capita GNP and personal beliefs and values supportive of democracy, suggesting that the political culture may be an important intervening variable in the relationship between development and democracy. As countries become richer and improvements in education and communications are felt, people have been observed to become politically more aware, effective, and defensive of their political and civil liberties. Evidence from Taiwan, Thailand, Turkey and Brazil has been adduced to support this hypothesis (Diamond, 1993a).

Again, the causal relationship is not necessarily in a single direction. The political culture influences behaviour and the operation of institutions, but is itself influenced by the development of new social forces, modes of socialization, leadership and international influences. Hence the political culture can sustain democracy despite relatively low levels of economic development. For example, both India and Costa Rica show 'surprising democratic persistence despite low or moderate economic development' because 'political culture at both the élite and mass levels clearly plays a strong supporting role' (Diamond, 1993a, 25).

Civil society and democratization

While stable and effective democracy is in part a function of the institutions negotiated and supported by political élites, it is also dependent on the way civil society is organized to influence policy makers, mobilize public opinion, hold governments at all levels to account, and make governments responsive to the expression of demands and needs (Diamond, 1996, 1997a). Such responsiveness and accountability require a civil society consisting of organizations that are autonomous, voluntary and protected by the rule of law. A civic community of neighbourhood associations, political parties, non-governmental organizations, associations, private voluntary bodies, grass-roots support organizations, and social movements complement state and market and form 'the informal sector of the polity' (Reilly, 1995, p. 7). Such bodies often proliferate in transitions to democracy, having, as in Brazil and the Philippines, originally been formed during the authoritarian regime when more overt forms of political participation were banned.

Civil society promotes the consolidation of democracy by monitoring the exercise of state power, stimulating political participation, educating people in democracy, representing interests, and providing an alternative to clientelism. It creates cross-cutting allegiances, throws up political leaders and disseminates political information. Associational autonomy entails a move away from clientelism, allowing people, especially the poor, to articulate their interests and so move from being clients to being citizens (Fox, 1994; Diamond, 1997a).

Parts of civil society are undoubtedly supportive of democracy and of the interests of groups hitherto excluded from political power, such as women, different categories of the urban and rural poor, and ethnic minorities. The development of civil society thus provides opportunities for the poor and disadvantaged to redress injustices as well as to practice democracy within their own associations (Diamond, 1992). Sustainable democracy requires 'democratic deepening', or the infusion of institutions with democratic practices. This requires the empowerment of associations in civil society to increase popular participation, making it more difficult for élites to manipulate democratic institutions (Luckham and White, 1996). A civil society supportive of democracy has to be embedded in a 'civic community' in which relations between civic associations are founded on trust, co-operation and reciprocity. A civic community increases the effectiveness of democratic government which in turn increases support for democracy.

However, some elements of civil society are distinctly un-civil, reactionary, authoritarian and in other ways uninterested in or opposed to democracy (White, 1996). Civil society may reflect the inequalities of resources, knowledge and mobilization that typically distinguish class and other interests in capitalist society (Grugel, 2002). The strength of civil society differs greatly between different regions of the Third World. In Africa, for example, civil society is 'male dominated and gerontocratic', and includes ethnic and fundamentalist religious associations unlikely to sponsor democratization (Kasfir, 1998, p. 136). In newly democratizing countries civil society may include groups that openly and freely co-operated with the previous authoritarian regime as well as criminal elements, drug mafias and paramilitary groups. Resistance to democratization may also come from a leadership of non-governmental organization that has been incorporated into political clientelism. In Latin America, while there has been some collective empowerment through credit unions, self-help housing and other community initiatives, new social movements have sometimes been subject to 'capture' by government and clientelist politics (Little, 1997).

Even when elements in civil society are pro-democratic it may not be easy for them to move from protest and political confrontation to constructive dialogue with governments (Hernandez and Fox, 1995). A contribution to democracy may be difficult when authoritarianism is deeply rooted, political representation a novel phenomenon, and political organizations traditionally monopolized by parties (Reilly, 1995). For example, the 'democratization of social life' creates a counterpoint to the state in Vietnam, when in the past social organizations (trade unions, youth movements and women's organizations) have been integrated into government and party. New social organizations are emerging to support the urban poor in their quest for housing, work and health care. But such participation is still limited because 'the constraints of the old centralized planning system still exist; the elements of civil society are still underdeveloped; and ways to attract and operationalize people's participation are as yet unreliable and ineffective' (Luan, 1996, p. 1890).

The balance of power

Theorizing about the conditions necessary for the survival of democracy includes using the methodology of comparative history to develop a 'balance of power' approach (Rueschmeyer et al., 1992). A balance of power between classes (and coalitions of classes), between the state and civil society, and between international and national pressures, is seen as the crucial determinant of whether democracies survive even under adverse conditions. The stability of democracy has been found to vary according to different historical contexts, depending on the overall balance of power.

In South and Central America the relative *power of social classes* was found to be dependent upon the reaction of the new middle class, emerging with the development of capitalist economies, to the rising power of the working class. The working class had supported democracy and the landed upper class had consistently opposed it, especially when controlling a large supply of cheap labour and forming a significant part of the economic élite, as was the case in South and Central America throughout the first half of the twentieth century. The relative weakness of the working class in Latin America has always been a contributory factor in the instability of democracy in the region.

The middle class has supported representative government, but opposed the inclusion of the working class. Middle-class support for democracy was apt to disappear when its interests were threatened by lower-class pressures, the middle class often supporting military intervention which curtailed civil rights and parliamentary government, even though it found its own access to the state restricted. Political parties were found to be crucial in consolidating a balance of power between classes, in mobilizing the working class, and in protecting the interests of economically dominant classes so that they had no need to resort to authoritarianism.

As we have already seen, a balance between *state power and civil society* is also necessary for the stability of democracy and the avoidance of authoritarianism. In developing countries the state's autonomy at the time of the emergence of mass pressure for democratization was greater than in the history of European democracy, tilting the balance in favour of the state. Autonomous social organizations, perhaps supported by religion, act as a counterbalance to the state, but their class content is important for democratic outcomes, as they have sometimes served as the repositories of authoritarian ideologies.

The importance of a countervailing power to that of the state is confirmed by post-colonial African history. Here the state has been 'the primary arena of class formation' and the 'primary means for the accumulation of personal wealth', leading to corruption, the concentration of power, the emergence of a parasitic bureaucratic bourgeoisie, and the absence of a middle class to demand 'the expansion of democratic rights and limitation of state power'. With a few exceptions, the state has not been balanced by a plurality of autonomous associations – intellectuals, traditional leaders, professionals, trade unions, business associations, religious groups, students, journalists and so on – that are necessary for stable, responsive and accountable government. In Asia, similarly, wherever bureaucratic and military dominance has restricted the autonomy of interest groups, voluntary bodies and political parties, a foundation of democracy has been removed with authoritarian consequences (Diamond, 1988, 21–7; Diamond et al., 1990).

The concept of *balance between international and national power* refers to the varying impact which foreign influences can have on the internal balance of power. Economic dependence on agrarian exports strengthens the power of large landholders. Capital-intensive industrialization using imported technology blocks the development of a working class. Foreign-owned mineral extraction for export, and import-substituting industrialization, weakens landowners, and strengthens urban classes, both the working class and the domestic bourgeoisie. When the repressive apparatus of the state is reinforced by foreign powers concerned about their strategic and economic interests, the balance between state and civil society is further altered (Rueschmeyer et al., 1992).

Institutional development

Political institutions and leadership also have implications for democratic stability. Institutions are seen as crucial to the key attributes of democracy – the rule of law, freedom, order, accountability, representation and administrative capacity. Institutions are also needed that can cope with ethnic demands for special treatment, including consociational democracy. State institutions are required to guarantee the effective exercise of citizenship.

Institutions have taken on renewed significance in comparative politics with theoretical developments known as the 'new institutionalism'. Institutions are the rules of the game, or humanly devised constraints on social interaction, and should be distinguished from organizations such as political parties. There are in fact different varieties of new institutionalism (Peters, 2005). Two have been applied to politics in developing countries, rational choice institutionalism and empirical institutionalism.

According to the rational choice version, the answer to fundamental questions about political and economic development in low income countries lies in institutions: the political institutions which influence decision-making; and the economic institutions (especially property rights and contracts) that are so important in the interaction between government and civil society. Attention is particularly paid to the administrative capacity of governments, especially in shaping the institutional environment of business. It applies economic reasoning to the rules of the game, to the decisions of individuals whether to obey existing rules, and to collective action to change the existing set of rules, assuming the individual's incentives depend on the behaviour patterns and cultural norms of the rest of society. Institutions are important for investment and economic innovation because property rights and contract enforcement mechanisms, supported by efficient, honest public administration, and the rule of law, provide incentives by lowering the costs of exchange. The supreme importance of the rule of law is a recurring theme in the New Institutionalism. Institutions are important in the alleviation of poverty and educational provision. Institutions are regarded as a form of social capital.

This type of institutional analysis can be applied to public policy analysis, reform of the legal system, tax administration, and the kind of bureaucracy needed to make it rational for citizens and clients to comply voluntarily with policy rules and participate in the policy-making process, thereby strengthening democracy. When confronted by the question of whether democracy or authoritarianism is best for economic development, this variant of the new institutionalism generally favours democracy. Democratic political institutions are more favourable to property rights than authoritarian, and the longer the duration of the regime, the stronger such rights will become. Many characteristics favourable to democracy are simultaneously supportive of good economic policy and property rights. For example, associations defending the interests of exporters, agricultural producers, and manufacturers improve economic efficiency, social welfare, and the distribution of income. The building of coalitions by élites on the basis of interest group support helps consolidate democracy. The efficient delivery of bureaucratically organized services to local communities, requires the existence of community organizations able to interact with central institutions, provide feedback on agency performance, and mobilize sufficient political resources to provide incentives for effective bureaucratic behaviour. Only democracies are likely to provide such an institutional environment.

Empirical institutionalism is concerned with the institutional weaknesses that have impeded attempts to sustain democracy in most regions of the Third World. Democracy in Asia has been threatened by the willingness of rulers to abuse their constitutional powers to strengthen their position. Military intervention in the region has often been preceded by the severe erosion of democratic constitutionalism by civil politicians seeking to perpetuate their power. A willingness to accept the consequences of democratic practices has been exceptional among Asian political leaders. In Latin America democratic instability has followed 'shifts in political leadership strategies and styles from consensus to confrontation, from accommodation to polarization'. In Africa the values and skills of political leaders have been crucial in undermining or sustaining democracy. Democracy in all regions of the Third World requires commitment to democratic values and an accommodating, compromising and consensual style on the part of political leaders (Diamond, 1989; Diamond and Linz, 1989; Diamond et al., 1990).

A growing institutionalizing of politics has been observed in Africa since 1990. There have been some notable exceptions, particularly Zimbabwe, but the general pattern that has emerged is that formal constitutional rules have come to matter more than the raw power of 'Big Men' who could only be removed from office by violence. More intensely contested elections have become more important in determining leadership successions. Political executives increasingly 'work *within*, rather than around, institutionalized channels' (Posner and Young, 2007, p. 134).

Institutional weaknesses have been reflected in political parties that are internally divided, unable to articulate interests clearly or mobilize a significant mass base. In Latin America stable democracy has been associated with parties that are coherent (in policy), complex (organizationally), autonomous (from the state) and adaptable (to social change). But in Africa weak 'input' institutions, and especially political parties, have excluded the mass of the population from constitutional politics, encouraging élitism and clientelism, and forcing people into 'non-formal' modes of participation (Diamond, 1988).

There is also evidence that a party system with only a small number of parties is most conducive to democratic stability. One reason why the military and bureaucracy have dominated politics in Thailand is because,

> with 143 parties crossing the Thai political stage between 1946 and 1981, political élites have been unable to build strong bases of popular support, to articulate, aggregate and mobilize political interests, to incorporate emerging interests into the political process, and to cooperate with one another in achieving policy innovations. (Diamond et al., 1990, p. 27)

Other institutional prerequisites of democracy that have been proposed include executive accountability to the legislature, a proportional electoral system, a bicameral legislature and judicial review. Vigorous legislative and judicial institutions capable of controlling an excessively zealous executive are also important: 'the strength and autonomy of the judiciary is roughly proportional to the condition of democracy' (Diamond, 1988, p. 31).

Considerable attention has also been paid to the form of executive, that is, whether democracy is best served by presidential or parliamentary government. A strong case has been made in favour of an executive recruited from among parliamentarians. Presidential executives, especially when combined with the personalistic and autocratic political traditions found in Latin America, allow directly elected presidents to claim mandates from the people entitling them to bypass elected representatives, organized interests and other mechanisms of accountability. The parliamentary system avoids conflicting executive and legislative mandates, gives greater flexibility of response when the executive loses the confidence of the legislature, and provides a stronger opposition and incentives for dialogue between government and opposition. When the head of state is not fused with the chief executive, it is more difficult for the incumbent to claim to represent the national interest rather than just a partisan position. It is also more compatible with a multiparty system, compared with the tendency for presidential systems to produce deadlock in executive–legislative relations, ideological polarization, and difficulties in coalition building (Mainwaring, 1993; Linz, 1994; Haufman, 1997). So a parliamentary system might have helped Brazil and Peru in the late 1980s 'where presidents whose programmes had failed catastrophically and whose political support had evaporated were forced to limp through their remaining terms with virtually no capacity to respond effectively to the deepening economic and political crises' (Diamond et al., 1990, p. 28).

However, comparative evidence is inconclusive. While one study found that 'the expected life of democracy under presidentialism is approximately 21 years, whereas under parliamentarianism it is 73 years' (Przeworski et al., 2000, p. 129), another involving a comparison of 56 transitions to democracy in the Third World between 1930 and 1995 found no evidence that constitutional type 'had any significant bearing on the success of Third World experiments in democracy' (Power and Gasiorowski, 1997, p. 144). Nor did they find that a multiparty system gave presidential executives particular problems. They were forced to conclude that institutional variables generally might be less important for democratic consolidation than had been thought.

Institutions can help with the consolidation of democracy by embedding appropriate sets of values that become routines of political life. However, the extent of deviation from democratic behaviour despite the institutions created as part of the process of democratization (such as competitive elections and constitutionally enshrined civil rights) strongly suggests that politics is only partially constrained by institutions. Whether norms of trust, accountability, toleration and other democratic values become institutionalized depends on the distribution of power within society: 'because institutions and the state are the outcomes of society-rooted politics, institutions can shape social outcomes only secondarily. Society-rooted politics is the primary determinant of outcomes' (Sangmpan, 2007, p. 220).

Foreign influence

Finally, interventions from abroad are clearly relevant to the consolidation of democracy. Such influence is currently supportive in the main, with regional and global trends towards democracy, and with powerful external actors making the promotion of democracy and human rights explicit foreign policy goals. Since 1980 the quality of governance in recipient countries has been an explicit aid objective. Democracy, human rights and good government, rather than economic reforms, have taken centre stage as aid conditionalities. This was prompted by a number of political developments. The collapse of the Soviet bloc made it unnecessary for the West to support anti-communist authoritarian regimes, and encouraged the view that political liberalization was necessary economic progress. Indigenous pro-democracy movements in countries in which democratization was already under way (in Latin America and parts of East and South East Asia such as Taiwan, South Korea and the Philippines) legitimized pro-democracy aid policies. Domestic political pressures in donor countries also demanded that democracy be a condition of aid. Bad governance was also used to justify cuts in overseas aid. The poor quality of governance was also blamed for the failure of structural adjustment and economic liberalization to achieve social and economic progress. Development, it is now believed within the aid community, needs the right political context. Demonstration effects from neighbouring states have been significant.

However, foreign powers can also work to undermine democracy (Haynes, 2001). For example, in 2001 US politicians and officials sought to influence the election in Nicaragua with money, propaganda and food aid. While the foreign policy of the USA is officially in favour of democratization, it has 'correlated poorly' with its other actions in international relations (Whitehead, 1986). In 2002 it was widely suspected of instigating an unsuccessful *coup* attempt against the democratically elected President of Venezuela. Not surprisingly, international effects on democracy (positive and negative) tend to be greater the smaller and more vulnerable the country.

Under pressure from the USA, UN and even the Commonwealth, at least 33 countries have enacted anti-terrorism legislation, with adverse consequences for the quality of democracy. However, before this is presented as foreign interference it should be noted that the 'pressure' has been largely symbolic and rhetorical, as there is no correlation between the adoption of anti-terror measures and the receipt of foreign investment or aid. Furthermore, in a number of countries, including India, Indonesia and Uganda, governments have been quick to use the limits on civil liberties and expanded law enforcement powers contained in the legislation to silence dissidents and punish political opponents. Elsewhere, including China, Egypt, Eritrea, Malaysia and Syria, where democracy is either absent or partial, existing authoritarian powers have been used against political opposition in the name of national security and the 'war on terror' (Whitaker, 2007).

Conclusion

With the dominant ideology in the world prescribing a free-market economy, there are very powerful pressures being applied to Third World countries to liberalize their economies and transform their polities in the direction of pluralism. Hence the current interest in what is needed to restore democracy as well as how to make it function effectively so that its legitimacy becomes firmly established. The significance of economic development to democracy shows how important it is to recognize that political reform cannot sensibly be pursued in isolation from measures designed to strengthen the performance of Third World economies. It is right to assert the importance of political prerequisites of democracy and the status of economic factors as necessary but not sufficient conditions for consolidation. But it is important that political preconditions should not be part of one's definition of democracy, lest theorizing becomes merely tautological.

It is also important to understand that democracy is a contested concept. The choice of a particular definition – electoral competition, decision-making procedures, civil and political rights, or the distribution of power within society – may reflect an ideological or normative position on the part of the user that should be acknowledged.

11
Conclusion: Democracy and Development

Democracy and modernization

A major challenge facing Third World societies is the creation of a political system with legitimacy in the eyes of the majority. Without legitimacy in government there can be no stability, and without stability, no social and economic progress. Legitimacy is increasingly seen to reside with democratic forms of government as pro-democracy movements gather momentum in most regions of the Third World. Yet the most pronounced feature of democratic regimes is their fragility. The establishment of peaceful, democratic politics is obstructed by civil war in Afghanistan, Burundi and Sudan, political assassination in Mexico, ethnic conflict and separatism in Rwanda, Somalia, Sri Lanka and Liberia, religious fundamentalism in Egypt and Algeria, bankrupt absolutism in Zaire and El Salvador, and the West's willingness to sell arms to any regime, no matter how repressive. The threat of economic crisis hangs over the fledgling democracies of Brazil, Malawi, Nepal, Uganda, Angola and Mozambique. Communal violence persistently mars India's democratic record. Many Third World countries are faced with accumulations of such factors, and some combine them with severe ecological problems, notably Somalia.

This chapter considers the prospects for Third World democracy in the light of the theories of political change discussed in the previous chapters, and examines the argument that development and democracy might not be compatible, especially in view of the success which some authoritarian states have had in developing their societies economically and socially. The concept of a 'developmental' state is considered in order to understand what qualities appear to be needed if any kind of state is to preside over economic growth and human development.

Although there have been impressive transitions away from military dictatorship in many parts of the Third World in the last decade, the military as a political force is present everywhere, growing stronger, and should never be underestimated politically. It remains dominant in parts of

Asia, the Middle East and Africa. The armed forces pose an overt threat to democracy in the Philippines, Haiti, Guatemala, Thailand, Uruguay, Chad, Venezuela, Cambodia, Nigeria, Mali, Peru, Sierra Leone and Gambia. Foreign intervention has often been a Third World democracy's only protection against the militarization of politics.

Much of the hope for stability in the new pluralist political systems rests on the organizational strength of political parties whose ideologies support the democratic process. How long some of the diverse coalitions for the restoration of democracy can survive the enormous expectations of them is a subject of much speculation. Elections in Mozambique, Kenya and Nepal have introduced competitive party politics into inhospitable social and economic environments. The African National Congress in South Africa encompasses a broad spectrum of regional, racial, cultural, class and ideological positions. Elsewhere parties themselves constitute the greatest threat to democracy, either because of their refusal to accept majority decisions (such as Renamo in Mozambique, Unita in Angola or ZANU-PF in Zimbabwe), or because of their inherent authoritarianism, contempt for human rights or religious intolerance.

The apparent globalization of political values and institutions represented by the dissolution of the communist regimes in the Second World and their replacement by systems of government broadly subscribing to liberal democratic beliefs and practices, has lent credence to the view that there is an inevitable trend towards a universal form of government on which all societies will eventually converge. Such interpretations of recent world history gain encouragement from the extent to which pluralist democracy has replaced military regimes or single-party states in Latin America and Africa.

There would seem to be echoes of modernization theory in such predictions and interpretations (Leftwich, 1993). Assumptions about the importance of the development of civil society as a counterbalance to the power of the state are reminiscent of the importance attached by modernization theory to the 'organic solidarities' which are a function of the increased complexity and specialization of modernizing social structures. Similarly ideas about 'good governance' which increasingly inform Western aid policy and which prescribe the separation of powers, the accountability and efficiency of public bureaucracy, and the rule of law as indispensable components of a democratic polity and free society, find their counterpart in the concept of structural differentiation that is central to political functionalism. The development of differentiated and specialized political structures serves to strengthen the extractive, regulative, distributive, symbolic and responsive capabilities of governments, as well as preserving the independence of different parts of the machinery of government, thus inhibiting the concentration of power in a small and personalized executive élite which is so often the hallmark of Third World politics.

However, modernization theory, unlike much contemporary Western political rhetoric, did not assume that democracy could take root regardless of economic and social conditions. Rather it sees economic development as preceding the modernization of politics – which is precisely what has happened in the newly industrializing states of the Third World, where democracy has until very recently been conspicuously absent in some of the fast growing capitalist economies, notably Brazil, Singapore, South Korea, Taiwan, Thailand and Indonesia (Leftwich, 1993).

The resurgence of religious fundamentalism in parts of the Third World appears to undermine much of modernization theory's conclusions about secularization as a feature of modern society and polity. However, the modernization theorists did not simply equate secularization with the separation of theology and politics. Secularization also meant a particular kind of rationalization seen as characteristic of efficient economic and political organization. In this respect modernization theory is relevant to the analysis of the performance of theocratic regimes, and of which category of autocratic regime they join – that with dismal records of social and economic development or that with records of economic growth and relatively high per capita incomes. The concepts of 'community' and 'association' are central to such analysis. Although the diversity of political developments in the Third World, and the absence of a clear direction of political change even in individual countries, obviate any theory of progress towards a single goal, the sociological concepts of modernization theory are indispensable for distinguishing between the different values that underpin social relationships and conflicts, especially those based on ethnicity.

Democracy and development

There have been different perspectives on whether democracy or authoritarianism is required to lift a poor country out of economic and social underdevelopment. The *conflict* perspective argues that economic development needs an authoritarian regime to push through policies to facilitate rapid growth in the face of resistance. Democracy is regarded as inherently unstable and permits the expression of powerful pressures to redistribute and consume resources rather than accumulate and invest them. Both tendencies hamper development. The *compatibility* argument claims democracies are as capable as authoritarian regimes of combining growth with redistribution, leading to expanded markets and economic growth. Democracy is also a precondition for a functioning market economy which promotes growth, human development and social equality. The *sceptical* view doubts whether there is any systematic relationship between democracy and development.

Different perspectives such as these can be attributed to the different time periods, countries, and political and economic indicators used by the researchers. Other methodological problems encountered when relating development to different types of regime include separating out the political from the multitude of factors affecting an economy, the absence of a single definition of democracy, and the fact that development has social as well as economic dimensions (Helliwell, 1994; Ersson and Lane, 1996; Blank, 2005).

Since most developmental states have been authoritarian rather than democratic during the decades of rapid economic growth and social development, it has sometimes been assumed that authoritarianism is a necessary condition of development. For example, in Taiwan the Kuomintang monopolized political power from 1949 to 1986, when the first free, multiparty elections were held, ruling by martial law. In Singapore the ruling People's Action Party has controlled all parts of the political process, including the media, and much of the economy. Human rights and political opposition have been restricted, as have other parts of civil society. In the developmental state, labour markets have been distinctly unfree when capitalist development has needed the repression of trade unions or state intervention in setting wage levels. The state's relations with civil society have been free from the pressures of organized labour and the peasantry, and supportive of emerging domestic capital (White, 1984; Pempel, 1999; Leftwich, 2000).

However, authoritarianism in the Third World generally has produced little development and has been distinguished more by corruption, rent-seeking, repression, the over-concentration of economic and social power, the impoverishment of the masses, and economic insecurity. In Africa, authoritarianism, whether civil or military, left a legacy of poverty, illiteracy, debt, displaced populations, corruption, political instability, and human rights violations: 'in the postcolonial era, the primary purpose of power and control of the state apparatus has been the private accumulation of wealth' (Agbese and Kieh, 2007, p. 13). Moreover, the majority of developmental states have performed better than average in respect for human rights. Political opposition persisted. Developmental states have not lacked legitimacy, mainly because the benefits of economic growth have been spread by investment in education, health care, housing and other social benefits, and by reductions in levels of social inequality.

Despite the authoritarian tendencies of developmental states it has been argued that development can equally well be achieved under a democratic regime, with the added bonus of political freedoms and civil liberties. However, if it is to be a 'pervasive' and participatory democracy rather than a purely procedural one, all interests, particularly disadvantaged groups, will have to be able effectively to voice demands for social welfare, poverty reduction, greater equality and an end to discrimination.

Development would have to be redistributive, 'inclusive' and not just about economic growth. It would also have to include political development, with strong institutions of representation and accountability, as well as empowering, through different forms of participation, a wide range of social groups. State autonomy would have to be based on consensus and inclusion, and 'embeddedness' would have to be in society in its broadest sense, and not just economic elites (White, 1998).

Such a democratic developmental state would require a number of contradictions to be resolved: between autonomous and accountable political leadership; growth and redistribution; political consensus and social inclusion; the concentration of power in state and business élites and public participation. These are 'fundamental contradictions which are difficult to resolve in the real world of politics' (White, 1998, p. 44). The institutional context would also have to be receptive: accountable bureaucracy; legal stability; a strong-knowledge base; and public–private co-operation, most of which are long-term projects and underline the importance of institution-building and the development of administrative capacity (Onis, 1991).

A developmental democracy also needs institutions to enforce property rights and contracts, providing incentives for investment and innovation. Investment in machinery, equipment, education and the financial sector ('keys to development') will not take place unless effective judicial and administrative institutions are in place. While both authoritarian and democratic regimes have been capable of protecting and neglecting property rights, there has been a 'substantial connection' between the institutions of representative government and individual rights of property and contract (Clague et al., 1997, p. 97). Long-lasting democracies provide better property rights than autocracies. However, causal effects are difficult to specify since there are factors favourable to both lasting democracy and property rights (and thus economic performance), such as equality or the absence of ethnic and racial divisions.

Democracy also contributes to development by providing a context for effective policy reforms. For example, political participation was necessary for educational reform in Burkina Faso. The rule of law enabled community-based resource management to go ahead in Tanzania. Democratic governance gives 'stakeholders' incentives and opportunities to improve public services. There is a reciprocal relationship here – sectoral reforms support democracy when they are designed to provide opportunities for participation, accountability and transparency, so generating social capital and providing experience of government mechanisms and processes (Brinkerhoff, 2000). South Asia's variable experience of democracy also suggests that context is important. In this region democracy provides a foundation of popular support for government that is necessary for economic and especially social development to occur (Blank, 2005).

Helliwell's comparative analysis of data for 125 countries between 1976 and 1985 found no significant causal influence of variable levels of democracy on economic growth, though there was evidence that democracy stimulates education and investment, both needed for economic development. Furthermore, democracy does not incur costs in terms of lost economic growth. Ersson and Lane (1996) similarly found that investment in physical capital and the availability of human capital had more impact on growth than level of democracy, but that democracy is positively correlated with human development generally. It should also be noted that the conditions that were crucial to economic success among the Asian Tigers – including a high rate of domestic savings and a large number of small and medium-sized enterprises – do not appear to be dependent on an authoritarian political regime (Sandschneider, 1991).

Democratic regimes also preside over economies generally paying higher wages, using labour more effectively, and benefiting more from technological progress than autocracies. Per capita incomes also grow faster in democracies. While some authoritarian regimes, notably the Asian Tigers, produced remarkable economic achievements, many others have not, notably in Africa. A comparison of 135 countries over a 40-year period showed that spectacular development is as likely under democracy as dictatorship, and produced not 'a shred of evidence that democracy need be sacrificed on the altar of development' (Przewroski et al., 2000, p. 271).

If confirmation were required that authoritarianism is no guarantee of development one need look no further than Zimbabwe and North Korea. In its determination to hold on to power the government of President Mugabe has undermined the independence of the judiciary, taken sweeping new security powers, brought an end to a free press, encouraged illegal occupations of farms and the murder of their owners, politicized the police, and incited Zanu-PF war veterans to violence and intimidation against opposition supporters which has ended in political murders, disappearances, unlawful detentions and assaults. The result has been to reduce sections of the population to starvation level, create hyperinflation at 165,000 per cent, increase unemployment to 50 per cent, and reduce real incomes by 75 per cent between 1998 and 2008. GDP is shrinking by between 2 and 5 per cent per annum.

An authoritarian cult of personality in North Korea has reduced its economy and society to one where transfers of food from abroad are required to stave off mass starvation, where GDP recorded negative growth during most of the 1990s and shrank by 1.1 per cent in 2006, where life expectancy is contracting, and nearly 8 million people are undernourished, including a third of all mothers and 37 per cent of children who are chronically malnourished. Aid agencies estimate that 2 million people have died since the mid-1990s because of economic mismanagement and natural disasters (Nanto and Chanlett-Avery, 2008).

The developmental democratic state

There does, however, appear to be agreement that for a democratic state to be developmental it requires institutions, political forces and socio-economic structures that are rarely found in developing countries. The *developmental* capacity of a democracy will depend partly on politics, especially levels of political equality and participation, and the type of party system. Politics, rather than regime type, determine whether a country is successful economically. To achieve development there needs to be a 'developmental state' rather than economic and political *laissez-faire*. State intervention has historically been associated with economic growth in the developing world.

One explanation of the economic success of East Asian countries such as South Korea, Taiwan, Singapore and Malaysia stresses the importance of the state having sufficient autonomy to guide private investment and intervene strongly in other areas of economic management so as to achieve high levels of growth. These 'developmental' states and their attendant approaches to public policy is owed to their independence from social forces such as landowners, private capital and labour, and their maintenance of a competent technocratic bureaucracy. Another interpretation of the relationship between state and class interests stresses the power of some economic groups (such as motor manufacturers in Korea) and the importance of co-operation with the state of at least those parts of civil society with an interest in industrialization, especially the business community.

The exceptional economic achievements of some East Asian countries initially prompted two theoretical claims. One was that success had been due to restrictions on state interventions, leaving as much economic activity as possible to be determined by market forces. The *laissez-faire* state's role was limited to supporting free enterprise by eliminating barriers to competition and investing in education and the physical infrastructure. The other claim related economic success to a highly interventionist state, controlling markets in favour of internationally competitive sectors selected by state technocrats. Here the state determined the scale and direction of economic growth to a greater extent than free markets, engaging in rational planning through incentives (e.g. credit and price controls), legislation (e.g. on investment, imports and taxation) and expenditure (e.g. on research and development) to ensure the development of manufacturing, high-technology production and selected industrial sectors (Henderson and Appelbaum, 1992; Hawes and Liu, 1993). It is now generally accepted that the latter view comes closer to explaining the policies of the developmental state, with a mixture of free market and state planning, and that development requires not less, but better, state intervention and structures (Leftwich, 2000).

The crucial political qualities of developmental states included a unified and competent bureaucracy, recruited on merit and offering stable and rewarding careers relatively free from political interference by sectional interests, such as traditional agrarian oligarchies, that might compromise the pursuit of economic growth. An example is South Korea, where merit recruitment into the service of the state has existed since 788 AD, where recruits are drawn from the best graduates of the best universities, and where the civil service enjoys a strong *esprit de corps* and social solidarity. In the developmental states bureaucratic cultures have been oriented towards developmental rather than embourgeoisement from corruption, fraud and nepotism, as in so many Third World states, though an efficient, well-trained and technocratic administration can co-exist with corruption, as the case of South Korea also shows. Meritocratic recruitment has provided the state with professional, technical and managerial talent, enabling economic planning to be placed in the hands of capable personnel with a sense of common purpose oriented towards national policy objectives and attracting the cooperation of business élites. Relatively small-scale bureaucracies have allowed control and accountability, and restricted interventions to strategic sectors of the economy (Onis, 1991; Weiss and Hobson, 1995; Evans, 1995; Leftwich, 2000).

The power relationship between government agencies appears to be another dimension of bureaucracy relevant to the developmental state. A comparison of industrialization policy in South Korea and India between 1950 and 1980 reveals that the greater level of success in South Korea can be attributed in part to inter-agency co-ordination and its absence in India. Internal cohesion within the state bureaucracy is secured not only by ensuring that bureaucrats pursue the public interest rather than their own, but also by the creation of a co-ordinating agency with powers to ensure compliance with government policy. In India, the Planning Commission had only advisory powers, whereas the Korean Economic Planning Board was empowered to compel Ministries to implement government policy, making Korean planning 'one of the most successful endeavours of its kind in the annals of development policy' (Chibber, 2002, p. 983).

Developmental states have also been characterized by a 'determined' set of nationalistic political and bureaucratic élites, relating to each other in shifting coalitions but all committed to developmental objectives. They have been motivated by a range of factors varying from country to country and including external threats to national security (e.g. Taiwan), shortages of raw materials (e.g. Singapore), relative material equality in the post-1945 period resulting from land reforms, and financial and technical assistance from the USA (e.g. Taiwan and South Korea). State élites have imposed nationalistic aims on civil society, partly through repression, but also by improving living standards, reducing inequality and raising levels of educational achievement and health. Political élites have also enjoyed credibility in their commitments to development, convincing the private sector, foreign and domestic, that it could risk investment. For example, South Korea's successful shift in policy in the 1960s towards exports demonstrated its credibility in world markets. Multinationals knew they could trust Singapore's government to live up to commitments because of its proven capacity to produce and implement sound economic policies (Onis, 1991; Castells, 1992; Huff et al., 2001).

Relations between the developmental state and society have entailed what Evans labels 'embedded autonomy'. States and entrepreneurial interests have 'shared projects', with the state providing incentives such as protection and subsidies, and firms responding according to prescribed standards of production and investment. The state also subordinates powerful pre-industrial groups and classes such as rural élites, and then 'coaxes' into existence economic groups such as industrialists and commercial farmers who share the state's objectives, whether they be industrial transformation, land reform, export oriented manufacturing, or control of foreign investment. Incentives and compulsion enable the state to engineer public–private cooperation, not only to secure economic objectives but also to curtail the power of organized labour and other pro-labour groups. A form of authoritarian corporatism was common, as in South Korea and Taiwan, providing restricted access to the state for selected economic interests and the repression of others. The state has consciously promoted the development of a capitalist class by providing the infrastructure needed by private enterprise, constraining working class power, mediating between different capitalist interests (industrial, financial and ethnic), and legislating in support of capital accumulation (Evans, 1995).

There has been a 'governed interdependence' between state and industry, though the state has had the power to choose which socio-economic interests to co-operate with. Linkages and collaboration between state agencies and leading private manufacturing firms, conglomerates, banks and trading companies have been established, and members of the political élite have 'circulated' between the bureaucracy, political executive and business. The integration of state and private sector (including foreign investors and MNCs) has been facilitated by joint ventures, state owned enterprises, and networks of government personnel and business interests, sometimes bound by a common ethnicity, as in Malaysia. 'Governed interdependence' and partnership with private industry, rather than its domination, were essential for effective state intervention (Polidano, 2001).

Policy formulation has not been monopolized by the state, which is not a single entity but internally divided as different state agencies respond to an increasingly diversified economy. Routine negotiations with organized interests to mobilize resources have arguably been more important than economic controls and political repression (Hawes and Liu, 1993; Weiss and Hobson, 1995; Polidano, 2001).

Democratic stability

As we saw in Chapter 9, democratic stability is unlikely to be achieved unless there is economic growth. However, this needs to be used to support social progress. Much will depend on whether opportunities for social betterment are provided for formerly excluded groups. Rapid economic growth may increase inequalities and lead to powerful expressions of political discontent, with destabilizing consequences. The economic and social conditions of the urban and rural poor are likely to decline, at least in the short term. Under the neo-liberal economic policies required by structural adjustment programmes, the correlates of political resistance remain of great significance to the analysis of politics among the Third World's poor. There are few countries where the poor are experiencing much progress. The drift from countryside to towns is unlikely to improve their position, either economically or politically, and therefore provides fertile ground in which to test theories of political action and inaction among marginalized people. The constraints on effective political mobilization among such groups remain strong, as does the inter-dependency between them and leaders from more prosperous and organized sections of society, such as the church in parts of Africa and Latin America, which mediate between them and the public authorities.

Hence the current interest within the international development community in the scope for 'empowering' the poor, through such measures as pro-poor coalitions, the removal of legal and other barriers to freedom of association, providing education and widely disseminated information in ways that reach the poor, and strengthening the Rule of Law to remove the illegalities which the poor encounter when they seek to exert political influence or enforce their rights: arbitrary arrest; police harassment; violence from thugs hired by economic élites; and bureaucratic discrimination (World Bank, 2001c). The importance of this package of measures can be seen from the experience of associations representing the rights of workers. In 2005, 115 trade unionists were murdered, over 1,600 were subjected to violent assault, and over 9,000 arrested while attempting to protect workers rights. Due to involvement with a union 10,000 lost their jobs and 1,700 were imprisoned. Violence and repression against trade unionists were particularly noticeable in Iran, El Salvador, China, India, Cambodia, Guatemala, Zimbabwe and Burma. Restrictions or total bans on freedom of association are in place in several Middle Eastern countries. Export zones, such as those in Bangladesh, India, Pakistan, the Philippines and Sri Lanka restrict or remove trade union rights as global companies force down production costs (ICFTU, 2006).

New democracies are also threatened by the possibility of a 'revolution' of rising expectations, as in countries where sharp increases in the prices of basic commodities have led to riots. Governments have to meet the expectations of a politically conscious and mobilized population for jobs, land, housing, safe water, health care and education, as in South Africa. Any economic crisis threatens the stability of democratic government.

Institutional developments and particularly the emergence of political parties strong enough to defend class interests in competitive politics, are crucial for democratic stability, and for the development of civil society as a counter-balance to the power of the state. Of particular significance here is the tendency for Third World parties to secure their support through patronage, clientelism and traditional affiliations, rather than by mobilizing people with a common socio-economic status. This makes it difficult to organize political action along class lines, and enables ruling élites to maintain their position even when faced with the need to secure mass support.

The reactions of dominant socio-economic groups to demands for greater social equality and political participation will also be crucial to the future of fragile democracies. The social dislocation and extended political mobilization occasioned by economic change and growth has often been associated with military intervention on behalf of sectional interests threatened by democratic politics. Political institutionalization has been found to provide some protection against a reactionary military-middle class alliance, which again points to the importance of mass political parties attracting support from across all regions and ethnic divisions. Military intervention has often responded to intra-class conflict by managing the state on behalf of fundamental economic and social structures that seemed threatened by the democratic process, or by siding with one middle-class faction (perhaps associated with a particular ethnic group) and dismantling the political institutions through which other factions articulated their interests.

The political culture may include anti-democratic values which endorse such authoritarian modes of government, especially among classes which believe their privileges to be threatened by a wider distribution of political power. There are still plenty of examples to remind us that in the rural areas of the Third World landlords are in a position to employ an armed force and a corrupt judicial system to ward off land reform.

External influences and democracy

The extent to which political autonomy is limited by external control of parts of a country's economy, and the internal power structure affected by dependency, remain significant in Third World politics. The ability of a country to secure substantial aid in return for buying arms from the aid donor, as evidenced by Malaysia's Pergau hydro-electric project, is indica-tive of the changing relationship between metropolitan centres and the wealthier of their former colonies. When aid is used to finance uneconomic projects as a 'sweetener' to secure arms deals in countries where the need for development assistance is much less than in many others, an ideal test-ing ground is provided for some of the contesting hypotheses in the neo-colonialism debate, especially those pertaining to the autonomy of governments to negotiate with richer countries and the beneficiaries of the outcomes of those negotiations within the Third World country concerned.

A key question for the future is how far Third World countries can diver-sify their economies and so reduce their reliance on the fluctuating values of a few vulnerable commodities. Indonesia, for example, reduced its export dependence on oil and gas from 80 per cent in 1981 to 35 per cent in 1989 by diversification into other minerals and timber. Malaysia has reduced its dependence on rubber and tin by manufacturing steel and motor cars and becoming the world's largest producer of electronic equipment. Such development requires substantial foreign investment of a kind which will always render a Third World economy vulnerable to the extraction of valuable surplus, growing disparities of income between the new industrial and business classes and the rural poor, and increasing international debt (Indonesia's foreign debt of over £50 billion is Asia's largest).

Dependency and peripherality may be significant for the success of attempts to strengthen democracy. Statistical analysis relating measures of democratization to measures of economic development in 40 countries between 1970 and 1998 found that countries on the periphery of the world economy achieve less in terms of democracy, and especially the enjoyment of human rights, than those closer to the core (Foweraker and Landman, 2004).

The effect on the domestic social structure of penetration by the global market of rapidly-growing economies in the Third World continues to pres-ent a challenge to political analysts. The exploitation of labour for low wages in unsafe working conditions is on the increase. Governments in the developing world which play host to multinationals and domestic indus-tries which cause heavy pollution and threats to the health of the poor, such as India and China, have strongly resisted recognizing the rights of communities to take legal action to restrict environmental destruction (for example, during the United Nation's World Summit on the Environment in 2002).

As inequalities increase it is difficult to see how governments can continue to suppress legitimate demands. While it may be good for such abstractions as growth rates and levels of production that investment by developed countries in developing economies, mainly Asian and Latin American, has increased, it is questionable how good it is for the people in the low-pay occupations and ecologically vulnerable regions that make these countries attractive to foreign investment. Economic liberalization has often been accompanied by very limited political liberalization. The latter is of much less concern than the former to private foreign investors. Hence the importance of concepts relating to dependency when analyzing the behaviour of foreign interests within the developing and industrializing society, their relations with indigenous interests, especially the local business class and political élite, and the consequences of these relationships for the urban and rural poor.

Bibliography

Abernethy, D. B. (1971) 'Bureaucracy and economic development in Africa', *The African Review*, vol. 1, no. 1.

Abrahamson, M. (1978) *Functionalism*. Englewood Cliffs, NJ: Prentice-Hall.

Adam, H. M. (1994) 'Formation and recognition of new states: Somaliland in contrast to Eritrea', *Review of African Political Economy*, no. 59.

Adam, H. M. (1995) 'Somalia: a terrible beauty being born?', in I. W. Zartman (ed.), *Collapsed States. The Disintegration of Legitimate Authority*. London: Lynne Rienner Publishers.

Adamolekun, L. (2002) 'Africa's evolving career civil service systems: three challenges – state continuity, efficient service delivery and accountability', *International Review of Administrative Sciences*, vol. 68, no. 3.

Agbese, P.O. and G.K. Kieh (eds) (2007) *Reconstituting the State in Africa*, Basingstoke: Palgrave Macmillan.

Ake, C. (1974) 'Modernisation and political instability: a theoretical explanation', *World Politics*, vol. 26, no. 4.

Ake, C. (1975) 'A definition of political stability', *Comparative Politics*, vol. 7, no. 2.

Alavi, H. (1971) 'The crisis of nationalities and the state in Pakistan', *Journal of Contemporary Asia*, vol. 1, no. 3.

Alavi, H. (1972) 'The state in post-colonial societies: Pakistan and Bangladesh', *New Left Review*, no. 74.

Alavi, H. (1990) 'Authoritarianism and legitimation of state power in Pakistan', in S. K. Mitra (ed.), *The Post-Colonial State in Asia: Dialectics of Politics and Culture*. London: Harvester Wheatsheaf.

Almond, G. A. (1960) 'Introduction', in G. A. Almond and J. Coleman (eds), *The Politics of the Developing Areas*. Princeton: Princeton University Press.

Almond, G. A. (1963) 'Political systems and political change', *American Behavioural Scientist*, vol. 6, no. 10.

Almond, G. A. (1965) 'A developmental approach to political systems', *World Politics*, vol. 17, no. 1.

Almond, G. A. (1987) 'The development of political development', in M. Weiner and S. P. Huntington (eds), *Understanding Political Development*. Boston: Little, Brown.

Almond, G. A. and G. B. Powell (1966) *Comparative Politics: A Developmental Approach*. Boston: Little, Brown.

Almond, G. A. and S. Verba (1963) *The Civic Culture: Political Attitudes and Decomocracy in Five Nations*. Princeton: Princeton University Press.

Amin, S. (1982) 'The disarticulation of economy within "developing societies"', in H. Alavi and T. Shanin (eds), *Introduction to the Sociology of 'Developing Societies'*. London: Macmillan.

Anderson, C. W., F. R. von der Mehden and C. Young (1974) *Issues of Political Development*, 2nd edn. Englewood Cliffs, NJ: Prentice-Hall.

Anglade, C. (1994) 'Democracy and the rule of law in Latin America', in I. Budge and D. McKay (eds), *Developing Democracy*. London: Sage.

Antunes, R. (2003) 'Trade unions and struggles', in R. H. Chilcote (ed.), *Development in Theory and Practice: Latin American Perspecives*, Lanham, MD: Rowan & Littlefield.

Apter, D. and C. G. Rosberg (1994) 'Changing African Perspectives', in Apter and Rosberg (eds), *Political Development and the New Realism in Sub-Saharan Africa*. Charlottesville, VA: University Press of Virginia.

Argyriades, D. (2007) ' "Resisting change": some critical remarks on contemporary narratives about reform', in D. Argyriades, O. P. Dwivedi and J. G Jabbra (eds.) *Public Administration in Transition. A Fifty-Year Trajectory Worldwide*. London: Vallentine Mitchell.

Ayoob, M. (1996) 'State-making, state breaking and state failure: explaining the roots of "Third World" insecurity', in L. van de Goor, K. Rupesinghe and P. Sciarone (eds), *Between Development and Destruction: An Enquiry into the Causes of Conflict in Post-Colonial States*. London: Macmillan.

Baburkin, S., A. C. Danopoulos, R. Giacalone and E. Moreno (1999) 'The 1992 coups attempts in Venezuela: causes and failure', *Journal of Political and Military Sociology*, vol. 27, no. 1.

Balogun, M. J. (2002) 'The democratization and development agenda and the African civil service: issues resolved or matters arising?', *International Review of Administrative Sciences*, vol. 68, no. 4.

Banuazizi, A. (1987) 'Socio-psychological approach to political development', in M. Weiner and S. Huntington (eds), *Understanding Political Development*. Boston: Little, Brown.

Baran, P. A. (1957) *The Political Economy of Growth*. New York: Monthly Review Press.

Barratt Brown, M. (1963) *After Imperialism*. London: Heinemann.

Batley, R. (2002) 'The changing role of the state in development', in V. Desai and R. B. Potter (eds), *The Companion to Development Studies*. London: Arnold.

Bauer, P. (1971) *Dissent on Development*. London: Weidenfeld & Nicolson.

Bauer, P. (1981) *Equality: The Third World and Economic Delusion*. London: Weidenfeld & Nicolson.

Becker, D. G. and R. L. Sklar (1987) 'Why post-imperialism?', in D. G. Becker, J. Frieden, S. P. Schatz and R. L. Sklar (eds), *Post-Imperialism. International Capitalism and Development in the Late Twentieth Century*. London: Lynne Rienner Publishers.

Berger, M. (1994) 'The end of the "Third World"?', *Third World Quarterly*, vol. 15, no. 2.

Berger, M. (2004) 'After the Third World? History, destiny and the fate of Third Worldism', *Third World Quarterly*, vol. 25, no. 1.

Berman, B. (1974) 'Clientelism and neocolonialism: centre–periphery relations and political development in African states', *Studies in Comparative International Development*, vol. 9, no. 1.

Berman, B. (1984) 'Structure and process in the bureaucratic states of colonial Africa', *Development and Change*, vol. 15, no. 2.

Bermeo, N. (1997) *The Power of the People*, Working Paper 1997/97, Madrid: Juan March Institute.

Bernstein, H. (1979) 'Sociology of underdevelopment vs. sociology of development', in D. Lehmann (ed.), *Development Theory: Four Critical Studies*. London: Frank Cass.

Bernstein, H. (1982) 'Industrialisation, development and dependence', in H. Alavi and T. Shanin (eds), *Introduction to the Sociology of 'Developing Societies'*. London: Macmillan.

Birch, A. H. (1978) 'Minority nationalist movements and theories of political integration', *World Politics*, vol. 30, no. 2.

Bisley, N. (2007) *Rethinking Globalization*. Basingstoke: Palgrave Macmillan.

Bjorkman, J. W. and K. Mathur (1996) 'India', in J. Blondel and M. Cotta (eds), *Party and Government: An Inquiry into the Relationship between Governments and Supporting Parties in Liberal Democracies*. London: Macmillan.

Blanco, L. and R. Grier (2007) 'Long live democracy: the determinants of political instability in Latin America', Department of Economics Working Paper, University of Oklahoma.

Bland, D. L. (1999) 'A unified theory of civil–military relations', *Armed Forces and Society*, vol. 26, no. 1.

Blank, J. (2005) 'Democratization and development', in D. T. Hagerty (ed.), *South Asia in World Politics*, Lanham, MD: Rowan & Littlefield.

Blomstrom, M. and B. Hettne (1984) *Development Theory in Transition*. London: Zed Books.

Bodenheimer, S. (1971) 'Dependency and imperialism: the roots of Latin American underdevelopment', in K. Fann and D. Hodges (eds), *Readings in United States Imperialism*. Boston: Porter Sargent.

Bowornwathana, B. (2000) 'Governance reform in Thailand: questionable assumptions, uncertain outcomes', *Governance: An International Journal of Policy and Administration*, vol. 13, no. 3.

Brass, P. R. (1991) *Ethnicity and Nationalism: Theory and Comparison*. London: Sage Publications.

Brecher, M. (1963) 'Political instability in the new states of Asia', in H. Eckstein and D. E. Apter (eds), *Comparative Politics: A Reader*. New York: Free Press.

Bretton, H. L. (1973) *Power and Politics in Africa*. London: Longman.

Brewer, A. (1980) *Marxist Theories of Imperialism: A Critical Survey*. London: Routledge & Kegan Paul.

Brinkerhoff. D. W. (2000) 'Democratic governance and sectoral policy reform: tracing linkages and exploring synergies', *World Development*, vol. 28, no. 4.

Brinkerhoff, D. W. and A. A. Goldsmith (2002) *Clientelism, Patrimonialism and Democratic Governance*. Cambridge, MA: Abt Associates Inc.

Brown, D. (1989) 'Ethnic revival: perspectives on state and society', *Third World Quarterly*, vol. 11, no. 4.

Brown, D. (2000) *Contemporary Nationalism: Civic, Ethnocultural and Multicultural Politics*. London: Routledge.

Brown, D. (2006) 'Contending nationalisms in South-East Asia', in G. Delanty and K. Kumar (eds), *The SAGE Handbook of Nations and Nationalism*. London: Sage Publications.

Bulloch, J. and H. Morris (1993) *No Friends but the Mountains: The Tragic History of the Kurds*. Harmondsworth: Penguin.

Cammack, P. (1997) *Capitalism and Democracy in the Third World: The Doctrine for Political Development*. London: Leicester University Press.

Cammack, P., D. Pool and W. Tordoff (1993) *Third World Politics: A Comparative Introduction*, 2nd edn. London: Macmillan.

Carbone, G. M. (2003) 'Political parties in a "no-party democracy". Hegemony and opposition under "Movement democracy" in Uganda', *Party Politics*, vol. 9, no. 4.

Cardoso, F. H. (1973) 'Associated-dependent development: theoretical and practical implications', in A. Stepan (ed.), *Authoritarian Brazil: Origins, Policies and Future*. New Haven, CN: Yale University Press.

Carey, S. C. (2002) 'A comparative analysis of political parties in Kenya, Zambia and the Democratic Republic of Congo', *Democratization*, vol. 9, no. 3.

Carnoy, M. (1984) *The State and Political Theory*. Princeton: Princeton University Press.

Carothers, T. (2002) 'The end of the transition paradigm', *Journal of Democracy*, vol. 13, no. 1.

Castells, M. (1992) 'Four Asian Tigers with a dragon head: a comparative analysis of the state, economy and society in the Asian Pacific rim', in R. Appelbaum and J. Henderson (eds), *States and Development in the Asian Pacific Rim*, Newbury Park, CA: Sage.

Castles, F. G. (1974) 'Political stability and the dominant image of society', *Political Studies*, vol. 22, no. 3.

Castron, C. (2002) 'The military and politics in Brazil, 1964–2000', in K. Koonings and D. Kruijt (eds), *Political Armies. The Military and Nation Building in the Age of Democracy*, London: Zed Books.

Chadda, M. (2000) *Building Democracy in South Asia, India, Nepal, Pakistan*. London: Lynne Rienner.

Chaliand, G. (1980) 'Introduction', in G.Chaliand (ed.), *People Without a Country: The Kurds and Kurdistan*, London: Zed Press.

Charlton, R. (1981) 'Plus ça change . . . a review of two decades of theoretical analysis of African *coups d'état*', *Culture et Developpement*, vol. 13, no. 2.

Chibber, V. (2002) 'Bureaucratic rationality and the developmental state', *American Journal of Sociology*, vol. 107, no. 4.

Chiriyankandath, J. (1994) 'The politics of religious identity: a comparison of Hindu nationalism and Sudanese Islamism', *Journal of Commonwealth and Comparative Politics*, vol. 32, no. 1.

Chowdhury, N. and B. J. Nelson (1994) 'Redefining politics: patterns of women's political engagement from a global perspective', in B. J. Nelson and N. Chowdhury (eds), *Women and Politics Worldwide*. New Haven, CN: Yale University Press.

Chu, Y.-H. (2001) 'The legacy of one-party hegemony in Taiwan', in L. Diamond and R. Gunther (eds), *Political Parties and Democracy*. Baltimore: The Johns Hopkins University Press.

Clague, C., P. Keefer, S. Knack and M. Olson (1997) 'Democracy, autocracy and the institutions supportive of economic growth', in C. Clague (ed.), *Institutions and Economic Development: Growth and Governance in Less-Developed and Post Socialist States*. Baltimore; The Johns Hopkins University Press.

Clapham, C. (1982) 'Clientelism and the state', in C. Clapham (ed.), *Private Patronage and Public Power: Political Clientelism in the Modern State*. London: Frances Pinter.

Clapham, C. (1985) *Third World Politics: An Introduction*. London: Croom Helm.

Clark, J. F. (2007) 'The decline of the African military coup', *Journal of Democracy*, vol. 18, no. 3.

Clay, J. W. (1989) 'Epilogue: the ethnic future of nations', *Third World Quarterly*, vol. 11, no. 4.

Coakley, J. (1993) 'The territorial management of ethnic conflict', *Regional Politics and Policy*, vol. 3, no. 1.

Cohen, B. J. (1973) *The Question of Imperialism: The Political Economy of Dominance and Dependence*. New York: Basic Books.

Coleman, J. S. (1954) 'Nationalism in Tropical Africa', *American Political Science Review*, vol. 48, no. 2.

Coleman, J. S. (1960) 'Conclusion: the political systems of the developing areas', in G. A. Almond and J. Coleman (eds), *The Politics of the Developing Areas*. Princeton: Princeton University Press.

Coleman, J. S. and C. G. Rosberg (eds) (1964) *Political Parties and National Integration in Tropical Africa*. Los Angeles: University of California Press.

Collier, D. (1979) 'The BA model: synthesis and priorities for future research', in D. Collier (ed.), *The New Authoritarianism in Latin America*. Princeton: Princeton University Press.

Compton, R. W. (2000) *East Asian Democratization. Impact of Globalization, Culture and Economy*, London: Praeger.

Connor, W. (1973) 'The politics of ethnonationalism', *Journal of International Affairs*, vol. 27, no. 1.

Connor, W. (1988) 'Ethnonationalism', in M. Weiner and S. P. Huntington (eds), *Understanding Political Development*. Boston: Little, Brown.

Coppedge, M. (2001) 'Political Darwinism in Latin America's lost decade', in L. Diamond and R. Gunther (eds), *Political Parties and Democracy*, Baltimore: The Johns Hopkins University Press.

Craske, N. (1999) *Women and Politics in Latin America*. New Brunswick, NJ: Rutgers University Press.

Creevy, L., P. Ngomo and R. Vengroff (2005) 'Party politics and different paths to democratic transitions: a comparison of Benin and Senegal', *Party Politics*, vol. 11, no. 4.

Crow, B. (1990) 'The state in Bangladesh: the extension of a weak state', in S. K. Mitra (ed.), *The Post-Colonial State in Asia. Dialectics of Politics and Culture*. London: Harvester Wheatsheaf.

Dahl, R. (1971) *Polyarchy: Participation and Opposition*. New Haven, CN: Yale University Press.

Dalton, R. J. and S. Weldon (2007) 'Partisanship and party system institutionalization', *Party Politics*, vol. 13, no. 2.

Danapoulos, C. and D. Zirker (2006) 'Governability and contemporary forms of military intervention: expanding Ecuadorian and Turkish models', *Journal of Security Sector Management*, vol. 4, no. 1.

Davies, J. C. (1972) 'Toward a theory of revolution', in D. H. Wrong and H. L. Gracey (eds) *Readings in Introductory Sociology*, 2nd edn. London: Collier-Macmillan.

Davin, D. (1996) 'Chinese women: media concerns and the politics of reform', in H. Afshar (ed.), *Women and Politics in the Third World*. London: Routledge.

de Kadt, E. (2002) 'The military in politics: old wine in new bottles', in K. Koonings and D. Kruijt (eds), *Political Armies. The Military and Nation Building in the Age of Democracy*, London: Zed Books.

Debray, R. (1967) 'Problems of revolutionary strategy in Latin America', *New Left Review*, no. 45.

Denoeux, G. (2002) 'The forgotten swamp: navigating political Islam', *Middle East Policy*, vol. 9, no. 2.

Diamond, L. (1988) 'Introduction: roots of failure, seeds of hope', in L. Diamond. J. J. Linz and S. M. Lipset (eds), *Democracy in Developing Countries*, vol. 2. *Africa*. Boulder, CO: Lynne Rienner Publishers.

Diamond, L. (1989) 'Introduction: persistence, erosion, breakdown and renewal', in L. Diamond, J. J. Linz and S. M. Lipset (eds), *Democracy in Developing Countries*, vol. 3, *Asia*. Boulder, CO: Lynne Rienner Publishers.

Diamond, L. (1992) 'Economic development and democracy reconsidered', in G. Marks and L. Diamond (eds), *Re-examining Democracy: Essays in Honor of Seymour Martin Lipset*. London: Sage.

Diamond, L. (1993a) 'Causes and effects', in L. Diamond (ed.), *Political Culture and Democracy in Developing Countries*. Boulder, CO: Lynne Rienner Publishers.

Diamond, L. (1993b) 'Introduction: political culture and democracy', in L. Diamond (ed.), *Political Culture and Democracy in Developing Countries*. Boulder, CO: Lynne Rienner Publishers.

Diamond, L. (1996) 'Is the Third Wave over?', *Journal of Democracy*, vol. 7, no. 3.

Diamond, L. (1997a) *Civil Society and the Development of Democracy*, Working Paper 1997/101. Madrid: Juan March Institute.

Diamond, L. (1997b) 'Introduction: in search of consolidation', in L.Diamond, M.F.Plattner, Y. Chu and H. Tien (eds), *Consolidating the Third Wave Democracies: Themes and Perspectives*, Baltimore, The Johns Hopkins University Press.

Diamond, L. (1998) *Political Culture and Democratic Consolidation*, Working Paper 1998/118. Madrid: Juan March Institute.

Diamond, L. and J. J. Linz (1989) 'Introduction: politics, society and democracy in Latin America', in L. Diamond, J. J. Linz and S. M. Lipset (eds), *Democracy in Developing Countries*, vol. 4, *Latin America*. Boulder, CO: Lynne Rienner Publishers.

Diamond, L., J. J. Linz and S. M. Lipset (eds) (1990) 'Introduction: comparing experiences with democracy', in L. Diamond, J. J. Linz and S. M. Lipset (eds), *Politics in Developing Countries. Comparing Experiences with Democracy*. London: Lynne Rienner Publishers.

Dirlik, A. (2004) 'Spectres of the Third World: global modernity and the end of the three worlds', *Third World Quarterly*, vol. 25, no. 1.

Dix, R. H. (1992) 'Democratisation and the institutionalisation of Latin American political parties', *Comparative Political Studies*, vol. 24, no. 4, January.

Dos Santos, T. (1973) 'The crisis of development theory and the problem of dependence in Latin America', in H. Bernstein (ed.), *Underdevelopment and Development*. Harmondsworth: Penguin.

Dowse, R. E. (1966) 'A functionalist's logic', *World Politics*, vol. 18, no. 4.

Dowse, R. E. (1969) 'The military and political development', in C. Leys (ed.) *Politics and Change in Developing Countries*. Cambridge: Cambridge University Press.

Eckstein, H. (1982) 'The idea of political development: from dignity to efficiency', *World Politics*, vol. 34, no. 4.

Eisenstadt, S. N. (1966) *Modernisation: Protest and Change*. Englewood Cliffs, NJ: Prentice-Hall.

Eisenstadt, S. N. and L. Roniger (1981) 'The study of patron–client relations and recent developments in sociological theory', in S. N. Eisenstadt and R. Lemarchand (eds), *Political Clientelism, Patronage and Development*. London: Sage.

Emmanuel, A. (1974) 'Myths of development versus myths of underdevelopment', *New Left Review*, no. 85.

Emmanuel, A. (1976) 'The multinational corporations and the inequality of development', *International Social Science Journal*, vol. 28, no. 4.

Enloe, C. H. (1973) *Ethnic Conflict and Political Development*. Boston: Little, Brown.

Enloe, C. H. (1976) 'Central governments' strategies for coping with separatist movements', in W. H. Morris-Jones (ed.), *The Politics of Separatism*, Collected Seminar Papers no. 19. London: University of London Institute of Commonwealth Studies.

Eriksen, T. H. (1993) *Ethnicity and Nationalism. Anthropological Perspectives*. London: Pluto Press.

Ersson, S. and J. E. Lane (1996) 'Democracy and development: a statistical exploration', in A. Leftwich (ed.), *Democracy and Development. Theory and Practice*. Cambridge: Polity Press.

Evans, P.B. (1995) *Embedded Autonomy. States and Industrial Transformation*, Princeton NJ: Princeton University Press.

Evans, P. B., D. Rueschmeyer and T. Skocpol (eds) (1985) *Bringing the State Back In*. Cambridge: Cambridge University Press.

Farsoun, S. K. and N. H. Aruri (2006) *Palestine and the Palestinians. A Social and Political History*. Boulder: Westview Press.

Fayemi, J. (2002) 'Entrenched militarism and the future of democracy in Nigeria', in K. Koonings and D. Kruijt (eds), *Political Armies. The Military and Nation Building in the Age of Democracy*. London: Zed Books.

Feardon, J. D. and D. D. Laitin, (2003) 'Ethnicity, insurgency, and civil war', *American Political Science Review*, vol. 97, no.1.

Filali-Ansary, A. (2003) 'The challenge of secularization', in L. Diamond, M. F. Plattner and D. Brumberg (eds), *Islam and Democracy in the Middle East*, Baltimore: The Johns Hopkins University Press.

Finer, S. E. (1962) *The Man on Horseback: The Role of the Military in Politics*. London: Pall Mall Press.

Finer, S. E. (1974) *Comparative Government*. Harmondsworth: Penguin.

First, R. (1972) *The Barrel of a Gun: Political Power in Africa and the Coup d'État*. Harmondsworth: Penguin.

Fitch, J. S. (1998) *The Armed Forces and Democracy in Latin America*. Baltimore: The Johns Hopkins University Press.

Foster-Carter, A. (1976) 'From Rostow to Gunder Frank: conflicting paradigms in the analysis of underdevelopment', *World Development*, vol. 4, no. 3.

Foweraker, J. and T. Landman (2004) 'Economic development and democracy revisited: why dependency theory is not yet dead', *Democratization*, vol. 11, no. 1.

Fox, J. (1994) 'The difficult transition from clientelism to citizenship', *World Politics*, vol. 46, no. 2.

Frank, A. G. (1966) 'The development of underdevelopment', *Monthly Review*, vol. 18, no. 4.

Frank, A. G. (1969a) *Capitalism and Underdevelopment in Latin America: Historical Studies of Chile and Brazil*. London: Monthly Review Press.

Frank, A. G. (1969b) *Latin America: Underdevelopment or Revolution*. New York: Monthly Review Press.

Frank, A. G. (1972a) 'Economic dependence, class structure and underdevelopment policy', in J. D. Cockcroft, A. G. Frank and D. L. Johnson (eds), *Dependence and Underdevelopment. Latin America's Political Economy*. New York: Doubleday.

Frank, A. G. (1972b) 'Sociology of development and the underdevelopment of sociology', in J. D. Cockcroft, A. G. Frank and D. L. Johnson (eds), *Dependence and Underdevelopment: Latin America's Political Economy*. New York: Doubleday.

Frazer, J. (1995) 'Conceptualising civil–military relations during democratic transition', *Africa Today*, vol. 42, nos 1–2.

Freedman, A. L. (2006) *Political change and Consolidation. Democracy's Rocky Road in Thailand, Indonesia, South Korea and Malaysia*. Basingstoke: Palgrave Macmillan.

Freedom House (2001) *Freedom in the World: Political Rights and Civil Liberties 2000–2001*. New York: Freedom House.

Freedom House (2007) *Countries at the Crossroads 2007*, www.freedomhouse.org

Freedom House (2008a) *Freedom in the World 2007*. New York: Freedom House.

Freedom House (2008b) *Global Press Freedom 2008. A Year of Global Decline*. New York: Freedom House

Fritzen, S. (2007) 'Discipline and democratize: patterns of bureaucratic accountability in Southeast Asia', *International Journal of Public Administration*, vol. 30, nos. 12–14.

Fukuyama, F. (1992) *The End of History and the Last Man*, New York: The Free Press.

Gasiorowski, M. J. (1998) 'Macro-economic conditions and political instability: an empirical analysis', *Studies in Comparative International Development*, vol. 33, no. 3.

Gates, S., H. Hegre, M. P. Jones, and H. Strand (2006) 'Institutional Inconsistency and political instability. polity duration 1900–2000', *American Journal of Political Science*, vol. 50, no. 4.

Ghai, Y. (2000) 'Ethnicity and autonomy: a framework for analysis', in Y. Ghai (ed.), *Autonomy and Ethnicity: Negotiating Competing Claims in Multi-ethnic States*. Cambridge: Cambridge University Press.

Ghassemlou, A. R. (1980) 'Kurdistan in Iran', in G. Chaliand (ed.), *People Without a Country*. London: Zed Press.

Gill, G. (2000) *The Dynamics of Democratization. Élites, Civil Society and the Transition Process*. Basingstoke: Macmillan.

Goldstone, J. A., R. H. Bates, T. R. Gurr, M. Lustik, M. G. Marshall, J. Ulfelder and M. Woodward, (2005) 'A global forecasting model of political instability', Paper presented to the Annual Meeting of the American Political Science Association, Washington, 1–4 September.

Goldstone, J. A., T. R. Gurr and F. Moshiri (eds) (1991) *Revolutions of the Late Twentieth Century*. Boulder, CO: Westview Press.

Goodwin, J. and T. Skocpol (1989) 'Explaining revolutions in the contemporary Third World', *Politics and Society*, vol. 17, no. 4.

Goulbourne, H. (1979) 'Some problems of analysis of the political in backward capitalist social formations', in H. Goulbourne (ed.), *Politics and State in the Third World*. London: Macmillan.

Gourevitch, P. A. (1979) 'The re-emergence of "peripheral nationalisms": some comparative speculations on the spatial distribution of political leadership and economic growth', *Comparative Studies in Society and History*, vol. 21. no. 2.

Government of Tibet in Exile (1996) *Tibet: Proving Truth From Facts*. London: The Office of Tibet, www.tibet.com/WhitePaper

Graham, B. D. (1993) *Representation and Party Politics: A Comparative Perspective*. Oxford: Blackwell Publishers.

Griffin, K. and J. Gurley (1985) 'Radical analyses of imperialism, the Third World, and the transition to socialism: a survey article', *Journal of Economic Literature*, vol. 23, no. 3.

Griffiths, R. J. (1996) 'Democratisation and civil military relations in Namibia, South Africa and Mozambique', *Third World Quarterly*, vol. 17, no. 3, September.

Grugel, J. (2002) *Democratization. A Critical Introduction*. Basingstoke: Palgrave Macmillan.

Gunther, R. and L. Diamond (2001) 'Types and functions of parties', in L. Diamond and R. Gunther (eds), *Political Parties and Democracy*, Baltimore: The Johns Hopkins University Press.

Gurr, T. R. and B. Harff (1994) *Ethnic Conflict in World Politics*. Boulder, CO: Westview Press.

Haggard, S. (1990) *Pathways from the Periphery: The Politics of Growth in the Newly Industrializing Countries*. Ithaca, NY: Cornell University Press.

Hah, C. and J. Martin (1975) 'Towards a synthesis of conflict and integration theories of nationalism', *World Politics*, vol. 27, no. 3, April.

Hammouya, M. (1999) *Statistics on Public Sector Employment: Methodology, Structures and Trends*. Geneva: International Labour Office.

Haque, M. S. (1999) 'Relationship between citizenship and public administration: a reconfiguration', *International Review of Administrative Sciences*, vol. 65, no. 3.

Haque, M. S. (2007) 'Theory and practice of public administration in Southeast Asia: traditions, directions, and impacts', *International Journal of Public Administration*, vol. 30, nos. 12–14.

Harris, N. (1970) 'The revolutionary role of the peasants', *International Socialism*, no. 41, December–January.

Haruna, P. F. (2003) 'Reforming Ghana's public service: issues and experiences in comparative perspective', *Public Administration Review*, vol. 63, no. 3.

Haufman, R. (1997) *The Next Challenge for Latin America*, Working Paper 1997/108. Madrid: Juan March Institute.

Hawes, G. and H. Liu (1993) 'Explaining the dynamics of the Southeast Asian political economy', *World Politics*, vol. 45, no. 4.

Hawthorne, G. (1992) 'Sub-Saharan Africa', in D. Held (ed.), *Prospects for Democracy. North, South, East, West*. Cambridge: Polity Press.

Haynes, J. (1993) *Religion in Third World Politics*. Buckingham: Open University Press.

Haynes, J. (1999) 'Conclusion', in Haynes (ed.), *Religion, Globalization and Political Culture in the Third World*. London: Macmillan.

Haynes, J. (2001) *Democracy in the Developing World*. Cambridge: Polity Press.

Haynes, J. (2003) 'Democratic consolidation in Africa: the problematic case of Ghana', *Commonwealth and Comparative Politics*, vol. 41, no. 1.

Heady, F. (1959) 'Bureaucratic theory and comparative administration', *Administrative Science Quarterly*, vol. 3, no. 4.

Hechter, M. (1975) *Internal Colonialism: The Celtic Fringe in British National Development, 1536–1966*. London: Routledge & Kegan Paul.

Hechter, M. (1985) 'Internal colonialism revisited', in E. A. Tiryakian and R. Rogowski (eds), *New Nationalisms of the Developed West*. London: Allen & Unwin.

Hechter, M. (2000) *Containing Nationalism*. Oxford: Oxford University Press.

Hechter, M., T. Kuyucu and A. Sacks (2006) 'Nationalism and direct rule', in G. Delanty and K. Kumar (eds), *The SAGE Handbook of Nations and Nationalism*, London: Sage Publications.

Heeger, G. A. (1973) 'Bureaucracy, political parties and political development', *World Politics*, vol. 25, no. 4.

Hein, W. and K. Stenzel (1979) 'The capitalist state and underdevelopment in Latin America: the case of Venezuela', in H. Goulbourne (ed.), *Politics and State in the Third World*. London: Macmillan.

Held, D. and A. McGrew (2000) 'The great globalization debate: an introduction', in D. Held and A. McGrew (eds), *The Global Transformation Reader. An Introduction to the Globalization Debate*. Cambridge: Polity Press.

Held, D., A. McGrew, D. Goldblatt and J. Perraton (1999) *Global Transformations: Politics, Economics and Culture*. Cambridge: Polity Press.

Helliwell, J. F. (1994) 'Empirical linkages between democracy and economic growth', *British Journal of Political Science*, vol. 24, no. 2.

Henderson, J. and R. Appelbaum, (1992) 'Situating the state in the East Asian development process' in R. Appelbaum and J. Henderson (eds), *States and Development in the Asian Pacific Rim*. Newbury Park, CA: Sage.

Hensman, R. (1996) 'The role of women in the resistance to political authoritarianism in Latin America and South Asia', in H. Afshar (ed.) *Women and Politics in the Third World*. London: Routledge.

Herbst, J. (1990) 'The structural adjustment of politics in Africa', *World Development*. vol. 18, no. 7.

Hernandez, L. and J. Fox (1995) 'Mexico's difficult democracy: grassroots movements, NGOs, and local government', in C. A. Reilly (ed.), *New Paths to Democratic Development in Latin America*. London: Lynne Rienner Publishers.

Higgott, R. A. (1978) 'Competing theoretical perspectives on development and underdevelopment', *Politics*, vol. 13, no. 1.

Higgott, R. A. (1983) *Political Development Theory: The Contemporary Debate*. London: Croom Helm.

Hilary, J. (2004) *Profiting From Poverty. Privatisation, Consultants, DFID, and Public Services*, London: War on Want.

Hilliard, V. G. and H. F. Wissink, (1999) 'Alternative administration: a southern African perspective', in K. M. Henderson and O. P. Dwivedi (eds), *Bureaucracy and the Alternatives in World Perspective*, Basingstoke: Macmillan.

Hirschmann, D. (1981) 'Development or underdevelopment administration?: a further "deadlock"', *Development and Change*, vol. 12, no. 4.

Hirst, P. and G. Thompson (1999) *Globalisation in Question: The International Economy and the Possibilities of Governance*, 2nd edn. Cambridge: Polity Press.

Hodder-Williams, R. (1984) *An Introduction to the Politics of Tropical Africa*. London: Allen & Unwin.

Holt, R. T. and J. E. Turner (1966) *The Political Basis of Economic Development*. Princeton, NJ: D. Van Nostrand Co.

Holt, R. T. and J. E. Turner (1972) 'The methodology of comparative research', in R. T. Holt and J. E. Turner (eds), *The Methodology of Comparative Research*. New York: Free Press.

Hoogvelt, A. M. M. (1978) *The Sociology of Developing Societies*, 2nd edn. London: Macmillan.

Hoogvelt, A. M. M. (1982) *The Third World in Global Development*. London: Macmillan.

Horowitz, D. L. (1985) *Ethnic Groups in Conflict*. Berkeley, CA: University of California Press.

Horowitz, D. L. (1994) 'Democracy in divided societies', in L. Diamond and M. F. Plattner (eds), *Nationalism, Ethnic Conflict and Democracy*. Baltimore: Johns Hopkins University Press.

Howell, J., A. Ishkanian, E. Obadare, H. Seckinelgin and M. Glasius (2006) *The Backlash against Civil Society in the Wake of the Long War on Terror*, Civil Society Working Paper No. 26. London: Centre for Civil Society, London School of Economics and Political Science.

HRW (2005) 'Entrenching impunity. Government responsibility for international crimes in Darfur', *Human Rights Watch*, vol. 17, no. 17(A).

HRW (2008) *Collective Punishment. War Crimes and Crimes Against Humanity in the Ogaden Area of Ethiopia's Somali Region*. New York: Human Rights Watch.

Huber, E., D. Rueschemeyer and J. D. Stephens (1993) 'The impact of economic development on democracy', *Journal of Economic Perspectives*, vol. 7, no. 3.

Huff, W. G. , G. Dewit and C. Oughton (2001) 'Building the developmental state: achieving economic growth through co-operative solutions: a comment on bringing politics back in', *Journal of Development Studies*, vol. 38, no. 1.

Hughes, O. E. (1998) *Public Management and Administration: An Introduction*, 2nd edn. London: Macmillan.

Hulme, D. and M. Turner (1990) *Sociology and Development: Theories, Policies and Practices*. London: Harvester Wheatsheaf.

Huntington, S. P. (1957) *The Soldier and the State: The Theory and Practice of Civil–Military Relations*. Cambridge, MA: Harvard University Press.

Huntington, S. P. (1965) 'Political development and political decay', *World Politics*, vol. 17, no. 2.

Huntington, S. P. (1968) *Political Order in Changing Societies*. New Haven, CN: Yale University Press.

Huntington, S. P. (1971) 'The change to change', *Comparative Politics*, vol. 3, no. 2.

Huntington, S. P. (1984) 'Will more countries become democratic?', *Political Science Quarterly*, vol. 99, no. 2.

Huntington, S. P. (1987) 'The goals of development', in M. Weiner and S. P. Huntington (eds), *Understanding Political Development*. Boston: Little, Brown.

Huntington, S. P. (1991) *The Third Wave: Democratization in the Late Twentieth Century*. Norman: University of Oklahoma Press.

Huntington, S. P. (1995) 'Reforming civil–military relations', *Journal of Democracy*, vol. 6, no. 4.

Huntington, S. P. (1996) *The Clash of Civilizations and the Remaking of World Order*, New York: Simon & Schuster.

Huntington, S. P. and J. I. Dominguez (1975) 'Political development', in F. I. Greenstein and N. W. Polsby (eds), *Micropolitical Theory*, Handbook of Political Science, vol. 3. Reading, MA: Addison-Wesley.

Hurwitz, L. (1973) 'Contemporary approaches to political stability', *Comparative Politics*, vol. 3, no. 3.

Hyden, G. (2006) *African Politics in Comparative Perspective*, Cambridge: Cambridge University Press.

Hymer, S. (1982) 'The multinational corporation and the law of uneven development', in H. Alavi and T. Shanin (eds), *Introduction to the Sociology of 'Developing Societies'*. London: Macmillan.

ICFTU (2006) *Annual Survey of Trade Union Rights Violations*. Brussels: International Confederation of Free Trade Unions.

Ikelegbe, A. (2001) 'Civil society, oil and conflict in the Niger Delta region of Nigeria: ramifications of civil society for a regional resource struggle', *Journal of Modern African Studies*, vol. 39, no. 3.

ILO (2007) 'Employment by sector', Geneva: International Labour Organization, www.ilo.org/public/employment/strat/kilm.pdf

Inglehart, R. and C. Welzel (2005) *Modernization, Cultural Change and Democracy*, Cambridge: Cambridge University Press.

Islam, N. (2004) '*Sifarish*, cyoophauls, power and collectivism: administrative culture in Pakistan', *International Review of Administrative Sciences*, vol. 70, no. 2.

Jackman, R. W. (1978) 'The predictability of *coups d'état*: a model with African data', *American Political Science Review*, vol. 72, no. 4.

Jackman, R. W. (1986) 'Explaining African *coups d'état*', *American Political Science Review*, vol. 80, no. 1.

Jacoby, U. (2007) 'Getting together. The new partnership between China and Africa for aid and trade', *Finance and Development*, vol. 44, no. 2.

Jahan, R. (1973) *Pakistan: Failure in National Integration*. New York: Columbia University Press.

Jain, R. B. (1992) 'Bureaucracy, public policy and socio-economic development', in H. K. Asmerom, R. Hope and R. B. Jain (eds), *Bureaucracy and Development Policies in the Third World*. Amsterdam: VU University Press.

Janowitz, M. (1970) *Political Conflict. Essays in Political Sociology*. Chicago: Quadrangle Books.

Jansen, K. (2001) 'Thailand, the making of a miracle?', *Development and Change*, vol. 32, no. 2.

Jaquette, J. S. (2001) 'Regional differences and contrasting views', *Journal of Democracy*, vol. 12, no. 3.

Jessop, R. (1977) 'Recent theories of the capitalist state', *Cambridge Journal of Economics*, vol. 1, no. 4.

Johnson, T. H., R. O. Slater and P. McGowan (1986) 'Explaining African military *coups d'état*', *American Political Science Review*, vol. 80, no. 1.

Jones, D. M. (1997) *Political Development in Pacific Asia*. Cambridge: Polity Press.

Judy, R. A. T. (1998) 'Islamiyya and the construction of the human being', in A. S. Moussalli (ed.), *Islamic Fundamentalism: Myths and Realities*. Reading, MA: Ithaca Press.

Kamat, S. (2004) 'The privatisation of public interest: theorizing NGO discourse in a neo-liberal era', *Review of International Political Economy*, vol. 11, no. 1.

Kamrava, M. (1995) *Politics and Society in the Third World*. London: Routledge.

Karl, T. L. (1996) 'Dilemmas of democratization in Latin America', in R. A. Camp (ed.), *Democracy in Latin America: Patterns and Cycles*. Wilmington: Scholarly Resources Inc.

Kasfir, N. (1983) 'Relating class to state in Africa', *Journal of Commonwealth and Comparative Politics*, vol. 21, no. 3.

Kasfir, N. (1998) 'Civil society, the state and democracy in Africa', *Journal of Commonwealth and Comparative Politics*, vol. 36, no. 2.

Kaufman, R. R., H. I. Chernotsky and D. S. Geller (1974) 'A preliminary test of the theory of dependency', *Comparative Politics*, vol. 7, no. 3.

Kay, G. (1975) *Development and Underdevelopment: A Marxist Analysis*. London: Macmillan.

Kedourie, E. (1992) *Politics in the Middle East*. Oxford: Oxford University Press.
Kellas, J. G. (1991) *The Politics of Nationalism and Ethnicity*. London: Macmillan.
'Kendal' (1980) 'Kurdistan in Turkey', in G. Chaliand (ed.), *People Without a Country*. London: Zed Press.
Keratnyky, A. (2002) 'Muslim countries and the democracy gap', *Journal of Democracy*, vol. 13, no. 1.
Kerr, P., (2002) 'Saved from extinction: evolutionary theorizing, politics and the state', *British Journal of Politics and International Relations*, vol. 4, no. 2.
Kiely, R. (1995) *Sociology and Development: The Impasse and Beyond*. London: UCL Press.
Kilson, M. L. (1963) 'Authoritarian and single-party tendencies in African polities', *World Politics*, vol. 15, no. 1.
Kohn, H. (1945) *The Idea of Nationalism: A Study of its Origins and Background*. London: Macmillan.
Koonings, K. and D. Kruijt (2002) 'Military politics and the mission of nation building', in K. Koonings and D. Kruijt (eds), *Political Armies. The Military and Nation Building in the Age of Democracy*, London: Zed Books.
Kostiner, J. (1997) 'State, Islam and opposition in Saudi Arabia: the post-Desert Storm phase', in B. Maddy-Weitzman and E. Inbar (eds), *Religious Radicalism in the Greater Middle East*. London: Frank Cass.
Kothari, R. (1968) 'Tradition and modernity revisited', *Government and Opposition*, vol. 3, no. 2.
Krasner, S.D. (1995) 'Compromising Westphalia', *International Security*, vol. 20, no. 3.
Krause, K. (1996) 'Armaments and conflict: the causes and consequences of military development', in L. van de Goor, K. Rupesinghe and P. Sciarone (eds), *Between Development and Destruction: An Enquiry into the Causes of Conflict in Post-Colonial States*. London: Macmillan.
Kuenzi, M. and G. Lambright (2001) 'Party system institutionalisation in 30 African countries', *Party Politics*, vol. 7, no. 4.
Kurer, O. (1997) *The Political Foundations of Development Policies*. London: University Press of America.
Laclau, E. (1971) 'Feudalism and capitalism in Latin America', *New Left Review*, no. 67, May/June.
Lall, S. (1975) 'Is "dependence" a useful concept in analysing underdevelopment?', *World Development*, vol. 3, no. 4.
Lane, R. (1994) 'Structural-functionalism reconsidered: a proposed research model', *Comparative Politics*, vol. 26, no. 4.
LaPalombara, J. and M. Weiner (eds) (1966) *Political Parties and Political Development*. Princeton: Princeton University Press.
Larrain, J. (1989) *Theories of Development: Capitalism, Colonialism and Dependency*. Cambridge: Polity Press.
Lawson, L. (2003) 'Globalization and the African state', *Commonwealth and Comparative Politics*, vol. 41, no. 3.
Leftwich, A. (1983) *Redefining Politics*. London: Methuen.

Leftwich, A. (1993) 'Governance, democracy and development in the Third World', *Third World Quarterly*, vol. 14, no. 3.

Leftwich, A. (2000) *States of Development*. Cambridge: Polity Press.

Lemarchand, R. (1981) 'Comparative political clientelism: structure, process and optic', in S. N. Eisenstadt and R. Lemarchand (eds), *Political Clientelism, Patronage and Development*. London: Sage.

Levine, D. (1986) 'Religion and politics in contemporary historical perspective', *Comparative Politics*, vol. 19, no. 1.

Levine, D. (1988) 'Assessing the impacts of liberation theology in Latin America', *The Review of Politics*, vol. 50, no. 2.

Leys, C. (1975) *Underdevelopment in Kenya: The Political Economy of Neocolonialism*. London: Heinemann.

Leys, C. (1976) 'The "overdeveloped" post-colonial state: a re-evaluation', *Review of African Political Economy*, vol. 5, no. 1.

Leys, C. (1977) 'Underdevelopment and dependency: critical notes', *Journal of Contemporary Asia*, vol. 7, no. 1.

Leys, C. (1978) 'Capital accumulation, class formation and dependency – the significance of the Kenyan case', in R. Miliband and J. Saville (eds), *The Socialist Register, 1978*. London: Merlin Press.

Leys, C. (1982) 'Samuel Huntington and the end of classical modernisation theory', in H. Alavi and T. Shanin (eds), *Introduction to the Sociology of 'Developing Societies'*. London: Macmillan.

Leys, C. (1996) *The Rise and Fall of Development Theory*. London: James Curry.

Lijphart, A. (1984) *Democracies: Patterns of Majoritarian and Consensus Government in Twenty-One Countries*. New Haven, CN: Yale University Press.

Linz, J. J. (1994) 'Presidential or parliamentary democracy: does it make a difference?', in J. J. Linz and A. Valenzuela (eds), *The Failure of Presidential Democracy*. Baltimore: The Johns Hopkins University Press.

Lipset, S. M. (1959) 'Some social requisites of democracy: economic development and political legitimacy', *American Political Science Review*, vol. 53, no. 1.

Lipton, M. (1977) *Why People Stay Poor: Urban Bias in World Development*. London: Temple Smith.

Little, W. (1997) 'Democratisation in Latin America, 1980–95', in D. Potter, D. Goldblatt, M. Kiloh and P. Lewis (eds), *Democratisation*. Cambridge: Polity Press.

Lloyd, P. C. (1973) *Classes, Crises and Coups: Themes in the Sociology of Developing Countries*. London: Paladin.

Long, N. (1977) *An Introduction to the Sociology of Rural Development*. London: Tavistock.

Love, J. L. (1980) 'The "Third World": a response to Professor Worsley', *Third World Quarterly*, vol. 2, no. 2.

Luan, T. D. (1996) 'Vietnam', in P. McCarney (ed.) *The Changing Nature of Local Government in Developing Countries*. Toronto: University of Toronto Centre for Urban and Community Studies and Federation of Canadian Municipalities.

Luckham, R. (1991) 'Militarism: force, class and international conflict', in R. Little and M. Smith (eds), *Perspectives on World Politics*, 2nd edn. London: Routledge.

Luckham, R. and G. White (1996) 'Introduction: democratizing the South', in R. Luckham and G. White (eds), *Democratization in the South: The Jagged Wave*. Manchester: Manchester University Press.

Luton, H. (1976) 'The satellite metropolis model: a critique', *Theory and Society*, vol. 3, no. 4.

Mack, A. and R. Leaver (1979) 'Radical theories of underdevelopment: an assessment', in A. Mack, D. Plant and V. Doyle (eds), *Imperialism, Intervention and Development*. London: Croom Helm.

Mackerass, C. (2001) 'Xinjiang at the turn of the century: the causes of separatism', *Central Asian Survey*, vol. 20, no. 3.

Macpherson, C. B. (1966) *The Real World of Democracy*. Oxford: Clarendon Press.

Mainwaring, S. (1992) 'Transitions to democracy and democratic consolidation: theoretical and comparative issues', in S. Mainwaring, G. O'Donnell and J. S. Valenzuela (eds), *Issues in Democratic Consolidation: The New South American Democracies in Comparative Perspective*. Notre Dame, IN: University of Notre Dame Press.

Mainwaring, S. (1993) 'Presidentialism, multipartism and democracy: the difficult combination', *Comparative Political Studies*, vol. 26, no. 2.

Mainwaring, S. (1998) 'Party systems in the Third Wave', *Journal of Democracy*, vol. 9, no. 3, July.

Mainwaring, S. and T. R. Scully (1995) 'Introduction: party systems in Latin America', in S. Mainwaring and T. R. Scully (eds), *Building Democratic Institutions: Party Systems in Latin America*. Stanford: Stanford University Press.

Mainwaring, S. and E. Zoco (2007) 'Political sequences and the stabilization of inter-party competition', *Party Politics*, vol. 13, no. 2.

Mamuya, I. (2008) 'What has gone wrong?', *Development and Cooperation*, vol. 35, nos. 7–8.

Manning, C. (2005) 'Assessing African party systems after the Third Wave', *Party Politics*, vol. 11, no. 6.

Mazrui, A. A. (1976) 'Soldiers as traditionalisers: military rule and the re-Africanisation of Africa', *World Politics*, vol. 28, no. 2.

McCourt, W. (2000) *Pay and Employment Reform in Developing and Transitional Societies*. New York: United Nations Research Institute for Social Development.

McGowan, P. J. (1976) 'Economic dependence and economic performance in Black Africa', *Journal of Modern African Studies*, vol. 14, no. 1.

McGowan, P. J. and T. H. Johnson (1984) 'African military *coups d'état* and under-development: a quantitative historical analysis', *Journal of Modern African Studies*, vol. 22, no. 4.

McGowan, P. J. and D. L. Smith (1978) 'Economic dependency in Black Africa: an analysis of competing theories', *International Organization*, vol. 32, no. 1.

McMichael, P., J. Petras and R. Rhodes (1974) 'Imperialism and the contradictions of development', *New Left Review*, no. 85.

McVey, R. (1984) 'Separatism and the paradoxes of the nation-state in perspective', in L. Joo-Jock and S. Vani (eds), *Armed Separatism in Southeast Asia*. Singapore: Institute of Southeast Asian Studies.

Meacham, C. E. (1999) 'Development administration and its alternatives in Latin America and the Caribbean: reforms and redirections', in K. M. Henderson and O. P. Dwivedi (eds), *Bureaucracy and the Alternatives in World Perspective*, Basingstoke: Macmillan.

Meier, G. (1976) *Leading Issues in Economic Development*, 3rd edn. New York: Oxford University Press.

Meillasoux, C. (1970) 'A class analysis of the bureaucratic process in Malawi', *Journal of Development Studies*, vol. 6, no. 2.

Melsom, R. and H. Wolpe (1970) 'Modernisation and the politics of communalism', *American Political Science Review*, vol. 64, no. 4.

Merkel, W. (1999) *Defective Democracies*, Working Paper 1999/132. Madrid: Juan March Institute.

Merton, R. (1952) 'Bureaucratic structure and personality', in R. Merton et al. (eds) *Reader in Bureaucracy*. Glencoe, IL: Free Press.

Migdal, J. S. (1974) *Peasants, Politics and Revolution: Pressures toward Political and Social Change in the Third World*. Princeton: Princeton University Press.

Migdal, J. S. (1988) *Strong Societies and Weak States: State–Society Relations and State Capabilities in the Third World*. Princeton, NJ: Princeton University Press.

Migdal, J. (1996) 'Integration and disintegration: an approach to society formation', in L. van de Goor, K. Rupesinghe and P. Sciarone (eds), *Between Development and Destruction: An Enquiry into the Causes of Conflict in Post-Colonial States*. London: Macmillan.

Migdal, J. S., A. Kohli and V. Shue (eds) (1994) *State Power and Social Forces: Domination and Transformation in the Third World*. Cambridge: Cambridge University Press.

Milne, R. S. (1972) 'Decision-making in developing countries', *Journal of Comparative Administration*, vol. 3, no. 4.

Misra, A. (2000) 'Tibet: in search of a resolution', *Central Asian Survey*, vol. 19, no. 1.

Mitra, S. K. (1995) 'The rational politics of cultural nationalism: subnational movements of South Asia in comparative perspective', *British Journal of Political Science*, vol. 25, no. 1.

Mohammed, N. A. L. (1999) 'Civil wars and military expenditures: a note', paper to Conference of World Bank's Development Economics Research Group, Washington.

Moore, B. (1973) *Social Origins of Dictatorship and Democracy: Lord and Peasant in the Making of the Modern World*. Harmondsworth: Penguin.

Moore, M. (1996) 'Is democracy rooted in material prosperity?', in R. Luckham and G. White (eds), *Democratization in the South: The Jagged Wave*. Manchester: Manchester University Press.

Moore, M. and J. Putzel (1999) *Politics and Poverty*, Background Paper for the World Development Report 2000/1. Washington: The World Bank.

Morgenstern, S. (2001) 'Organized factions and disorganised parties. Electoral incentives in Uruguay', *Party Politics*, vol. 7, no. 2.

Morgenthau, R. S. (1964) *Political Parties in French-Speaking West Africa*. Oxford: Clarendon Press.

Mouzelis, N. (1989) 'State and politics in the parliamentary semi-periphery', in C. Thomas and P. Saravanamuttu (eds), *The State and Instability in the South*. London: Macmillan.

Muller, E. N. (1988) 'Democracy, economic development and income inequality', *American Sociological Review*, vol. 53, no. 1.

Muller, E. N. and M. A. Seligson (1987) 'Inequality and insurgency', *American Political Science Review*, vol. 81, no. 2.

Muller, E. N., M. A. Seligson and H. Fu (1989) 'Land inequality and political violence', *American Political Science Review*, vol. 83, no. 2.

Munck, R. (2003) *Contemporary Latin America*, Basingstoke: Palgrave Macmillan.

Muni, S. D. (1979) 'The Third World: concept and controversy', *Third World Quarterly*, vol. 1, no. 3.

Nafziger, E. W. (1972) 'Economic aspects of the Nigerian civil war', in R. Higham (ed.), *Civil Wars in the Twentieth Century*. Lexington: University of Kentucky Press.

Nafziger, E. W. and W. L. Richter (1976) 'Biafra and Bangladesh: the political economy of secessionist conflict', *Journal of Peace Research*, vol. 13, no. 2.

Nanto, D. K. and E. Chanlett-Avery (2008) *The North Korean Economy: Leverage and Policy Analysis*, Washington, DC: Congressional Research Service.

Nash, M. (1963) 'Approaches to the study of economic growth', *Journal of Social Issues*, vol. 29, no. 1.

Neuberger, B. (2006) 'African nationalism', in G. Delanty and K. Kumar (eds), *The SAGE Handbook of Nations and Nationalism*, London: Sage Publications.

Niles, K. J. (1999) 'Economic adjustment and targeted social spending: the role of political institutions', Background Paper for the World Development Report 2000/2001. Washington, DC: The World Bank.

Nkrumah, K. (1965) *Neo-Colonialism: The Last Stage of Imperialism*. London: Nelson.

Nordlinger, E. (1987) 'Taking the state seriously', in M. Weiner and S. P. Huntington (eds), *Understanding Political Development*. Boston: Little, Brown.

Norris, P. and R. Inglehart (2004) *Sacred and Secular. Religion and Politics Worldwide*, Cambridge: Cambridge University Press.

Nove, A. (1974) 'On reading Andre Gunder Frank', *Journal of Development Studies*, vol. 10, nos. 3–4.

Nursey-Bray, P. (1983) 'Consensus and community: the theory of African one-party democracy', in G. Duncan (ed.), *Democratic Theory and Practice*. Cambridge: Cambridge University Press.

Nyerere, J. K. (1973) *Freedom and Development*. London: Oxford University Press.

O'Brien, D. C. (1972) 'Modernisation, order and the erosion of a democratic ideal: American political science 1960–70', *Journal of Development Studies*, vol. 8, no. 4.

O'Brien, P. J. (1975) 'A critique of Latin American theories of dependency', in I. Oxaal, T. Barnett and D. Booth (eds), *Beyond the Sociology of Development. Economy and Society in Latin America and Africa.* London: Routledge & Kegan Paul.

O'Connor, J. (1970) 'The meaning of economic imperialism', in R. I. Rhodes (ed.), *Imperialism and Underdevelopment.* New York: Monthly Review Press.

O'Donnell, G. (1979) 'Tensions in the bureaucratic authoritarian state and the question of democracy', in D. Collier (ed.), *The New Authoritarianism in Latin America.* Princeton: Princeton University Press.

O'Donnell, G. (1992) 'Transitions, continuities and paradoxes', in S. Mainwaring, G. O'Donnell and J. S. Valenzuela (eds), *Issues in Democratic Consolidation: The New South American Democracies in Comparative Perspective.* Notre Dame, IN: University of Notre Dame Press.

O'Donnell, G. (1998) *Polyarchies and the (Un)rule of Law in Latin America.* Working Paper 1998/125. Madrid: Juan March Institute.

O'Kane, R. H. T. (1981) 'A probabalistic approach to the causes of *coups d'état*', *British Journal of Political Science*, vol. 11, no. 3.

O'Kane, R. H. T. (1986) 'Explaining African *coups d'état*', *American Political Science Review*, vol. 80, no. 1.

Olson, M. (1963) 'Rapid growth as a destabilising force', *Journal of Economic History*, vol. 23, no. 4.

Omid, H. (1992) 'Theocracy or democracy? The critics of "westoxification" and the politics of fundamentalism in Iran', *Third World Quarterly*, vol. 13, no. 4.

Onis, Z. (1991) 'The logic of the developmental state', *Comparative Politics*, vol. 24, no. 1.

Oommen, T. K. (2006) 'Nation and nationalism in South Asia', in G. Delanty and K. Kumar (eds), *The SAGE Handbook of Nations and Nationalism*, London: Sage Publications.

Orridge, A. W. (1981) 'Uneven development and nationalism', *Political Studies*, vol. 29, nos 1&2, March and June.

Ortiz, R. D. (2002) 'Insurgent strategies in the post-cold war: the case of the Revolutionary Armed Forces of Colombia', *Studies in Conflict and Terrorism*, vol. 25, no. 2.

Oyediran, O. and A. Agbaje (1991) 'Two-partyism and democratic transition in Nigeria', *Journal of Modern African Studies*, vol. 29, no. 2.

Ozkirimli, U. (2000) *Theories of Nationalism. A Critical Introduction*, Basingstoke: Palgrave.

Parsa, M. (2000) *States, Ideologies and Social Revolutions.* Cambridge: Cambridge University Press.

Parsons, T. (1951) *The Social System.* Glencoe, IL: Free Press.

Parsons, T. (1960) *Structure and Process in Modern Societies.* Chicago, IL: Free Press.

Parsons, T. (1966) *Societies: Evolutionary and Comparative Perspectives.* Englewood Cliffs, NJ: Prentice-Hall.

Payne, S. (1975) *Basque Nationalism.* Reno: University of Nevada Press.

Peeler, J. (1998) *Building Democracy in Latin America.* London: Lynne Rienner.

Pempel, T. J. (1999) 'The developmental regime in a changing world economy', in M. Woo-Cumings (ed.), *The Developmental State*, Ithaca, NY: Cornell University Press.

Perlmutter, A. (1971) 'The praetorian state and the praetorian army: toward a taxonomy of civil–military relations in developing polities', in J. L. Finkle and R. W. Gable (eds), *Political Development and Social Change*, 2nd edn. London: John Wiley.

Peters, B. G. (2005) *Institutional Theory in Political Science*, London: Continuum.

Petras, J. F. (1975) 'New perspectives on imperialism and social classes in the periphery', *Journal of Contemporary Asia*, vol. 5, no. 3.

Petras, J. F. (1981) *Class, State and Power in the Third World*. London: Zed Press.

Petras, J. (2006) '"Centre-left" regimes in Latin America: history repeating itself as farce?', *Journal of Peasant Studies*, vol. 33, no. 2.

Phadnis, U. and R. Ganguly (2001) *Ethnicity and Nation-Building in South Asia*. London: Sage.

Philip, G. (1984) 'Military-authoritarianism in South America: Brazil, Chile. Uruguay and Argentina', *Political Studies*, vol. 32, no. 1.

Philip, G. (1990) 'The political economy of development', *Political Studies*, vol. 38, no. 3.

Philip, G. (2003) *Democracy in Latin America. Surviving Conflict and Crisis?*, Cambridge: Polity Press.

Phillips, A. (1977) 'The concept of "development"', *Review of African Political Economy*, vol. 8, January–April.

Pinkney, R. (1993) *Democracy in the Third World*. Buckingham: Open University Press.

Polese, M. (1985) 'Economic integration, national policies and the rationality of regional separatism', in E. A. Tiryakian and R. Rogowski (eds), *New Regionalisms of the Developed West*. London: Allen & Unwin.

Polidano, C. (2001) 'Don't discard state autonomy: revisiting the East Asian experience of development', *Political Studies*, vol. 49, no. 3.

Posner, D. N. and D. J. Young (2007) 'The institutionalization of political power in Africa', *Journal of Democracy*, vol. 18, no. 3.

Post, K. (1972) '"Peasantisation" and rural political movements in western Africa', *European Journal of Sociology*, vol. 13, no. 2.

Posusney, M. P. (2005) 'The Middle East's democracy deficit in comparative perspective', in M. P. Posusney and M. P. Angrist (eds), *Authoritarianism in the Middle East. Regimes and Resistance*, London: Lynne Rienner.

Potter, D. (1992) 'Democratization in Asia', in D. Held (ed.), *Prospects for Democracy: North, South, East, West*. Cambridge: Polity Press.

Potter, D., D. Goldblatt, M. Kiloh and P. Lewis (eds) (1997) *Democratization*. Cambridge: Polity Press.

Powell, J. D. (1970) 'Peasant society and clientelist polities', *American Political Science Review*, vol. 64, no. 2.

Power, T. J. and M. J. Gasiorowski (1997) 'Institutional design and democratic consolidation in the Third World', *Comparative Political Studies*, vol. 30, no. 2.

Pratt, R. P. (1973) 'The underdeveloped political science of development', *Studies in Comparative International Development*, vol. 8, no. 1.

Przeworski, A. (1986) 'Some problems in the study of the transition to democracy', in G. O'Donnell, P. Schmitter and L. Whitehead (eds), *Transitions from Authoritarian Rule: Tentative Conclusions about Uncertain Democracies.* Baltimore: The Johns Hopkins University Press.

Przeworski, A. (1995) *Sustainable Democracy.* Cambridge: Cambridge University Press.

Przeworski, A., M. E. Alvarez, J. A. Cheibub and F. Limongi (2000) *Democracy and Development: Political Institutions and Well-Being in the World, 1950–1990.* Cambridge: Cambridge University Press.

Putnam, R. D. (1967) 'Toward explaining military intervention in Latin American polities', *World Politics*, vol. 20, no. 1.

Pye, L. W. (1966) *Aspects of Political Development.* Boston: Little, Brown.

Pye, L. W. (1971) 'Armies in the process of political modernisation', in J. L. Finkle and R. W. Gable (eds), *Political Development and Social Change*, 2nd edn. London: John Wiley.

Ram, H. (1997) 'Exporting Iran's Islamic revolution: steering a path between Pan-Islam and nationalism', in B. Maddy-Weitzman and E. Inbar (eds), *Religious Radicalism in the Greater Middle East.* London: Frank Cass.

Randall, V. (1988) *Political Parties in the Third World.* London: Sage.

Randall, V. (2004) 'Using and abusing the concept of the Third World: geopolitics and the comparative study of political development', *Third World Quarterly*, vol. 25, no. 1.

Rapaport, D. C. (1962) 'A comparative theory of military and political types', in S. P. Huntington (ed.), *Changing Patterns of Military Politics*, International Yearbook of Political Behavior Research, vol. 3. Glencoe, IL: Free Press.

Ray, D. (1973) 'The dependency model of Latin American underdevelopment: three basic fallacies', *Journal of Interamerican Studies and World Affairs*, vol. 15, no. 1.

Reilly, C. A. (ed.) (1995) *New Paths to Democratic Development in Latin America: The Rise of NGO–Municipal Collaboration.* London: Lynne Rienner.

Rejai, M. and C. H. Enloe (1969) 'Nation-state and state-nations', *International Studies Quarterly*, vol. 13, no. 2.

Rhodes, R. I. (1968) 'The disguised conservatism in evolutionary development theory', *Science and Society*, vol. 32, no. 3.

Riggs, F. W. (1957) 'Agraria and Industria', in W. J. Siffin (ed.) *Toward the Comparative Study of Public Administration.* Bloomington, IL: Indiana University Press.

Riggs, F. W. (1963) 'Bureaucrats and political development', in J. LaPalombara (ed.) *Bureaucracy and Political Development.* Princeton: Princeton University Press.

Riggs, F. W. (1964) *Administration in Developing Countries: The Theory of Prismatic Society.* Boston: Houghton Mifflin.

Riley, S. P. (1991) *The Democratic Transition in Africa: An End to the One-Party State?*, Conflict Studies 245. London: Research Institute for the Study of Conflict and Terrorism.

Riley, S. P. (1992) 'Political adjustment or domestic pressure: democratic politics and political choice in Africa', *Third World Quarterly*, vol. 13, no. 3.

Robinson, W. I. (1998) '(Mal)Development in Central America: globalisation and social change', *Development and Change*, vol. 29, no. 3.

Robinson, W. I. (1999) 'Latin America in the age of inequality: confronting the new "Utopia"', *International Studies Review*, vol. 1, no. 3.

Robinson, W. I. (2001) 'Social theory and globalisation: the rise of a transnational state' *Theory and Society*, vol. 30, no. 2.

Robles, A. C. (2008) 'Whose service?', *Development and Cooperation*, vol. 35, nos. 7–8.

Roniger, L. (1994a) 'The comparative study of clientelism and the changing nature of civil society in the contemporary world', in L. Roniger and A. Gunes-Ayata (eds), *Democracy, Clientelism and Civil Society*. London: Lynne Rienner.

Roniger, L. (1994b) 'Conclusions: the transformation of clientelism and civil society', in L. Roniger and A. Gunes-Ayata (eds), *Democracy, Clientelism and Civil Society*. London: Lynne Rienner.

Rosen, G. and W. Jones (1979) 'The radical theory of development', in A. Mack, D. Plant and U. Doyle (eds), *Imperialism, Intervention and Development*. London: Croom Helm.

Rothstein, R. L. (1977) *The Weak in the World of the Strong: The Developing Countries in the International System*. New York: Columbia University Press.

Rouquie, A. (1986) 'Demilitarization and the institutionalisation of military-dominated politics in Latin America', in G. O'Donnell, P. C. Schmitter and L. Whitehead (eds), *Transitions from Authoritarian Rule*. Baltimore: The Johns Hopkins University Press.

Rowat, D. C. (1990) 'Comparing bureaucracies in developed and developing countries: a statistical analysis', *International Review of Administrative Sciences*, vol. 56, no. 2.

Roxborough, I. (1979) *Theories of Underdevelopment*. London: Macmillan.

Rueschmeyer, D. (1991) 'Different methods – contradictory results? Research on development and democracy', in C. C. Ragin (ed.), *Issues and Alternatives in Comparative Social Research*. Leiden: Brill.

Rueschmeyer, D., E. H. Stephens and J. D. Stephens (1992) *Capitalist Development and Democracy*. London: Polity Press.

Russett, B. M. (1964) 'Inequality and instability: the relation of land tenure to polities', *World Politics*, vol. 16, no. 3.

Rustow, D. A. (1967) *A World of Nations: Problems of Political Modernisation*. Washington, DC: The Brookings Institution.

Sandbrook, R. (1976) 'The crisis in political development theory', *Journal of Development Studies*, vol. 12, no. 2.

Sandschneider, E. (1991) 'Successful economic development and political change in Taiwan and South Korea', in J. Manor (ed.), *Rethinking Third World Politics*. London: Longman.

Sangmpan, S. N. (2007) 'Politics rules: the false primacy of institutions in developing countries', *Political Studies*, vol. 55, no. 1.

Sartori, G. (1970) 'Concept misinformation in comparative polities', *American Political Science Review*, vol. 64, no. 4.

Saul, J. (1974) 'The state in post-colonial societies: Tanzania', in R. Miliband and J. Saville (eds), *The Socialist Register, 1974*. London: Merlin Press.

Schedler, A. (2001) 'Taking uncertainty seriously: the blurred boundaries of democratic transition and consolidation', *Democratization*, vol. 8, no. 4.

Schuurman, F. J. (1993) 'Introduction: development theory in the 1990s', in F. J. Schuurman (ed.), *Beyond the Impasse: New Directions in Development Theory*. London: Zed Books.

Seers, D. (1981) 'Development options: the strengths and weaknesses of dependency theories in explaining a government's room to manoeuvre', in D. Seers (ed.), *Dependency Theory: A Critical Reassessment*. London: Francis Pinter.

Shanin, T. (1982) 'Class, state and revolution: substitutes and realities', in H. Alavi and T. Shanin (eds), *Introduction to the Sociology of Developing Societies*. London: Macmillan.

Shivji, I. G. (1973) 'Tanzania: the silent class struggle', in L. Cliffe and J. S. Saul (eds), *Socialism in Tanzania*. Nairobi: East African Publishing House.

Shivji, I. G. (1976) *Class Struggles in Tanzania*. London: Heinemann.

Singer, J. D. (1996) 'Armed conflict in the former colonial regions: from classification to explanation', in L. van de Goor, K. Rupesinghe and P. Sciarone (eds), *Between Development and Destruction: An Enquiry into the Causes of Conflict in Post-Colonial States*. London: Macmillan.

SIPRI (2005) *SIPRI Yearbook, 2005*. Stockholm: Stockholm International Peace Research Institute.

Sirowy, L. and A. Inkeles (1991) 'The effect of democracy on economic growth and inequality', in A. Inkeles (ed.), *On Measuring Democracy: Its Consequences and Concomitants*. New Brunswick: Transaction Books.

Smith, A. D. (1971) *Theories of Nationalism*. London: Duckworth.

Smith, A. D. (1979) 'Towards a theory of ethnic separatism', *Ethnic and Racial Studies*, vol. 2, no. 1.

Smith, A. D. (1995) *Nations and Nationalism in a Global Era*. Cambridge: Polity Press.

Smith, A. D. (2001) 'Nations and history', in M. Guibernau and J. Hutchinson (eds), *Understanding Nationalism*. Cambridge: Polity Press.

Smith, B. C. (1988) *Bureaucracy and Political Power*. Brighton: Wheatsheaf.

Smith, B. C. (2007) *Good Governance and Development*. Basingstoke: Palgrave Macmillan.

Smith, M. (2002) 'Army politics as an historical legacy: the experience of Burma', in K. Koonings and D. Kruijt (eds.), *Political Armies. The Military and Nation Building in the Age of Democracy*, London: Zed Books.

Snyder, L. L. (1976) *Varieties of Nationalism: A Comparative Study*. Hinsdale: Dryden Press.

So, A. Y. (1990) *Social Change and Development: Modernization, Dependency and World System Theories*. London: Sage.

Soeters, J. L. and M. T. Tessema (2004) 'Public management in developing countries', *International Review of Administrative Sciences*, vol. 70, no. 4.

Sridharan, E. and A. Varshney (2001) 'Toward moderate pluralism: political parties in India', in L. Diamond and R. Gunther (eds), *Political Parties and Democracy*, Baltimore: The Johns Hopkins University Press.

Stein, H. (1985) 'Theories of the state in Tanzania: a critical assessment', *Journal of Modern African Studies*, vol. 23, no. 1.

Stockton, H. (2001) 'Political parties, party systems and democracy in East Asia', *Comparative Political Studies*, vol. 34, no. 1.

Strange, S. (1996) *The Diffusion of Power in the World Economy*. Cambridge: Cambridge University Press.

Sutcliffe, B. (1972) 'Imperialism and industrialization in the Third World' in R. Owen and B. Sutcliffe (eds), *Studies in the Theory of Imperialism*, London: Longman.

Symmons-Symonolewicz, K. (1965) 'Nationalist movements: an attempt at a comparative typology', *Comparative Studies in Society and History*, vol. 7, no. 2.

Taylor, D. (2005) 'Religion and politics', in D. T. Hagerty (ed.), *South Asia in World Politics*, Lanham, MD: Rowan & Littlefield.

Taylor, J. G. (1979) *From Modernisation to Modes of Production: A Critique of the Sociologies of Development and Underdevelopment*. London: Macmillan.

Therborn, G. (1979) 'The travail of Latin American democracy', *New Left Review*, nos. 113–14, January–April.

Tinker, H. (1981) 'The nation-state in Asia', in L. Tivey (ed.), *The Nation-State: The Formation of Modern Politics*. Oxford: Martin Robertson.

Tipps, D. (1973) 'Modernization theory and the comparative study of societies: a critical perspective', *Comparative Studies in Society and History*, vol. 15, no. 2.

Toye, J. (1987) *Dilemmas of Development: Reflections on the Counter-Revolution in Development Theory and Policy*. Oxford: Blackwell.

Transparency International (2007) *Global Corruption Barometer 2007*, www.transparency.org/policy_research/surveys_indeces/gcb

Turner, M. and J. Halligan (1999) 'Bureaucracy and the alternatives in East and Southeast Asia', in K. M. Henderson and O. P. Dwivedi (eds), *Bureaucracy and the Alternatives in World Perspective*. Basingstoke: Macmillan.

Turner, M. and D. Hulme (1997) *Governance, Administration and Development: Making the State Work*. London: Macmillan.

Twitchett, K. J. (1965) 'Colonialism: an attempt at understanding imperial, colonial and neo-colonial relationships', *Political Studies*, vol. 13, no. 3.

UNDP (1993) *Human Development Report 1993*. Oxford: Oxford University Press.

UNDP (1999) *Debt and Sustainable Human Development*, Technical Advisory Paper No. 4. New York: United Nations Development Programme.

UNDP (2001) *Human Development Report 2001: Making New Technologies Work for Human Development*. New York: United Nations Development Programme.

UNDP (2006) *Human Development Report 2006.Beyond Security: Power, Poverty and the Global Water Crisis*. New York: United Nations Development Programme.

UNDP (2007) *Human Development Report 2007/2008: Fighting Climate Change. Human Solidarity in a Divided World*. New York: United Nations Development Programme.

Valenzuela, J. S. (1992) 'Democratic consolidation in post-transitional settings: notion, process and facilitating conditions', in S. Mainwaring, G. O'Donnell and J. S. Valenzuela (eds), *Issues in Democratic Consolidation: The New South American Democracies in Comparative Perspective*. Notre Dame, IN: University of Notre Dame Press.

Vanley, I. S. (1980) 'Kurdistan in Iraq', in G. Chaliand (ed.), *People Without a Country*. London: Zed Press.

Varma, B. N. (1980) *The Sociology and Politics of Development: A Theoretical Study*. London: Routledge & Kegan Paul.

Vengroff, R. (1977) 'Dependency and underdevelopment in Black Africa: an empirical test', *Journal of Modern African Studies*, vol. 15, no. 4.

Wallerstein, I. (1960) 'Ethnicity and national integration in West Africa', *Cahiers d'Etudes Africaines*, no. 3, October.

Wallis, M. (1989) *Bureaucracy: Its Role in Third World Development*. London: Macmillan.

Ware, A. (1996) *Political Parties and Party Systems*. Oxford: Oxford University Press.

Warren, B. (1973) 'Imperialism and capitalist industrialization', *New Left Review*, no. 81.

Warren, B. (1980) *Imperialism: Pioneer of Capitalism*. London: New Left Books.

Webber, M. (1993) 'The Third World and the dissolution of the USSR', *Third World Quarterly*, vol. 13, no. 4.

Weber, H. (2004) 'The "new economy" and social risk: banking on the poor?', *Review of International Political Economy*, vol. 11, no. 2.

Weiner, M. (1965) 'Political integration and political development', *The Annals of the American Academy of Political and Social Science*, no. 358, March.

Weiner, M. (1987) 'Empirical democratic theory', in M. Weiner and E. Ozbundun (eds) *Competitive Elections in Developing Countries*. Durham, NC: Duke University Press.

Weiss, L. (1998) *The Myth of the Powerless State: Governing the Economy in a Global Era*. Cambridge: Polity Press.

Weiss, L. and J. M. Hobson (1995) *States and Economic Development: A Comparative Historical Analysis*. Cambridge: Polity Press.

Wells, A. (1974) 'The *coup d'état* in theory and practice: independent Black Africa in the 1960s', *American Journal of Sociology*, vol. 79, no. 4.

Westlake, M. (1991) 'The Third World (1950–1990) RIP', *Marxism Today*, August.

Whalen, G. (1996a) 'Analysing women in the politics of the Third World', in H. Afshar (ed.), *Women and Politics in the Third World*. London: Routledge.

Whalen, G. (1996b) *Gender in Third World Politics*. Boulder, CO: Lynne Rienner.

Whitaker, B. E. (2007) 'Exporting the Patriot Act? Democracy and the "war on terror" in the Third World', *Third World Quarterly*, vol. 28, no. 5.

White, C. P. (1974) 'The Vietnamese revolutionary alliance: intellectuals, workers and peasants', in J. W. Lewis (ed.), *Recent Rebellion and Communist Revolution in Asia*. Stanford: Stanford University Press.

White, G. (1984) 'Developmental states and socialist industrialization in the Third World', *Journal of Development Studies*, vol. 21, no. 1.

White, G. (1996) 'Civil society, democratisation and development', in R. Luckham and G. White (eds), *Democratization in the South: The Jagged Wave*. Manchester: Manchester University Press.

White, G. (1998) 'Constructing a democratic developmental state', *Democratization*, vol. 5, no. 3.

Whitehead, L. (1986) 'International aspects of democratization', in G. O'Donnell, P. Schmitter and L. Whitehead (eds), *Transitions from Authoritarian Rule: Tentative Conclusions about Uncertain Democracies*. Baltimore: The Johns Hopkins University Press.

Williams, D and T. Young (1994) 'Governance, the World Bank and liberal theory', *Political Studies*, vol. 42, no. 1.

Wiseman, J. A. (1996) *The New Struggle for Democracy in Africa*. Aldershot: Avebury Press.

Woddis, J. (1977) *Armies and Politics*. London: Lawrence & Wishart.

Wolf-Phillips, L. (1987) 'Why Third World?', *Third World Quarterly*, vol. 1, no. 1.

Wolfe, E.R. (1968) *Peasant Wars of the Twentieth Century*, New York: Harper & Row.

Wood, G. D. (1977) 'Rural development and the post-colonial state: administration and the peasantry in the Kosi region of North-East Bihar, India', *Development and Change*, vol. 8, no. 3.

Wood, G. D. (1984) 'State intervention and bureaucratic reproduction: comparative thoughts', *Development and Change*, vol. 15, no. 1.

Wood, G. D. (2000) 'Prisoners and escapees: improving the institutional responsibility square in Bangladesh', Institute for International Policy Analysis, University of Bath.

Wood, J. R. (1981) 'Secession: a comparative analytical framework', *Canadian Journal of Political Science*, vol. 14, no. 1.

World Bank (1990) *World Development Report 1990: Poverty*. Oxford: Oxford University Press.

World Bank (1991) *World Development Report 1991: The Challenge of Development*. Oxford: Oxford University Press.

World Bank (1993) *World Development Report 1993: Investing in Health*. Oxford: Oxford University Press.

World Bank (1997) *World Development Report 1997: The State in a Changing World*. Washington, DC: The World Bank.

World Bank (1999) *Global Economic Prospects and the Developing Countries 1998/99. Beyond Financial Crisis*, Washington, DC: The World Bank.

World Bank (2001a) *Global Development Finance 2001: Building Conditions for Effective Development Finance*. Washington, DC: The World Bank.

World Bank (2001b) *World Development Indicators 2001*. Washington, DC: The World Bank.

World Bank (2001c) *World Development Report 2000–2001: Attacking Poverty*. New York: Oxford University Press.

World Bank (2006) *World Development Report 2006: Equity and Development*, Washington, DC: The World Bank.

World Bank (2007a) *Global Economic Prospects 2007: Managing the Next Wave of Globalization*. Washington, DC: The World Bank.

World Bank (2007b) *World Development Indicators, 2007*. Washington, DC: World Bank.

World Bank (2007c) *World Development Report 2007. Development and the Next Generation.* Washington, DC: World Bank,

World Bank (2008a) *Rising Food Prices: Policy Options and World Bank Response* Washington, DC: World Bank, http://go.worldbank.org/QLBJFC7X10

World Bank (2008b) *World Development Report 2008. Agriculture for Development.* Washington, DC: The World Bank.

Worsley, P. (1984) *The Three Worlds: Culture and World Development.* London: Weidenfeld & Nicolson.

Worthley, J. A. and K. K. Tsao (1999) 'Reinventing government in China: a comparative analysis', *Administration and Society*, vol. 31, no. 5.

Wriggins, H. (1966) 'National integration', in M. Weiner (ed.), *Modernization.* New York: Basic Books.

Wright, R. (1996) 'Islam and liberal democracy: two visions of Reformation', *Journal of Democracy*, vol. 7, no. 2.

Wright, T. P. (1976) 'South Asian Separatist Movements', in W. H. Morris-Jones (ed.), *The Politics of Separatism*, Collected Seminar Papers no. 19. London: University of London Institute of Commonwealth Studies.

Yanai, N. (1999) 'Why do political parties survive?: an analytical discussion', *Party Politics*, vol. 5, no. 1.

Ziemann, W. and M. Lanzendorfer (1977) 'The state in peripheral societies', in R. Miliband and J. Saville (eds), *The Socialist Register 1977.* London: Merlin Press.

Zubaida, S. (1978) 'Theories of nationalism', in G. Littlejohn (ed.), *Power and the State.* London: Croom Helm.

Index